The Blue Guides

  S0-BHZ-414

City Guide
Venice

Alta Macadam

A&C Black • London
WW Norton • New York

Seventh edition
Published by A & C Black (Publishers) Limited
37 Soho Square, London W1D 3HD

A CIP catalogue record of this book
is available from the British Library.

ISBN 0–7136–5455–4

Published in the United States of America by
WW Norton and Company, Inc
500 Fifth Avenue, New York, NY 10110

Published simultaneously in Canada by
Penguin Books Canada Limited
10 Alcorn Avenue, Toronto, Ontario M4V 3B2

ISBN 0–393–32248–3 USA

The author and the publishers have done their best to ensure the accuracy of all the information in Blue Guide Venice; however, they can accept no responsibility for any loss, injury or inconvenience sustained by any traveller as a result of information or advice contained in the guide.

Alta Macadam has been a writer of Blue Guides since 1970. She lives in Florence with her family, the painter Francesco Colacicchi and their children, Giovanni and Lelia. Combined with work on writing the guides she has also been associated in Florence with the Bargello Museum, the Alinari photo archive, and Harvard University at the Villa I Tatti in Florence. As author of the Blue Guides to Rome, Venice, Sicily, Florence, Tuscany, and Umbria she travels extensively in Italy every year to revise new editions of the books.

The History of Venice © **John Law** (M.A. D.Phil. F.R. Hist.S.), University of Wales, Swansea. Contributor to the Further Reading and Topography sections. Dr Law is a historian of late medieval and Renaissance Italy. His interests in Venice extend to the 19C and 20C.

Cover picture: Santa Maria della Salute and gondolas, Gettyone Stone.

Printed and bound in Great Britain by Butler and Tanner Ltd, Frome and London.

Contents

The islands of the Venetian lagoon

Maps and plans

Street map of Venice ~ Atlas section 2–16

Foreword

Since the sixth edition of the Blue Guide was published in 1998 the much-heralded *Giubileo*—millennium year—has come and gone. Planned as for a military campaign in anticipation of throngs of pilgrims en route to Rome, funds were made available under a special law financing an extensive programme for renovating ecclesiastical buildings—convents and monasteries—providing a valuable addition to the city's lodging capacity. Although this is still insufficient to meet the demands of an increasingly extended tourist season, the rapidly expanding conversion of former family palaces and houses into hotels, pensions and bed and breakfasts, is deplored by the Mayor, who would prefer increased economic productivity to be engendered by business investment.

At present tourism remains the economic mainstay of the historic centre—remembering that the lagoon city is the minor partner in the dual municipality of Venice–Mestre, having only a third of the total population. The increasing numbers of day visitors thronging Piazza San Marco and its access routes make it all the more rewarding for enterprising visitors to explore the less frequented *sestiere* of Cannaregio and Castello, following the trail of Venice in Peril's work throughout the city.

The Venice in Peril Fund

The fund was set up in 1971, succeeding the Italian Art and Archives Rescue Fund instituted in November 1966 in response to the emergency caused by devastating floods in Florence and Venice. As a member of the Association of 25 international voluntary committees dedicated to the conservation of the city's monuments, works of art and historic urban fabric, recognised by UNESCO as a Non-Governmental Organisation, it works in close collaboration with the Ministry for Cultural Heritage, the municipal and ecclesiastical authorities and with many national and local environmental and conservation bodies.

To follow an itinerary of projects undertaken by Venice in Peril over the past 30 years leads the curious and discerning reader all over the city. Three of the major projects are indeed in Piazza San Marco; the Loggetta, designed by Sansovino at the foot of the soaring bell tower; the elaborate Porta della Carta of the Doge's Palace and the 14th and 15th century original capitals for the columns bearing the loggia of the Palace, which are now in the ground floor museum. But away from the crowds in the Piazza, the first project undertaken, up on the north shore of Cannaregio, was the imposing Gothic church of the Madonna dell'Orto, much admired by John Ruskin. The interior has been completely damp-proofed, the symmetric brick façade with its fine stone sculptures cleaned and consolidated, the organ finally restored to concert standard. Further west, at the end of the Cannaregio canal where the old slaughter houses have been re-structured to accommodate the Faculty of Economic Tourism of Venice University, a 16th century derelict house belonging to the Municipality is to be renovated to provide flats for tenants. The Fund is financing the survey and technical studies drawn upon by the Superintendency of Architecture which, in agreement with the Municipality's Public Works division, will be the basis of the restoration project.

In the south-west area of Dorsoduro, close to the Maritime Station, one of the Fund's most successful projects was the global restoration of San Nicolò dei

Mendicoli, a church founded in the eighth century on the extreme fringes of the city, a parish of poor fishermen now enlivened by the expanding re-use of the ex-cotton factory and obsolete port buildings for the University of Architecture. In the nearby majestic church of Santa Maria del Carmelo the Altar of the Scuola dei Carmini, restored in a joint project with the Confraternity, has saved the remarkable frescoes by Sebastiano Ricci in the vault.

Other projects in the churches of San Zulian, Santa Maria Formosa, San Francesco della Vigna and Santa Maria Mater Domini have tackled the problems of air and water pollution, for which Venice is unfortunately an ideal laboratory. Destructive sulphation of stone and marble surfaces is a continuing chemical phenomenon, even though noxious emission has been controlled by legislation, and specialised biennial courses in stone conservation conducted by the International Centre for Conservation in Rome together with the Venice University of Architecture are also supported by the Fund, making use of the monumental surfaces of these churches as work sites providing practical experience for conservators, museum directors and chemists attending the courses from all over the world. Since 1975 qualified craftsmen and site managers have been offered specialised multi-disciplinary courses, organised by the Council of Europe's *Centro Europeo Venezia* on the island of San Servolo, in conservation of the architectural heritage. Venice in Peril has for several years provided an annual bursary for a British craftsman.

The most recent major project on the cemetery island of San Michele in Isola is the hexagonal Cappella Emiliani, adjunct to the beautiful Codussi façade of the church. The remarkable range of precious marble in its sculpted interior is particularly vulnerable to the humidity caused by rising damp, condensation and infiltration from the leaking circular roof, while its foundations are at risk from the devastating scourge of the *moto ondoso*—waves created by the continual passage of vaporetti and speeding motor-boats which are a major threat to the whole city.

Since the destruction of the Fenice theatre in 1996 little progress has been made towards its reconstruction, not for lack of funds but because of prolonged discussion over contractual procedures: it would be inadvisable to predict a firm date for its re-opening. Meanwhile, the orchestra and company continue to perform not only in the PalaFenice tent on the Tronchetto but now in the historic Teatro Malibran, re-opened after renovation in May.

Although subsidence is a relatively minor factor in the threat from the water, the effects of global climate change on rising sea levels in the Adriatic are causing more frequent medium-high tides out of season. The programme of cleaning out the city's canals, raising the lowest-lying fondamente where necessary, proceeds systematically, simultaneously with work on the ecosystem of the lagoon while the long-studied mobile flood barrier system is being revised to take into account long-term forecast of eustasism.

But funds are urgently needed to keep pace with the seemingly inexhaustible list of endangered buildings, monuments, sculpture and works of art which are beyond the resources of the local Superintendencies: donations will be most gratefully received at the **Venice in Peril Fund** (the British appeal for the Preservation of Venice, reg. charity number 262146), Morley House, 314–322 Regent St, London W1B 3BE, ☎ 020 7636 6138, 📠 020 7636 6139, ✉ venice-inperil@btclick.com, www.veniceinperil.org. We are immensely indebted to Alta

Macadam and to the publishers of the Blue Guides for continuing to give us access to their vast readership whose knowledge and understanding of Venice will help her to survive into the succeeding millennia.

Frances Clarke
President
The Venice in Peril Fund
Dorsoduro 1113
Venice

Introduction

Venice, in Italian Venezia, is considered by many the most beautiful city in the world. It is in a unique position, built on an archipelago of islets or shoals, a few kilometres from the mainland, in a lagoon protected from the open sea by the natural breakwater of the Lido. The seawater enters the lagoon through three channels. The splendid buildings of Venice, on foundations of Istrian limestone which withstand the corrosion of the sea, are supported on piles of pine driven down about 7.5 metres beneath the water to a solid bed of compressed sand and clay. Boats provide the only means of transport along a system of over one hundred canals, the main thoroughfare being the Grand Canal, and the remark-ably peaceful atmosphere in the city is due to the total absence of cars.

Although traces have recently been found of prehistoric and Roman settlements in the lagoon, the island of Torcello, first inhabited in the 5C–6C, became important in the 7C. Venice was an independent Byzantine province by the 9C with its centre on the islands of the Rialto. The great Venetian maritime Republic, much influenced by the Eastern Empire, flourished as a commercial power from then onwards. The strength of the Republic, one of the most glorious and long-lasting in history, lay in its remarkable political structure. A rigid constitution provided elective offices for numerous citizens who acknowleged the sacredness of Venice's political institutions, personified by St Mark and his symbol of the winged lion. The power of the doge was carefully kept in check, and he was seldom more than the figurehead of the Republic, although at the end of the 13C an oligarchic system of government was introduced. Throughout most of her remarkably stable history Venice led a cautious foreign policy, favouring neutrality and peace where possible, earning her the name of Serenissima, the 'most serene'. Her political independence was soon acknowledged by both the Pope and Emperor. Merchants who traded in foreign goods and established Venice as a central distribution point between the East and Europe, played a decisive role in Venetian society.

The splendid monuments in the city today, contained geographically within virtually the same limits as at the height of the Republic, are testimony to her remark-able civilisation. There are numerous Gothic and Renaissance palaces, as well as beautiful churches from all periods. The population of the historic centre decreased at an alarming rate in the 1980s and 1990s, and is now only about 67,000 compared with one of 200,000 when the Republic was at its zenith (and 123,000 in 1966).

Important scientific research has been carried out in the last few decades in an attempt to preserve the delicate ecological balance between the open sea and the enclosed lagoon, but after many years of discussions and delays, urgent measures are now required to solve the problem of how to protect the buildings of the city from the periodic floods caused by exceptionally high tides (*acqua alta*). The proposed project of flood barriers and the conservation work in progress in the lagoon are outlined on page 75. Private committees funded from numerous countries have been working in conjunction with the Italian authorities since 1966 on the restoration of buildings (so far more than eighty monuments and nine hundred works of art have been restored).

Since about 10 million people visit Venice every year, the city can become uncomfortably crowded at certain periods, especially during Carnival (February), over Easter, and in September. At these times it is best to stay away from Piazza San Marco and the Rialto during the daytime, and explore areas such as the beautiful Dorsoduro, Cannaregio and the northern districts near the church of the Madonna dell'Orto, or the waterfronts on the Giudecca canal.

Acknowledgements

As in all previous editions of this guide I have to thank first and foremost **Frances Clarke** who has always provided me with generous help during the preparation of each new edition. She is deeply knowledgeable about Venice and has long been admired as one of her most important citizens. I am extremely grateful to her for her friendship and for keeping me so closely in touch with all that is going on in Venice. **Laura Corti**, another friend who lives in Venice, has also helped me in countless ways during work on the book, and offered me her companionship on a number of expeditions. Many warm thanks also to **John Millerchip**, committee member of the Venice in Peril Fund and co-ordinator of the international committees for the safeguarding of Venice, who was always ready to answer all my queries about restoration projects and conservation issues. I am also indebted to **Maria Turchetto** for detailed information on restaurants, and in particular for up-to-date information on the best *bacari* to be found in Venice.

Philip Rylands kindly checked the section on the Peggy Guggenheim collection. **Cesare Battisti**, of the Venice tourist office, supplied much useful practical information.

How to use the guide

Italian words have been used in the text for topographical descriptions (ie. *campo, calle, rio, fondamenta, salizzada*, etc.); these are explained on p 72. Names of streets, canals, etc. are written up in the Venetian dialect and often change when repainted; the names found in situ have generally been used in the text but it should be borne in mind that the spelling of a word can be changed by a letter or two. Water-buses are referred to as *vaporetti* (sing., *vaporetto*) and *motoscafi* (sing., *motoscafo*).

Map references References to the **16-page atlas** at the back of the book appear in the text as follows, (Pl. 1; 1). The first figure refers to the page, the second to the square. References to **ground plans** are given in the text as a bracketed single figure or letter.

Hotels listed on pp 20–27 have been keyed on the atlas at the back of the book by letters and 🛏.

Abbreviations In addition to generally accepted and self-explanatory abbreviations, the following occur in the guide:

ACTV	Azienda del Consorzio Trasporti Veneziano (the company that runs the Venetian transport system)
APT	Azienda di Promozione Turistica (official local tourist office)
C	century
fest.	festa, or festival (i.e. holiday, including Sunday)
fl.	floruit (flourished)

Churches are taken as being orientated, with the entrance at the west end and the altar at the east end, the south aisle on the right and the north aisle on the left. Opening times are given within the text.

Museum opening times, entrance fees, and telephone numbers are given in the list on pp 44–48; only the opening times are given within the main text. The following **symbols** have been used:

☎	telephone	✉	e-mail/web-site addresses
🖷	fax	⛴	vaporetto landing stage

Currency Since the Euro (€) is to replace the Italian lire as the official monetary unit in Italy on 1 January 2002, but the Italian lire will stay in circulation for a few months, prices have been given in both currencies. The fixed exchange rate for one Euro is Lire 1936.270. The Euro equivalents are given only as a guide, and can only be approximate at the time of going to press. For further information see p 14.

Highlights of Venice

Venice is one of the most beautiful and best preserved cities in the world, and a walk through any of the narrow streets or quiet squares or along the picturesque canals can be as rewarding as a visit to its great monuments. The *vaporetti* along the Grand Canal or in the wider Giudecca canal provide superb views of the city.

The most famous place in Venice is the spectacular **Piazza San Marco**, with its two most important buildings, the **Basilica di San Marco**, a splendid Byzantine church, famous for its mosaics, and the **Palazzo Ducale**, the residence of the doges, which has a beautiful Gothic exterior and contains sumptuous rooms decorated in the 16C and 17C by Venetian painters including Veronese and Tintoretto.

The **Grand Canal** (best seen from vaporetto no. 1), which winds through the city, is bordered on either side with a continuous line of lovely old buildings, many of them grand palaces, including the splendid **Ca' d'Oro** (which is also open as a museum). Other palaces on the canal include the 15C Gothic Palazzo Contarini-Fasan, Ca' Foscari, and Palazzo Dario; the 16C Renaissance Palazzo Corner, Palazzo Corner-Spinelli, Palazzo Grimani, and Palazzo Loredan Vendramin Calergi; the 17C Ca' Pesaro and Ca' Rezzonico, and the 18C Palazzo

Grassi. The Grand Canal is crossed by the **Rialto Bridge**, a famous Venetian landmark built in 1588.

The secluded district of **Dorsoduro** is one of the most delightful parts of the city. Here is the famous **Galleria dell'Accademia** which contains the most important collection of Venetian paintings in existence, with Giovanni Bellini, Titian, Tintoretto and Veronese well represented.

The island of the **Giudecca**, with the church of the **Redentore**, a masterpiece of Palladio, is also a peaceful district seldom visited by tourist groups. Nearby is another church by Palladio, **San Giorgio Maggiore**, in a magnificent position on a small island in the basin of San Marco (with a good view from its bell-tower).

Other churches of particular interest include the huge Gothic church of **Santi Giovanni e Paolo**, with numerous funerary monuments to doges, some of them Renaissance masterpieces by Pietro and Tullio Lombardo, and the equestrian statue of Bartolomeo Colleoni by Verrocchio outside. The huge Gothic Franciscan church of the **Frari** has more good funerary monuments and paintings by Giovanni Bellini and Titian. **San Zaccaria** and **Santa Maria Formosa** are interesting for their architecture and paintings. **Santa Maria della Salute** is the masterpiece of Baldassare Longhena, in a splendid position at the beginning of the Grand Canal. **San Sebastiano** is decorated with superb paintings by Paolo Veronese. The charming little church of **Santa Maria dei Miracoli** is a masterpiece of the Renaissance by Pietro Lombardo. The **Madonna dell'Orto**, in a lovely quiet area of the city, contains important works by Tintoretto. **La Pietà** has a fine 18C interior, and **San Stae** has 18C paintings.

The interesting buildings which belonged to the Scuole, or lay confraternities dedicated to charitable works during the Republic, include the **Scuola Grande di San Rocco**, with over 50 paintings by Tintoretto, one of the most remarkable pictorial cycles in existence; the **Scuola Grande del Carmini**, with beautiful frescoes by Giambattista Tiepolo; and the **Scuola di San Giorgio degli Schiavoni**, charmingly decorated with paintings by Vittore Carpaccio.

Museums of great interest (beside the Galleria dell'Accademia), include: the **Museo Correr**, the city museum with historical collections and some fine paintings; the **Ca' d'Oro**, with some very fine Venetian sculptures; the **Museo Querini-Stampalia**, with Venetian paintings; and the **Ca' Rezzonico**, a palace on the Grand Canal with splendid 18C decorations including frescoes by the Tiepolo (to be reopened in 2001). **The Archaeological Museum** has some fine ancient Greek and Roman sculpture. The **Peggy Guggenheim collection** contains one of the most representative displays of 20C art in Europe. The **Museo Storico Navale** is an excellent naval museum.

In the beautiful **Venetian Lagoon** there are numerous islands worth a visit. The most evocative place is the tiny island of **Torcello**, with its beautiful cathedral. **Burano** is a charming little island with brightly painted houses on miniature canals. **Murano** is interesting for its glass works, and glass museum, and its Byzantine basilica.

PRACTICAL INFORMATION

 Planning your trip

When to go

Since Venice is one of the most visited places in the world, it is only relatively empty of tourists in January, late November and early December. This is the best time to see the city, even though the weather can be very cold and wet, and thick sea mists can shroud the city for days at a time. The most crowded seasons are Easter, September, October, Christmas and New Year, and Carnival time (ten days around the beginning of February before Lent). At these times the city can more than double its population, and the presence of thousands of visitors can mar a visit; but even so it is always possible to escape from the crowds which tend to congregate around Piazza San Marco and the Rialto bridge. In July and August the city is very crowded during the day, but most of the tourists do not stay overnight.

The climate of Venice is conditioned by its position on the sea; although it is subject to cold spells in winter and oppressive heat on some summer days, there is almost always a refreshing sea breeze. As everywhere in Italy Venice is crowded with Italian school parties from March until early May.

Passports

Passports are necessary for all travellers from Britain and North America entering Italy. Visitors from Australia and New Zealand do not require visas, but those from South Africa do. A lost or stolen passport can be replaced by the British or US embassy in Rome (information from the Consulates in Venice and Milan, see p 50). You are obliged to carry some means of identity with you when in Italy.

Italian Tourist Boards

The Italian State Tourist Office (**ENIT**, *Ente Nazionale Italiano per il Turismo*) provides detailed information about Italy at its website, www.italiantourism.com.
Australia c/o Italian Chamber of Commerce and Industry, Level 26, Market St, Sydney, ☎ 02 9262 1666; ☐ 02 9262 5745.
Canada 1 Place Ville Marie, Suite 1914, Montreal, Quebec, H3B 2C3, ☎ 001 514 886 7667; ☐ 514 392 1429; ✉ initaly@ucab.net.
Netherlands Stadhoudeskade 2, 1054 ES Amsterdam, ☎ 003 120 616 8244; ☐ 120 618 8515.
UK 1 Princes Street, London W1R 8AY, ☎ 020 7408 1254 or 020 7355 1557; ☐ 020 7493 6695; ✉ enitlond@globalnet.co.uk, www.enit.it.
USA 630 Fifth Avenue, Suite 1565, New York, NY 101111, ☎ 001 212 245 5633; ☐ 212 586 9249; ✉ enitny@italiantourism.com. 500 North Michigan Avenue, Suite 2240, Chicago I, IL 60611, ☎ 001 312 644 0996, ☐ 312 644 3012; 12400 Wilshire Blvd, Suite 550, Los Angeles, CA 90025, ☎ 310 820 1898, ☐ 310 820 6357; ✉ enitala@earthlink.net.

Venice web sites
www.turismovenezia.it
ACTV transport system: www.actv.it

Tour operators

Among those which offer package holidays to Venice from the UK are:

Abercrombie & Kent Travel, Sloane Square House, Holbein Place, London SW1W 8NS, ☎ 020 7559 8500, 📠 020 7730 9376, ✉ info@abercrombie kent.co.uk, www.abercrombiekent.co.uk.

Citalia (CIT Holidays Ltd), Marco Polo House, 3–5 Lansdowne Road, Croydon, Surrey CR9 1LL, ☎ 020 8686 5533, ✉ www.citalia.co.uk.

CTS Travel (UK) Ltd, 44 Godge Street, London W1P 2AD, ☎ 020 7436 4878, 📠 020 7580 5675, ✉ www.ctstravel.co.uk.

Italiatour (part of Alitalia), 9 Whyteleafe Business Village, Whyteleafe Hill, Whyteleafe, Surry CR3 0AT, ☎ 01883 621 900, 📠 01833 625 255, ✉ www.alitalia.it/italiatour. In the US ☎ 800 845 3365; in Canada ☎ 888 515 5245.

Magic of Italy, King's House, 12–42 Wood Street, Kingston-upon-Thames, Surrey KT1 1JF, ☎ 02700 270 500 for reservations, 0990 462 442 for brochures, ✉ www.magictravelgroup. co.uk.

Martin Randall Travel Ltd, 10 Barley Mow Passage, London W4 4PH, ☎ 020 8742 3355, 📠 020 8742 7766, ✉ info@martinrandall.co.uk.

Prospect Music & Art Tours Ltd, 36 Manchester Street, London W1U 7LH, ☎ 020 7486 5704, 📠 020 7486 5686, ✉ enquiries@prospecttours.com.

Sunvil, Sunvil House, Upper Square, Old Isleworth, Middlesex TW7 7BJ, ☎ 020 8758 4722, 📠 020 8568 8330, ✉ www.sunvil.co.uk.

Travelscene, 11–15 St Ann's Road, Harrow Middlesex HA1 1LQ, ☎ 020 8863 2787, 📠 020 8861 5083, ✉ www.travelscene.co.uk.

Health and insurance

British citizens, as members of the EU, have the right to claim health care in Italy if they have the E111 form issued by the Department of Health and available at main post offices. For additional cover they may want to take out a private insurance policy, and this is certainly advisable for visitors from outside the EU. Keep the receipt (*ricevuta*) and medical report (*cartella clinica*) to present to your insurer.

Currency

On 1 January 2002 the Euro (€) is to replace the Italian lire as the official monetary unit. The fixed exchange rate for one Euro is Lire 1936.270. There will be bank notes of 5, 10, 20, 50, 100, 200 and 500 Euro, and coins of 1, 2, 5, 10 and 50 Eurocents as well as 1, and 2 Euro. For a few months the Lire will stay in circulation also, but will then be withdrawn. Travellers' cheques and Eurocheques are the safest way of carrying money while travelling, and most credit cards are now generally accepted in shops, hotels, and restaurants, and at some petrol stations. Outside banks in the centre of Venice there are numerous cashpoints called Bancomat (check with your own bank about any charges associated with their use), and also automatic machines which change foreign bank notes.

Disabled travellers

Italy is as last catching up with the rest of Europe in the provision of facilities for the disabled. All new public buildings are now obliged by law to provide access for the disabled, and specially designed facilities. In the annual list of hotels in Venice published by the *APT*, hotels which are able to provide hospitality for the disabled are indicated. Airports and railway stations in Italy provide assistance, and for rail travel the disabled are entitled to a 'carta blu' which allows a discount on the price of the fare. Trains equipped to carry wheelchairs are listed in the railway timetable published by the *FS* and available at news-stands. Museums and galleries should all now have facilities for the disabled, including specially designed toilets.

Access to public transport in Venice is greatly facilitated by the fact that wheel-chairs can be wheeled straight on to the vaporetti (but not motoscafi; see p 39). Although it has been estimated that some 40 per cent of the most important buildings in Venice can be reached without having to cross a bridge, the greatest obstacles in the city remain the numerous bridges. Ponte delle Guglie (Pl. 3; 5) over the Cannaregio canal has been equipped with a ramp. A mechanical lift is in operation on Rio dei Fuseri (Pl. 8; 6); the key is at present kept nearby at the shop of Testolini (with copies at the *APT* and **Municipio**). Other lifts have been installed on Riva del Carbon (Palazzo Dolfin-Manin; Pl. 8; 4), near San Lio (Pl. 9; 3), on Murano at Ponte Santa Chiara, and on Burano. There are plans to install another lift between Campo Santo Stefano and Campo Sant'Angelo (Pl. 8; 5). On the *APT* maps of Venice the areas in yellow are accessible to the disabled. A map entitled *Veniceforall* gives more information (available from the local health authority offices **ULSS** at 3493 Dorsoduro, near Piazzale Roma). For further information contact the *APT* in Venice, the Comune (☎ 041 976 435 or 041 529 5711), or *Informahandicap*, ☎ 041 534 1700.

Getting there

By air

Direct daily air services operate throughout the year between London and Venice, and from numerous European cities, including Amsterdam, Brussels, Frankfurt, Munich, Lugano, Zurich, and Paris. From the US there are non-stop flights to Milan, with connecting flights on to Venice. Credit card bookings can be made on the web, where information on cut price tickets can also be found.

From the UK *Alitalia* (☎ 0870 544 8259; ✉ www.alitalia.co.uk) from London Gatwick.
British Airways (☎ 0990 444 000 or 0345 222 111; ✉ www.british-airways.com) from London Heathrow.
Go (☎ 0845 6054321; ✉ www.go-fly.com) from London Stansted.
  There are also services from regional airports.

From the USA and Canada *Alitalia* (☎ 1 800 223 5730; ✉ www. alitaliausa.com) from New York (JFK or Newark), San Francisco, and Los Angeles to Milan.
American (☎ 212 489 7004, ✉ www.aa.com) from Chicago to Milan.
Continental (☎ 1 800 231 0856, ✉ www.continental.com) from New York to Rome.

Delta (☎ 1 800 241 4141, ✉ www.delta-air.com) and *TWA* (☎ 1 800 892 4141, ✉ www.twa.com) from New York to Milan.
Air France, *British Airways*, *KLM*, *Lufthansa* and *Sabena* offer flights connecting through Paris, London, Amsterdam, Frankfurt, Munich and Brussels which are often cheaper than direct flights.

By rail

There are now frequent trains from London Waterloo through the Channel Tunnel via Calais to Paris Gare du Nord in c 3 hours. Venice can be reached by the over night sleeper from Paris Gare de Lyon. For details, contact *European Rail Ltd* (☎ 020 7387 0444; ▤ 020 7387 0888, ✉ www.raileurope.co.uk).

The luxury *Venice Simplon Orient-Express* runs twice a week for most of the year from London via Paris, Zurich, and Innsbruck to Venice (details from *Venice Simplon Orient Express Ltd*, ☎ 020 7805 5100, and in the US ☎ 800 524 2420.

In the North America, information on rail travel is available from *CIT*: New York, ☎ 212 697 1394; Los Angeles, ☎ 310 338 8616; Montreal, ☎ 514 845 9109; Toronto, ☎ 416 927 7712.

Rail websites

www.fs-on-line.com (the *Italian State Railway* website)
www.freedomrail.co.uk
www.itwg.com/home.asp
www.railchoice.co.uk (arranges rail travel between London and Italy via Paris, and will also issue tickets for travel within Italy)

By coach

Eurolines (☎ 01582 404 511; ✉ www.eurolines.com) operates services from London Victoria to Milan or Bologna, the nearest centres for Venice. There are discount fares for the unders 26s, but even so the fare is still high compared to the cut-price air tickets now available.

By car

You are strongly advised to approach the city by rail or air, rather than by road, if possible, since you have to leave your car in a multi-storey garage or an open-air car park, none of which are free, and space can be very limited. If, however, you are travelling by car, Venice is approached by a network of motorways. It is connected by motorway with Milan (via Brescia, Verona, Vicenza, and Padua), and with Rome, Florence, and Bologna (via Ferrara and Padua); both these routes meet at *Padova Est* and the exit for Venice is at *Mestre*. The motorway from Trieste and the Dolomites converge at *Mestre Est*, the most convenient exit for Venice.

By sea

Steamers and **cruise ships** usually anchor at the *Stazione Marittima* on the Giudecca canal and at San Basilio (1401 Zattere; Pl. 12; 2), ☎ 041 533 4860. Smaller ships sometimes anchor at the quays alongside Rive dei 7 Martiri (Pl. 10; 8). Steamer services operate from Turkey, Egypt, Greece and the Middle East. For boats from Padua along the Brenta canal, see p 52.

Private boats can sometimes find moorings at the Diporto Velico Veneziano, Sant'Elena (Pl. 16; 6); the port on the Isola di San Giorgio Maggiore (Cini Foundation); or near the Punta della Dogana on the Giudecca canal. More space is available at Punta Sabbioni. The *Port Authority Office* (Capitaneria di Porto) is on the Fondamenta delle Farine (Pl. 8; 8), ☎ 041 533 4111.

Arriving in Venice

By air

Venice airport—*Marco Polo*—is at Tessera on the lagoon 9 kilometres north of the city (☎ 041 260 6111; arrivals information, ☎ 041 260 9240; departures information; ☎ 041 260 9250; lost property office, ☎ 041 260 6436). It has direct flights from London and many other European cities, and internal services from Milan and Rome. The best way of reaching Venice from the airport is by the motorboat service called *Alilaguna* (☎ 041 523 5775) which runs at least every hour from 06.15 to 00.20. It approaches the city across the lagoon via Murano, and calls at the Lido, the Arsenal, San Marco and the Zattere (the entire trip takes 1hour 20 minutes). *Alilaguna* also runs an hourly service at peak hours from the airport direct to the Fondamente Nuove, going on to call at Santa Giustina, Riva degli Schiavoni and terminating at San Marco (the entire trip takes just one hour). It costs Lire 17,000.

A less pleasant (but cheaper and faster) approach to the city from the airport is via the mainland by *ACTV* bus to Piazzale Roma (Pl. 6; 1), which has services about every half hour (from 04.40 to 00.40). There is also an excellent bus service which takes 20 minutes run by *ATVO* (blue coaches; ☎ 520 5530) in conjunction with flight arrivals and departures between the airport and Piazzale Roma (departures from the airport between 08.50 and 23.20).

From Piazzale Roma there are 24 hour vaporetti services to all destinations (see below). Radio taxis are also available 24 hours at the airport, ☎ 041 541 5084 (by motorboat) or by car to Piazzale Roma.

By train

The **railway station**—*Stazione Santa Lucia* (Pl. 2; 8)—is right on the Grand Canal, near its west end. For information, ☎ 147 888 088; lost property, ☎ 041 785 238. Venice was first connected by rail to the mainland in 1846; the station was rebuilt in 1955. It has a restaurant, a left luggage office (always open), a bank, information offices, public toilets and shower-rooms. Vaporetti, motor-boat taxis, and gondolas operate from the quay outside.

By car

Venice was connected to the mainland by a causeway (Ponte della Libertà) in 1933, and you have to leave your car at one of the garages or open air car parks (unless you are going on to the Lido in which case you board the car ferry at Tronchetto; see below). Parking space is very limited (the garages are used also by Venetian residents). At the most crowded times of year automatic signs on the motorway approaches indicate the space available at the time of arrival in the various car parks and garages.

Car parks Piazzale Roma (Pl. 6; 1). The most convenient car park (multi-storey garages) with a landing-stage (served by water-bus nos **1**, **52**, and **82**, and an all-night service) on the Grand Canal, and a taxi-stand. The garage at the end of the bridge is the *Autorimessa Comunale di Venezia* (municipal car park) used almost exclusively by Venetian residents (Lire 30,000 or c €15 every 24hrs). Other garages here charge considerably more (around Lire 8000 or c €4 every 2hrs). For information ☎ *ASM* 041 272 7211. It is forbidden to park outside in Piazzale Roma; cars are towed away by the police to Via Torino, Mestre.

Isola del Tronchetto (beyond Pl. 6; 1). Garage parking for 3500 cars (open 24hrs) which costs Lire 30,000 or c €15 every 24hrs. ☎ 041 520 7555. This is also served by vaporetti services to San Marco (no. **82**, and an all-night service), see below.

Open-air car parks (cheaper than the garages) are also open at certain times of the year (carnival time, Easter and in the summer) at **San Giuliano** (see atlas 16), and at **Fusina** (see p 73). When open (for information, *ASM*, ☎ 041 272 7211), these are also connected to Venice by vaporetti services.

If the car parks are full, cars have to be left on the mainland in **Mestre** or **Marghera**, both connected by frequent bus and train services to Venice. One of the cheapest car parks is in front of Mestre station (trains to Venice every 10 minutes in 8 minutes). There are also car parks on the far (east) side of the lagoon at **Punta Sabbioni**, **Treporti**, and **Cavallino**. These are much further away from Venice, but are sometimes less full. They are also connected to Venice by vaporetti services (less frequent than the main services, see below).

Information and hotel booking offices

The following **information offices** supply an up-to-date list of opening times of museums and churches, a list of hotels, a free map of Venice, details of annual festivals, and other information on request.

APT information offices in Venice: Venice Pavilion, Giardinetti Reali (Pl. 8; 8), ☎ 041 522 5150 open daily 10.00–18.00; and 71 c/f San Marco (Pl. 8; 6), ☎ 041 529 8740, usually open 09.00–16.00.

APT head office: Calle del Rimedio, 4421 Castello (Pl. 9; 3).

Smaller *APT* branches at the railway station (open 08.00–19.00), Piazzale Roma car park, and the airport. There is usually an office open also at the Marghera exit from the Milan autostrada. In summer there is an office on the Lido in Viale Santa Maria Elisabetta.

On arrival, **hotel booking facilities** are run by the *Associazione Veneziana Albergatori* (*AVA*) at the above subsidiary *APT* offices, the airport and the car parks at Piazzale Roma (in the Autorimessa Comunale garage) and Tronchetto. ☎ 041 523 8032; last minute booking (toll free number) 800 843006. There is also a toll-free number for tourist complaints: 800 355920.

There are now numerous agencies and hotel representatives in Britain and America who specialise in making hotel reservations (normally for 5-star and 4-star hotels only). Information about hotels in Venice can be obtained abroad from the *ENIT* offices (see National Tourist Boards, p 13).

 Where to stay

Hotels

There are five official categories of hotels in Italy from the luxury 5-star hotels to the most simple 1-star establishments. These categories are bound to disappoint many travellers, however, for they are now based on the services offered (television in each room, private telephone, and *frigobar*, for example) and often do not reflect quality. 3-star and 4-star hotels in Venice are not always on a par with hotels with the same designation in the other large European cities. Often hotels in the same category differ greatly in quality.

Accommodation may also be booked through agencies in the **UK** including *HPS Hotel Reservations*, Archgate, 823–825 High Road, Finchley, London N12 8UB, ☎ 020 8446 0126, 🖨 020 8446 0196, ✉ www.hotel-reserve.com and *Hotel Connect*, Birkley House, 18–24 High Street, Edgeware HA8 7RP, ☎ 020 8381 3131, ✉ enquiries@hotelconnect.co.uk, ✉ www.go-fly.com (via *Go* airline's website).

Every hotel has to declare its **prices** annually. Prices change according to the season, and can be considerably less in off peak periods. In the foyer there should be a list of all the rooms in the hotel with their rates, and the total charge for a room (excluding breakfast) should be displayed on the back of the room door. For tax purposes hotels are obliged by law to issue an official receipt (*ricevuta fiscale*).

In all hotels service charges are included in the rates, so tipping is not necessary. You should beware of **extra charges** added to the bill. Drinks from the *frigobar* in your room are extremely expensive, so it is always best to buy drinks yourself from a shop outside the hotel. Telephone calls are also more expensive if made from your room; there is usually a pay telephone in the lobby which is the most economical way of telephoning and is more convenient than using the public telephones in the streets. A large supplement is usually charged for breakfast served in your room.

Breakfast (*prima colazione*) can be disappointing and costly. By law it is an optional extra charge, although a lot of hotels try to include it in the price of the room. When booking, always specify if you want breakfast or not. If you are staying in a one- two- or three-star hotel, it is usually a good idea to go round the corner to the nearest *pasticceria* or bar for breakfast. In some of the more expensive hotels good buffet breakfasts are now provided, but even here the standard of the 'canteen' coffee can be poor: you can always ask for an *espresso* or *cappuccino* instead.

Hotels are all listed with their rates in the annual (free) publication of the *APT*, *Venezia: Hotels, Residences, Campings* (available from tourist information offices). Many of the luxury five-star and four-star hotels are near San Marco, on the Grand Canal, or on Riva degli Schiavoni. Numerous more simple hotels, often in attractive and quieter positions, are also situated near these areas.

One of the most pleasant parts of the city in which to stay is the Dorsoduro, an area less crowded with tourists. Rooms in Venetian hotels tend to be particularly small because of the way the city is built. The hotels near Piazzale Roma and the station (mostly in Lista di Spagna; Pl. 3; 5) are convenient (and easy to reach with luggage) but in a much less attractive part of the town. If all the hotels in Venice are full it is worth staying in Treviso or Padua (see pp 52 and 53 and *Blue Guide Northern Italy*), both only half an hour away by train, rather than in Mestre and the industrial area of Marghera, the nearest places to Venice on the mainland, which have numerous hotels, but provide no substitute for a stay in Venice itself.

As Venice has a great number of visitors, it is **essential to book well in advance**, especially in September and October, in spring, at Carnival time, around Christmas and the New Year, and at weekends (particularly those which fall near Italian public holidays). To confirm the booking a deposit is usually required (often the price of the room for one night): this can often be made by credit card (you have the right to claim this back if you cancel the booking at least 72 hours in advance).

Prices are raised from 15 March–15 November, and 20 December–2 January, and at Carnival. Payment by credit card is becoming more and more common, but not every hotel accepts them. For complaints, ☎ 800 355 920, toll free.

Venice is divided into six *sestieri* (districts) (San Marco, Dorsoduro, Castello, San Polo, Santa Croce, and Cannaregio), and the houses are numbered consecutively within these districts. When writing to a hotel the only address necessary is the name of the sestiere and its number, as given in the list below.

Venice has about 200 hotels and only a small selection has been given below. Some hotels are closed in winter. The hotels given below are listed according to category and location. The keys refer to the atlas section at the back of the book.

Five-star hotels

Gritti Palace (b; Pl. 8; 7), San Marco 2467, ☎ 041 794 611, ▤ 041 520 0942, ✉ res073.grittipalace@luxurycollection.com. An old-established hotel in a 16C palace at the beginning of the Grand Canal, furnished with great taste in Venetian style. Less grand than the *Daniele*, with just under a hundred rooms, it is one of the smaller luxury-class hotels in the city, in a quiet position near San Marco, with a particularly friendly atmostphere. Its restaurant is on a terrace built out on to the Grand Canal, and it has a renowned foyer bar. Owned by the *Starwood* hotel group, with private motor-boat service to the *Excelsior* and *Des Bains* hotels on the Lido (with swimming pools and sea bathing). John and Effie Ruskin stayed here in 1851.

Danieli (a; Pl. 9; 5, 6), Castello 4196, ☎ 041 522 6480, ▤ 041 5200208, ✉ res072.danieli@luxurycollection.com. One of the most famous hotels in Venice opened in 1822. It has a *fin de siècle* atmosphere and distinguished visitors have included George Sand, Alfred de Musset, Charles Dickens, Ruskin, Wagner, Debussy, and Proust. It is a rather gloomy neo-Gothic palace on the busy Riva degli Schiavoni, a few steps from the Palazzo Ducale (an extension built in 1948 is one of the most ugly buildings in Venice). Now owned by the *Sheraton* hotel group (see above), it has over two hundred rooms (the best and most expensive are those overlooking the lagoon), and an elegant bar. The luxury class restaurant on the roof has unattractive furniture but a superlative view of the lagoon.

Palazzo dei Dogi (ca; Pl. 4; 3), Fondamenta Madonna dell'Orto, Cannaregio 3500, ☎ 041 220 8111, ▤ 041 220 8999, ✉ grandhoteldeidogi@boscolo.com. Recently opened. The special attraction of this hotel is that it is in an exceptionally peaceful and attractive area of the city, a long way from the tourists, and therefore highly recommended for those who wish to have a quiet holiday. It has a long walled garden, with fine trees, which stretches all the way to the lagoon (looking towards the island of San Michele), with its own private watergate, and delightful terrace on the waterfront. The 70 bedrooms are pleasantly furnished, although the bathrooms a little bit small. There are seven particularly grand rooms (more expensive) with high ceilings and chandeliers. The restaurant is tastefully decorated and there are lovely marble floors. It is part of the *Boscolo* group of hotels.

Four-star hotels

Cipriani (d; Pl. 15; 5), Giudecca 10, ☎ 041 520 7744, ▤ 041 520 3930, ✉ info@hotelcipriani.it. The hotel is in a secluded part of the city, on the island of the Giudecca (with a private motor-boat service), with a large swimming pool, a tennis court, and a renowned restaurant, surrounded by lovely gardens. Favoured by the rich and famous. It was founded by Giuseppe Cipriani of **Harry's Bar** in an undistinguished building of 1958, with a rather banal decor where the colour brown predominates. It is open from the end of March to the beginning of November, but it now has a small dependence, in the handsome Palazzo Vendramin, open all year.

Colombina (cb; Pl. 9; 3), Calle del Remedio, 4416 Castello, ☎ 041 277 0525, ▤ 041 277 6044, ✉ info@hotelcolombina.com. Opened in 1999, with just 32 rooms, it does not take groups. No-smoking rooms are available on request. It is in a pretty palace on the Rio di Palazzo (at the end of the canal can be seen the Bridge of Sighs), with its own watergate. Although in a very central position, it is on a quiet calle and canal. Three of the rooms have balconies on the canal and two rooms on the fourth floor have *altane* (roof terraces), with splendid views (reached by short flights of steps). The marble floors are '*alla veneziana*' and there are nice marble bathrooms. The rooms on the inside overlooking a courtyard cost less (but are larger). No restaurant.

Europa & Regina (h; Pl. 8; 8), San Marco 2159, ☎ 041 240 0001, ▤ 041 523 1533, ✉ res075.europa&regina@westin.com. In three palaces (including the 17C Palazzo Tiepolo) on the Grand Canal opposite the church of Santa Maria della Salute. The most attractive and largest rooms are those with cool marble floors and neo-Classical furniture, others are much simpler and carpeted. Owned by the **Starwood** hotel group, it has friendly and efficient staff, and most of its clients are American or Japanese. Approached on foot through a very secluded campo. It has a delightful luxury-class restaurant on the waterfront.

Monaco & Grand Canal (e; Pl. 8; 8), San Marco 1325, ☎ 041 520 0211, ▤ 041 520 0501, ✉ mailbox@hotelmonaco.it. Also at the beginning of the Grand Canal near San Marco. Furnished in an undistinguished style, somewhat lacking in atmosphere. Owned by the **Benetton** group with seventy rooms recently renovated. It has a luxury-class restaurant on the Grand Canal.

Other four-star hotels

Near San Marco *Luna Baglioni* (f; Pl. 8; 6), San Marco 1243, ☎ 041 528 9840, ▤ 041 528 7160, ✉ prenotazioni@baglionihotels.com, www.baglioni hotels.com; *Cavalletto & Doge Orseolo* (n; Pl. 8; 6), San Marco 1107, ☎ 041 520 0955, ▤ 041 523 8184, ✉ cavalletto@sanmarcohotels.com, www.san-marcohotels.com; *Saturnia & International* (i; Pl. 8; 5), San Marco 2399, ☎ 041 520 8377, ▤ 041 520 7131, ✉ info@hotelsaturnia.it, www.hotelsatur-nia.it; *Starhotel Splendid Suisse* (g; Pl. 8; 4), San Marco 760, ☎ 041 520 0755, ▤ 041 528 6498, ✉ splendidsuisse.ve@starhotels.it, www.starhotels.it; *Concordia* (p; Pl. 9; 5), San Marco 367, ☎ 041 520 6866, ▤ 041 520 6775, ✉ info@hotelconcordia.it, www.hotelconcordia.com.

Near the Rialto *Giorgione* (cc; Pl. 4; 8), Cannaregio 4587, ☎ 041 522 5810, ▤ 041 523 9092, ✉ giorgione@hotelgiorgione.com, www.hotelgiorgione.com.

On Riva Degli Schiavoni *Gabrielli Sandwirth* (j; Pl. 10; 5), Castello 4110 ☎ 041 523 1580, ▤ 041 520 9455, ✉ hotelgabrielli@libero.it; *Londra Palace* (k; Pl. 9; 6), Castello 4171, ☎ 041 520 0533, ▤ 041 522 5032, ✉ info@hotelondra.it,

www.hotelondra.it; *Metropole* (l; Pl. 9; 6), Castello 4149, ☎ 041 520 5044, 🗏 041 522 3679, ✉ Venice@hotelmetropole.com, www.hotelmetropole.com/.
Near the station *Amadeus* (ee; Pl. 3; 5), Cannaregio 227, ☎ 041 220 6000, 🗏 041 220 6020, ✉ booking@gardenahotels.it, www.gardenahotels.it; *Bellini* (yy; Pl. 3; 5), Cannaregio 116, ☎ 041 524 2488, 🗏 041 715 193, ✉ reservation@bellini.boscolo.com, www.boscolohotels.com; *Principe* (gg; Pl. 3; 5), Cannaregio 146, ☎ 041 220 4000, 🗏 041 220 4020, ✉ booking@gardenahotels.com, www.gardenahotels.it.

Three-star hotels

Locanda ai Santi Apostoli (bs; Pl. 4; 8), Cannaregio 4391, ☎ 041 521 2612, 🗏 041 521 2611, ✉ aisantia@tin.it, www.veneziaweb.com/santiapostoli. A charming little hotel on the third floor, very imaginatively designed, with a main room overlooking the Grand Canal. The eleven rooms, with wooden ceilings and Venetian marble floors, are particularly spacious. Extra charge for the two rooms on the Grand Canal. Family run.

San Cassiano, Ca' Favretto (ao; Pl. 4; 7), Santa Croce 2232, ☎ 041 524 1768, 🗏 041 721 033, ✉ info@sancassiano.it, www.sancassiano.it. In a spacious old palace on the Grand Canal with a lovely ground floor, splendidly furnished with tapestries and chandeliers. The rooms on the floors above have high ceilings (the best are the seven on the Grand Canal). There is no lift. There is a tiny terrace on the waterfront and a little entrance court with tables outside.

Flora (t; Pl. 8; 8), San Marco 2283a, ☎ 041 520 5844, 🗏 041 522 8217, ✉ info@hotelflora.it. A hotel with an extremely friendly atmosphere, and lovely little garden. The rooms are well furnished. It is also equipped to take disabled guests.

Kette (nn; Pl. 8; 6), San Marco 2053, ☎ 041 520 7766, 🗏 041 522 8964, ✉ info@hotelkette.com, www.hotelkette.com. In a peaceful position, a well run hotel, with a very friendly atmosphere. Pleasantly furnished, with good bathrooms.

Locanda Remedio (bu; Pl. 9; 3); Castello 4412, ☎ 041 520 6232, 🗏 041 521 0485. A pleasant little hotel in an extremely narrow quiet calle, off a rio near Santa Maria Formosa, and only a short distance from Piazza San Marco. It is in a nice old palace with a rather choosy proprietor.

Accademia Villa Maravege (ah; Pl. 7; 8), Dorsoduro 1058, ☎ 041 521 0188, 🗏 041 523 9152, ✉ info@pensioneaccademia.it, www. pensioneaccademia.it. A well-known old-established hotel in the quiet area of Dorsoduro, with a garden and secluded garden court for breakfast. Since it is also reasonably priced for its category, it is necessary to book well in advance. Some of the rooms and bathrooms are very small.

Carpaccio (bb; Pl. 7; 4), San Polo 2765, ☎ 041 523 5946, 🗏 041 524 2134. A small simple hotel notable for its position in the 16C Palazzo Barbarigo on the Grand Canal. Six rooms overlook the Grand Canal, and twelve are on the smaller Canale di San Polo.

Santo Stefano (aq; Pl. 7; 6), San Marco 2957, ☎ 041 520 0166, 🗏 041 522 4460, ✉ info_htl.sstefano@tin.it, www.hotelscelio.sstefano.com. A small hotel in a Gothic palace on the pleasant large Campo Santo Stefano near the foot of the Accademia Bridge. It has tiny rooms, but good bathrooms.

Savoia & Jolanda (z; Pl. 9; 6), Castello 4187, ☎ 041 520 6644, 🗏 041 520 7494, ✉ savoia.ve.san@iol.it, www.elmoro.com/savoia&jolanda. A pleasant late 19C building on the Riva degli Schiavoni, with a fine view of the Isola di San Giorgio Maggiore. Residents are allowed a 25 per cent discount at the restaurant.

Most of the rooms are small; the more spacious ones cost considerably more. It is in the process of renovation, and the newer rooms are rather heavily furnished. It has a quieter annex in Campo San Zaccaria. It may become a 4-star hotel.

La Calcina (ai; Pl. 13; 4), Dorsoduro 780, ☎ 041 520 6466, ▤ 041 522 7045, ✉ la.calcina@libero.it, www.lacalcina.com. In a delightful position on the Zattere overlooking the Giudecca canal, where Ruskin stayed in 1877. The rooms overlooking the waterfront are more expensive. Modernised bathrooms. There is terrace built out onto the water for the use of guests.

Locanda Sturion (za Pl. 8; 4), Calle Sturion, San Polo 679, ☎ 041 523 6243, ▤ 041 522 8378, ✉ info@locandasturion@com, www.locandasturion.com. A small hotel near the Rialto but in a peaceful position. On the top floor (with no lift), it has some rooms overlooking the Grand Canal. It is furnished in a heavy 19C style, but has Venetian marble floors.

Other three-star hotels

Near San Marco *Bridge* (m; Pl. 9; 3), Castello 4498, ☎ 041 520 5287, ▤ 041 520 2297, ✉ info@hotelbridge.com, www.hotelbridge.com; *Ala* (o; Pl. 8; 7), San Marco 2494, ☎ 041 520 8333, ▤ 041 520 6390, ✉ alahtlve@gpnet.it, www.hotelala.it; *Bonvecchiati* (q; Pl. 8; 6), San Marco 4488, ☎ 041 528 5017, ▤ 041 528 5230, ✉ hbonvecc@tin.it, www.hotelinvenice.it; *Boston* (r; Pl. 8; 6), San Marco 848, ☎ 041 528 7665, ▤ 041 522 6628, ✉ bostonhotel@libero.it, www.bostonhotel.it; *Casanova* (s; Pl. 8; 6), San Marco 1284, ☎ 041 520 6855, ▤ 041 520 6413, ✉ hotel.casanova.ve@iol.it, www.side7.it/casanova; *La Fenice et des Artistes* (u; Pl. 8; 5), San Marco 1936, ☎ 041 523 2333, ▤ 041 520 3721, ▤ 041 520 3721, ✉ fenice@fenicehotels.it. www.charmerelax.com; *Lisbona* (oo; Pl. 8; 6, 8), S. Marco 2153, ☎ 041 528 6774, ▤ 041 520 7061, ✉ info@hotellisbona.com, www.hotellisbona.com; *San Zulian* (zb; Pl. 9; 3), San Marco 534, ☎ 041 522 5872, ▤ 041 523 2265, ✉ h.sanzulian@iol.it, www.hotelsanzulian.it; *Santa Marina* (zc, Pl. 9; 3), Campo Santa Marina, Castello 6068, ☎ 041 523 9202, ▤ 041 520 0907, ✉ info@hotelsanta marina.it, www.hotelsantamarina, it; *Montecarlo* (v; Pl. 9; 5), San Marco 463, ☎ 041 520 7144, ▤ 041 520 7789, ✉ mail@venicehotelmontecarlo.com, www.venicehotelmontecarlo.com; *San Marco* (w; Pl. 8; 6), San Marco 877, ☎ 041 520 4277, ▤ 041 523 8447, ✉ marcohtl@tin.it, www.sanmarcohotel.com/sanmarco; *Ambassador Tre Rose* (y; Pl. 8; 6), San Marco 905, ☎ 041 522 2490, ▤ 041 522 2490, ▤ 041 522 2123, ✉ ambassador@samarcohotels.com, www.sanmarcohotels.com; *Panada* (ii; Pl. 9; 3), San Marco 646, ☎ 041 520 9088, ▤ 041 520 9619, ✉ info@hotel panada.com, www.hotelpanada.com; *Do Pozzi* (hh; Pl. 8; 7), San Marco 2373, ☎ 041 520 7855, ▤ 041 522 9413, ✉ hotel.dopozzi@flashnet.it, www.hoteldopozzi.it; *San Moisè* (pp; Pl. 8; 6), San Marco 2058, ☎ 041 520 3755, ▤ 041 521 0670, ✉ info@sanmoise.it, www.sanmoise.it; *Ateneo* (qq; Pl. 8; 6), San Marco 1876, ☎ 041 520 0777, ▤ 041 522 8550, ✉ ateneo@ateneo.it, www.ateneo.it; *Scandinavia* (ar; Pl. 9; 3), Castello 5240, ☎ 041 522 3507, ▤ 041 523 5232, ✉ info@scandinaviahotel.com, www.scandinaviahotel.com; *Firenze* (mm; Pl. 8; 6), San Marco 1490, ☎ 041 522 2858, ▤ 041 520 2668, ✉ info@hotel-firenze.com, www.hotel-firenze.com; *Violino d'Oro* (cd; Pl. 8; 6), San Marco 2091, ☎ 041 277 0841, ▤ 041 277 1001, ✉ violino@violinodoro.com, www.violinodoro.com.

Near Riva degli Schiavoni *Bisanzio* (aa; Pl. 9; 6), Castello 3651, ☎ 041 520 3100, 📠 041 520 4114, ✉ email@bisanzio.com, www.bisanzio.com; *Commercio & Pellegrino* (ww; Pl. 9; 6), Castello 4551, ☎ 041 520 7922, 📠 041 522 5016, ✉ htlcomm@tin.it, www.commercioepellegrino.com/.

Near the Rialto *Tintoretto* (bt; Pl. 4; 5), Cannaregio 2316, ☎ 041 721 522, 📠 041 721 791, ✉ hoteltintoretto@hoteltintoretto.com, www.hotel tintoretto.com; *Malibran* (an; Pl. 8; 2), Cannaregio 5864, ☎ 041 522 8028, 📠 041 523 9243, ✉ info@hotelmalibran.it, www.hotelmalibran.it. *Da Bruno* (tt; Pl. 9; 3), Castello 5726a, ☎ 041 523 0452, 📠 041 522 1157.

On Dorsoduro *American* (zz; Pl. 13; 2, 4), Dorsoduro 628, ☎ 041 520 4733, 📠 041 520 4048, ✉ hotameri@tin.it, www.hotelamerican.com.

Near the Station *Alle Guglie* (c; Pl. 3; 5), Cannaregio 1523, ☎ 041 717 351, 📠 041 717 715, ✉ info@alleguglie.it, www.hotelalleguglie.it; *Al Sole* (dd; Pl. 6; 4), S. Croce 136, ☎ 041 710 844, 📠 041 714 398, ✉ info@alsole palace.com, www.alsolepalace.com; *Continental* (ff; Pl. 3; 5), Cannaregio 166, ☎ 041 7155 122, 📠 041 524 2432, ✉ continental@ve.nettuno.it, www. hotelguide.com; *Abbazia* (kk; Pl. 2; 6), Cannaregio 66, ☎ 041 717 333, 📠 041 717 949, ✉ abbazia@iol.it, www.venezialberghi.com; *Santa Chiara* (ap; Pl. 6; 2), S. Croce 548, ☎ 041 520 6955, 📠 041 522 8799, ✉ conalve@ doge.it, www.santachiara. com; *Gardena* (ab; Pl. 6; 2), S. Croce 239, ☎ 041 220 5000, 📠 041 220 5020, ✉ booking@gardenahotels.it, www.gardenahotels.it.

Two-star hotels

Agli Alboretti (al; Pl. 7; 8), Dorsoduro 882/4, ☎ 041 523 0058, 📠 041 521 0158, ✉ alborett@gpnet.it. A little family-run hotel, with small modernised rooms, in the quiet Dorsoduro next to the Gallerie dell'Accademia. It has a restaurant in an open courtyard behind.

Antica Locanda Montin (at; Pl. 13; 1), Dorsoduro 1147, ☎ 041 522 7151, 📠 041 520 0255, ✉ locandamontin@libero.it. A few rooms above the restaurant of *Montin*, very popular with the British. On a charming small rio in Dorsoduro. *La Residenza* (ag; Pl. 10; 5), Castello 3608, ☎ 041 528 5315, 📠 041 523 8859, ✉ info@venicelaresidenza.com, www.venicelaresidenza.com. A small hotel in a lovely old Gothic palace in the peaceful Campo Bandiera e Moro beside the church of San Giovanni in Bragora. It has a splendid old frescoed portego on the piano nobile with a piano and comfortable chairs and where breakfast is served. The rooms are pleasant, and the bathrooms have been modernised.

Seguso (aj; Pl. 13; 4), Dorsoduro 779, ☎ 041 528 6858, 📠 041 522 2340. A charming old-fashioned pensione on the Zattere overlooking the wide Giudecca canal. The bedrooms are large and pleasantly furnished, with marble floors. It does not take groups, and in the high season it is obligatory to have at least one meal a day at the restaurant.

Alla Salute da Cici (ak; Pl. 14; 3), Dorsoduro 228, ☎ 041 523 5404, 📠 041 522 2271, ✉ hotel.salute.dacici@iol.it. A reliable hotel in a very quiet position in Dorsoduro (Rio delle Fornace). However, it is big enough to take group bookings, so can be noisy if full. It is rather unimaginatively furnished, but has a courtyard where breakfast is served in summer.

Wildner (vv, Pl. 9; 6) 4161 Riva degli Schiavoni, ☎ 041 5227463, 📠 041 5265615, ✉ wildner@veneziahotels.it, www.veneziahotels.com/wildner.htlm. A simple, family run hotel with a restaurant, in a lovely position on the Riva degli Schiavoni overlooking the lagoon. All the rooms have bathrooms.

Other two-star hotels

On Dorsoduro *Messner* (ak; Pl. 14; 3), Dorsoduro 216, ☎ 041 522 7443, 📠 041 522 7266, ✉ messner@doge.it; *Tivoli* (ad; Pl. 7; 3), Dorsoduro 3838, ☎ 041 524 2460, 📠 041 522 2656, ✉ h.tivoli@tin.it.

Near San Marco *Al Piave* (bv; Pl. 9; 3, 4), Castello 4838, ☎ 041 528 5174, 📠 041 523 8512, ✉ hotel.alpiave@iol.it, www.elmoro.com/al piave; *Astoria* (jj; Pl. 8; 6), S. Marco 951, ☎ 041 522 5381, 📠 041 520 0771, ✉ info@astoria.it, www.astoriahtl.it; *Gallini* (ll; Pl. 8; 5), S. Marco 3673, ☎ 041 520 4515, 📠 041 520 9103, ✉ hgallini@tin.it; *Serenissima* (ss; Pl. 8; 6), S. Marco 4486, ☎ 041 520 0011, 📠 041 522 3293, ✉ serenhtl@tin.it ; *Rio* (bc; Pl. 9; 3), Castello 4356, ☎ 041 523 4810, 📠 041 520 8222, ✉ info@aciugheta-hotelrio.it, www.aciugheta-hotelrio.it.

Near Riva Degli Schiavoni *Bucintoro*, 2135 Riva San Biagio (zd; Pl. 10; 8), ☎ 041 522 3240, 📠 041 523 5224; *Campiello* (ze; Pl. 9; 6), Campiello del Vin, Castello 4647, ☎ 041 520 5764, 📠 041 520 5798, ✉ campiello@hcampiello.it, www.hcampiello.it; *Paganelli* (vv; Pl. 9; 6), Castello 4182, ☎ 041 522 4324, 📠 041 523 9267, ✉ hotelpag@tin.it, www.gp net.it/paganelli.

Near the station *Hesperia* (ac; Pl. 3; 5) Cannaregio 459, ☎ 041 715 52512, 📠 041 715 112, ✉ hesperia@shineline.it.

One-star hotels

Locanda Fiorita (af; Pl. 8; 5), 3457 San Marco, ☎ 041 523 4754, 📠 041 522 8043, ✉ locafior@tin.it, www. locandafiorita.com. A tiny hotel near Campo Santo Stefano, in a very quiet position.

Villa Rosa (be; Pl. 2; 6), 389 Calle Misericordia, Cannaregio, ☎ 041 718976, 📠 041 716 569, ✉ villarosa@ve.nettuno.it. A pleasant little hotel in an attractive house with a walled courtyard where you can sit or have breakfast in the summer. Although very close to the station off the Lista di Spagna, it is in a peaceful position at the end of Calle Misericordia (past numerous other less pleasant hotels). The rooms are all very different, some with views over the rooves and balconies, and most of them well lit. One single room, and a number of family rooms. Friendly atmosphere and good value.

Locanda Ca'Foscari (ch; Pl. 7; 4), 3887B Calle della Frescada, Dorsoduro, ☎ 041 710 401, 📠 041 710 817, ✉ valtersc@tin.it. Just 11 very pleasant rooms on the second and third floor with lovely views (some overlooking the calle and some an internal garden). No lift, non-smokers preferred. Efficiently run by a family. The quiet rooms have marble floors and all have showers or baths. It does take small groups so you need to book well in advance.

Al Gambero (ba; Pl. 8; 6), Calle dei Fabbri 4687, San Marco, ☎ 041 522 4384, 📠 041 520 0431, ✉ hotgambero@tin.it. A delightful small hotel with 27 rooms on three floors (no lift), some overlooking the canal and others the calle, with marble bathrooms. The pleasantest rooms are on the first floor with pretty windows. No groups taken. Charming breakfast room. It may become a 2-star.

Other one-star hotels

Near San Marco *Riva* (am; Pl. 9; 3), Castello 5310, ☎ 041 522 7034, 📠 041 528 5551; *Locanda Silva* (bd; Pl. 9; 5), Castello 4423, ☎ 041 523 7892,

041 528 6817; *Noemi* (rr; Pl. 8; 6), S. Marco 909, ☎ 041 523 8144, 041 277 1005, ✉ hotelnoemi@tin.it, www.hotelnoemi.com.
On Dorsoduro *Galleria* (zf; Pl. 7; 8), 878 Accademia (at the foot of the Accademia bridge), ☎ 041 520 4172, 041 520 4172, ✉ galleria@tin.it, www.hotelgalleria.it.
Near Riva Degli Schiavoni *Casa Linger* (bw; Pl. 10; 5), Castello 3541, ☎ 041 528 5920, 041 528 4851.
Near the Rialto *Al Vagon* (bg; Pl. 8; 2), 5619 Cannaregio, ☎ 041 528 5626, 041 528 5626.
Near the station *Al Gobbo* (zg; Pl. 3; 5), Cannaregio 312, ☎ 041 715 5001, and numerous others.

Hotels in the lagoon

The **Lido** (see p 250) is a resort with numerous hotels, most of them closed in winter. Some of them have swimming-pools, tennis courts and private beaches. The Lido is a pleasant place to stay in summer but if you want to savour the unique atmosphere of Venice you are strongly advised to choose a hotel in the city itself.
Five-star hotel. *Westin Excelsior*, Lungomare Marconi 41, ☎ 041 526 0201, 041 526 7276, ✉ res077.excelsior@westin.com, www.westin.com. **Four-star hotels.** *Des Bains*, Lungomare Marconi 17, ☎ 041 526 5921, 041 526 0113, ✉ res078.desbains@starwoodhotels.com, www.sheraton.com; *Hungaria Palace*, 28 Gran Viale, ☎ 041 242 0060, 041 526 4111, ✉ info@hungaria.it, www.hungaria.it, with a good restaurant; *Quattro Fontane*, 16 Via 4 Fontane, ☎ 041 526 0227, 041 526 0726, ✉ info@quattro-fontane.com; *Villa Mabapa*, 16 Riviera S. Nicolò, ☎ 041 526 0590, 041 526 9441, ✉ info@villamabapa.com, www.villamabapa.com; *Le Boulevard*, 41 Gran Viale, ☎ 041 526 1990, 041 526 1917, ✉ boulevard@leboule-vard.com, www.boulevard.com; *Villa Laguna*, 6 Via San Gallo, ☎ 041 526 0342, 041 526 8922, ✉ info@bagaglino.it, www.bagaglino.it; *Biasutti*, 24 Via Dandolo, ☎ 041 526 0120; 041 526 1259, ✉ biasuttiho-tels@tin.it. **Three-star hotels.** *Riviera*, 5 Gran Viale Santa Maria Elisabetta, ☎ 041 526 0031, 041 526 5979, ✉ riviera-htl@libero.it; *Helvetia*, Gran Viale Santa Maria Elisabetta 4/6, ☎ 041 526 0105, 041 526 8903, ✉ info@hotelhelvetia.com, www.hotelhelvetia.com; *Rigel*, 13 Via E. Dandolo, ☎ 041 526 8810, 041 276 0077; *Atlanta Augustus*, 15 Via Lepanto, ☎ 041 526 0569, 041 526 5604, info@hotelatlanta.net, www.hotelatlanta.net; *Petit Palais*, 54 Lungomare Marconi, ☎ 041 526 5993, 041 526 0781, ✉ info@hotelpetitpalais.com, www.hotelpetitpalais.com. Also two-star and one-star hotels.

On the coast north of the Lido the resorts of **Cavallino** and **Lido di Jesolo** are both well supplied with hotels.

On the island of **Torcello**, the *Locanda Cipriani* (Isola di Torcello, 29; ☎ 041 730 150; 041 735 433) has 6 rooms (three doubles and three singles), renovated in 2000. Famous for its luxury class restaurant, this is one of the most delightful and peaceful places to stay in Venice in winter (although it is closed in January), but prices are the equivalent of a four-star hotel.

On the charming little island of **Burano** *Raspo de ua* (Piazza Galuppi, 560 Burano, ☎ & 041 730 095), with a garden, is the only one-star hotel on an island in the lagoon. Reached by a regular boat service from the Fondamente Nuove in 40 minutes.

At the south end of the lagoon, **Chioggia** and **Sottomarina** (see p 257) also have a number of hotels.

Locande

These are tiny hotels with fewer than 7 rooms so not officially allowed to be classified as hotels, although not all hotels entitled Locanda fall into this group as some of them have over 7 rooms and therefore do appear in the offical list of hotels.

Locanda al Leon (cf; Pl. 9; 5), Campo Santi Filippo e Giacomo 4270 Castello, ☎ 041 277 0393, 🖷 041 521 0348, ✉ leon@hotelalleon.com. In a very central location, just off Campo San Filippo e Giacomo, with just six rooms in a family house. Opened in 1998, it has a delightful atmosphere, and is particularly popular with Americans. The door on the street leads straight into a pretty little hall with the staircase. No smoking. All the rooms (including a family room which sleeps four), simply furnished with great taste, have bathrooms with showers, and overlook the campo, campiello, or calle. Prices change according to the season. An ideal place to stay.

Locanda Casa Querini (ce; Pl. 9; 3), Campo San Giovanni Novo, 4388 Castello, ☎ 041 241 1294; 🖷 041 241 4231, ✉ parpayola@libero.it. Another particularly delightful place to stay, opened at the end of 1999. Six charming spacious high-ceilinged rooms, well furnished, overlooking a very quiet campo. It has air conditioning and rooms for non-smokers. In summer you can sit outside in the campo for breakfast.

Hostels

The *Venice Youth Hostel* (*Ostello per la Gioventù*) is on the Giudecca (Fondamenta Zitelle 86; Pl. 14; 6), in a splendid position (260 beds) ☎ 041 523 8211, 🖷 041 523 5689. A bed here costs Lire 27,000 or c €14 a night. It is closed for the last two weeks in January. Bookings should be made in advance in writing.

Italian Youth Hostels Association (*Associazione Italiana Alberghi per la Gioventù*), 44 Via Cavour, 00184 Roma, ☎ 06 474 1256, ✉ www.hostels-aig.org. In Venice, the AIG has offices in Calle di Castelforte (near San Rocco), 3101 San Polo, ☎ 041 520 4414.

Most hostels are run by religious organisations, and they are listed in the annual *APT* hotel list. They charge betwen 21,000 and 50,000 a night and include: the *Istituto Canossiano*, Ponte Piccolo, 428 Giudecca (women only), ☎ 041 522 2157, the *Foresteria Valdese* (run by the Waldensians), Palazzo Cavagnis, Calle Lunga Santa Maria Formosa, 5170 Castello, ☎ /🖷 041 528 6797, and the *Casa Cardinal Piazza*, 3539a Fondamenta Contarini, Cannaregio, ☎ 041 721 388; 🖷 041 720 233.

Among the institutes which offer lodgings for young tourists in the summer period are the following: *Domus Cavanis*, Sant'Agnese, 912 Dorsoduro, ☎ 041 522 2826; *Domus Civica*, S Polo 3082, ☎ 041 721 103; the *Patronato Salesiano Leone XIII*, Giardini di Castello 1281, ☎ 041 240 3611; *Suore Salesie*, Rio delle Eremite, Dorsoduro 108 (women only), ☎ 041 522 3691; and *Santa Fosca*, Cannaregio 2372, ☎ 041 715 775.

Rooms and apartments for rent

The *APT* supplies a list of Venetians who have rooms to rent *(affittacamere)* in private lodgings. Short lets are available (also for just a week or even a weekend) through real estate agencies (list from the Venice tourist board). These include *New Ital Tourist*, 4700 San Marco, ☎ 041 520 8848, 🖹 041 522 6043; *ABC Immobiliare*, ☎ 041 523 7759; and *House Deal Consulting*, ☎ 041 520 9352; 🖹 041 528 9671.

Camping

Camp sites are listed in the annual *APT* hotel list, from the most expensive four-star sites, to the simplest and cheapest 1-star sites. Their classification and rates charged must be displayed at the camp site office.

The sites nearest Venice on the mainland are on the outskirts of Mestre and Marghera, near Marco Polo airport (four-star *Alba d'Oro*, at Ca' Noghera, ☎ 041 541 5102, open April–Sept), at Tessera (one-star *Marco Polo*, ☎ 041 541 6033, closed mid Nov–mid Feb), and at Fusina (two-star *Fusina*), near Malcontenta, ☎ 041 547 0055; 🖹 041 547 0050 (open all year). On the mainland north of the Lido there are numerous camp sites along the coast at Punta Sabbioni, Cavallino, Lido di Jesolo, Eraclea Mare, Cáorle, and Bibione, and there are also sites in the southern part of the lagoon at Chioggia and Sottomarina.

 # Food and drink

Venetian specialities

First courses

Risotto is a favourite Venetian first course. The rice is often cooked with fish (*risotto di pesce*), or with inkfish (cuttlefish) in their ink (*risotto nero* or *risotto di seppie*). *Risotto primavera* is a vegetable risotto, while *risi e bisi* is a risotto served in spring cooked with fresh peas, celery and ham. As in the rest of Italy, pasta is served in numerous ways in Venice (see the menu below), fish sauces (such as *pasta alle vongole*, spaghetti with clams) being the most common. A winter dish is *pasta e fagioli*, a bean soup made from haricot beans and short pasta seasoned with bay and dressed with olive oil. Polenta in Venice is made from a particularly fine grained maize from the Friuli region and tends to be white, and served in a more liquid form than the more usual yellow polenta popular in the rest of Italy.

A delicate first course, only available in season, is baby grey shrimps (*schie*) served with polenta. Cold hors d'oeuvre include *sarde in saor*, fried sardines, marinated in vinegar and onions, and *granseola*, dressed crab in its shell. Mussels (*cozze*) in their shells are also often served in Venice: if they are *in bianco* they are lightly cooked with parsley and garlic, whereas *cozze al pomodoro* is a richer spicier dish.

In summer raw (cured) ham (*prosciutto crudo*) is particularly good (the best come from San Daniele in Friuli or Parma) served with melon or green figs.

Second courses

Meat Among the meat dishes is the famous *fegato alla veneziana*, calf's liver thinly sliced and fried with onions; otherwise Venetians tend to prefer poultry to red meat, although *Carpaccio*, raw beef sliced very thinly and sometimes served with bitter green salad and parmesan cheese, was invented in Venice.

Fish The chief speciality of Venetian cooking is fish, which is always the most expensive item on the menu. Especially good (but expensive) is fish such as *dentice* (dentex) or *orata* (bream) of a size suitable for one person, often best served grilled. The cheapest fish dish is usually *fritto misto*, small fried fish, including octopus, squid, cuttlefish, and prawns. Crustaceans include *scampi* (the Venetian word for shrimp), which are often served grilled, or boiled and dressed with olive oil, lemon, salt, and pepper.

Among the more unusual fish dishes are *seppie*, cuttlefish (or inkfish), usually cooked in their own ink and served with polenta. Eel (*anguilla* or *bisato*) is often available: it is sometimes grilled, or *alla Veneziana*, cooked in lemon with tuna fish, or marinated in oil and vinegar (with a bay leaf) and then fried with wine and tomato. Crab is also a favourite Venetian dish: *granseola* is dressed crab served cold in its shell; *molecche* (or *moeche*) are soft shelled tender baby crabs, stuffed with egg and fried and served hot (they are only available in early Spring); *mezancolle* are also a variety of crab. Scallops are called *capesante*, and clams are *caparozzoli*. *Baccalà* is salt cod: when called *baccalà mantecato* it is cooked in milk, oil, and garlic, and blended into a creamy mixture, and when simmered in milk it is called *baccalà alla vicentina*. *Stoccafisso* is unsalted cod. *Sampiero* is John Dory and *Coda di rospo* is angler fish (served grilled or baked). *Zuppa di pesce*, fish stew made with a variety of fish, is a meal in itself.

Vegetables which are particularly good in spring include locally grown asparagus and artichokes. A vegetable found almost exclusively in Venice and the Veneto is *radicchio rosso*, bitter red chicory usually served grilled.

It is worth spending time looking (if not buying!) at the splendid Rialto markets, open every morning except Sunday (see Ch. 17) where the local fish and vegetables can be seen in all their splendour.

Desserts Although Venice has numerous cake shops which sell delicious confectionary the city is not famous for its desserts. However, the rich *Zabaione*, made with beaten egg yolk and Marsala, and *tiramisù*, made with biscuits, coffee, mascarpone, and eggs are sometimes served in restaurants.

A great variety of delicious biscuits are baked in Venice, and sold at *pasticcerie* (cake-shops and bars), bakeries, or grocery stores. They include *zaeti*, made partly from cornmeal, and *Bussai buranei*, made in Burano. The Venetians are very fond of the simple biscuits (rather similar to rusks) known as *baicoli*, made from wheat flour, sugar, salt, and yeast. Fritters (*frittelle*) are often served in bars in winter (especially at Carnival time), flavoured with raisins, pine nuts or lemon peel. Charming biscuits in the form of St Martin on horseback, decorated with sugar and chocolate are widely available all over the city on the feast of San Martino in early November. At this time *cotognata* (or *persegada*), a sweet made from quinces is also sold. After Christmas, for Epiphany, *pinsa* is made from cornmeal, fennel seeds, raisins, candied fruit and dried figs.

Drinks

A tradition persists in Venice and the Veneto of taking an *ombra* or *ombreta* (usually before dinner): a glass of white or red wine (or sparkling white wine, *prosecco*) in a *bacaro* or *osteria* (a selection of these is given on p 35). The word *ombra* means shadow and there was once a stall in the shadow of the campanile in Piazza San Marco which sold wine by the glass. Some people prefer a cocktail: *spritz* is a typical Venetian cocktail made from white wine, bitters, and lemon soda, and the *Bellini* is a famous cocktail invented at the **Bar Cipriani**, the ingredients of which include champagne and peach juice. *Mimosa* is a cocktail made with orange juice. *Ombre* or cocktails are served with delicious savoury snacks (*cicchetti*), a great Venetian speciality, usually a small fish, a piece of cooked vegetable, or a piece of tasty cheese.

Wine

In restaurants it is often advisable to accept the house wine (*vino della casa* or *vino sfuso*); white and red are usually available. This varies a great deal, but is normally a vin ordinaire of average standard and reasonable price. Bottled wines from the Verona area include the well-known *Valpolicella* (red), *Soave* (white), and *Bardolino* (red or rosé). The wines from Friuli can be excellent, particularly those from the Collio region (the white Tocai, Pinot grigio, and Sauvignon, and the red Merlot, Cabernet, and Pinot nero). Good white wines from the Alto Adige are also sometimes available (for example those from Tramin, Lake Caldaro, and Novacella). Prosecco, a sparkling white wine from Conegliano-Valdobbiadene (the best is often Cartizze), is popular as an aperitif.

The menu

A selection of typical Italian dishes, which often appear on menus all over the country, are listed below (for Venetian specialities, see above).

Hors d'ouevres ~ *antipasti*

Antipasto di mare is a seafood hors d'oeuvre, whereas an *antipasto misto* usually has a variety of raw hams and salami, olives, and *crostini*, small pieces of toast or bread with a type of paté made out of chicken livers, capers, and anchovies.

Affettati usually include Parma ham, *salami* and *finocchiona* or *sbriciolona* (a delicious salami cured with fennel). In summer raw ham (*prosciutto crudo*) is served with melon or figs. *Pinzimonio* is a plate of fresh raw vegetables (artichokes, fennel, celery, carrots, etc.) which are dipped in a dressing (usually oil and lemon).

In the autumn *fettunta* or *bruschetta* is sometimes served: toasted bread with garlic and oil straight from the olive press.

First courses ~ *primi piatti*

Italy is famous for its numerous pasta dishes and often the first course in a restaurant is the best part of the meal. Various types of pasta are served with a tomato sauce (*al pomodoro*) or a meat sauce (*al ragù* or *al sugo di carne*), made with minced meat, sausage, herbs, and tomato andcooked at length. *Penne all'arrabbiata* or *penne strascicate* is short pasta in a rich spicy tomato sauce, and *penne all'Amatriciana*, is short pasta served with a sauce of salt pork and tomato. *Pappardelle alla lepre* are large flat noodles made with flour and egg with a rich hare sauce. *Fettuccine* or *tagliatelle*, are ribbon noodles usually freshly made on the premises, often served with a meat sauce or with *porcini* mushrooms. *Taglierini* or *tagliolini* is thin pasta served with a sauce or in broth. *Spaghetti alla carbonara* is spaghetti with bacon, beaten egg, and black pepper sauce. *Lasagne* or *pasticcio* is layers of pasta with meat or fish filling and cheese and tomato sauce. *Cannelloni* are rolled pasta 'pancakes' with meat filling and cheese and tomato sauce. *Ravioli* is pasta filled with spinach and ricotta cheese (or minced veal), and *cappelletti*, are a form of ravioli often served in broth. *Malfatti* are ricotta and spinach balls, usually served with butter and sage, and *tortellini*, small coils of pasta, filled with a rich stuffing served either in broth or with a sauce.

Gnocchi is a heavy pasta made from potato, flour, and eggs, usually served with a simple tomato sauce, and *gnocchi alla parigina*, or *alla romana*, is pasta made from maize.

Minestra or *zuppa* is a thick soup, and *brodo* is a clear soup. *Stracciatella* is broth with eaten egg and parmesan cheese. *Minestrone* is a thick vegetable soup with chopped vegetables (and sometimes pasta). In winter this is made with the addition of bread, cabbage and white beans and called *ribollita* or *minestra di pane.*

In summer, *panzanella* is often served, a cold salad made with bread, raw onions, tomatoes, cucumber, basil, oil and vinegar. Bread is also the basic ingredient in *pappa al pomodoro*, usually served hot or tepid, cooked with tomato sauce and basil. Haricot beans (*fagioli*) and chick peas are a favourite winter dish; beans are cooked with sage and dressed with oil, or in a tomato sauce *all'uccelletto*, or served with short pasta (*pasta e fagioli*). Lentils (*lenticchie*) are usually cooked with celery and garlic. *Ceci* are chick peas, usually cooked with oil, garlic and rosemary.

Main courses ~ *secondi piatti*

Meat ~ *carne* such as steak (*bistecca*) is often served simply grilled (*alla griglia*) or roasted (*arrosto*), in particular *agnello* (lamb) or *maiale* (pork). *Arista* is a joint of pork ribs cooked in the oven. *Manzo* (beef) or *vitella* (veal) is sometimes stewed slowly for a long time in red wine and a tomato sauce: there are a number of variations generally known as *stufato* (often served in slices), or *spezzatino* (a veal stew, usually with pimento, tomato, onion, peas, and wine). Veal is served also in numerous other ways: *Ossobuco* is stewed shin of veal, and veal escalopes (*braccioline*) are often served either cooked in lemon or wine (*scaloppine al marsala*). Veal cutlets with ham, covered with melted cheese are known as *costoletta alla bolognese*, whereas *costolette milanese* are veal cutlets fried in bread-crumbs, and *saltimbocca* is rolled veal with ham and herbs. *Involtini* are thin rolled slices of meat in a sauce.

Rabbit (*coniglio*) is often served, usually *in umido* or *alla cacciatora*, stewed in tomato sauce. The meat of rabbit and *faraona* (guinea fowl, almost always served roasted) is usually of better quality than chicken (*pollo*). *Pollo* or *coniglio alla cacciatore* is a chicken or rabbit dish made with herbs, and (usually) tomato, onion and pimento sauce.

Liver (*fegato*) is a favourite Venetian dish, but now harder to find are other traditional dishes using offal (*frattaglie*) such as brains (*cervello*), sliced kidneys sautéed with parsley (*rognoncini trifolata*), and sweetbreads (*animelle*). *Trippa* (tripe) is an unusual traditional dish, usually served cold.

Fish ~ *pesce* is always the most expensive item on the menu but can be extremely good in restaurants specialising in it. Among the most succulent and expensive are *dentice* (dentex), *orata* (bream) and *triglie* (red mullet) usually cooked simply *arrosto* (baked) or *alla griglia* (grilled). *Fritto di pesce* or *fritto misto di mare* has various types of small fried fish and crustacea almost always including *calamari* (squid) and *seppie* (cuttlefish), and is usually the most inexpensive fish dish on the menu. Seafood, often served cooked in white wine with garlic and parsley, includes *cozze* (mussels) and *vongole* (clams). These can also be served as a sauce for spaghetti. A good fish dish often to be found in simpler restaurants is *baccalà*, salt cod, usually served cooked in tomato sauce, but in Venice it is served in an unusual variety of ways (see above, Venetian specialities). *Zuppa di pesce* is a rich fish stew made with a wide variety of fish: if cooked with tomato sauce it is called *alla Livornese* since it is a speciality of Livorno, a Tuscan port.

Other fish include: *pesce spada*, sword-fish, *aragosta*, lobster (an expensive delicacy), *calamari*, squid, *sarde*, sardines, *coda di rospo*, angler fish, *branzino*, sea bass, *sgombro*, mackerel, *cefalo*, grey mullet, *sampiero*, John Dory, *sogliola*, sole, *tonno*, tuna fish, *trota*, trout, *gamberi*, prawns, *polipi*, octopus, *cannocchie* (or *pannocchie*), mantis shrimp, *acciughe*, anchovies, *capesante*, scallops, *molecche* or *mezancolle*, baby crabs.

Vegetarian dishes ~ *piatti vegetariani*

There are numerous excellent first courses without meat. The most nourishing include risotto, cannelloni, ravioli, malfatti, gnocchi, polenta. Pulses include haricot beans (*fagioli*), cooked in a variety of ways with or without tomato and sometimes together with short pasta, and chick peas (*ceci*) and lentils (*lenticchie*). *Melanzane alla parmigiana*, aubergine cooked in the oven with a cheese and tomato sauce and *peperonata*, stewed peppers, often with aubergine, onion, tomato, and potato, are particularly rich vegetable dishes. Large wild mushrooms (*porcini*) make an excellent second course (best grilled), although they are an expensive delicacy (only served in season, October–December and around Easter). Vegetable *tortini* are similar to omelettes and are good made with artichokes (*carciofi*) or courgettes (*zucchini*). Some type of cheese is almost always available.

Vegetables ~ *contorni*

The most popular vegetable dish is salad (*insalata*); *insalata verde* is green salad (only lettuce), and *insalata mista* usually includes tomatoes (*pomodori*) and raw carrot. Cooked vegetables include *spinaci*, spinach, *broccoletti*, tender broccoli, *fagiolini*, French beans, and *zucchini*, courgettes. Peas (*piselli*) are often cooked *al prosciutto*, that is with bacon, fresh garlic, and parsley. Artichokes (*carciofi*) are cooked in numerous ways and are best in spring: they are almost always served young and small and usually eaten whole. They may be *alla giudia* (deep fried) or *alla Romana* (stuffed with wild mint and garlic, and then stewed in olive oil and water).

Some restaurants serve excellent lightly fried vegetables, including courgette slices, artichoke hearts, courgette flowers, onions, tomatoes, and sage.

In spring *gobbi* (a vegetable related to the artichoke) are usually good. *Fagioli* (dried haricot beans) usually served as a first course (see above), are also considered a vegetable dish.

Fennel (*finocchio*) is a vegetable with a very distinctive taste, which is good both raw and cooked. Asparagus (*asparagi*), available in spring, are usually served with oil and lemon, or used in risotto.

Melanzane, aubergine are cooked in numerous ways, often grilled and served with oil and garlic; *melanzane alla parmigiana*, is a delicious dish made with a rich cheese and tomato sauce. Peppers (*peperoni*) are also served grilled with oil and garlic; *peperonata* is stewed peppers, often with aubergine, onion, tomato, and potato.

Potatoes (*patate*) are less popular in Italy than they are in Britain, and are usually not particularly good: they can be served boiled (*(lessi)* or fried *(patatine fritte)*.

Dessert ~ *dolci*

Italians usually prefer fresh fruit for dessert and sweets are considered the least important part of the meal. In many simple restaurants and trattorie often only fruit is served at the end of the meal. *Macedonia* (or *insalata di frutta*), fruit salad, is often available and is usually made with fresh friut in season. Otherwise you can order *frutta fresca* (fresh fruit) which varies according to what is in season but normally includes apples (*mele*) and pears (*pere*). Oranges (*arance*), mandarins and clementines (*mandarini* and *clementini*) are at their best in November and December, and grapes (*uva*) best in September. In summer peaches (*pesche*), apricots (*albicocche*), and cherries (*ciliege*) are often available. Particularly refreshing at the end of a meal in summer is melon (*melone*) and water melon (*anguria* or *cocomero*). Figs (*fichi*) are also sometimes served in summer, also as an hors d'ouvre with Parma ham. In spring strawberries (*fragole*) are served, usually with fresh lemon juice or in red wine. *Fragoline di bosco*, are tiny wild strawberries.

Crostata is a fruit flan, and *torta*, a tart made with nuts, chocolate, lemon, etc. *Zuppa inglese* is a rich trifle sometimes offered in smarter restaurants. *Torta della nonna* is a good pastry filled with custard and garnished with almonds. *Tiramisù* is a rich pudding based on mascarpone cheese, mixed with egg, chocolate, biscuits, and sometimes a liqueur. *Monte Bianco* is a rich dessert made from a purée of chestnuts. *Saint honoré* is a meringue cake. *Zabaione* is a hot sweet made with beaten egg yolks and Marsala wine. Ice-cream (*gelato*) is also widely available (but is not usually home-made in restaurants). *Cassata* is an ice cream cake.

You can also usually order cheese (*formaggio*) at the end of a meal. *Pecorino*, a sheep's cheese, is almost always available, and in spring is eaten with fresh raw broad beans. *Gorgonzola* is another well known Italian cheese. Goat's cheese is called *formaggio di capra*.

Where to eat

It has become extremely difficult to recommend **restaurants** in Venice (*ristoranti, trattorie*) since they change hands frequently and the standard often deteriorates once they become well known. Many of the numerous restaurants near San Marco cater for the international tourist market. Simpler trattorie (often better value) are to be found away from this area in the smaller campi. In the simplest trattorie the food is usually good, and considerably cheaper than in the more famous restaurants, though furnishings and surroundings can be a lot less comfortable. Although some restaurants serve excellent fish (always more expensive than meat) the general standard of Venetian cooking can be disappointing. Most restaurants display a menu outside which gives you an idea of the prices: however, many simpler restaurants do not, and here, although the choice is usually limited, the standard of the cuisine is often very high.

Lunch is normally around 13.00 and is the main meal of the day, while dinner is around 20.00 or 21.00. It is always acceptable to order a first course only, or to skip the first course and order only a main course. The most usual closing day is Monday. Restaurants have been very slow to introduce no smoking areas.

Service charges Prices are almost always inclusive of service, so always check whether or not the service change has been added to the bill before leaving a tip (if in doubt, ask the waiter). It is customary to leave a few thousand lire on the table to convey appreciation. For tax purposes restaurants are now obliged by law to issue an official receipt to customers (*ricevuta fiscale*); you should not leave the premises without this document. A cover charge (coperto— shown separately on the menu) is still sometimes added to the bill, although it has been officially abolished.

A selection of a few restaurants—divided into five categories according to price per person for dinner (bottled wine excluded)—is given below. Those in the lower categories are almost invariably the best value, particularly those in ££ range, but they can be crowded and are usually much less comfortable than the trattorie and restaurants in the higher price ranges.

£££££   above 100,000 lire or c €50 a head
££££   around 60,000 lire or c €30 a head
£££   around 40–60,000 lire or c €20–30 a head
££   around 30–40,000 lire or €15–20 a head
£   around 30,000 lire or c €15 a head, or less

Luxury (£££££)
Harry's Bar, Calle Vallaresso (Pl. 8; 8), ☎ 041 528 5777.
Quadri, 120 Piazza San Marco (Pl. 9; 5), ☎ 041 522 2105.
Taverna La Fenice, Campiello della Fenice (Pl. 8; 5), ☎ 041 522 3856 (closed while the building site of the new Fenice theatre is still in operation).
Osteria Da Fiore, Calle del Scaleter (Pl. 7; 4), ☎ 041 721 308.
   The restaurants in the following hotels (see above) have superb positions:
Gritti (Pl. 8; 7), ☎ 041 794 611.
Danieli (Pl. 9; 5, 6), ☎ 041 522 6480.
Cipriani (Pl. 14; 5), ☎ 041 520 7744.
Monaco and Grand Canal (Pl. 8; 8), ☎ 041 520 0211.

First-rate restaurants (££££)
Da Ivo, Ramo dei Fuseri, 1809 San Marco (Pl. 8; 4, 6), ☎ 041 520 5889.
Poste Vecie, 1608 Pescheria (Pl. 8; 1), ☎ 041 721 822.
Da Arturo, Calle degli Assassini (Pl. 8; 5), ☎ 041 528 6974.
Harry's Dolci, near Sant'Eufemia on the Giudecca (Pl. 13; 5) in a splendid position run by *Cipriani*, also a snack bar, ☎ 041 522 4844.
Malamocco, Campiello del Vin (Pl. 9; 6), ☎ 041 522 7438.
Al Theatro (also an elegant pizzeria), Campo San Fantin (Pl. 8; 5), ☎ 041 522 1052.
Carampane, Rio Terrà Rampani, near Campo San Polo (Pl. 8; 1), ☎ 041 524 0165.
La Corte Sconta, 3886 Calle del Pestrin (Pl. 10; 5), ☎ 041 522 7024.

Restaurants and trattorie (£££)
Alle Testiere, Calle del Mondo Novo (San Lio), 5801 Castello (Pl. 9; 3), a tiny restaurant, booking essential, ☎ 041 522 7220.
Da Remigio, 3416 Castello (Pl. 9; 4), ☎ 041 523 0089.

Antica Besseta, Salizzada Zusto (near San Giacomo dell'Orio; Pl. 3; 8), ☎ 041 721 687.

Da Ignazio, Calle dei Saoneri (Pl. 7; 4), ☎ 041 523 4852.

Alla Madonna, Calle della Madonna (Pl. 8; 2), ☎ 041 522 3824.

Antica Locanda Montin, Fondamenta di Borgo (Pl. 7; 1), ☎ 041 522 7151.

Riviera, 1473 Fondamenta delle Zattere (Pl. 13; 1, 3), ☎ 041 522 7621.

Altanella, Calle dell'Erbe, Giudecca (Pl. 13; 6), ☎ 041 522 7780.

Vini da Gigio, 3628 Fondamenta San Felice (Pl. 4; 6), ☎ 041 528 5140.

Trattoria da Gianni, 4377 Strada Nova (Pl. 4; 8), ☎ 041 523 7268.

Metropole, 4149 Riva degli Schiavoni (Pl. 9; 6) in a 4-star hotel with a set price buffet, ☎ 041 520 544.

Il Milion, behind the church of San Giovanni Crisostomo (Pl. 8; 2), ☎ 041 522 9302.

Simple trattorie of good value (££)

Antica Mola, Fondamenta degli Ormesini (Pl. 3; 4), ☎ 041 717 492.

Santo Stefano, Campo Santo Stefano (Pl. 8; 5), ☎ 041 523 2467.

La Zucca, Calle Larga, off Campo San Giacomo dell'Orio (Pl. 3; 8), ☎ 041 524 1570.

Al Giardinetto, 4928 Ruga Giuffa (Pl. 9; 3, 4), with a large garden, ☎ 041 528 5332.

La Donna Onesta, 3922 Calle Donna Onesta (off the Crosera near Ca'Foscari; (Pl. 7; 5), ☎ 041 710 586.

Le Bandierette, 6671 Barbaria delle Tole (Pl. 9; 2), ☎ 041 522 0619.

Ca' d'Oro ('alla vedova'), 3912 Calle del Pistor (Pl. 4; 7), ☎ 041 528 5324.

Melograno, 458 Calle Riello (Pl. 3; 5), ☎ 041 524 2553

Da Sandro, 2753 Calle Lunga San Barnaba (Pl. 7; 5, 7), ☎ 041 523 0531.

L'Incontro, Rio terrà Canal (Campo Santa Margherita; Pl. 7; 5), ☎ 041 522 2404.

Osterie or bacari (£)

Osterie or *bacari* (as they are known in Venice) are cheap eating places which sell wine by the glass and good simple food (usually crowded and often less comfortable than normal trattorie). Many of these are open only at lunch time and closed at weekends.

Ai Assassini, Rio Terrà degli Assassini (Pl. 8; 5), ☎ 041 528 7986.

Vivaldi, 1457 Calle Madonetta, off Campo San Polo (Pl. 8; 3), ☎ 041 523 8185.

Da Alberto, Calle Larga Giacinto Gallina (Pl. 9; 1) (closed Sun), ☎ 041 523 8153.

Osteria al ponte (often called *alla patata*), Calle dei Saoneri (Pl. 7; 4), with seating, ☎ 041 523 7238.

Al Mascaron, Calle Lunga Santa Maria Formosa (Pl. 9; 3, 4), ☎ 041 522 5995.

Al Volto, Calle Cavalli (Riva del Carbon; Pl. 8; 4), ☎ 041 522 8945.

Do Mori, off Ruga Vecchia San Giovanni Elemosinario; (Pl. 8; 1), no seating, ☎ 041 522 5401.

Osteria Antico Dolo, Ruga Vecchia San Giovanni, near Calle del Paradiso, San Polo (Pl. 8; 1), ☎ 041 522 6546.

Pietro Panizzolo (Carla), Corte Contarina, San Marco 1535A (Pl. 8; 6), ☎ 041 523 7855.

Osteria ai Postali, 821 Rio Marin, Santa Croce (Pl. 7; 1), ☎ 041 715 156.

Vini da Beppe, Pescheria (Pl. 8; 1).

Aciugheta, Campo Santi Filippo e Giacomo (Pl. 9; 5), ☎ 041 522 4292.

Bistro Veneziano, Calle dei Fabbri (Pl. 8; 4), ☎ 041 523 6651.
Schiavi (or Al Bottegon), Fondamenta Nani (Rio San Trovaso; Pl. 7; 8).
La Rivetta, Ponte San Provolo (Pl. 9; 6), ☎ 041 528 7302.
La Mascareta, Calle Lunga Santa Maria Formaosa (Pl. 9; 3), ☎ 041 523 0744.
San Giobbe, Fondamenta di San Giobbe (Pl. 2; 4), specialising in tripe .
Al Paradiso Perduto, 2540 Fondamenta della Misericordia (Pl. 4; 6), ☎ 041 720 581.
Caffè, Campo S. Margherita (Pl. 7; 5), ☎ 041 528 7998.
da Codroma, 2540 Ponte del Soccorso (Pl. 6; 6), with seating, ☎ 041 524 6789
ai Canottieri, 690 Fondomento di San Giobbe (Pl. 2; 4), ☎ 041 717 999.

These last four are popular with young people; they open until late and sometimes have music. There are also other *osterie* or *bacari* in Calle Lunga San Barnaba (Pl. 7; 5, 7); Calle dei Saoneri (Pl. 7; 4); and on the Fondamenta delle Zattere (Pl. 14; 4).

Pizzerie and self-service restaurants

There are a number of self-service restaurants in the centre of the city (notably in the *Frezzeria* Pl. 8; 6). Pizzas and other good hot snacks are served in a *pizzeria*, *Rosticceria*, and *tavola calda*. Some of these have no seating and sell food to take away or eat on the spot. There is a good simple pizzeria in the Ghetto called *Pizzeria al Faro* (1181 Ghetto Vecchio; Pl. 3; 3), and others with tables outside on the Zattere (Pl. 13; 3, 4). There are good *rosticcerie* in Sottoportego Calle della Bissa (Pl. 8; 4), and near the Teatro Goldoni.

Restaurants specialising in certain types of food, include the Jewish restaurant (*Gam-Gam*) near the entrance to the Ghetto by Ponte delle Guglie (Pl. 3; 5), an Syrian restaurant (*Sahara*) on Fondamenta della Misericordia (Pl. 4; 5), ☎ 041 721 077, and several Chinese restaurants near the Rialto.

Restaurants in the Venetian Lagoon

Murano, has a number of simple trattorie, including the *Osteria del Duomo*, at the foot of Ponte San Donato on Fondamenta Maschio. There is also a good bakery on this fondamenta.

Burano, has a number of fish restaurants, notably *Da Romano*, ☎ 041 730 030. The *Trattoria alla Maddalena* is a good restaurant on the island of **Mazzorbo**.

Torcello, has the famous luxury restaurant *Locanda Cipriani*, ☎ 041 730 150 (closed in January), and the cheaper *Al trono di Attila*, ☎ 041 730 094, much frequented by groups.

Lido, *Trattoria Andri*, 21 Via Lepanto; *al Porticciolo*, *Da Valentino*, and *Africa*, among others; *Da Nane al Canton*, and *Da Memo* at San Pietro in Volta.

Chioggia, has good fish restaurants including *El Gato*, Campo S. Andrea, and *Garibaldi* at Sottomarina. A cheaper trattoria (and pizzeria) is *Vecio Foghero*, 91 Via Scopici.

Isola di Sant'Erasmo, *Vignotto* (agriturismo) in Via Forti; *Isola delle Vignole*. *Trattoria Vignole Nuove all'Oasi* (open May–Sept).

Places to picnic

The most beautiful place to picnic in the lagoon is on the island of **Torcello** (it has no shops, so food must be bought in Venice). Other pretty places in the lagoon to picnic include **Malamocco** and **Alberoni** at the southern end of the Lido, and **Mazzorbo** and **Burano**.

The biggest public gardens in Venice are the **Giardini Pubblici** and the adjoining **Giardini Garibaldi** (inset Pl. 16) in Castello, both of which are pleasant places to picnic. The **Giardinetti Reali** is a small public garden, with a few benches, between Piazza San Marco and the waterfront. There are also public gardens near the railway station: in Canareggio, off Campo San Geremia; and the **Giardino Papadopoli** across the Grand Canal. Some of the larger campi have benches (including Campo di San Giacomo dell'Orio, Campo Santa Margherita, Campo Bandiera e Moro, Campo San Polo, and Campo del Ghetto Nuovo) and there are small grassy patches outside the churches of San Trovaso and San Pietro di Castello. There are also benches on the sunny Zattere overlooking the Giudecca canal (towards the Maritime station), and on the fondamente on the Giudecca (near the Zitelle).

Food for picnics Bars sell ready-made sandwiches (*tramezzini*) which can be very good (one of the best places to find freshly made sandwiches is the *Bar dei Nomboli*, 2717c Rio terrà dei Nomboli, Pl. 7; 4). Sandwiches (*panini*) can also be made up on request at grocery shops (*alimentari*). *Fornai* (bakeries) often sell delicious individual pizze, cakes, etc. There are excellent food markets open in the mornings (except Sunday) at the Rialto and in Rio Terrà San Leonardo and supermarkets in Campo Santa Margherita, on the Zattere (near the Stazione Marittima), and in Salizzada San Lio.

Cafés

Cafés and bars which are open from early morning to 20.00 or 21.00 (those with tables outside remain open longer on summer evenings), serve numerous varieties of excellent refreshments which are usually eaten standing up. You should pay the cashier first, and show the receipt to the barman in order to get served. Italians sometimes leave a small tip for the barman, but this is certainly not expected. If you sit at a table you are charged considerably more (at least double) and given waiter service (you should not pay first).

The two most famous cafés in the city are *Florian* and *Quadri* in Piazza San Marco (Pl. 8; 6/9; 5), with tables outside and orchestras; you are charged extra for your magnificent surroundings. *Harry's Bar* (Pl. 8; 8) is the most celebrated cocktail bar, but the *Danieli* and *Gritti* hotels also have foyer bars, renowned for their cocktails, décor and atmosphere.

Among the best cafés for ice-cream (*gelaterie*) are *Nico*, on the Zattere (Pl. 13; 4), *Paolin* in Campo Santo Stefano (Pl. 8; 5), and *Causin* in Campo Santa Margherita (Pl. 7; 5).

The best cake-shops (*pasticcerie*) include *Colussi* in the Calle Lunga San Barnaba (Pl. 7; 5, 3), *Marchini* in Calle del Spezier (Pl. 8; 5), *Vio* in Ramo Manin (Pl. 8; 4), *Rosa Salva*, four shops in Merceria San Salvador (Pl. 8; 4), Campo S. Luca (Pl. 8; 3), Calle Fiubera (Pl. 8; 6), and Campo Santi Giovanni e Paolo (Pl. 9; 1). *Dal Cò*, Calle dei Fabbri (Pl. 8; 6); *Tonolo*, near San Pantalon (Pl. 7; 3); *Canonica*, Campo Santi Filippo e Giacomo (Pl. 9; 5); *Rizzardini*, Campiello dei Meloni (near Campo San Polo; Pl. 7; 4); *Didovich*, Campo Santa Marina, near Campo di Santa Maria Formosa (Pl. 9; 3); and *Boscolo*, Campiello dell'Anconetta, near San Marcuola (Pl. 3; 6).

Getting around

Water-buses ~ vaporetti

An excellent service is run by *ACTV* (*Azienda del Consorzio Trasporti Veneziano*). Their headquarters are in Corte dell'Albero next to the Sant'Angelo landing-stage on the Grand Canal; information and ticket offices at Piazzale Roma, ☎ 041 528 7886, and Calle dei Fuseri, San Marco 1810 (Pl. 8; 6). A plan of the transport in the city is on pp 42–43. Transport information, ☎ 041 528 7886 or 041 240 9150, ✉ www.actv.it.

Tickets (in 2001, Lire 6000 or c €3) can be bought at tobacconists (*tabacchi*), newsagents, and most landing-stages, although since some landing-stages are not manned, and at others there can be long queues it is always best to buy a number of tickets at one time. If you board without a ticket, you can buy one from the conductor. Tickets must be stamped at automatic machines on the landing-stages before each journey.

Travelcards. It is usually well worthwhile buying one of the multiple journey tickets: either a 24hr (Lire 18,000 or c €9), a 72hr (Lire 35,000 or c €18) or a 7-day ticket (Lire 60,000 or c €30), which gives unlimited travel on all the lines. They are available at all manned landing stages (and need to be stamped just once at the automatic machine). A return ticket, which allows you to make two trips in one day on any line, costs Lire 10,000 or c €5. There are also 'family' tickets for groups of 3, 4 or 5 people valid for one journey or for 24hrs. There are also 3 'itinerary tickets', which cost Lire 15,000 or c €7, and allow unlimited travel for 12hrs on the Grand Canal, or in the lagoon to the north of Venice (including Murano, Burano, and Torcello), or on the route to Chioggia via the Lido and Pellestrina.

Student and youth fares. Young visitors in possession of the *Rolling Venice* card (see p 58) are entitled to special *ACTV* tickets which allows unlimited use of the system for 72 hrs (Lire 25,000 or c €13), sold at the manned landing stages.

It is also possible for non-residents to purchase a *tessera di abbonamento* which can only be obtained in person at the *ACTV* office at Piazzale Roma and must bear the photograph of the holder (it is valid for 3 years, and costs Lire 10,000 or c €5, plus a one-month season ticket). It entitles the holder to purchase monthly season tickets or single tickets at greatly reduced fares.

The *vaporetti* (nos 1 and 82) which serve the centre of the city, can carry up to 220 people and are more comfortable and provide better views for the visitor than the smaller and quicker *motoscafi* (nos 41, 42, 51, and 52) which make two circular routes of the city and carry around 130 people. Most of the services run at frequent intervals (every 10 minutes).

Timetables are usually available on request, free of charge, at the manned landing-stages; the summer timetable comes into force around 15 June and usually operates until the last day of September. All the services stick to a rigid timetable and are extremely reliable. Many landing-stages now have automatic illuminated signs listing the imminent departures. Despite the efficient service, well signposted landing stages and the courteous seamen who usually announce each stop when the boat docks, some services on the Grand Canal now also have automatic loud-speaker announcements and illuminated signs inside the cabin indicating the next stop. Some of the services (including no. 52) are suspended or modified during fog, although the Giudecca ferry, and the services to the Lido, and between Fondamente Nuove and Murano should be kept open whatever the weather conditions (using radar).

There are frequent variations in the routes taken by some of the *ACTV* services, and the numbers tend to change from one year to the next. Up-to-date information is always available at each landing-stage, or at the information offices.

Navigation services

Vaporetti routes serving the Grand Canal and the Giudecca

1 • (every 10 minutes by day, from 05.00 to 23.43). A comfortable vaporetto which runs slowly up and down the Grand Canal stopping at all landing stages on both banks, and providing superb views of the city. It takes just under an hour with 20 stops between Piazzale Roma and the Lido.
Piazza Roma (car park)–*Ferrovia* (Railway Station)–*Riva di Biasio–San Marcuola– San Stae* (Ca' Pesaro)– *Ca' d'Oro–Rialto–San Silvestro–Sant'Angelo–San Tomà* (Frari)–*Ca' Rezzonico–Accademia–Santa Maria del Giglio–Santa Maria della Salute–San Marco* (Vallaresso)–*San Zaccaria–Arsenale–Giardini–Sant'Elena– Lido*

82 • (vaporetto every 10 minutes, from 04.49 to 23.00). *San Zaccaria–San Giorgio Maggiore–Zitelle–Redentore–Palanca–Sant' Eufemia* (temporarily closed)–*Zattere–San Basilio–Sacca Fisola–Tronchetto–Piazza le Roma–Ferrovia* (Scalzi)–*San Marcuola–Rialto–Sant'Angelo-San Tomà–San Samuele–Accademia–San Marco* (Vallaresso). It takes the same route on the return journey

These two routes are substituted at night by a service (**N**) every 20 minutes calling at *San Zaccaria–San Giorgio Maggiore–Zitelle–Redentore–Palanca–Zattere–Palanca–San Basilio-Sacca Fisola–Tronchetto–Piazzale Roma–Ferrovia–San Marcuola–San Stae–Ca' d'Oro–Rialto–San Tomà–San Samuele–Accademia–Vallaresso–San Zaccaria– Giardini–Lido*. It takes the same route on the return journey

Traghetto. The ferry across the Giudecca canal from Zattere to Giudecca (Palanca) comes into operation at certain times of day

Circular *motoscafo* routes serving the Guidecca, Fondamente Nuove, and Murano and the Lido

41 • (every 20 minutes, circular route of the city in an anti-clockwise direction). *Murano* (Venier, Museo, Navagero, Faro, and Colonna stops)–*Cimitero–Fondamente Nuove– Madonna dell'Orto–Sant'Alvise–Cannaregio canal* (Tre Archi and Guglie stops)–*Ferrovia– Piazzale Roma–Santa Marta–Sacca Fisola–Palanca–Redentore–Zitelle–San Zaccaria–Arsenale–Giardini–Sant'Elena–Bacini–Celestia–Ospedale–Fondamente Nuove–Cimitero–Murano* (Colonna, Faro, Navagero, Museo, and Venier stops)

42 • (every 20 minutes, circular route of the city in a clockwise direction). *Murano* (Venier, Museo, Navagero, Faro, and Colonna stops)–*Cimitero–Fondamente Nuove–Ospedale–Celestia–Bacini–Sant'*

Elena–Giardini–Arsenale–
San Zaccaria–Zitelle–
Redentore–Palanca–Sacca
Fisola–Santa Marta–
Piazzale Roma–
Ferrovia–Cannaregio
canal (Guglie and Tre
Archi stops)–Sant'
Alvise–Madonna dell'
Orto–Fondamente Nuove–
Cimitero–Murano
(Colonna, Faro, Navagero,
Serenella, Venier, Museo
and Venier stops)

51 • (every 20 minutes,
circular route of the city
in an anti-clockwise
direction). Lido–San
Pietro di Castello–Bacini–
Celestia–Ospedale–
Fondamente Nuove–
Madonna dell'Orto–
Sant'Alvise–Cannaregio
canal (Tre Archi and
Guglie stops)–Ferrovia–
Piazzale Roma–Santa
Marta–Zattere–San
Zaccaria–Giardini–Sant'
Elena–Lido

52 • (every 20 minutes,
circular route of the city
in a clockwise direc-
tion). Lido–Sant'Elena–
Giardini–San Zaccaria–
Zattere–Santa Marta–
Piazzale Roma–Ferrovia–
Cannaregio canal (Guglie

and Tre Archi stops)–
Sant'Alvise–Madonna
dell'Orto–Fondamente
Nuove–Ospedale–
Celestia–Bacini–San
Pietro di Castello–Lido

61 • every 20 minutes
from Piazzale Roma–
Santa Marta–San
Basilio–Zattere–Arsenale
–Sant'Elena–Lido

62 • every 20 minutes
from Lido–Sant'Elena–
Arsenale–Zattere-San
Basilio–Santa Marta–
Piazzale Roma

Lagoon services

6 • San Zaccaria–Lido
(direct), by steamer
every 20–40 minutes
(offering fine views of
the city on the
approach from the Lido)

12 • (every 30–60 minutes). Fondamente
Nuove–Murano
(Faro)–Mazzorbo–
Torcello–Burano–Treporti.
To Torcello in 35 min-
utes; to Burano in 40
minutes; and to Treporti
in 65 minutes

14 • (every hour)
steamer from Ponte della
Paglia (Riva degli

Schiavoni)–Lido (Santa
Maria Elisabetta)–Punta
Sabbioni. Connection
from Punta Sabbioni by
vaporetto to Treporti,
Burano, and Torcello. To
Punta Sabbioni in 40
minutes; to Treporti in
70 minutes; to Burano
in 85 minutes; and to
Torcello in 90 minutes

13 • (c every hour)
Fondamente Nuove–
Murano (Faro)–Vignole–
Sant'Erasmo
(Capannone)–Lazzaretto
Nuovo (on request)–
Sant'Erasmo (Chiesa, and
Punta Vela stops). Some
services continue to
Treporti

20 • (service by small
motorboat) Riva degli
Schiavoni–San Servolo–
Isola di San Lazzaro degli
Armeni

11 • (runs c every hour).
The service leaves from
Riva degli Schiavoni for
Pellestrina and Chioggia
(bus connections are
used for part of the jour-
ney) Lido–Alberoni–Santa
Maria del Mare–
Pellestrina–Chioggia. The
trip takes about 1.5 hrs

Car ferry (no. 17; c every hour) from Tronchetto non-stop via the Giudecca canal
to the Lido in 30 minutes (the boat docks near San Nicolò (north of S.M. Elisabetta).
Summer services There are frequent variations in the services which operate
in summer. There is normally a direct vaporetto service from Tronchetto to San
Marco via the Grand Canal, and from the station via the Giudecca to San
Zaccaria. The latest services and timetables have to be checked on the spot.

By water taxi

Water taxis (motor-boats) charge by distance, and tariffs are officially fixed.
However, it is always wise to establish the fare before hiring a taxi. It is also possi-

ble to hire a taxi for sightseeing (hourly tariff). Taxi-stands are on the quays in front of the station (☎ 041 716 286), Piazzale Roma (☎ 041 716 922), Rialto (☎ 041 523 0575), San Marco (☎ 041 522 9750), the Lido (☎ 041 526 0059) and the airport (☎ 041 541 5084). Radio taxis: ☎ 041 723 112, 041 522 2303.

By gondola

Gondolas are of ancient origin and peculiar build, with the gondolier standing behind the passenger. By the 18C they had assumed their present form. The curious toothed projection forward, called the Ferro, is supposed to represent the six sestiere (districts) of the city. In 1562, in order to minimize the rivalry between noble houses, it was decreed that all gondolas should be painted black. Few noble Venetian families still maintain a private gondola. The wooden shelter, or felze, which used to protect passengers in bad weather is now no longer used. See also p 177.

To hire a gondola it is best to agree the fare at the start of the journey. They can be hired for 50 minute periods and the tariffs are fixed, with a night surcharge (after 20.00). There are gondola stands at the Station, Piazzale Roma, Calle Vallaresso (San Marco), Riva degli Schiavoni, Rialto, among other places.

Gondola ferries or *traghetti* cross the Grand Canal in several places (usually marked by green signs on the waterfront, and yellow signs in the nearest Calle), either straight (*diretto*) or diagonally (*trasversale*). They are a cheap and pleasant way of getting about in Venice and provide the opportunity to board a gondola for those who cannot afford to hire one (passengers usually stand for the short journey, which costs Lire 700 or c €14 cents). The fare is traditionally placed on the gunwale of the boat. There have been gondola ferries across the Grand Canal for centuries, and up until the 16C each ferry had its own guild.

At present they run at Calle Vallaresso to the Punta della Dogana; Campo Santa Maria del Giglio to the Salute area; San Barnaba (near Ca' Rezzonico) to San Samuele; San Tomà (near the Frari) to Santo Stefano and Sant'Angelo; Riva del Carbon to Riva del Vin in the Rialto area; Santa Sofia (near Ca' d'Oro) to the Rialto markets, San Marcuola to the Fontego dei Turchi; and at the Railway Station. They normally operate from 06.00 or 08.00–18.00 or 19.00 including fest., but some of them close at lunch time. Those at San Barnaba, Riva del Carbon and the Railway Station operate on a reduced timetable (mostly only in the morning), and the Santa Sofia ferry operates from 07.00–20.55 (fest. 07.30–18.55), and that at San Tomà until 20.30 or 21.00. Services are suspended in bad weather.

An association for the protection of gondolas has been instituted, for further information, ☎ 041 528 5075.

Buses on the Lido

These are run by *ACTV*. Tickets (which cost Lire 1400 or c €7 cents) are stamped at automatic machines on board. From Piazzale Santa Maria Elisabetta (at the vaporetti landing-stage) Service **A** to San Nicolò al Lido, and via Lungomare Marconi, to the Casinò and Excelsior Hotel; Service **B** to Alberoni via Malamocco. Bus No. **11** runs the entire length of the Lido (via Malamocco and Alberoni) and has a connecting ferry from Alberoni (Santa Maria del Mare) to San Pietro in Volta and Pellestrina (see above).

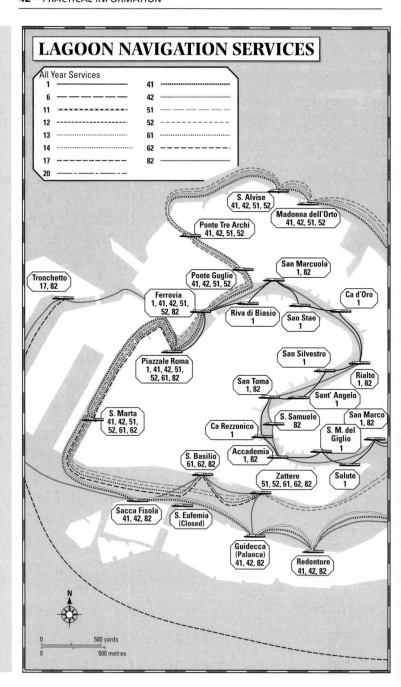

LAGOON NAVIGATION SERVICES

All Year Services

1 ————————	41 ····················
6 — — — — —	42 ═══════════
11 ▬▬▬▬▬▬	51 — — — — —
12 — — — — — —	52 — — — — —
13 ····················	61 ····················
14 ····················	62 — — — — —
17 — — — — — —	82 ═══════════
20 — · — · — · —	

S. Alvise
41, 42, 51, 52

Madonna dell'Orto
41, 42, 51, 52

Ponte Tre Archi
41, 42, 51, 52

San Marcuola
1, 82

Tronchetto
17, 82

Ponte Guglie
41, 42, 51, 52

Ca d'Oro
1

Ferrovia
1, 41, 42, 51,
52, 82

Riva di Biasio
1

San Stae
1

Piazzale Roma
1, 41, 42, 51,
52, 61, 82

San Silvestro
1

Rialto
1, 82

San Toma
1, 82

Sant' Angelo
1

S. Marta
41, 42, 51,
52, 61, 62

Ca Rezzonico
1

S. Samuele
82

San Marco
1, 82

**S. M. del
Giglio**
1

S. Basilio
61, 62, 82

Accademia
1, 82

Zattere
51, 52, 61, 62, 82

Salute
1

Sacca Fisola
41, 42, 82

S. Eufemia
(Closed)

**Guidecca
(Palanca)**
41, 42, 82

Redentore
41, 42, 82

N

0 ———— 500 yards
0 ———— 500 metres

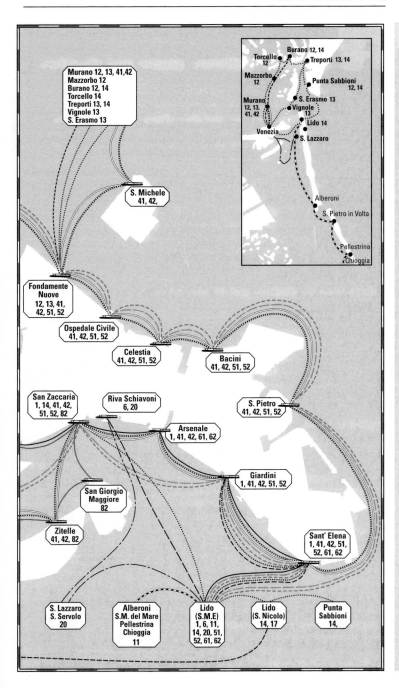

Murano 12, 13, 41,42
Mazzorbo 12
Burano 12, 14
Torcello 14
Treporti 13, 14
Vignole 13
S. Erasmo 13

Burano 12, 14
Torcello 12
Mazzorbo 12
Treporti 13, 14
Punta Sabbioni 12, 14
Murano 12, 13, 41, 42
S. Erasmo 13
Vignole 13
Lido 14
Venezia
S. Lazzaro
Alberoni
S. Pietro in Volta
Pellestrina
Chioggia

S. Michele 41, 42,

Fondamente Nuove 12, 13, 41, 42, 51, 52

Ospedale Civile 41, 42, 51, 52

Celestia 41, 42, 51, 52

Bacini 41, 42, 51, 52

San Zaccaria 1, 14, 41, 42, 51, 52, 82

Riva Schiavoni 6, 20

S. Pietro 41, 42, 51, 52

Arsenale 1, 41, 42, 61, 62

Giardini 1, 41, 42, 51, 52

San Giorgio Maggiore 82

Zitelle 41, 42, 82

Sant' Elena 1, 41, 42, 51, 52, 61, 62

S. Lazzaro S. Servolo 20

Alberoni S.M. del Mare Pellestrina Chioggia 11

Lido (S.M.E) 1, 6, 11, 14, 20, 51, 52, 61, 62

Lido (S. Nicolo) 14, 17

Punta Sabbioni 14,

Museums, galleries, *scuole* and churches

The table below gives the hours of admission, entrance fees, and telephone numbers of the various museums, galleries, *scuole*, and monuments in Venice in force in 2001. **Opening times vary and often change without warning**; those given below should therefore be accepted with reserve. A current list of the opening times is always available at the *APT* offices in Venice. Monday is no longer the standard closing day for State-owned museums, and many of these are now open seven days a week. At certain times of the year the opening hours of some museums may be prolonged (when financed by sponsor companies). Some museums are closed on the main public holidays: 1 January, Easter, 1 May, 15 August, and Christmas Day, although there is now a policy all over Italy to keep at least some of them open on these days: information can be obtained about these from the *APT* offices.

Admission charges are normally between Lire 4000 (c €2) and Lire 13,000 (c €7). There is a combined ticket for Palazzo Ducale, the Museo Correr, the Museo Archeologico, Palazzo Mocenigo, the Glass Museum in Murano, and the Lace Museum in Burano (Lire 18,000 or c €9, with a validity of 90 days).

Reductions for students and the over 65s. Citizens of member countries of the EU under the age of 18 and over the age of 65 are entitled to free admission to State-owned museums and monuments in Italy (on production of an identity card proving your age). EU students between the ages of 18 and 26 are now entitled to a reduction (usually 50%) to State-owned museums, and some other museums have special tickets for students.

For one week during the year (the *Settimana per i Beni Culturali e Ambientali*), usually in early December or March, there is free entrance to all state-owned museums in Italy, and others are opened specially.

Opening times

The following codes have been used to identify the ownership of museums in the table below.

(S): State-owned museums. Information from the *Soprintendenza ai Beni Artistici e Storici di Venezia*, 63 Piazza San Marco (☎ 041 521 0577).

(C): museums owned by the Comune of Venice. Information from the *Musei Civici di Venezia*, 52 Piazza San Marco (☎ 041 522 5625).

The **ticket offices** close one hour before the museum closes. Opening hours for Sundays apply also to holidays (*giorni festivi*).

Accademia Galleries (S). Lire 12,000 or c €6; combined ticket with the Ca' d'Oro and Museo Orientale, Lire 18,000 or c €9. 08.15–19.15, Mon 08.15–14.00. ☎ 041 522 2247. One of the great collections of Italian paintings in the country, and the best in existence of Venetian paintings, with Giovanni Bellini and Tintoretto particularly well represented.

Accademia (reserve collection) by appointment on Tues 15.00–17.30. ☎ 041 522 2247. An interesting collection displayed in a hall designed by Palladio, including works by Carpaccio, Titian, and Tintoretto.

Archaeological Museum (S). Combined ticket, Lire 18,000 or c €9; Lire 10,000 or c €5 for students aged 14–29; Lire 6000 or c €3 for children aged 6–14, with Palazzo Ducale, Museo Correr, Libreria Marciana, Palazzo Mocenigo, Murano glass museum, and the Burano lace museum. Open daily 09.00–19.00 (1 Nov–31 Mar 09.00–17.00). ☎ 041 522 4951. The ticket office closes an hour and a half before closing time. Now entered through the Correr Museum this is a very fine collection of Greek and Roman sculptures made in the 16C by Cardinal Grimani.

Basilica of San Marco: **Treasury and Pala d'Oro**. Lire 3000 or c €2. Admission, see p 79. The Treasury preserves some splendid Byzantine goldsmiths' works, and the Pala d'Oro is an exquisite medieval altar frontal decorated with gold, enamels, and precious stones. **Loggia & Museo della Basilica**. Lire 3000 or c €2. Admission, see p 79. The loggia has a superb view of Piazza San Marco and the museum contains the four famous gilded bronze horses from the façade, thought to be Roman works.

Biblioteca Marciana *see* Libreria.

Burano: Scuola di Merletti. Lire 8000 or c €4; or combined ticket, Lire 18,000 or c €9; Lire 10,000 or c €5 for students aged 14–29; Lire 6000 or c €3 for children aged 6–14, with Palazzo Ducale, Museo Correr, Archaeological Museum, Libreria Marciana, Palazzo Mocenigo and the Murano glass museum. Open daily 10.00–16.00 or 17.00, closed Tues. Demonstrations of lace making Tues–Fri. ☎ 041 730 034. A charming display of lace in a building which once housed a lace-making school.

Ca' d'Oro (S). Lire 6000 or c €3; combined ticket with the Galleria dell'Accademia and Museo Orientale, Lire 18,000 or c €9. Open daily 08.15–19.15; Monday 08.15–14.00. ☎ 041 520 0345. In one of the most famous Gothic palaces in Venice on the Grand Canal, the collection includes paintings, detached frescoes and exquisite Venetian sculptures.

Ca' Pesaro *see* Museo d'Arte Moderna, and Oriental Museum.

Ca' Rezzonico *see* Museo del Settecento Veneziano.

Campanile di San Giorgio Maggiore. Lire 5000 or c €3. Open 09.30–12.30, 14.30– 17.00. ☎ 041 522 7827. From the top, reached by a lift, there is a breathtaking view of Venice and the lagoon.

Campanile di San Marco. Lire 10,000 or c €5. Open daily 09.00–dusk (16.45 in winter; 19.00 in spring; 21.00 in summer). It is closed for mainentance for 20 days in January. ☎ 041 522 4064. A lift ascends to the summit from which there is a superb view of the city and, on a clear day, the Alps.

Casa Goldoni (C). Closed. ☎ 041 523 6353. A charming little Venetian palace, the birthplace of Carlo Goldoni, which contains mementoes of this famous 18C Venetian playwright.

Centro Studi Storia del Tessuto e del Costume *see* Museo di Palazzo Mocenigo.

Cini (Vittorio) Collection *see* Galleria di Palazzo Cini.

Correr Museum (C). Open daily 09.00–19.00 (1 Nov–31 Mar 09.00–17.00); the ticket office closes an hour and a half before closing time. Combined ticket, Lire 18,000 or c €9; Lire 10,000 or c €5 for students aged 14–29; Lire 6000 or c €3 for children aged 6–14, with Palazzo Ducale, Libreria Marciana, Museo Archeologico, Palazzo Mocenigo, Murano glass museum, and the Burano lace museum. ☎ 041 522 4951. The municipal museum with extensive collections illustrating the history of Venice, and a fine picture gallery.

Doges' Palace *see* Palazzo Ducale.

Galleria dell'Accademia *see* Accademia Galleries.

Galleria di Palazzo Cini. Lire 8000 or c €4. Usually open Mar–June, Sept and

Oct 10.00–13.00, 14.00–18.00, except Mon. ☎ 041 521 0755. An interesting collection of Tuscan paintings (including a portrait by Pontormo) and decorative arts assembled by Vittorio Cini. Exhibitions are held on the second floor.

Goldoni's House *see* Casa Goldoni.

Guggenheim (Peggy) Collection. Lire 12,000 or c €6; Lire 8000 or c €4 for students. Open 10.00–18.00, 1 Apr–31 Oct Sat 10.00–22.00 closed Tues; sometimes closed 6 Jan–1 Feb. ☎ 041 240 5411. One of the most visited museums in the city, it has a particularly representative collection of modern art, from 1910 onwards.

Icons, Museum of *see* Museo Dipinti Sacri Bizantini.

Jewish Museum. Lire 5000 or c €3; reduction for students, Lire 3000 or c €2. Open 10.00–17.30, Fri 10.00–15.30; closed Sat & Jewish holidays. ☎ 041 715 359. A small collection of Jewish treasures in the heart of the former Jewish ghetto of the city. Tickets for the **guided tour**, in English and Italian, of the museum and **synagogues of the Ghetto** can be bought from the museum in the campo of the Ghetto Nuovo; Lire 12,000 or c €6, reduction for students, Lire 9000 or c €5. Admission 10.30–16.30 or 17.30; Fri 10.00–14.30; closed Sat & Jewish holidays (the museum and normally three synagogues are shown at 10.30, 11.30, 12.30, 13.30, 14.30, 15.30 and 16.30). The **Old Jewish Cemetery** on the Lido is open on Sunday at 14.30; guided tour; Lire 12,000 or c €6.

Lace Museum *see* Burano: Scuola di Merletti.

Libreria Marciana (S). Open daily 09.00–19.00 (1 Nov–31 Mar 09.00–17.00); the ticket office closes an hour and a half before closing time. Combined ticked, Lire 18,000 or c €9; Lire 10,000 or c €5 for students aged 14–29; Lire 6000 or c €3 for children aged 6–14, with Palazzo Ducale, the Correr Museum, Museo Archoeologico, Palazzo Mocenigo, Murano glass museum, and Burano lace museum. ☎ 041 522 4951. Now entered from the Archeological Museum, the great hall is decorated by the Venetian Mannerists and contains photocopies of the precious books owned by the library including the Grimani Breviary and Fra Mauro's map of the world. The vestibule has a fresco by Titian.

Monastero Mekhitarista *see* San Lazzaro degli Armeni.

Murano Glass Museum *see* Museo Vetrario di Murano.

Museo Civico Correr *see* Correr Museum.

Museo Communità Israelitica see Jewish Museum.

Museo d'Arte Moderna (Ca' Pesaro) (C). Closed for restoration (☎ 041 721 127). In a fine palace on the Grand Canal. This collection of modern (mostly Italian) art (19C and 20C) has been undergoing rearrangement for many years.

Museo Diocesano d'Arte Sacra. Donation—opened by volunteers. Open weekdays 10.30–12.30. ☎ 041 522 9166. A collection of works of art, including paintings and silver, from closed churches in Venice.

Museo Dipinti Sacri Bizantini. Lire 7000 or c €4. Open 09.00–12.30, 13.30–16.30; fest. 10.00–17.00. ☎ 041 522 6581. A room of Byzantine icons, mostly 16C–17C, many of them painted in Venice.

Museo Fortuny (C). Closed for restoration. ☎ 041 241 0110. A splendid old palace which preserves its atmosphere as the home of the painter Mariano Fortuny (1871–1949) who here designed the famous Fortuny silks.

Museo di Palazzo Mocenigo (C). Lire 8000 or c €4; or combined ticket, Lire 18,000 or c €9, with Palazzo Ducale, Museo Correr, Archaeological Museum, Biblioteca Marciana, the Glass Museum in Murano, and the lace museum in Burano. Open 10.00–16.00 or 17.00, closed Mon. ☎ 041 721 798. A well-preserved late 17C Venetian residence, with interesting paintings and frescoes.

Museo Querini Stampalia. Lire 12,000 or c €6. Open 10.00–13.00, 15.00–18.00; Fri & Sat also 18.00–22.00, closed Mon. ☎ 041 271 1411. A palace, partly redesigned by Carlo Scarpa, with a good collection of Venetian paintings (including Palma Vecchio and Giambattista Tiepolo), and Venetian furniture.

Museo Storico Navale. Lire 3000 or c €2. Open 08.45–13.30, closed Sun. ☎ 041 520 0276. A large well-displayed collection of boats and ships, giving a vivid idea of the maritime Republic.

Museo del Settecento Veneziano (C). To reopen in 2001. ☎ 041 241 0100. In the splendid Ca'Rezzonico on the Grand Canal, a collection of 18C art arranged in well furnished 18C rooms with frescoes by Giambattista Tiepolo, and charming detached frescoes by his son Gian Domenico.

Museo di Torcello. Lire 3000 or c €2; or combined ticket with the basilica and bell-tower, Lire 10,000 or c €5. Open Apr–Oct 10.30–17.30, Nov–March 10.00–16.30, closed Mon. ☎ 041 730 761. A small museum preserving treasures from the island of Torcello including 7C mosaic fragments, and a 13C silver altar frontal.

Museo Vetrario di Murano (C). Lire 8000 or c €4; or combined ticket, Lire 18,000 or c €9, with Palazzo Ducale, Museo Correr, Archaeological Museum, Libreria Marciana, Palazzo Mocenigo and the Glass museum in Burano. Open 10.00–16.00 or 17.00, closed Wed. ☎ 041 739 586. A very fine collection of glass, much of it made on Murano from the 15C onwards. There is also a display illustrating how glass is made.

Natural History Museum. Closed. ☎ 041 524 0885. Well arranged collection in a restored Veneto-Byzantine palace on the Grand Canal with exhibits from the Sahara as well as from the Venetian lagoon.

Naval Museum *see* Museo Storico Navale.

Oratorio dei Crociferi. Lire 3000 or c €2. Open 1 Apr–31 Oct Thurs, Fri, Sat 10.00–13.00; closed Nov–Mar. ☎ 041 270 2464. A 16C chapel with a complete cycle of paintings by Palma Giovane, once part of a hospital founded in the mid-12C for crusaders.

Oriental Museum (S). Lire 4000 or c €2; combined ticket, Lire 18,000 or c €9, with the Galleria dell'Accademia and Ca' d'Oro. 08.15–14.00, closed Mon. ☎ 041 524 1173. A good collection of Far Eastern works of art, particularly interesting for its Chinese and Japanese paintings, lacquer-work, and bronzes.

Ospedaletto *see* Sala della Musica.

Palazzo Ducale. Combined ticket, Lire 18,000 or c €9; Lire 10,000 or c €5 for students aged 14–29; Lire 6000 or c €3 for children aged 6–14, with the Correr Museum, the Museo Archeologico, the Libreria Marciana, Palazzo Mocenigo, Murano glass museum, and the Burano lace museum. Open daily 09.00–19.00 (1 Nov–31 Mar 09.00–17.00); the ticket office closes an hour and a half before closing time. ☎ 041 522 4951. Guided tours of the *itinerari segreti* (lesser known parts of the palace) usually every day except Wed at 10.00 & 12.00 (by appointment). The vast and magnificent Doges' Palace decorated in the 16C–17C by Tintoretto, Veronese and numerous other Venetian painters with huge historical and allegorical canvases celebrating the glory of Venice.

Palazzo Labia. By appointment, Wed, Thurs & Fri 15.00–16.00. ☎ 041 781 277. Famous for its magnificent ballroom with frescoes by Giambattista Tiepolo of Antony and Cleopatra.

Sala della Musica and Ospedaletto (Santa Maria dei Derelitti). Open Apr–Sept Thurs, Fri & Sat 16.00–19.00; Oct–Mar same days 15.00–18.00. ☎ 041 270 2464. The church and music room of one of Venice's historic hospitals.

San Lazzaro degli Armeni (Island of). Lire 8000 or c €4. Open daily 15.20–17.00. ☎ 041 526 0104. Island monastery of Armenian Mekhitarian Fathers who show visitors the precious library and mementoes of Byron.

Scala Contarini del Bovolo. Lire 3000 or c €2. Open Apr–Oct daily 10.00–18.00. ☎ 041 270 2464. Exterior spiral staircase and loggia built in the late 15C which has a unique view of Venice without the lagoon.

Scuola Grande dei Carmini. Lire 8000 or c €4. Open 09.00–16.00 or 18.00; fest. 09.00–16.00. ☎ 041 528 9420. One of the famous Venetian confraternities. Its main hall probably designed by Longhena contains nine ceiling paintings by Giambattista Tiepolo.

Scuola Grande di San Rocco. Lire 9000 or c €5. Open 09.00–17.30 (Nov–Mar 10.00–16.00). ☎ 041 523 4864. The largest and most important of the Venetian *scuole*, famous for its pictoral cycle of over fifty paintings, the masterpiece of Tintoretto.

Scuola di San Giorgio degli Schiavoni. Lire 5000 or c €3. Open 10.00–12.30, 15.30–18.00, Sun 10.00–12.30, closed Mon. ☎ 041 522 8828). A charming little scuola with delightful paintings by Carpaccio (1502–08).

Scuola di San Giovanni Evangelista. At present only open by appointment, ☎ 041 718 234 and for concerts. With a 15C staircase by Mauro Codussi, and a main hall decorated with a cycle of paintings by 16C Venetian painters.

Seminario Patriarcale. Open by appointment. ☎ 041 520 8565. The Manfrediana Picture Gallery has an interesting collection of paintings and terracotta busts by Alessandro Vittoria.

Synagogues of the Ghetto *see* Jewish Museum.

Torcello Basilica and bell-tower. Lire 5000 or c €3 and Lire 4000 or c €2; or combined ticket, Lire 10,000 for the basilica, bell-tower and museum. ☎ 041 270 2464. Open 10.30-17.30 (Nov–Mar 10.00–16.30). The basilica is one of the most beautiful churches in Venice with extremely important Byzantine mosaics. The bell-tower can be climbed to see the wonderful view of the lagoon.

Torcello Museum *see* Museo di Torcello.

Torre dell'Orologio. Closed for restoration. A clock tower designed by Mauro Codussi at the end of the 15C. Steps (no lift) lead up to the top to see the mechanism of the clock (at present being restored).

Churches

For some years now there have been various projects to open as many churches as possible for certain hours of each day: the latest scheme, instituted in 1998 and called *Chorus*, provides access to 13 churches (**Santa Maria del Giglio, Santo Stefano, Santa Maria Formosa, Santa Maria dei Miracoli**, the **Frari, San Polo, San Giacomo dell'Orio, San Stae, Sant'Alvise**, the **Madonna dell'Orto, San Pietro di Castello**, the **Redentore**, and **San Sebastiano**). These are open Monday–Saturday 10.00–17.00; Sunday, except in July and August, 13.00–17.00, except for the Frari which is open Mon–Sat 09.00–18.00; Sunday (including July and August) 13.00–18.00, and San Sebastiano which is open Mon–Sat 10.00–17.00 and Sunday 15.00–17.00. There is a single admission ticket (Lire 3000 or c €2) or combined ticket (Lire 15,000 or c €8) available at any of these churches. Information from the office of the Curia, ☎ 041 275 0462.

Six other churches are kept open by the *Associazione S. Apollonia*, ☎ 041 270 2464: **San Pantalon**, Sun–Fri 16.00–18.00; the **Carmini**, Mon–Sat 14.30–17.00; **San Trovaso** Mon–Sat 15.00–18.00; **San Giovanni in Bragora** Mon–Sat 15.30–17.30; **San Cassiano** Wed–Sat 09.00–12.00, and **San Salvador** Mon–Sat 09.00–12.00, 15.00–18.00. This association also keeps open the basilica and bell-tower of Torcello.

A list of approximate opening times of some other churches is also usually available at *APT* offices.

The opening times of other churches vary a great deal but the majority are open from 07.30 or 08.30 to 12.00. In the afternoon many remain closed until 16.00 or even 17.00 and close again at 18.00 or 19.00; some do not reopen at all in the afternoon. A few churches open for services only. Where possible the normal opening times have been given in the text.

Lights (coin operated) have now been installed in almost every church to illuminate frescoes and altarpieces, which are often otherwise impossible to see. As a result it is essential to carry a great deal of change on you (but if you run out of coins, the sacristan or custodian can usually help). Some churches now ask that sightseers do not enter during a service, but normally visitors not in a tour group may do so, provided you are silent and do not approach the altar in use. If you are wearing shorts or have bare shoulders you can sometimes be stopped from entering San Marco. Churches in Venice are very often not orientated. In the text the terms north and south refer to the liturgical north (left) and south (right), with the high altar at the east end. A torch and binoculars are always useful when visiting a church. The sacristan will often unlock closed areas on request (and a donation is usually expected).

 General information

Acqua alta

Acqua alta is an exceptionally high tide (above 110cm) which now occurs frequently throughout the year (especially between September and April) flooding many of the low-lying areas of the city (sometimes up to about 130 cm). A watch is kept on the level of the lagoon, and when an *acqua alta* is imminent sirens are sounded throughout the city. The period of the flood tide usually lasts 2 or 3 hours, and *passarelle* or duck-boards (raised gangplanks) are laid out in Piazza San Marco, by the landing-stages and in other thoroughfares. This raised thoroughfare throughout the city totals about 4 kilometres. A map showing the calli which do not usually get flooded and where the duckboards are set up is provided in the *ACTV* timetable and posted up in the *ACTV* landing-stages. However, it is not possible to get about the city on these occasions without wellington boots. In addition, some of the *ACTV* waterbuses (including nos **41**, **42**, **51** and **52**) are suspended during an *acqua alta* because they are unable to pass below the road and rail bridges near the station. The *Centro Previsioni e Segnalazioni Maree* (Palazzo Cavalli, San Marco 4090, ☎ 041 274 8787) gives information on tides. For a 24hr recorded message, ☎ 041 520 6344 or 041 520 7722.

Banking services

Banks are usually open Mon–Fri 08.30–13.30, and for one hour in the afternoon (usually 14.45–15.45, or 15.15–16.15); Sat and holidays usually closed, although some banks now stay open on Sat morning. **Note**. They close early (about 11.00) on days preceding national holidays. There are now automatic machines for changing foreign bank notes, and Bancomat machines (which take overseas cards), outside many banks in the city.

The commission on cashing travellers' cheques can be quite high (but is usually lowest at banks). Money can also be changed at exchange offices (*cambio*), in travel agencies, some post offices, at the airport and the station (usually open seven days a week). At some hotels, restaurants, and shops money can be exchanged (but usually at a lower rate). For further information, see p 14.

Chemists see *Pharmacies*

Church services

Roman Catholic services On Sunday and, in the principal churches, often on weekdays, Mass is celebrated from the early morning up to 12.00 and from 17.30 until 19.00 in the evening. High Mass, with music, is celebrated in San Marco at 10.00 on Sunday. At 11.00 the Gregorian chant is sung at San Giorgio Maggiore. Mass in English is held at San Zulian at 12 o'clock on Sundays in summer.
Non-Catholic churches Anglican, St George's, Campo San Vio; Lutheran, Campo Santi Apostoli; Greek Orthodox, Ponte dei Greci; Waldensian Evangelical and Methodist, 5170 Calle Lunga Santa Maria Formosa. Jewish **Synagogue**. Scola Spagnola and Scola Levantina, Ghetto Vecchio.
Religious festivals On saints' days Mass and vespers with music are celebrated in the churches dedicated to the saints concerned. On the Feast of St Mark (25 April) special services are held and the Pala d'Oro exposed on the high altar (also displayed at Christmas and Easter). For the Feasts of the Redentore (3rd Sunday in July) and of Santa Maria della Salute (21 November), see below.

Consulates

There is an Honorary British Consul in Venice (Palazzo Querini, Accademia, Dorsoduro 1051, ☎ 041 522 7207). In Milan there is a US Consul (1 Largo Donegani, ☎ 02 290351) and a British Consul General. The British, American, Canadian, Australian, Irish, and New Zealand embassies are in Rome.

Crime and personal security

For all emergencies, ☎ 113.
Venice is a comparitively safe city and pickpocketing is not as widespread as in other Italian towns. However, it is always advisable not to carry valuables in handbags, and always watch out on public transport.

Help is given to British and American travellers in Italy who are in difficulty by the British and American embassies and consulates, see above. They will replace lost or stolen passports, and will give advice in emergencies.

You are strongly advised to carry some means of identity with you at all times while in Italy, since you can be held at a police station if you are stopped and found to be without one.

There are three categories of **policemen** in Italy: *Vigili Urbani*, municipal police who wear blue uniforms in winter and light blue during the summer and have helmets similar to those of London policemen. ☎ 041 274 8207. They have an office at Piazzale Roma, ☎ 041 522 4576 or 041 274 7070. *Carabinieri* (military police who wear black uniform with a red stripe down the side of the trousers). Their headquarters is at Piazzale Roma, ☎ 041 523 5333. The *Polizia di Stato* (state police who wear dark blue jackets and light blue trousers). The Central Police Station (the Questura) is at San Polo (Castello), ☎ 041 270 5511.

Crime should be reported at once, theft to either the Polizia di Stato or the Carabinieri. A detailed statement has to be given in order to get an official document confirming loss or damage (*denuncia di smarrimento*), which is essential for insurance claims. Interpreters are usually provided.

Lost property. For the municipal police office, ☎ 041 522 4576. For the railway lost property, ☎ 041 785 238; and for objects lost on *ACTV* water-buses, ☎ 041 272 2179.

To report the loss of theft of a credit card, call: *Topcard Visa*, ☎ 800862079 *Mastercard*, ☎ 800870866, *American Express*, ☎ 06 72282.

Cultural institutions and libraries

Ateneo Veneto, Scuola di San Fantin, San Marco 1897; *Giorgio Cini Foundation*, Isola di San Giorgio Maggiore; *German Institute*, Palazzo Barbarigo della Terrazza, Ramo Pisani, San Polo; *Istituto Veneto di Scienze, Lettere, ed Arti*, Palazzo Loredan, Campo Santo Stefano 2945 and Palazzo Franchetti; *Conservatorio di Musica B. Marcello*, Palazzo Pisani, Santo Stefano 2810; *Scuola di Musica Antica di Venezia* (International School of early music), 426 San Marco; *Fondazione Levi*, Palazzo Giustiniani-Lolin, San Marco 2893; *Istituto Ellenico di Studi Bizantini e post-Bizantini*, Ponte dei Greci 3412; *Archivio Storico delle Arti Contemporanee*, the Biennale archives and art and media library, Ca' Corner della Regina; *Istituzioni di Ricovero e di Educazione Venezia (IRE)*, a public institution which provides assistance for the elderly and minors and owns a number of charitable institutions and monuments in Venice, 27 Giudecca; *Istituto di Studi Teatrali*, Casa Goldoni, San Tomà; *Venice European centre for the trades and professions of the Conservation of Architectural Heritage* (also known as the *Associazione Europea Pro Venezia Viva*), Isola di San Servolo; *Associazione Culturale italo-tedesco* (German-Italian Cultural Association), Palazzo Albrizzi, Strada Nuova, 4118 Cannaregio.

UNESCO Venice Offices: regional office for Science and Technology for Europe (ROSTE), 1272/A Dorsoduro; and Liaison Office (for Culture), 63 Piazza San Marco. Both offices should be moved in the near future to Palazzo Zorzi which is being restored with special law funding.

Organisations for the safeguarding and restoration of Venice

The *Association of International Private Committees for the Safeguarding of Venice* operates in conjunction with *UNESCO* from the *UNESCO* Liaison office at 63 Piazza San Marco, ☎ 041 520 9989, fax 041 520 9988. Among the 30 members of the Association are the *Venice in Peril Fund* (website: venicein-peril.org; see p 8) and the *World Monuments Fund* (both with their headquarters here) and the *Save Venice Inc. New York* which has its headquarters at San Vidal, San Marco 2887. The *Associazione Amici dei Musei e Monumenti Veneziani* also have offices at 63 Piazza San Marco, and *Italia Nostra* is at 1260 San Marco.

The *Venice International Foundation*, Ca'Rezzonico supports the local municipal museums.

Libraries

Nazionale Marciana, San Marco 7; *Archivio di Stato*, Campo dei Frari 3002; *Cini Foundation*, see above; *Fondazione Querini-Stampalia*, Santa Maria Formosa 4778; *Correr*, Piazza San Marco; *Archivio Storico delle Arti Contemporanee*, see above; *Centro Studi di Storia del Tessuto e del Costume*, Palazzo Mocenigo at San Stae.

Days out

Although it is unlikely you will feel inclined to leave the peace of Venice, however long your stay, there are places on the mainland close to Venice which are of great interest.

The most important town close by is **Padova** (Padua) which is only 30 minutes away by train on the main line to Bologna (frequent services). There are also *ATP* bus services via the autostrada every half hour, and *ACTV* services via the Brenta every hour. *APT* Information, ☎ 049 8750655. Fully described in *Blue Guide Northern Italy*, Padua, famous for its university, one of the oldest in Europe, and with a particularly lively atmosphere with several large daily markets, is one of the most interesting large towns in northern Italy. It is famous for the Cappella Scrovegni which contains Giotto's best preserved fresco cycle, one of the most beautiful chapels in Italy. The Basilica, known as Il Santo, has important sculptures by Donatello, and in the piazza outside is his celebrated equestrian monument to Gattamelata. The 14C Salone in the Palazzo della Ragione is another splendid sight.

Padua is connected to Venice by the **Brenta canal** (also fully described in *Blue Guide Northern Italy*), lined by numerous beautiful villas built by the Venetian aristocracy in the 16C–18C, and typified in Shakespeare's *Merchant of Venice* by Portia's villa of Belmont. In these country houses, often surrounded by gardens, orchards, and farms, the Venetians would spend the early summer. Many of them have now fallen into disrepair, and only a few are open to the public. The best way of seeing the Riviera del Brenta is from a motor-launch. There are usually services between Venice and Strà from April to the end of October operated by: *Il Burchiello*, ☎ 049 660944; *I Battelli del Brenta*, ☎ 049 8760233, and *Delta tour*, ☎ 049 8700232. The Burchiello is named after a 17C boat which followed the same route between Padua and Venice. Boats usually leave Venice on three days a week and Padua on three, and take about 8 hours and 30 minutes (returning by coach). Passengers are transported by coach between Strà, which has the largest villa open to the public, the Villa Pisani, and Padua. Services starts from San Marco and calls at Malcontenta (see below), Oriago, Mira, and Dolo, before terminating at Strà (the price includes lunch and visits to the villas at Strà, Mira, and Malcontenta). There is also a bicycle path along the banks of the canal.

At **Malcontenta**, at the mouth of the Brenta canal, 12.5km from Venice by road, is the famous *Villa Foscari* (open May–Oct Tues & Sat, 09.00–12.00). One of the most successful and earliest suburban villas built by Palladio(completed by 1560), it was extremely influential in European country house architecture. It was built for the brothers Nicolò and Alvise Foscari on the last stretch of the Brenta canal before it reaches the lagoon. The temple-like façade has a tall Ionic portico, thermal windows, and four characteristic

Venetian chimneys. The interesting interior plan provided for two identical apartments for the brothers on the piano nobile, on either side of the central hall which contains damaged frescoes by Battista Franco and Giovanni Zelotti. There is a bus to Malcontenta from Piazzale Roma in Venice, and the Brenta canal motor-launches usually stop here.

Treviso is only 30 minutes away from Venice by train (on the Udine line, frequent services). *APT* information office, ☎ 0422 547632. If hotels are full in Venice, Treviso makes a very pleasant place to stay as an alternative. It is a picturesque small town, with a number of canals, and has interesting churches and museums. It is also described in *Blue Guide Northern Italy*, together with the rest of the Veneto, including Vicenza, famous for its Palladian villas in and around the town.

Electric current
The electricity supply is 220 watts. Visitors may need round, two-pin Continental plugs for some appliances.

Emergencies
For all emergencies, ☎ 113: the switchboard will coordinate the help you need. For first aid emergencies, ☎ 118

First aid services (*Pronto Soccorso*) are available at hospitals, railway stations, and airports. The most central hospital is Ospedale Civile, Santi Giovanni e Paolo, ☎ 041 529 4111), where first aid services are available. For emergency first aid and ambulance service, ☎ 041 523 0000. First-aid and ambulance emergency 24hr service, ☎ 118, fire brigade, ☎ 115, ☎ road assistance, ☎ 116

For all other emergencies, see under 'Crime' above.

Entertainment
September is traditionally the best month in Venice for cultural activities. Concerts, exhibitions, and lectures throughout the year are advertised in the local press, on wall posters, in the *ACTV* landing-stages, and in the free quarterly publications *Pocket Venice* and *Leo Bussola*, and the monthly *Un Ospite di Venezia* (A Guest in Venice), all available (free) through the tourist offices, hotels, and agencies. Detailed information is also always available at the *APT* offices. Daily events are also list in the local newspaper *La Nuova* and *Il Gazzettino*.

Casinòs The famous Venice **Casinò Municipale** is open in summer at the Lido and in winter (Oct–Mar) at Palazzo Vendramin on the Grand Canal. Play (including roulette and chemin de fer) begins at 15.00 and continues until about 04.30. There is also a restaurant here. Direct vaporetto services from 13.45 from the station, Piazzale Roma, and San Zaccaria every 30 minutes to and from the casinò on the Lido. Another widely advertised casinò has been opened on the mainland near the airport, but it has slot-machines and could be anywhere in the world and has and none of the elegant almosphere of the Venice casinò.

Concerts There are excellent concerts throughout the year, usually of Venetian Baroque music, in the Scuola Grande di San Rocco and the Scuola Grande di San Giovanni Evangelista, the churches of La Pietà, San Stae, and Santo Stefano, and in the church of Santa Maria dei Derelitti in the Ospedaletto. Concerts held in other churches (and widely advertised through hotels) are usually of a much lower standard. Organ recitals are often held in the Frari, and in St Mark's in July and August. Concerts are also held at the Fondazione Giorgio Cini.

Exhibitions Exhibitions are held in the Accademia Gallery, Museo Correr, Palazzo Ducale, Palazzo Grassi, Ca' Pesaro, the Cini Foundation, Palazzo Fortuny and Le Zitelle. The Biennale is one of the most famous international exhibitions of modern art, first held in 1895. Since 1993 it has been held in odd years, usually from June to early October. It takes place in the Giardini Pubblici (see Ch. 25) in permanent pavilions. Exhibitions are held in other parts of the city during the Biennale, in the Antichi Granai (old grain warehouses) on the Giudecca and in the Corderie, Campo della Tana (the old rope works of the Arsenal). The Biennale also organises a famous annual Film Festival (founded in 1932), usually held in early September on the Lido.

Opera La Fenice (Pl. 1; 5), Campo San Fantin, one of the most famous opera-houses in Italy (see Ch. 9), was destroyed by fire in 1996. It is to be rebuilt, but meanwhile the company is using a temporary pavilion set up on the Tronchetto and known as the **Palafenice** (Pl. 6;1). The **Teatro Malibran**, behind San Giovanni Crisostomo, reopened in 2001 so that now fully-staged performances can be held there until the Fenice is reopened. There is a booking office for the Fenice (open during banking hours) in the Cassa di Risparmio, Campo San Luca (☎ 041 521 0161). The Fenice does not operate in August. For information, ☎ 147 882 211.

Theatres and cinemas Theatres include the *Carlo Goldoni*, Calle Goldoni, *L'Avogaria*, Calle de l'Avogaria, Dorsoduro, and *Fondamenta Nuove*, 5013 Fondamente Nuove. The **Ridotto** in Calle Valleresso is probably to be restored. There are cinemas near the Accademia on Dorsoduro, and in the sestiere of San Marco (*Centrale*, *Olimpia*, and *Rossini*). The *Olimpia* sometimes shows films in English. A film festival is held in late May at the Teatro Fondamenta Nuove. For the Biennale film festival, see above.

Festivals

The Venetian **Carnival** was famous throughout the Republic when it lasted from 26 December to the first day of Lent. Parties and pageants were organised by special societies, and it was a time when the authority of the Church and State was ignored and the masked inhabitants enjoyed a period of freedom and anarchy. In this century the spirit of Carnival died out, but since 1980 the week or ten days in February before Lent, has been celebrated in Venice by ever increasing numbers of Italians and foreigners, and it has become the most crowded (and expensive) time of year in Venice. The city is invaded by merry-makers in fancy dress and masks, and numerous theatrical and musical events take place, both in theatres, and outside in the calli and campi. On some days during Carnival week the city more than doubles its population. The festivities end on Shrove Tuesday when a huge ball is usually held in Piazza San Marco. For information, contact the Consorzio Carnevale di Venezia, ☎ 041 717 065.

The **Vogalonga** (literally long row) takes place on a Sunday in May. First held in 1975 it has become a very popular Venetian event. The Vogalonga is open to anyone prepared to row from the mouth of the Giudecca canal around the east end of Venice (Sant' Elena) up past Murano, through the Mazzorbo canal, around Burano, past San Francesco del Deserto and back down past the islands of Sant' Erasmo and Vignole, through the main canal of Murano, and back to Venice via the Cannaregio canal and the Grand Canal to the Punta della Dogana; a course of 32 kilometres. Any type or size of boat may participate with any number of oarsmen in each boat. A small participation fee is paid on enrolment. The departure is at 9 o'clock (best seen from the Zattere or Riva degli Schiavoni and the Giardini) and the first boats usually arrive back in the city at 11.00 or 11.30 (seen from the Cannaregio canal and the Grand Canal). It is a non-competitive course and the last oarsmen usually return around 15.00. Normally, some 1500 boats and over 5000 people take part in the event in a remarkable variety of boats, some of them elaborately decorated.

On the **Festa del Redentore** (3rd Saturday and Sunday in July) a bridge of boats is constructed across the Giudecca canal; its vigil is celebrated with acquatic concerts and splendid fireworks (best seen from the Giudecca, the Zattere, or from a boat). Motor-boats are excluded from the Basin of St Mark's after 21.00.

The **Festa della Salute** (21 November) is also celebrated by a bridge of boats across the Grand Canal at the Dogana.

The **Regata Storica** (first Sunday in September) starts with a procession on the Grand Canal of the historic bissone, boats of a unique shape with their high prows richly decorated. This is followed by the most famous of the Venetian regattas with four different races, culminating in that of the two-oar gondolini, rowed by expert Venetian oarsmen. Other Regate are held from June–September in the lagoon near Sant 'Erasmo, Murano, Pellestrina and Burano.

The **Festa della Sensa** takes place on the Sunday after Ascension Day (usually in May). This was celebrated throughout the Republic when the Doge ceremonially cast a ring into the lagoon at San Nicolò al Lido (see p 254) symbolising the marriage of Venice with the sea. For the occasion, the doge was transported from Venice in the elaborate Bucintoro. It is now celebrated by the Mayor and Patriarch and other Venetian authorities. They depart from the Bacino di San Marco and proceed to San Nicolò al Lido.

The **Venice Marathon** is held on a Sunday at the end of October. A marathon race of some 42 kilometres, the course begins in Strà and follows the Brenta canal to Mestre, crosses Ponte della Libertà, and then continues via the Zattere to end at Riva degli Schiavoni.

Internet centres

Cafè Noir, 3805 Calle Lunga San Pantalon, Dorsoduro; *Internet Cafè*, 664 Santa Croce; *Omniservice*, Fondamenta dei Tolentini; *Play the Game*, 6187 Calle Lunga Santa Maria Formosa; *Venetian Navigator*, 5269 Calle delle bande, Castello.

Newspapers and magazines

The local Italian newspapers in Venice are the *Gazzettino* and *La Nuova*. Other national papers include *Corriere della Sera* (of Milan), *La Stampa* (of Turin), and *La Repubblica*. Foreign newspapers are obtainable at most kiosks. The *International Herald Tribune*, published daily in Bologna, carries news on Italy.

Free publications include *Leo Bussola* and *Pocket Venice* (both quarterlies), and *Un'ospite a Venezia*, published once a month (or more frequently in summer). They all give up to date information on the city (also in English) and are available through the *APT* information offices, hotels, and agencies.

Nightlife

Up-to-date listings of discos and bars with live music open till late can be found in the free publication *Pocket Venice*. For the casinò, see p 53.

Opening hours

Shops are normally open from 08.00 or 09.00–13.00 and 15.00 or 15.30–19.30 or 20.00, although recently the local authority in Venice has allowed shops to adopt whatever opening hours they wish. Most of the year, some food shops are closed on Wednesday afternoon (in July and August they are closed instead on Saturday afternoon); although now many of them only close on Sunday. Clothes shops, hairdressers, etc. are usually closed on Monday morning. For banking hours, see p 50.

Pensioners

There is free admission to all State-owned galleries and monuments for British citizens over the age of 65 (you should carry your passport for proof of age and nationality). There are no concessions for foreign pensioners on public transport.

Pharmacies

Pharmacies or chemists (*farmacie*) are identified by their street signs, which show a luminous green cross. They are usually open Monday–Friday 09.00–13.00, 16.00–19.30 or 20.00. Some are open 24hrs a day. A few are open on Saturdays, Sundays (and holidays), and at night: these are listed on the door of every chemist and in the daily. Five or six chemists remain open all night in various parts of the city (daily information in the local newspapers, *Un ospite di Venezia*, or at ☎ 041 523 0573).

Photography

Rules about photography vary in museums, so it is always best to ask first for permission (the use of a flash is often prohibited).

Porters

Porters in Venice are distinguished by their hats (with *portabagaglio* on the badge) and they are available in various parts of the city to help visitors with heavy luggage to their hotels (they will accompany you on the vaporetti). Although tariffs are fixed, you should establish the price for each piece of luggage before hiring a porter.

Public holidays

The main holidays in Italy, when offices, shops, and schools are closed, are as follows:

1 January	New Year's Day
25 April	Liberation Day and the Festival of St Mark
Easter Monday	
1 May	Labour Day
15 August	Assumption
1 November	All Saints' Day
21 November	Festa della Salute
8 December	Immaculate Conception
25 December	Christmas Day
26 December	St Stephen

The festival of the Redentore (**3rd Sat & Sun in July**) is also usually considered a public holiday in Venice.

Museums are usually closed on 24 June, Easter Sunday and 15 August, although sometimes some of the State museums are kept open on these days. There is usually no public transport on 1 May and the afternoon of Christmas Day. For annual festivals, see above.

Shopping

Masks are sold in little shops all over the city throughout the year (but especially near Carnival time): some of the most original can be found in **Mondonovo**, between Ponte dei Pugni and Campo Santa Margherita (Dorsoduro 3063). Fine hand-made paper and stationery is sold at the *Antica Legatoria Piazzesi*, near Santa Maria del Giglio (San Marco 2511) and at *Alberto Valese-Ebrù*, Campo Santo Stefano (San Marco 3471). Venetian glass is sold in numerous glass factories and shops on the island of Murano and all over Venice, including *Paolorossi*, Campo San Zaccaria (Castello 4685) and *Amadi*, Calle Saoneri (San Polo 2747). Beautiful silk furnishings, scarves, etc modelled on the Fortuny silks are sold at **Venetian Studium**, Calle Larga 22 Marzo (San Marco 2403). *Campiello di Arras* at Campiello Squellini (Dorsoduro 3234) sells hand-woven clothes. A shop specialising in Venetian music is *Nelesso*, Calle del Spezier (San Marco 2765). Models of boats and nautical curiosities are made by **Gilberto Penzo**, Calle II dei Saoneri (San Polo 2681), and another interesting shop is *Anticlea Antiquariato*, Calle San Provolo (Castello 4719).

Bookshops Among the best stocked bookshops in Venice are **Sansovino**, Bacino Orseolo, San Marco 84; *Goldoni*, Calle dei Fabbri, San Marco 4742; *Fantoni*, near Campo Manin, San Marco 4121; *Alla Toletta*, Calle della Toletta, Dorsoduro 1214 (with a large selection of discount books). *Filippi*, near Santa Maria Formosa, in Calle del Paradiso (Castello 5763), and in the Casselleria (Castello 5284) specialises in selling and publishing books on Venice.

Open-air markets The most important food market in Venice is the Rialto market which sells a superb variety of produce every morning except Sundays. The colourful vegetables include locally grown asparagus and artichokes, and the wholesale market is particularly lively in the early morning when boats put in laden with food. The large fish market here has excellent fresh fish. There is a small daily produce market in Campo Santa Margherita, and, nearby, on Rio di San Barnaba, fruit and vegetables are sold from a picturesque boat. Another small local market is in the popular district of Castello at the end of Via Garibaldi.

There are some small food supermarkets in various parts of Venice, including **Billa**, on Fondamenta delle Zattere (near the Maritime station) which is also open all day on Sunday.

There are stalls catering for tourists, selling mementoes of Venice on the approaches to the Rialto bridge and near San Marco (on Riva degli Schiavoni and in front of the Giardinetti Reali).

Sport and leisure

There are public **beaches** on the sea at the extreme north and south ends of the Lido, at San Nicolò (bus A) and Murazzi and Alberoni (bus B). The big hotels on the sea-front have their own beaches and the other hotels share private beaches on the Lungomare Marconi. Beach huts at some of these may be hired by the day.

There is a municipal **swimming pool** (closed mid-July–mid-Sept) on the residential island of Sacca Fisola, connected to the Guidecca by a bridge, and at Sant'Alvise. There is an 18-hole **golf course** at Alberoni at the south end of the Lido. **Tennis courts** are available on Dorsoduro and near the Arsenal (there are also clubs on the Lido).

Boats to hire by the hour at Brussa, 331 Cannaregio (Ponte delle Guglie), ☎ 041 715 787. Great care should be taken when there is an exceptionally low tide. There are strict speed limits for private boats, and some canals are one-way, or reserved for gondolas. The Grand Canal is only open to private boats from 15.00 to midnight, and there are plans to close it to private boats at all times. Information on the latest regulations from the *Vigili Urbani*, Calle Cavalli, 4094 San Marco (near Campo San Luca), ☎ 041 270 8766.

Bicycles can be hired on the Lido by the vaporetto landing stage (Piazzale S.M. Elisabetta), in the Gran Viale S.M. Elisabetta, and in Via Zara.

Students and young visitors

If you are between the age of 14 and 29 you can buy a special card (*Rolling Venice*) for Lire 5000 or c €3 at the office of the *Comune* (*Assessorato alla Gioventù*), Corte Contarina 1529, San Marco, ☎ 041 274 7651; 🖹 041 274 7642. This is open Mon–Fri 09.30–13.00; Tues & Thurs also 15.00–17.00. The card, valid one year, entitles you to discounts in the city in certain restaurants, hotels, hostels, shops, and museums. It also gives access to the university canteen in Palazzo Badoer, Calle del Magazen 2840, San Polo (closed in Aug). The *Rolling Venice* card allows you to purchase a special ticket (Lire 25,000 or c €13) for use on nearly all *ACTV* services for 72 hours (available at *ACTV* ticket offices).

An information office run by the Comune for young visitors called *Informagiovani* can be contacted by ☎ 041 534 6268.

EU members under 18 are allowed free entrance to State-owned museums, and EU students between the ages of 18 and 26 are now entitled to half-price tickets for State-owned museums, and sometimes reductions for the young are available in other museums (see the Museum timetable on p 44).

Youth and student hostels are listed on p 27, and cheap eating places are described on pages 35–36. For internet centres see p 55.

Telephones and postal services

There are numerous public telephones all over the city in kiosks in the campi, and in bars and restaurants. They are operated by coins or telephone cards (5000, 10,000 or 20,000 lire; or c €3, €5, €10) which can be bought from tobacconists displaying a blue 'T' sign, bars, some newspaper stands, and post offices. For international calls there are also now various prepaid telephone cards (available as above) which you do not insert in the public telephones, but they can be used from any telephone by dialling a toll free number.

Numbers that begin with 800, called *numero verde*, are toll-free, but require a deposit. **Telephone numbers** in Italy can have from seven to eleven numbers. All now require the area code, whether you are making a local call or a call from outside Venice. Placing a local call costs Lire 200 or c €10 cents. For directory assistance (in Italian), dial 12.

Most cities in the world can be dialled direct from Italy. International telephone cards (Lire 10.000–50,000 or c €5–€25), which offer considerable savings, are now widely available from the same outlets as above. For information about international calls, ☎ 176. For person-to-person, collect and credit card calls, ☎ 170. The cheapest times to make telephone calls are from 22.00 to 08.00 and all day Sunday and holidays.

Venice area code 041.

dialling UK from Italy (0044) + number.

dialling US from Italy (001) + number.

The **head post offices** is in the Fondaco dei Tedeschi (Pl. 8; 2), at the foot of the Rialto bridge, with the telephone exchange and the poste restante, *Fermo Posta*. It is open 08.10–19.25, and on Sunday 08.30–19.30, except on the last day of the month when it is open 08.15–12.00. There are branch offices (open 08.00–14.00) in various parts of the city including Calle dell' Ascensione (near the west end of Piazza San Marco).

For information about the Italian postal services, ☎ 160.

Stamps are sold at tobacconists (displaying a blue 'T' sign) as well as post offices. Stamps for postcards and letters weighing up to 20g cost Lire 800 or c €40 cents for Italy and the EU and Lire 900 or c €46 cents for other destinations.

A **priority postal service** (for which special stamps must be purchased) for Italy and abroad, which promises delivery within three days, was introduced in 1999. *CAIpost* is a guaranteed, but much more expensive, express postal service which gives you a receipt. At post offices there are special boxes for letters abroad.

Tipping

Most prices in hotels and restaurants include a service charge, and so tipping is far less widespread in Italy than in North America. Even taxi-drivers rarely expect more than a few thousand lire added to the charge (which officially includes service). In restaurants prices are almost always inclusive of service, so always check whether or not the service charge has been added to the bill before leaving a tip (if in doubt, ask the waiter for explanation). In hotels, porters who show you to your room and help with your luggage, or find you a taxi, usually expect a few thousand lire.

Toilets

As in the rest of Italy, there is a notable shortage of public toilets in Venice. However, in recent years more have been opened and at present there are 9 in operation in the centre of the city, most of them open from 08.00–20.00 (Lire 500 or c €26 cents), and with facilities for the disabled:

Near San Marco there are toilets in Calle dei Preti behind Calle dell' Ascension (Pl. 8; 6) and in the Giardinetti Reali (Pl. 9;5), and near the Rialto in Calle della Bissa off Campo San Bartolomeo (Pl. 8; 4), and on the other side of the Rialto bridge. There are also toilets at the foot of the Accademia bridge (outside the Galleria dell'Accademia; Pl. 7; 8), as well as at Piazzale Roma and the railway station. Also rio terrà San Leonardo (Pl. 3; 6), near San Giovanni in Bragora (Pl. 10; 5), and the Giardini Garibaldi (Pl. 11; 7). There are also public toilets on the Lido, the island of San Michele, Murano, Torcello and Burano. For further information, contact *AMAV* (*Azienda Multiservizi Ambientali Veneziana*), ☎ 041 521 7011. Nearly all museums now have toilets. Many bars (cafés) have toilets available to the public (generally speaking the larger the bar, the better the facilities).

BACKGROUND INFORMATION

The history of Venice

By John Law

In memory of Professor Sir John Hale (1923–99)

> *Ay, because the sea's the street there, and 'tis arched by what you call*
> *Shylock's bridge with houses on it, where they kept the carnival:*
> *I was never out of England—it's as if I saw it all.*

In Robert Browning's poem *A Toccata of Galuppi's* (1842), the speaker addressing the Venetian composer, Baldassare Galuppi (1706–85) says that he already knows Venice although he has never been there, such is its reputation. The modern visitor may feel even more familiar with Venice, having absorbed the city by osmosis in a Rialto or Lido café, at a performance of Shakespeare's *The Merchant of Venice* (c 1596) or Gilbert and Sullivan's *Gondoliers* (1889), during a screening of David Lean's *Summer Madness* (1955) or Nicholas Roeg's *Don't Look Now* (1973), before a Turner seascape or a study of Venetian society—or 'society'— by Sargent, while listening to the music of Antonio Vivaldi. They may have read Henry James's *The Aspern Papers* (1889) or Thomas Mann's *Death in Venice* (1913)—on which the film by Luchino Visconti (1973) and the opera by Benjamin Britten (1973) are based—or Michael Dibdin's thriller *Dead Lagoon* (1994) and the detective fiction of Donna Leon.

In spite of such exposure, one never fails to be startled by Venice's remarkable situation and appearance: a city surrounded by the sea and built on a collection of natural and man-made islands, with canals instead of streets. As early as the 6C the homes of the Venetians were described as 'built like sea-birds' nests, half on sea and half on land', and its unusual setting also inspired artists like Vittore Carpaccio (c 1465–1523) and Giovanni Antonio Canal, or Canaletto (1697–1768). Moreover, the unusual setting helps one to understand much of Venice's history, contributing to what is known as the Myth of Venice. The Myth is a body of observations and explanations about the city; dating from the Middle Ages and ranging from the supernatural, to the plausible to the factual, it was rehearsed and elaborated upon by Venetians and foreigners alike.

Origins and early history

In the first place, how did a city become established in the lagoons at the head of the Adriatic? A possible answer—applicable through much of Italy—that the city had Roman or pre-Roman origins, does not work for Venice. The Romans knew the lagoons, but they founded their cities on the mainland. The Myth provided various explanations: the site had been divinely indicated to the Apostle Mark, later the city's patron saint; or noble, Christian families from the Roman province of Venetia fled to the lagoons to escape the invasions of Attila the Hun in the 5C.

Modern historians now accept that the major exodus from north-eastern Italy to the relative safety of the lagoons took place in the 6C in the face of the Lombard invasions, but the image of Venice as a safe haven—literally and figuratively—has an abiding place in the city's Myth. In the mid-14C, the poet Petrarch described Venice as 'the one haven sought out by those whose ships have been shaken by tyranny and the storms of war', sentiments echoed later, for example in the 16C by the Welsh traveller William Thomas, who acknowledged the 'liberty' enjoyed by 'strangers' (foreigners). Enthusiastic rhetoric aside, there is no doubt that constant immigration contributed crucially to the growth, economic activity and cultural life of Venice.

The Myth underlined the special, providential, quality of Venice's secure location by stressing that its 'walls' were natural: the sea. In fact, the Venetians did at various times reinforce these defences—fortifications did guard the principal entrances to the lagoons—but undoubtedly to attack the city was a formidable undertaking, especially since the community which eventually emerged in the 11C as the 'Commune of the Venetians' was established on the 'high bank' (the *rivus altus*, or Rialto) in the centre of the lagoons. Only three times before 1797 did the city face an enemy or a hostile coalition with the resources to force an invasion or blockade. In 809 Pepin, the son of the western Emperor Charlemagne, tried to take the city. In the War of Chioggia (1378–81) Venice confronted a coalition led by its principal maritime rival, Genoa; at the outset of the War of the League of Cambrai (1508–17) the lagoons were threatened by the armies of France and the Empire. On all these occasions Venice managed to survive. It was only in 1797 that the city lost its independence, this time to Napoleon, but that was the consequence of intimidation and capitulation rather than assault. The only close siege Venice endured, and lost, was in 1848–49 when the city attempted to rebel against Austrian rule. Then its site could not protect it from aerial attack, by balloon, and from specially mounted artillery.

The lagoons which defended Venice also helped to make the city one of the major ports of the Mediterranean. However, as an anchorage it was not ideal and navigating in its waters was difficult. When threatened with invasion, the Venetians pulled up the markers that indicated the navigable channels, and even in the Middle Ages vessels with a deep draught had to unload their cargoes at sea rather than at the city's wharves. But the *lidi*, the sandbanks separating the lagoons from the open sea, afforded greater shelter to shipping than other ports of the Adriatic, and this introduces a further reason why the site of Venice favoured its economic growth.

Situated at the head of the Adriatic, close to the mouths of then navigable rivers, like the Po and the Adige, Venice was geographically situated to become an entrepot port with the Venetians as middlemen between the Mediterranean, northern Italy and central Europe. Moreover the lagoons themselves produced valuable trading commodities in game, fish and salt, the last a major item in the economy of the Middle Ages, and beyond. That the area was relatively barren in other respects provided a further stimulus to Venetian trade. Most of what was needed to sustain a growing community had to be imported: construction materials for buildings and ships, and foodstuffs, in particular grain. Even water had to be brought in to supplement supplies collected in cisterns.

Growth, government and social structure

Of course, Venice did not emerge suddenly as a major commercial power. Initially, trade was local or regional—a sphere of commercial activity which remained crucial throughout its history—but by the 9C Venetian merchants had reached the important inter-continental market of Alexandria. And the growth of trade was not only encouraged by an appetite for new goods and markets, developments in shipping and an increasing population. The Venetians also benefited from their historic ties with the Byzantine—the Eastern Roman—Empire, its capital at Constantinople another major inter-continental market.

In geo-political terms Venice was situated within a frontier province of the Byzantine Empire, with its magistrates—its tribunes and then its duke, or doge—being regarded as officers of that Empire. Gradually, from the 8C, the realities of Byzantine sovereignty and military protection weakened, and from the 9C onwards the Venetians are found sending fleets to aid Byzantium against enemies in the eastern Mediterranean and southern Italy. This shift in the balance of power had important repercussions.

The collapse of the Byzantine presence in the Adriatic allowed Venice to emerge, de facto, as a self-governing and sovereign commune, with a broadly republican constitution. Moreover, the despatch of war fleets to aid Byzantium earned the city a privileged commercial position at Constantinople and within the Empire. The increasingly one-sided nature of this relationship provoked a reaction against Venetian commercial hegemony in the 12C which in turn encouraged Venice to take a leading role in the western crusade which was diverted from its original destination—Moslem Egypt—to capture Constantinople and overthrow the Empire (1204). The four bronze horses, copies of which grace the façade of the basilica of San Marco, were part of the booty of that enterprise, from which flowed further commercial privileges. And the foundations of a Venetian Empire were laid in the Balkans, the Aegeaen and the eastern Mediterranean. The city did indeed hold parts of 'the gorgeous east in fee'.

Finally, the city's site may have shaped its history both socially and politically. Venice appears to present a contrast to many other states in late medieval and early modern Europe in that its history was not punctuated by periods of faction and civil war, by dynastic conflicts or by popular uprisings. This is made all the more remarkable by the fact that from around 1300 the city's government was in the exclusive hands of a self-made, hereditary and virtually closed nobility drawn from the city's merchant families. In the Renaissance the relative stability and continuity demonstrated by Venice drew admirers from Florence, France, England and Holland, as well as uncritical praise from its own historians and political thinkers.

For such subscribers to the Venetian Myth, the explanation for this phenomenon was to be found in the quality and character of the nobility itself: a ruling class disciplined enough to sink personal and family interests for the common good, not only of themselves but of their subjects in Venice and its territories in the east and on the Italian mainland. From the 14C an explanation was also found in the commune's constitution, alleged by its admirers to be a balance of three elements: monarchy (the doge, the head of state), aristocracy (the inner councils of the government) and democracy (the entire nobility sitting in the Greater Council, or *Maggior Consiglio*).

No aspect of the Venetian Myth more provoked its enemies than this, and to the modern historian exploding it can come deceptively easily. In its early history, rival factions allied to the opposing empires of east and west struggled for hegemony, while some leading families sought to control the office of doge, like the Orseoli (c 1000) or the Tiepolo in the 13C. Even in more settled times, in the Renaissance, divisions can be found within the nobility, over the extent of Venetian involvement in the mainland, for example. Corruption and self-interest can easily be detected, while among the members of the *Maggior Consiglio*, wealth, office and honours were not distributed equitably. Far from being self-effacing, individuals and families sought to promote themselves through the building of urban palaces and rural villas, by seeking the patronage of the Church and the control of its higher offices, and commissioning portraits and tomb monuments. In practice, if not in law, the courts offered the nobility preferential treatment.

Yet the fact remains that Venetian history does display a remarkable degree of continuity. There were attempts to overthrow the state, led by disaffected nobles (1310) and a disillusioned doge, Marino Falier (1354), but they were isolated incidents which attracted little support and were quickly put down. And when Venice found itself under threat (1378–81 and 1508–17) its enemies were unable to exploit internal resentment.

The possible explanations for the city's stability are several. Some may appear rather negative. In the aftermath of the failed coup of 1310, the commune established a security magistracy, the Council of Ten, which could be ruthless in hunting down internal and external enemies. The city's sailors, probably the largest element in the work force, were normally in no position to organise a challenge to the government given their diverse geographical origins, their mobility and the variety of their occupations; they even lacked guild status.

But more positive reasons for Venetian stability and continuity can be advanced. Although the nobility made up a small proportion of the population, its numbers were relatively large, if not to modern eyes: in the early 14C, out of a total population of c 100,000 just over 1000 were hereditary members of the Greater Council. That Council embraced most families with a perceived right to rule, and it is now understood to have been less closed—at least into the 15C—than was once assumed. Poverty did not deprive a family of its nobility; membership of the *Maggior Consiglio* continued to offer the chance to hold office and influence policy, if only through the sale of votes! In terms of residence, nobles did not isolate themselves from commoners and their palaces were not fortresses. The many *palazzi* that can still be identified testifies not only to the number of noble families that once existed, but also to their social integration across the city.

Moreover, from the rest of the population a citizen class was also recognised. It was made up of established but non-noble families with backgrounds in trade or the professions, and it was granted privileged access to posts in the commune's secretariat and in the often wealthy and prestigious religious confraternities of Venice, the *scuole*. These institutions had a welfare as well as a devotional role which, together with hospitals and other charitable bodies, may have helped to alleviate serious poverty and distress. The city's trade and craft guilds, if excluded from and supervised by the government, were in practice afforded a considerable degree of autonomy. Again, as the city expanded so the government realised the need to ensure a regular supply of foodstuffs, available at affordable prices in times of need.

The regular staging of elaborate processions—as on the feast days associated with the patron saint, Mark—may have helped to inculcate a sense of community, a sense that was possibly further encouraged by Venice's location. It required a constant effort to maintain the fabric and health of the city, to keep canals and channels navigable; the once prosperous community on Torcello declined due to the spread of malarial swamps and the silting up of the principal waterways. Venice also had to preserve the *lidi* that protected the lagoons from the Adriatic, and to control the estuaries of the mainland rivers. All such projects necessitated the intervention of the commune, the state, and may have helped foster a sense of common identity, a 'life-boat mentality', among the Venetians.

Empires won and lost

There was no clearer indication of the importance of the sea to Venice than the annual ceremony of the *Sposalizio*, the Marriage of the Sea. It dated in part from the departure of a warfleet on Ascension day 1000 to assert Venetian authority in Istria, in part from the pope's grant of a ring to the doge in 1177 to symbolise the city's lordship over the Adriatic. In the ceremony, the doge was rowed on the state barge, the *bucintoro*, out of the lagoons to the open sea where he cast a blessed ring into the waves, with the words, 'We wed you, O Sea, as a sign of our perpetual lordship'. The *Sposalizio* had become a major tourist attraction by the 18C—though by then the city had become the 'Ocean's bride' rather than its lord!

Earlier visitors, when Venice was still a major Mediterranean power, were impressed by a more practical expression of the city's aspirations to rule the waves, its *Arsenale* or dockyard. This had been begun in 1104 and was steadily expanded until the 16C. Behind fortifications, galleys were built and repaired, and all manner of marine equipment—rigging, oars, sails, anchors, armaments—were stockpiled. The *Arsenale* was where naval squadrons were prepared to defend Venetian colonies and commercial interests overseas, as well as patrol the rivers of north-eastern Italy. But the galleys fitted out here also had a key commercial role. In the 14C and 15C they operated in state-directed protective convoys over set routes at fixed times of year. Their combined use of oars and sails meant they had to carry large crews, but it gave them speed and manoeuvrability, and suited them to the transportation of items of low bulk but high value—fine textiles, spices, dyes, drugs—as well as pilgrims bound for the Holy Land.

Galley operations were supplemented by the activities of a much large number of privately operated sailing ships with a greater cargo capacity, suitable for the transport of such items as timber, salt and grain. At its height, from the 14C to the 16C, Venetian maritime trade reached from the English Channel to the Black Sea, though individual Venetians could venture still further afield, like the Polo family who reached China in the late 13C. The Venetian gold ducat became one of the major trading currencies in the Mediterranean and beyond. The Rialto, in addition to its role as a local market, became an international centre for commercial information, exchange and banking.

Also sustaining Venetian trade were the colonies it acquired in the aftermath of the Fourth Crusade (like Crete, 1204) or later (like Cyprus, 1489). But the arming of warfleets and the acquisition of colonies and naval bases overseas are reminders that Venetian expansion and commercial activity did not go unchallenged. Early in its history Venice had to overcome the competition of other communities in the lagoon area. From the late 13C to the late 14C a series of exhausting wars were fought with the rival commercial city of Genoa, and if on balance Venice emerged as the victor here this was not the case when she came to face the rising power of the Ottoman Turks in the Balkans, the Aegeaen and the eastern Mediterranean from the 15C.

In the 14C, and nearer home, the city's trade routes—indeed its safety—were threatened by various Italian powers of which the Carrara lordship of Padua (1337–88, 1390–1405) was the most dangerous. In 1404, this persuaded Venice to embark on a series of campaigns which led to the acquisition of a mainland empire—the *stato di terra*—covering the Veneto and much of Lombardy.

To its enemies, Venice appeared in pursuit of the lordship of Italy, and for some Venetians in the 15C and 16C the Republic's expansion on the mainland was a mistake, provoking the hostility of other Italian and European powers and diverting the Venetians themselves away from the real source of the city's greatness—overseas maritime trade. However, the major reason for Venice's decline from great power status in commercial, naval, military and imperial terms, was the emergence of new rivals in the Mediterranean and elsewhere.

From the late 15C the Ottoman Empire steadily reduced the extent of the *stato di mar* until at the fall of the Republic (1797) it included only the Ionian islands and Istria. The foreign invasions of Italy from 1494 and the War of the League of Cambrai saw the city losing territory on the Italian mainland and acquiring the greatly increased Habsburg Empire as a neighbour. In the wider world, the discoveries of America and the sea route to India in the late 15C meant that Venice no longer held such a key position in international trade. Other powers, like England and Holland, taking advantage of these developments and with more secure access to timber, began to outclass Venice at sea. In addition, piracy on the Dalmatian coast threatened Venetian trade at the mouths of the lagoons.

But Venice did not experience a sudden or steady decline. The trade in oriental goods via Alexandria recovered—if not permanently—from the immediate impact of the Portuguese voyages of discovery around 1500. The gold ducat retained its value until 1797; Venice remained a centre of commerce if in a more regional sense. Watchful diplomacy and powerful fortresses prevented any sudden collapse in its empire, while as a still significant naval force the city participated in the alliance of Christian powers that defeated the Turks at Lepanto (1571). In the late 17C the Republic recovered—if briefly—her imperial role with the reconquest of territory in the Greek Peloponnese.

But the transitory nature of these gains, surrendered in 1718, underlined the relative decline of Venice whose aristocratic constitution, once so admired in Europe, had become an object of criticism and ridicule by the 18C. Hence it was as a powerless anachronism that Venice fell, virtually without a fight, to the French revolutionary armies in 1797. The *bucintoro*, for centuries associated with the city's claim to rule the sea, was destroyed, and the four bronze horses from the façade of San Marco, again identified as symbols of the Republic's grandeur and independence, were carted off to Paris. The newly-created Democratic Republic had only an ephemeral existence as Napoleon had already ceded the city and its remaining subject territories to Austria. Habsburg rule was challenged by a rebellion led by the Venetian patriot, Daniele Manin, in sympathy with wider movements for Italian independence, the Risorgimento. After stubborn resistance, Austrian rule was reimposed in 1849 and brought to an end only in 1866 when Venice was joined to the Kingdom of Italy.

Culture and society

Throughout its history Venice attracted outsiders. In the Medieval and Renaissance periods there were various reasons for this: its economic activity; its galley sailings to the Holy Land; its own significance as a religious centre with a large number of churches and important relics, ranging from the reputed body of St Mark (acquired in the early 9C) to what was believed to be his autograph Gospel (acquired in the early 15C). The fact that it was the capital of an empire, with a need for soldiers and sailors, also has to be taken into account.

The pragmatic attitude of a mercantile community, traditionally wary of the secular power of the Church, and relatively tolerant towards other religions and forms of Christianity, also attracted outsiders. Hence some immigrants established substantial communities, like the Armenians (from the 12C) and the Albanians (from the 15C). A large Jewish community achieved a permanent residence from the 16C. This was settled in the *ghetto* an area close to the Rialto once known for the casting of metals (*gettare*: to cast or mould). Its walls separated and protected Jews and Christians, and its size and economic importance helped ensure that *ghetto* was a word Venice gave to a generally less tolerant world. Finally, the proximity of Padua, whose famous university was privileged from the 15C as the only university of the Venetian state, was another attraction.

It is hardly surprising, therefore, that the cosmopolitan character of the city contributed to its cultural vitality. The presence of Greek exiles from Turkish rule, together with the city's importance from the late 15C as a centre for the printing and distribution of printed books, facilitated the production of Greek texts by the Roman publisher Aldus Manutius (1449–1515). Aldus introduced the first Greek type, but the Aldine press was more than a printing house: it was an academy actively promoting the study and use of Greek.

Painters, sculptors and architects were drawn to Venice by the abundance of on-going public, private and ecclesiastical building projects and the plentiful supply of materials, from marbles to pigments. For some their stay was short, as with the painter Gentile da Fabriano whose frescoes (c 1420) decorated the Greater Council hall of the ducal palace. For others, Venetian residence became permanent, as in the case of the Lombardi sculptors and architects in the 15C.

Tullio Lombardo's tombs in the Dominican church of SS Giovanni e Paolo for the doges Andrea Vendramin (d. 1478) and Giovanni Mocenigo (d. 1485) can still be admired, but the climate of Venice was hostile to fresco painting and Gentile's work in the ducal palace soon deteriorated. The much more durable, and expensive, medium of mosaic was chosen to decorate the shrine of the city's patron saint at San Marco. The introduction of oil painting on canvas gave large scale works by Venetian painters a greater permanence, and a higher profile to the 'Venetian school' from the late 15C, with figures like Giovanni Bellini (1428–1516) and Giorgione, from Castelfranco on the mainland (c 1478–1511). This in turn attracted more artists, and raised the reputation of Venetian painting to the extent that by the late 16C artists like Titian (c 1477–1576), Veronese (1528–88) and Tintoretto (1512–94) had acquired international reputations. This helped ensure that in the 18C Venice became one of the major centres on the Grand Tour, despite lacking a classical past. And depictions of Venice could always find a market, from Jacopo de' Barbari's 'bird's eye' view of the lagoons (1500) to the work of Antonio da Canale, 'Canaletto' (1697–1768) and Francesco Guardi (1712–93) in the 18C.

It was not only the visual that drew admiring visitors. As in Renaissance Florence and Rome, Flemish musicians made an important contribution, especially with the appointment of Adrian Willaert to direct the music of San Marco in 1527. He developed the madrigal and in San Marco exploited the church's architecture and acoustics to great effect by using a double choir, achievements taken further by talented and productive native composers who acquired international fame—helped again by the printing press—like Andrea Gabrieli (1510–68) and his nephew Giovanni (1557–1612). Claudio Monteverdi was attracted to Venice in 1613, and from the 17C opera began to flourish. The prolific composers Antonio Lotti (c 1667–1740) and Antonio Vivaldi (1678–1741) helped ensure that continuing vitality, and reputation, of Venetian music.

Decline and rediscovery

Another prolific composer was Baldassare Galuppi (1705–85), whom Browning uses in his *Toccata of Galuppi's* to evoke 18C Venice.

> *Did young people take their pleasure when the sea was warm in May?*
> *Balls and masks begun at midnight, burning ever to mid-day,*
> *When they made up fresh adventures for the morrow, do you say?*

The society conjured up is pleasure-seeking, and this introduces a further element in Venice's reputation—a city of the senses, of licence and indulgence, of the libertine, adventurer and author Giacomo Girolamo Casanova (1725–98). Its annual carnival delighted Lord Byron, who enthused to a friend in 1818: 'I have had some curious masking adventures this Carnival; but, as they are not yet over, I shall not say on. I will work the mine of my youth to the last veins of the ore'. From the Middle Ages the number and boldness of its prostitutes—and higher class courtesans—fascinated visitors. It was also a centre of gambling. The pioneering, but then discredited, Scottish financier, John Law, died there an unsuccessful gambler in 1729. Eighteenth century society was satirised by the popular and prolific Venetian dramatist Carlo Goldoni (1707–93) author of *The Servant of Two Masters* and *The Spendthrift Miser*.

But *A Toccata of Galuppi's* is also infused with melancholy and unease, alluding to the superficial gaiety of society and anticipating Venice's fall:

> *As for Venice and her people, merely born to bloom and drop,*
> *Here on earth they bore their fruitage, mirth and folly were the crop:*
> *What of soul was left, I wonder, when the kissing had to stop?*

Certainly the impression made on some 19C observers was of decay, with its black and silent gondolas no longer seen as transports of delight. The theme of death finds its most famous literary expression in Thomas Mann's *Death in Venice* (1913).

In the early 19C this impression of a city in decline stemmed in part from a negative view of Venetian government, controlled by a sinister, vindictive, narrow oligarchy. Others, with different political sympathies, lamented the

Republic's loss of independence (1797), though Wordsworth's famous sonnet *On the Extinction of the Venetian Republic* dates from five years after that event:

> *And what if she had seen those glories fade,*
> *Those titles vanish, and that strength decay;*
> *Yet shall some tribute of regret be paid*
> *When her long life hath reached its final day:*
> *Men are we, and must grieve when even the Shade*
> *Of that which once was great, is passed away.*

More generally, the city's physical and economic decline struck the traveller; writing in 1869, Mark Twain observed that Venice had 'fallen a prey to poverty, neglect and melancholy decay.'

However, even before the end of Habsburg rule in 1866 a process of re-discovery and re-evaluation took place. An important figure was John Ruskin (1819–1900) whose enthusiastic and minute studies of Venetian architecture not only encouraged the eventual restoration of such central monuments as the Ducal Palace and the Basilica of San Marco, but helped broadcast the city's appeal. The construction of a railway bridge to the mainland (1846) and the unification of Venice with Italy (1866) increased the influx of visitors and foreign residents. Small, but influential and well-connected, foreign communities— French, American and British—were established in the late 19C.

Ruskin's infectious enthusiasm for the art and architecture of the Middle Ages was paralleled by the pioneering work of the historian Rawdon Brown (1806–83), who published material relating to the British Isles from the massive government archives of the defunct Venetian Republic and other souces. Brown was also of invaluable—if under-recognised—assistance to Ruskin as well as to other scholars, collectors and visitors from Britain, America and France. However, foreign visitors and residents were drawn by more than the city's beauty and past; they were also encouraged by its low rents, its business opportunities, its cosmopolitan society and by—for some—its less censorious morals. To cater for visitors, hotels were built and upgraded, bathing facilities were introduced on the Lido—and even in the lagoons. Consulates proliferated and Protestant churches were founded.

One of the most sympathetic observers of late 19C Venice was the American William Howells, consul from 1861 to 1865, but the real hey-day of the foreign community followed the unification with Italy. To summarise the character of that diverse and changing society is hard, but some impression can be suggested by two contrasting individuals. Alexander Robertson (1846–1933) established himself as the Scottish Presbyterian minister in Venice in 1890. A disciple of Ruskin, his enthusiasm for the city was expressed prolifically in books and journalism. He became a guide and point of contact, taking the aspiring poet Ezra Pound under his wing. Robertson found in Venetian history a rejection of papal authority, and his championship of the Protestant cause provoked the sarcasm of the writer Frederick Rolfe (1860–1913), otherwise known as the Baron Corvo. Rolfe was generally hard up, but mocked the more respectable members of the English community in Venice—from whom he expected support—while consorting with gondoliers. His autobiographical *Desire and Pursuit of the Whole*, set in Venice, was written in 1909, but was judged too scandalous for publication until 1934.

Venice today

Although the Arsenale remained an active naval base until comparatively recently, Venice emerged relatively unscathed by the two World Wars. However, the threats it now faces are among the greatest in its history. A combination of high tides and strong winds, the *acqua alta*, means that the city has always suffered from flooding, but this has now been exacerbated by the sinking of the city and the rise in the water level. The fabric of Venice is also endangered by heavy, diesel-driven traffic in the canals and by shipping in the lagoons, as well as by air and water pollution.

In addition, there are social and economic problems. The economy depends heavily on tourism which threatens to turn the city into a museum or theme park as well as exposing it to increasing wear and tear. The resident population is steadily decreasing as Venetians look for a wider range of employment, more convenient and conventional housing and more time with their motor cars on the mainland.

But if it is easy to list the problems facing Venice their solution has proved harder. The fundamental and long-term measures needed to treat unemployment and preserve the environment have been frustrated by the sheer enormity of such problems, by vested interests, by political inertia or in-fighting.

However, it would be wrong to paint too negative or pessimistic a picture. The expertise to restore buildings and works of art exists, encouraged by such bodies as the Venice in Peril Fund, and is now being successfully employed. An international centre for the study and application of conservation techniques has been established on the island of San Servolo. The cultural life of the city is sustained by learned societies like the *Istituto Veneto*, the *Ateneo Veneto*, the *Fondazione Giorgio Cini* and an energised university. Its rich archives, libraries, galleries and collections continue to mesmerise scholars worldwide. Private enterprise has made a significant contribution to the cultural vitality of Venice: the Guggenheim Foundation supports the Peggy Guggenheim Collection; Fiat has restored the Palazzo Grassi as an exhibition and conference centre; the Delmas Foundation of New York encourages the study of Venice in Britain and the United States.

Traditional festivals have been preserved, like that of the Redentore (the Redeemer), in July, or re-invented, like the Regata in September or the Carnival before Lent. Venice hosts the Biennali, biennial festivals for the fine arts and film, as well as holding frequent exhibitions. Tourism does help to sustain craft forms —like glass manufacture—which in turn contribute to conservation.

In 1996, the famous 18C La Fenice theatre (1792) was burnt to the ground, the victim of an arson attack. Prophetically named (*fenice*; phoenix), the theatre has survived other fires, rising from the ashes in 1836. Work is still underway to restore the building to its former glory. Hopefully, one day La Fenice will be seen as a metaphor for the city as a whole, triumphant over disaster. Certainly, the 'temporary'—but successful—opera house on the Tronchetto can be seen as an expression of the traditional Venetian virtues of ingenuity and pragmatism, while the recent reopening of the historic Teatro Malibran will give opera in Venice a more magnificent temporary home.

The Doges of Venice

[697–717	Paoluccio Anafesto]	1253–1268	Ranier Zeno
[717–726	Marcello Tegalliano]	1268–1275	Lorenzo Tiepolo
726–737	Orso Ipato	1275–1280	Jacopo Contarini
737–742	[interregnum]	1280–1289	Giovanni Dandolo
742–755	Teodato Ipato	1289–1311	Pietro Gradenigo
755–756	Galla Gaulo	1311–1312	Marino Zorzi
756–764	Domenico Monegario	1312–1328	Giovanni Soranzo
764–775	Maurizio Galbaio	1329–1339	Francesco Dandolo
787–804	Giovanni Galbaio	1339–1342	Bartolomeo Gradenigo
804–811	Obelario degli Antenori	1343–1354	Andrea Dandolo
811–827	Agnello Particiaco	1354–1355	Marin Falier
827–829	Giustiniano Particiaco	1355–1356	Giovanni Gradenigo
829–836	Giovanni Particiaco I	1356–1361	Giovanni Dolfin
836–864	Pietro Tradonico	1361–1365	Lorenzo Celsi
864–881	Orso Particiaco I	1365–1368	Marco Corner
881–887	Giovanni Particiaco II	1368–1382	Andrea Contarini
887	Pietro Candiano I	1382	Michele Morosini
888–912	Pietro Tribuno	1382–1400	Antonio Venier
912–932	Orso Particiaco II	1400–1413	Michele Steno
932–939	Pietro Candiano II	1414–1423	Tommaso Mocenigo
939–942	Pietro Particiaco	1423–1457	Francesco Foscari
942–959	Pietro Candiano III	1457–1462	Pasquale Malipiero
959–976	Pietro Candiano IV	1462–1471	Cristoforo Moro
976–978	Pietro Orseolo I	1471–1473	Nicolò Tron
978–979	Vitale Candiano	1473–1474	Nicolò Marcello
979–991	Tribuno Memmo	1474–1476	Pietro Mocenigo
991–1008	Pietro Orseolo II	1476–1478	Andrea Vendramin
1008–1026	Otto (or Orso) Orseolo	1478–1485	Giovanni Mocenigo
1026–1032	Pietro Centranico	1485–1486	Marco Barbarigo
1032–1043	Domenico Flabanico	1486–1501	Agostino Barbarigo
1043–1071	Domenico Contarini	1501–1521	Leonardo Loredan
1071–1084	Domenico Selvo	1521–1523	Antonio Grimani
1084–1096	Vitale Falier	1523–1538	Andrea Gritti
1096–1102	Vitale Michiel I	1539–1545	Pietro Lando
1102–1118	Ordelafo Falier	1545–1553	Francesco Donà
1118–1130	Domenico Michiel	1553–1554	Marcantonio Trevisan
1130–1148	Pietro Polani	1554–1556	Francesco Venier
1148–1156	Domenico Morosini	1556–1559	Lorenzo Priuli
1156–1172	Vitale Michiel II	1559–1567	Girolamo Priuli
1172–1178	Sebastiano Ziani	1567–1570	Pietro Loredan
1178–1192	Orio Mastropiero	1570–1577	Alvise Mocenigo I
1192–1205	Enrico Dandolo	1577–1578	Sebastiano Venier
1205–1229	Pietro Ziani	1578–1585	Nicolò Da Ponte
1229–1249	Giacomo Tiepolo	1585–1595	Pasquale Cicogna
1249–1253	Marin Morosini	1595–1605	Marino Grimani

1606–1612	Leonardo Donà	1676–1684	Alvise Contarini
1612–1615	Marcantonio Memmo	1684–1688	Marcantonio Giustinian
1615–1618	Giovanni Bembo	1688–1694	Francesco Morosini
1618	Nicolò Donà	1694–1700	Silvestro Valier
1618–1623	Antonio Priuli	1700–1709	Alvise Mocenigo II
1623–1624	Francesco Contarini	1709–1722	Giovanni Corner II
1625–1629	Giovanni Corner I	1722–1732	Alvise Mocenigo III
1630–1631	Nicolò Contarini	1732–1735	Carlo Ruzzini
1631–1646	Francesco Erizzo	1735–1741	Alvise Pisani
1646–1655	Francesco Molin	1741–1752	Pietro Grimani
1655–1656	Carlo Contarini	1752–1762	Francesco Loredan
1656	Francesco Corner	1762–1763	Marco Foscarini
1656–1658	Bertucci Valier	1763–1778	Alvise Mocenigo IV
1658–1659	Giovanni Pesaro	1779–1789	Paolo Renier
1659–1675	Domenico Contarini	1789–1797	Lodovico Manin
1675–1676	Nicolò Sagredo		

The topography of Venice

The irregular plan of Venice is crossed by some 170 canals of which the Grand Canal divides the city into two unequal parts. The other canals, called *Rii* (sing. *rio*), with the exception of Cannaregio, have an average breadth of 4–5 metres and are often winding. They are spanned by c 430 bridges, mostly of Istrian stone (others are built in iron or wood). Almost all the bridges remained without parapets up until the 19C when numerous elegant wrought-iron balustrades were added. Also at this time many bridges were rebuilt in iron or cast-iron. The bridges are used also to carry gas pipes, the acqueduct, and electricity cables thoughout the city.

The city is supported on piles of pine, driven down about 7.5 metres to a solid bed of compressed sand and clay, and many of the buildings are built above a foundation course of Istrian limestone which withstands the corrosion of the sea. Pine is the only wood which hardens with time (and becomes almost fossilised) when exposed to water (and protected from the air).

The typical Venetian palace has a ground floor, *androne*, with a water-gate and sometimes a portico, and a courtyard, often with a well. The main rooms are on the first floor or *piano nobile*, arranged on either side of the *portego*, a large central hall, narrow and long, which sometimes extends for the whole depth of the building. It is lit by tall windows on the façade. On the upper floors there were sometimes protruding loggie (*liagò*), and on the roof characteristic open wooden balconies (*altane*). Venetian chimneys have a particularly charming shape.

The streets, nearly all narrow, are called *calle;* the more important thoroughfares, usually shopping streets, are known as *calle larga, ruga*, or *salizzada* (the name given to the first paved streets in 1676). Smaller alleys are called *caletta* or *ramo*. A street alongside a canal is called a *fondamenta;* a *rio terrà* is a street in the course of a filled-in rio. A *riva* was a wharf. A *sottoportego* (or *sottoportico*) passes beneath buildings. *Piscina* is a place where a basin of water connected to a canal formerly existed; and *sacca* a strech of water where canals meet. *Lista* is a lane which led up to an ambassador's palace.

The only *piazza* is that of St Mark; there are two *piazzette*, one in front of the Doge's Palace, the other the *Piazzetta dei Leoncini* (now *Giovanni XXIII*). Other squares in Venice are called *campo, campiello*, or *corte* according to their size.

A notable feature of some of the campi is the *vera da pozzo*, or well-head, which stands above a cistern into which rain-water was collected through grilles in the pavement. Below ground level the water filtered through sand before reaching the central well shaft.

Names of the streets and canals are often written up in Venetian dialect and changed when renewed. Some of the most curious corruptions of the Venetian dialect are: San Stae = Sant'Eustachio, San Marcuola = Santi Ermagora e Fortunato, and San Trovaso = Santi Gervasio e Protasio.

Houses are numbered consecutively throughout each of the six *Sestieri* or districts into which the city was divided in the 12C (San Marco, Castello, Dorsoduro, San Polo, Santa Croce, and Cannaregio).

A note on place names

In most Italian cities a large number of place names recall relatively recent events in the nation's history, with the main focus being on the Risorgimento and the First World War which united Italy almost bringing it to its present frontiers. These events and their participants are also acknowledged in Venice. There are monuments to Giuseppe Garibaldi (1807–82), Giuseppe Mazzini (1805–82) and King Vittorio Emanuele II of Savoy (1820–76), as well as to Venice's own hero of the Risorgimento, Daniele Manin (1804–57). The *partigiani* (partisans) who joined the Allies in 1943 to defeat Fascism in northern Italy are also commemorated.

However, most Venetian place names date from earlier periods in the city's history. This is in part a reflection of the city's strong sense of identity; it can also be explained from the fact that the urban fabric of Venice was relatively unchanged in the 19C and 20C, while the city's suburbs have been built on the mainland. Place names still preserve the memory of Venetian noble families (Calle Molin); foreign communities (Riva degli Schiavoni: the quay of the Slavs); economic activities (the Zattere, where rafts of timber were broken up). Many indicate the local church (Campo Santa Maria Formosa). Some names carry social or peronal references: the Calle della Stua recalls the presence of a bath-house or brothel (*stufa*; stew); the Corte del Milion is the reputed address of Marco Polo who described his eastern travels in his *Il Milione*. Other names are purely topographical such as the Calle dietro la Chiesa—the alley that runs behind the church.

The Terraferma

Venice is connected to the **mainland** by a road bridge (over 3.5km long), Ponte della Libertà, built in 1931–33, and a (parallel) railway bridge which dates from 1841–46 (widened in 1977).

Mestre (184,000 inhabitants), a dull modern town 8km from Venice is where many Venetians now live. Of Roman origin, it became part of the Venetian Republic in 1337. Since 1926 it has been incorporated in the municipality of Venice which it has outgrown, although in the 1990s the two cities voted to remain united as one municipality. The station of Venezia-Mestre is an important rail junction.

Nearby is **Marghera**, a large commercial harbour and oil refinery constructed in the 1920s and 30s, without thought to the consequences for the lagoon and the city of Venice. It has altered the delicate physical balance between the lagoon, the open sea, and the mainland. Discussions continue about how to lower the pollution caused by the petro-chemical industries here accused of producing radio-active waste and a high degree of cancer-caused deaths amongst its workers, and how to lessen the risk from the continual passage of oil tankers across the lagoon.

The **Brenta canal** between Padua and Venice (see p 52) reaches the lagoon at **Fusina**, which was the place where boats were boarded for Venice, before the railway line was built in the 19C. The trip took about one and a half hours and provided a splendid approach across the lagoon to the city (described by numerous travellers, including William Hazlitt in 1826 and Charles Dickens in 1846). There is now a car park here open at the most crowded periods of the year (when it is connected to Venice by a special vaporetto service).

The Venetian Lagoon

The hauntingly beautiful Venetian Lagoon is separated from the Adriatic by the low and narrow sand-bars of the Lido and Pellestrina which are pierced by three channels, the Porto di Lido, the Porto di Malamocco, and the Porto di Chioggia. A shallow expanse of water, with an average depth of 1 metre, and an area of 544sq km, it is the largest coastal lagoon in the Mediterranean, and the only one in the world which supports a large town in its centre. On some of the islands townships and monasteries were established in the Middle Ages, most of which have now diminished in importance, except for Murano, with its glass manufactories. On others, isolation hospitals were built, and after a fire in the Arsenal in 1569, many of the smaller islands were used as forts or stores for gunpowder. The Lido became a famous resort in the early 20C. The future of some of the islands, abandoned in the 1960s and 1970s, is uncertain. There is an excellent service of public vaporetti to all the inhabited islands.

The ecology of the lagoon

The survival of the lagoon and Venice itself depends on an extremely delicate ecological balance between the open sea and the enclosed lagoon, and from as early as the 12C work was being carried out to preserve it. Canals were dug between the early 16C and the 18C to divert the silt-bearing rivers (notably the Brenta and Bacchiglione, the Piave and Sile) away from the area so that they could flow directly into the sea to the north and south of the lagoon. In the 18C a great sea wall (the *murazzi*) was constructed out of pozzolana and Istrian stone at Pellestrina to control the eroding waters of the Adriatic, and in the 19C and early 20C outer breakwaters were built up at the three entrances. The salt marshes, the extent of which has dramatically diminished in this century, still protect a great number of aquatic species, although marine life is threatened by the increase in sea-weed in the waters of the lagoon.

Since the early years of the 16C, the lagoon has been protected by a board presided over by the Magistrato alle Acque. In 1987 this board, which has become the local office of the Italian Ministry of Public Works, granted a licence to a private consortium of firms called the Consorzio Venezia Nuova to undertake studies, present projects, and carry out the work necessary to safeguard the lagoon and the city. The division of the responsibility for the preservation of the lagoon between the municipality and the Regional and central governments continues to cause problems and delays. However, a great deal of valuable scientific research has been carried out on the lagoon in the last few decades.

It is now known that much damage was caused in the 1920s and 30s by the growth of the port of Marghera, and the decision in the 1950s to set up the second largest oil refinery in Italy inside the lagoon itself, only a short distance from Venice. The three sea entrances were subsequently deepened to allow tankers into the lagoon, and a channel 12 metres deep was excavated in the 1960s so that these ships could cross the lagoon from Malamocco, actions which accelerated the process of erosion in the lagoon. The discharge of nitrogen and the creation of dump sites inside the lagoon also caused serious problems. It is widely recognised that the passage of oil tankers today represents a very real hazard, and urgent measures have been called for to eliminate this traffic by the installation of pipe lines. In 2001 ships carrying dangerous cargo without a double hull were banned from the lagoon. Further damage was caused when the natural process of subsidence in the lagoon was increased by the construction of artesian wells for industrial use (drilling has officially been prohibited since the 1970s, but the extraction of liquids or gas in the Adriatic and the lagoon area has still not been totally halted). There is a suggestion that a buffer zone of artificial wetlands should be created in order to preserve the lagoon from pollution from the terraferma.

The navigable channels in the lagoon are marked by piles in the water, and the only way to see the remote parts of the lagoon is to hire a private boat (see p 58). However, much of it can also be seen from the ACTV public transport service of vaporetti. A particularly good view of the lagoon can be had from the walk around the outside of the walls of the island of the Lazzaretto Nuovo (see p 262; there is also a little observation post here in one of the towers), and from the top of the bell-tower of Torcello cathedral which is now open to visitors daily.

The *Consorzio Venezia Nuova* offices in Venice are in Palazzo Morosini, 2803 San Marco, ☎ 041 5293511. For information on the *WWF* (*World Wide Fund for Nature*) reserve in the southern part of the lagoon at Valle Averto, ☎ 041 5382820 or 041 5185068.

The conservation of Venice

At present the greatest problem facing Venice is the notable increase in the last few years of the number of days on which the city suffers from *acqua alta* (a flood tide over 110cm above mean sea level), which damages the buildings of the city (see p 49). One day in 2000 there was an exceptionally high tide of 144cm which meant that over 90% of the city was under water for a few hours. *Acqua alta* is caused not only by the subsidence of the lagoon, but also by the gradual rise in the mean sea level.

A project first discussed in 1970, and finalised in 1984, planned to regulate tides above the height of 1 metre by the installation of moveable barriers at the three entrances to the lagoon, using a system similar to those already in use in the Netherlands and Britain. These sluice gates are designed to lie on the bed of the sea, and be raised only when a particularly high tide is expected (it was originally estimated that such an occasion would probably arise only about seven times a year). Each barrier measures some 20 metres across, and is 18–30 metres high, and 4–5metres thick: to close all three entrances to the lagoon, some 128 of these would be needed. They could be activated in about 30 minutes once a high tide was forecast, and would remain raised for anything between two and five hours.

Although a prototype (known as Mo.S.E.; *modulo sperimentale elettromeccanico*) was installed at the Porto di Lido entrance to the lagoon in 1988, and exhaustive scientific experiments were carried out, this project, seen by many engineers to be the only possible solution to the problem of *acqua alta*, was halted in 1995 to be re-examined by an Italian government committee for its impact on the environment. In 1998 a commission of five international experts reported in favour of the project, giving it their conditional approval and stating that in their opinion the barriers would not adversely effect the ecology of the lagoon. In the same year, a commission appointed by the Ministry of the Environment pronounced a negative verdict.

Finally in 2000 the *Comitatone*, an inter-ministerial working group on the safeguarding of the city, under the chairmanship of the Magistrato alle Acque, were unable to take a decision on Mo.S.E. owing to the irreconcilable opinions of the Minister for Public Works and the Minister for the Environment, and they passed responsibility to the Cabinet of Ministers in Rome. No action has been taken to date since they have declared that more time is need to carry out yet further studies.

There is political opposition from the environmentalists who are worried about its impact on the ecology of the lagoon, and it has also now been recognised that the sea-level is rising due to global warming (it is estimated that by 2200 there will be a rise of 100cm in the mean sea level) and so the barriers might no longer be adequate to protect the city from the sea. There is also an urgent need to find a more reliable method for forecasting exceptionally high tides. Even if a decision were to be taken to go ahead with the project it is estimated that at least a decade would be needed before it was operational.

In the meantime detailed scientific studies of the lagoon continue, the sea defences are being strengthened, the beaches on the sea at Pellestrina and Cavallino reclaimed, some of the grass-grown shoals which emerge from the lagoon and the mud banks normally awash at high tide reconstructed, the polluted waters cleaned, and the fish-farms in the marshes (where eels, mullet, and sea bream are caught) reopened to tidal flow. Since 1997 **Insula**, a consortium for urban maintenance, under the direction of the Municipality, has been carrying out a programme of dredging and cleaning canals and raising the level of the lower-lying fondamente where possible to 1.20 metres above mean sea level (work has been completed near San Niccolò dei Tolentini, and is under way on the Giudecca canal). Since up to now it has appeared to be impossible to impose speed limits on motorboats throughout the city and lagoon, a revolutionary new boat has been designed to lessen the wash or wave damage (*moto ondoso*) caused by speeding motorboats which damages the foundations of all Venetian buildings and the quays on the main canals. This may one day replace some of the *ACTV* fleet. Called the *mangiaonda* (or 'wave-eater') its bow-wave is absorbed and converted into a source of propulsive energy.

However, despite these few encouraging signs it is generally recognised that all necessary action to deal with the pollution and ecology of the lagoon has not yet been taken. This is even more worrying since a series of indispensable actions have already been stipulated in various Special Laws for Venice since 1973.

Further reading

General background
Christopher Hibbert, *Venice: Biography of a city* (1988)
Hugh Honour, *Companion Guide to Venice* (1997)
Joe Links, *Venice for Pleasure* (1995)
Jan Morris, *Venice* (1993)

Social history
David Chambers and Brian Pullan, *Venice: a Documentary History* (2001)
Shirley Guiton, *No Magic Eden* (1972) (on Torcello, Burano, and Murano in
  particular) and *A World by itself* (sequel)
Mary MacCarthy, *Venice Observed* (1972)
Ed. Logan Pearsall Smith, *Life and Letters of Sir Henry Wotton*, (2 vols); a
  vivid insight into life in Venice in the early 17C (1907)
John Pemble, *The Mediterranean Passion* (1987), *Venice Rediscovered* (1995)
Brian Pullan, *Rich and Poor in Renaissance Venice: the social institutions of a Catholic
  state to 1620* (1971)
B. Redford, *Venice and the Grand Tour* (1996)

History
M. Brion, *Venice the Masque of Italy* (1962)
G. Bull, *Venice the Most Triumphant City* (1980)
D.S. Chambers, *The Imperial Age of Venice* (1971)
Frederick C. Lane, *Venice, a Maritime Republic* (1973)
P. Lauritzen, *Venice: a Thousand Years of Culture and Civilisation* (1978)
W. H Macneill, *Venice* (1974)
Jan Morris, *The Venetian Empire. A Sea Voyage* (1990)
John Julius Norwich, *The Rise to Empire* (1977), and *The Greatness and the Fall*
  (1981) (2 vols); reissued in 1982 in paperback as *The History of Venice*
Maurice Rowdon, *The Fall of Venice* (1970)

Some older histories and descriptions
Horatio Brown, *Life on the Lagoons* (1884), *Venice. An Historical Sketch* (1895), *In
  and around Venice* (1905), *Studies in Venetian History* (1907)
William Howells, *Venetian Life* (1866)
E. Hutton, *Venice and Venetia* (1911)
Henry James, *Italian Hours* (1909)
E.V. Lucas, *A Wanderer in Venice* (1914)
Pompeo Molmenti, *Venice* (1926)
Thomas Okey, *Venice and its Story* (1910)
Margaret Oliphant, *The Makers of Venice* (1898)
Lonsdale and Laura Ragg, *Venice* (1916); *Things Seen in Venice* (1920)
Alexander Robertson, *Venetian Sermons*, (1905)
Margaret Symonds, *Days Spent on a Doge's Farm* (1893)
Alethea Wiel, *Venice* (1894)

Art history

J. Clegg, *Ruskin and Venice* (1981)
E. Concina, *A History of Venetian Architecture* (1998)
P. Fortuny Brown, *The Renaissance in Venice* (1997), *Venice and Antiquity* (1996)
Richard Goy, *Venice: the City and its Architecture* (1999)
J. Halsby, *Venice. The Artist's Vision* (1990)
Robert Hewison, *Ruskin and Venice* (1978)
P. Hills, *Venetian Colour—marble, mosaic, and glass 1250–1550* (1998)
D. Howard, *Venice and the East* (2000)
P. Humfrey, *Painting in Renaissance Venice* (1996)
R. Lieberman, *Renaissance Architecture in Venice* (1982)
Mary Lutyens, ed, *Effie in Venice* (1965)
M. MacDonald, *Palaces in the Night. Whistler in Venice* (2001)
Sarah Quill, *Ruskin's Venice. The Stones Revisited* (2000)
J. Ruskin, *Stones of Venice* (3 vols) (1851)
J. Steer, *Venetian Painting* (1970)
A. Whittick, *Ruskin's Venice* (1976)

Literary works

Robert Browning, '*A Toccata of Galuppi's*'
Lord Byron, '*Childe Harold's Pilgrimage*', '*Marino Faliero*', '*Two Foscari*'
Henry James, *The Princess Casamassima*, *The Aspern Papers*, *The Wings of a Dove*
Ben Jonson, *Volpone*
Thomas Mann, *Death in Venice* (1913)
Marcel Proust, *Albertine Disparue* (1925)
William Shakespeare, *The Merchant of Venice* and *Othello*
William Wordsworth, '*On the Extinction of the Venetian Republic*'

Modern works and anthologies

Michael Dibdin, *Dead Lagoon* (1995)
Milton Grundy, *Venice. An Anthology Guide* (1998)
L.P. Hartley, *Eustace and Hilda* (1947)
Donna Leon, *The Anonymous Venetian* (1995), *Death in a Strange Country* (1995),
  Acqua Alta (1997), *Fatal Remedies* (2000)
I. Littlewood, *Venice. A Literary Companion* (1991)
D.C. McPherson, *Shakespeare, Jonson and the Myth of Venice* (1990)
M. Marqusee, *Venice. An Illustrated Anthology* (1987)
Frederick Rolfe (Baron Corvo), *The Desire and Pursuit of the Whole* (for an attempt
  to solve the mystery of the 'Baron's' life: A.J.A. Symons, *The Quest for Corvo*,
  1934)
Muriel Spark, *Territorial Rights* (1979)
Barry Unsworth, *Stone Virgin* (1985)
Salley Vickers, *Miss Garnet's Angel* (2000)

THE GUIDE

1 • The Basilica of San Marco

The basilica is the most important church in Venice and is one of its most splendid buildings, with superb Byzantine mosaics (only illuminated at certain times) and sculptural decorations. The four famous ancient bronze horses are kept in the Museo di San Marco which should therefore not be missed; an entrance fee is charged for it as well as for the treasury and the Pala d'Oro (the gilded and enamelled main altarpiece), which are also well worth seeing. The basilica must be the most visited building in Venice, and the authorities don't appear to have yet understood how to cope with the incessant crowds of tourists here. There are postcard shops in inappropriate places within the basilica itself which sometimes has a rather shabby atmosphere, and the attendents are not always as friendly as they might be. The campanile is well worth visiting for the view.

The Basilica of San Marco (Pl. 9; 5) stands high in importance among the churches of Christendom. Founded in 832 its sumptuous architecture retains the original Greek-cross plan derived from the great churches of Constantinople, and in particular, from the (destroyed) 6C Justinian church of the Holy Apostles. Its five onion domes are Islamic in inspiration. This famous shrine has been embellished over the centuries by splendid mosaics, marbles, and carvings. It contains outstanding art treasures, the origins of some of which are still uncertain (including the bronze horses and the columns which support the baldacchino in the sanctuary). Numerous different styles and traditions have been blended in a unique combination of Byzantine and Western art.

As the Doge's Chapel the basilica was used throughout the Republic's history for State ceremonies; it replaced San Pietro (see Ch. 25) as the cathedral of Venice only in 1807.

- **Admission** The basilica is open daily 09.45–16.30 or 17.00; fest. 14.00–16.30 or 17.00. However the **mosaics are only lit for one hour** on weekdays, 11.30–12.30, and on Sundays and holidays from 14.00–17.00. The **Treasury and Pala d'Oro** are open from 10.00–18.00; fest. 15.00–18.00 (admission charge). The **Loggia on the façade** and the **Museo della Basilica** (admission charge) are open 10.00–16.30. Other areas of the basilica, including the crypt, baptistery, and Cappella Zen, normally kept locked, can usually be seen by special request at the offices of the Proto of San Marco (the architects in charge of the fabric of the building) inside the basilica; enquire about procedure from one of the uniformed guards.
- **Ground plans** The Roman and Arabic numerals in the text refer to the Plan on pp 82–83; the letters refer to the Plan of the mosaics on p 89.

Building history

The first church built by Doge Giustiniano Particiaco was consecrated in 832 but damaged by fire in a popular rising (976) against Doge Pietro Candiano IV and radically restored, if not rebuilt by Doge Pietro Orseolo I.

Doge Domenico Contarini restructured the building in 1063, and work was continued by Doge Domenico Selvo (1071–84). This church, consecrated in 1094 by Doge Vitale Falier is thought to have had basically the same form as the first church, and is that which exists today.

The mosaic decoration begun at the end of the 11C is the work of centuries. After 1159 the walls were faced with marble from Ravenna, Sicily, Byzantium, and the East. During the Fourth Crusade (1204) and sack of Constantinople many of the greatest treasures which now adorn the basilica (including the four bronze horses) were transported to Venice. The sculptural decoration of the upper façade dates from the end of the 14C and beginning of the 15C. In the 16C Jacopo Sansovino carried out important restoration work to consolidate the structure of the building; a task which still continues.

Exterior

The sumptuous **main façade** is in two orders, each of five arches, those below supported by clusters of numerous columns and those above crowned by elaborate Gothic tracery, pinnacles, sculptures, and tabernacles. A balcony with waterspouts separates the two orders and copies of the famous bronze horses stand here.

Lower order of the façade. The columns are of different kinds of marble, many from older buildings, and most of them have fine capitals. Between the arches are six bas-reliefs: Hercules carrying the Erymanthean Boar, St Demetrius, Hercules and the Hydra, St George, the Virgin Orans, and the Angel Gabriel; the first is a Roman work; the second was made by a Byzantine craftsman in the late 12C, and the others are 13C in the Veneto-Byzantine style. At either end of the façade, between the columns, are statuettes of water-carriers.

At the left end of the façade a huge single column with a fine capital supports three porphyry columns.

Door of Sant'Alipio (I). In the arch above the door is a ***mosaic** of the

---

The legend of St Mark

According to legend St Mark the Evangelist anchored off the islands of the Rialto, while on a voyage from Aquileia to Rome. While he was there he had a vision of an angel who greeted him with the words *Pax tibi, Marce evangelista meus. Hic requiescet corpus tuum.* ('Peace be with you, Mark my evangelist. Here will be your resting place'). This portent was supposed to have been fulfilled in 828 when two Venetian merchants brought the body of St Mark from the Arab port of Alexandria and placed it in charge of Doge Giustiniano Particiaco who ordered the first church on this site to be built. When this church was rebuilt in the 10C the body of St Mark, which had been hidden for safekeeping, was lost, only to be miraculously 'rediscovered' by Doge Vitale Falier in 1094. The name and symbol of St Mark (a winged lion) have been emblematic of Venice since the 9C. There are numerous stone lions all over the city. The lion of St Mark can also still be seen on columns in piazze or decorating public buildings in many towns which were once subject to Venice, in the Veneto and further afield.

Translation of the Body of St Mark to the Basilica (1260–70). This is the only original remaining mosaic on the façade, and is the earliest representation known of the exterior of the basilica (the bronze horses are already in place). Beneath it is a fine arched lunette with early 14C bas-reliefs of the symbols of the Evangelists and five pretty arches decorated with fretwork, Islamic in style. The architrave above the door is formed by a long 13C Venetian bas-relief in the early Christian style. Superb capitals surmount the columns on either side of the door which dates from 1300 (by Bertuccio).

Second doorway (II). The mosaic of *Venice venerating the relics of St Mark* dates from 1718 (cartoon by Sebastiano Ricci). Above the door is a window with Gothic tracery surrounded by fine carvings of Christ and two Prophets on a mosaic ground. These doors are also by Bertuccio.

The **central doorway** (III) is crowned by a mosaic of the *Last Judgement* (1836). Among the columns flanking the doorway eight are in red porphyry. The three *arches have beautiful carvings dating from c 1240 (first inner arch) to c 1265 (third outer arch). These constitute one of the most important examples of Romanesque carving in Italy, showing the influence of Benedetto Antelami, the most prominent sculptor of 12C Italy. The main outer arch has, on the soffit, carvings showing Venetian trades (such as boat building and fishing), and, on the outer face, Christ and the Prophets. The middle arch depicts the months and signs of the zodiac on the soffit and the Virtues and Beatitudes on the outer face. The smallest arch shows Earth, the Ocean, and seven pairs of animals on the soffit, and, on the outer face, scenes of daily life from youth to old age. The very fine Byzantine **doors** date from the 6C. In the lunette is a marble carving of the *Dream of St Mark* by the school of Antelami (13C).

The **fourth doorway** (IV) has a mosaic of *Venice welcoming the Arrival of the Body of St Mark* (by Leopoldo dal Pozzo from cartoons by Sebastiano Ricci, early 18C), and 13C reliefs above a Gothic window.

Above the **fifth doorway** (V) is a mosaic showing the *Removal of the Body of St Mark from Alexandria* (also by dal Pozzo). The Moorish window has Byzantine reliefs and mosaics.

Upper order of the façade. The central window is flanked by arches filled with mosaics (left to right, *Descent from the Cross*, *Descent into Hell*, *Resurrection*, and *Ascension*) rearranged by Luigi Gaetano (1617–18) from designs by Maffeo da Verona. Before the central window stand copies of the famous gilded bronze horses made in 1980: the originals are now displayed in the Museo della Basilica (see p 94).

The façade is crowned by fine Gothic sculpture (better seen from the balcony, see p 94), begun in the early 15C by the Dalle Masegne brothers and continued by Lombard and Tuscan artists (including the Lamberti. Between the arches are figures of water-carriers by a Lombard master of the 15C. The central arch has fine carving by Pietro di Niccolò Lamberti. Above is the gilded lion of St Mark, and, crowning the arch, a statue of St Mark (by Niccolò Lamberti). The two outer tabernacles contain the Annunciatory Angel and the Virgin Annunciate attributed to Jacopo della Quercia. At the south-west angle of the balcony, overlooking the piazzetta, was a porphyry head (8C), said to be a portrait of Justinian II (d. 711) but this has been removed for many years.

South façade (towards Palazzo Ducale). This continues the design of the west façade. The first doorway (VI), which was blocked by the construction of

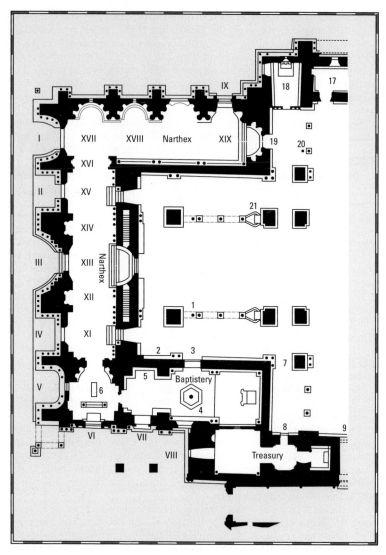

the Cappella Zen (see below) was formerly one of the main entrances to the basilica and the first to be seen from the water-front. The columns are surmounted by
two marble griffins (12C–13C). The second arch (VII) contains the bronze doors
(14C) of the Baptistery and a Gothic window. The two upper arches are finely
decorated; between them and above a small 10C door, is a Byzantine mosaic of
the *Madonna in Prayer* (13C), in front of which two lamps are lit every night in
fulfilment of a vow of a sea-captain after he survived a storm at sea. The Gothic
sculpture which crowns the arches is partly the work of Niccolò Lamberti. The

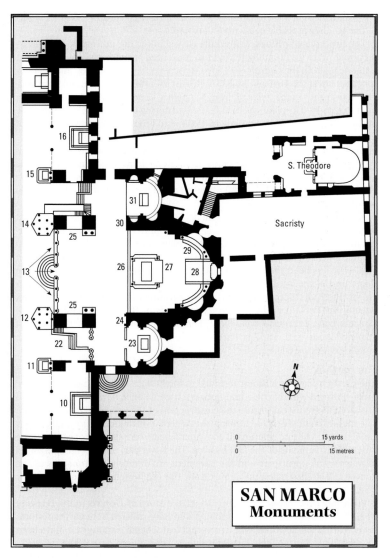

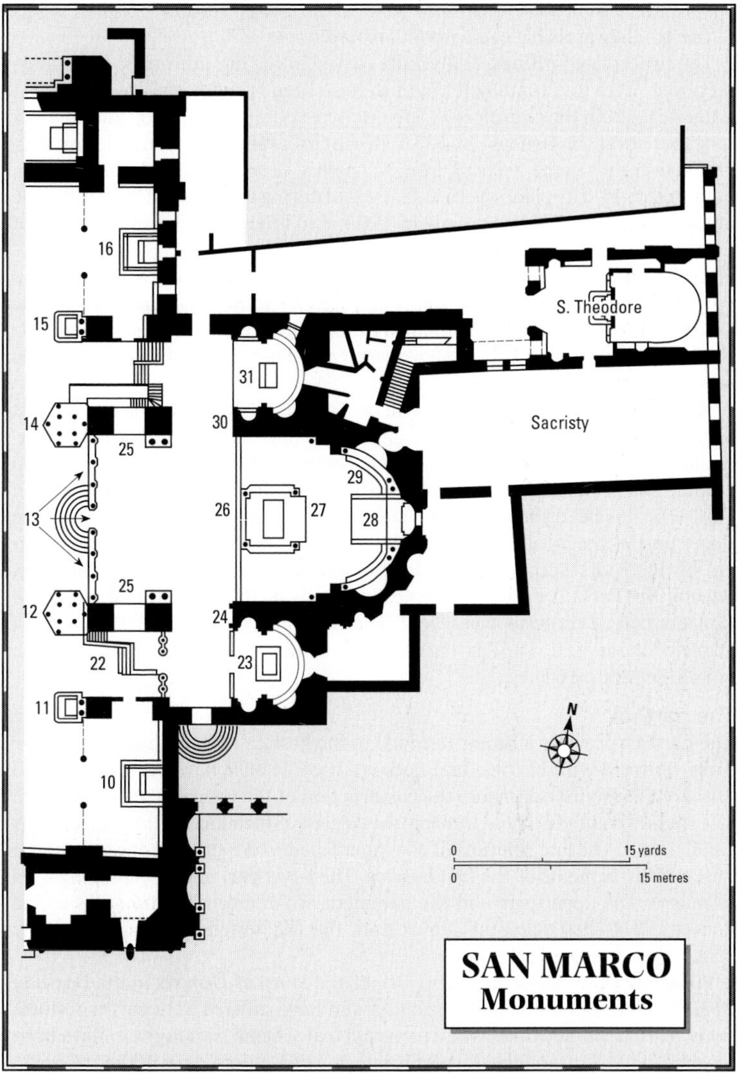
16
15
14
25
13
25
12
22
11
10
31
30
26
27
28
29
24
23
S. Theodore
Sacristy
N
0
15 yards
0
15 metres
SAN MARCO
Monuments

two rectangular walls of the Treasury (VIII) stand beside the Porta della Carta of Palazzo Ducale. These are richly adorned with splendid marbles and fragments of ambones and plutei (9C–11C). The front of the bench at the foot of the wall bears an inscription of the late 13C with one of the earliest examples of the Venetian dialect.

On the corner are two delightful sculptured groups in porphyry known as the ***Tetrarchs**, thought by some scholars to represent Diocletian and three other emperors, and by others the four sons of Constantine. Their symbolic embrace apparently was meant to represent political harmony. Probably Egyptian works of the 4C, they probably come from Constantinople.

The two isolated **pillars**, beautifully carved in the 6C, in front of the baptistery door, were traditionally thought to have been brought by Lorenzo Tiepolo (later doge) from the church of St Saba in Acre (now part of Israel) after his victory there over the Genoese in 1256. Recent excavations in Istanbul have suggested that they came, instead, from the palace church of St Polyeuktos there, built in AD 524. The pillars were in fact seized during the Sack of Constantinople at the time of the Fourth Crusade in 1204, and brought back to Venice at that time.

At the south-west corner of the façade is the **Pietra del Bando**, a stump of a porphyry column thought to come from Acre, from which decrees of the Venetian government were proclaimed from 1256 onwards. It was hit when the Campanile collapsed in 1902, but at least it saved the corner of the church from serious damage.

North façade (facing the Piazzetta dei Leoncini). This was probably the last to be finished. Between the arches and in the bays are interesting bas-reliefs, including one showing Alexander the Great conducted to Heaven by two Griffins (between the first two arches). The last of the four arches, the Porta dei Fiori (IX) has beautifully carved 13C arches enclosing a Nativity scene. The upper part of the façade has statues by Niccolò Lamberti, and fine water-carriers by Piero di Niccolò Lamberti (also attributed to Jacopo della Quercia). Beyond the Porta dei Fiori the projecting walls of the Mascoli and St Isidore Chapels bear Byzantine bas-reliefs. The sarcophagus contains the body of Daniele Manin (X; d. 1857 in Paris), ruler of the short-lived Venetian Republic (1848–49; see p 161).

The narthex

The narthex provides a fitting vestibule to the basilica (although it is often now sadly cluttered with barriers and notices). It could once have been approached also from the south side before the construction of the Cappella Zen (see above). The slightly pointed arches, probably the earliest of their kind in Italy, support six small domes. The fine columns of the inner façade were either brought from the East or are fragments of the first basilica. The lower part of the walls is encased in marble; the upper part and the pavement are mosaic. The *mosaics of the domes and arches represent stories from the Old Testament, and are mainly original work of the 13C.

First bay (XI). *Mosaics (1200–10) of the *Story of Genesis* to the *Death of Abel*. The mosaics are in poor condition and have suffered from earlier restorations. The carefully worked out iconographical scheme is thought to have been inspired by the Cotton Bible (probably late 5C) miniatures, once in the collection of Sir Robert Bruce Cotton (1571–1631) whose library is now in the British Museum. The 24 episodes are divided into three bands; in the centre of the dome, *Creation of the Sky, Earth, and Firmament*; in the middle band, *Creation of the Sun, Moon, Animals, and Man*; third band, *Stories of Adam and Eve*. In the pendentives are four winged Seraphs. The **door of San Clemente** (protected by outer doors), cast in the East, is traditionally supposed to be a gift from the Byzantine Emperor Alexius Comnenus. It is decorated with figures of saints (their names in Greek). The Byzantine capitals of the columns flanking the doorway are beautifully decorated with birds. The **first arch** (XII) has mosaics showing the story of **Noah and the Flood**. Here lies Doge Vitale Falier (d. 1096) who consecrated the basilica in 1094, and who was responsible for much of the work on it. The tomb, made up of Byzantine fragments, is the oldest surviving funerary monument in the city.

Second bay (XIII), in front of the main door. Two tiers of niches contain unrestored *mosaics, the earliest in the basilica (c 1063). They represent the **Madonna with the Apostles Peter, Paul, James, Andrew, Simon, Thomas, Philip,** and **Bartholomew**, and, beneath, the four Evangelists. In the semi-dome, **St Mark in Ecstasy** (on a cartoon attributed to Lorenzo Lotto, 1545). Two Byzantine angels stand on the columns flanking the arch. The **great door** (between two wooden doors) was executed by order of Leone da Molino (1113–18), Procurator of San Marco (1112–38) and modelled on the Byzantine doors of San Clemente (see above).

The slab of red Verona marble with a white marble lozenge in the pavement traditionally marks the spot where the Emperor Frederick Barbarossa was forced to kneel before Pope Alexander III in 1177. This marked a significant moment in the history of Venice's rise to power as the city, which had at first joined the Lombard League against Barbarossa, under the dogeship of Sebastiano Ziani had been chosen as the scene for the reconciliation between the Papacy and the Empire. The little door on the right leads up to the Museo della Basilica and the Loggia (described on p 94).

The **second arch** (XIV) has mosaics showing the **Death of Noah** and the **Tower of Babel**. The tomb of the wife of Doge Vitale Michiel (d. 1101) is made up of plutei and transennae of the 11C.

Third bay (XV). In the dome and the arch above the door, mosaics of the **Story of Abraham** (c 1230) and, in the pendentives, four tondi with **Prophets**. In the lunette above the door there is a Byzantine mosaic of St Peter. **Third arch** (XVI). Mosaics of **Saints Alipio and Simon**, and, in the centre, a tondo with **Justice** (c 1230).

Fourth bay (XVII). Tomb of Doge Bartolomeo Gradenigo (d. 1342) by a Pisan sculptor. The north wing of the narthex was probably added before 1253. The mosaics along this side of the narthex were partly re-made in the 19C; they portray the **Story of Joseph**, and, in the pendentives, the **Prophets**.

In the **fifth bay** (XVIII) is the recomposed tomb of Doge Marin Morosini (d. 1253), with a 13C relief. The **seventh bay** (XIX) has mosaics with the **Story of Moses** and a bust of Pope John XXIII (the first stage in his canonisation by took place in 2000), by Giacomo Manzù, a well-known 20C Italian sculptor (d. 1991).

Interior

Five great domes cover the Greek-cross of the interior, alternating with barrel vaults; each of the four arms has vaulted aisles in which the numerous columns with exquisite foliated capitals support a gallery (formerly the *matroneum*), fronted by a parapet of ancient plutei (dating from the 6C–11C). The sanctuary, where the religious and political ceremonies of the Republic were held, is raised above the crypt, and separated from the rest of the church by a rood-screen. The whole building is encased by eastern marbles below, and splendid mosaics on a gold ground above, illuminated high up by small windows (the rose window in the south transept and the arch opened at the west end are later additions which alter the delicate effect of dim lighting). At the centre of the nave hangs a huge Byzantine chandelier, while red lamps decorate the side chapels.

The 12C ***pavement**, which has subsided in places, has a geometric mosaic of antique marble with representations of beasts and birds. Part of it is covered with unattractive and untidy modern floor coverings which replace the pretty old carpets which once protected the floor. The light in the interior of the church changes constantly so it should be visited at different times of the day.

The mosaics

The mosaics (only lit at certain times, see p 79), which cover a huge area of the basilica, were begun after 1063. They were badly damaged by fire in 1106, and work continued on them up until the 20C. The original medieval iconographical scheme has been largely preserved. Some mosaics were repaired, others renewed, often following the original designs. In the 12C and 13C the Venetian school of mosaicists flourished, much influenced by Byzantine prototypes, and the decoration of the interior was completed by 1277. In the 14C and 15C mosaics were added to the baptistery and other chapels, with the help of Tuscan artists including Paolo Uccello and Andrea del Castagno.

In the early 16C many well-known Venetian painters (Titian, Salviati, Tintoretto, Palma Giovane) provided cartoons for mosaicists including the Zuccato brothers, and the partial replacement of the mosaics took place. In this way, paintings were reproduced in mosaic, and the art of true mosaic decoration was lost. From 1715–45 Leopoldo Dal Pozzo carried out restoration work and added new mosaics. Many of the mosaics were cleaned in the 1970s when a remarkable survey of them was undertaken by the celebrated art historian, Otto Demus.

The central ***Dome of the Ascension** (A) is the work of Venetian masters of the late 12C. Around the Ascension in the centre are the Virgin and two angels and the twelve Apostles; between the windows, the sixteen Virtues of Christ; in the pendentives, the Evangelists above four figures representing the rivers of Paradise. The ***mosaics** on the arch (B) towards the nave also date from the late 12C and portray scenes of the Passion: the Kiss of Judas; Crucifixion; Marys at the Tomb (15C copy); Descent into Limbo; and the Incredulity of St Thomas.

Over the nave rises the ***Dome of the Pentecost** (C), dating from the early 12C and probably the first of the five domes to be decorated with mosaics. The fine composition shows the Descent of the Holy Spirit; between the windows, the Converted Nations; in the pendentives, four colossal angels. Lower down above the west door into the narthex, is a brightly coloured ***lunette** (D) of Christ enthroned between the Madonna and St Mark (13C; restored). In the barrel vault stretching to the façade (also seen through glass from the narthex and from the organ gallery above, see below) are scenes of the Last Judgement, from a cartoon by Tintoretto, Aliense, and Maffeo da Verona (1557–1619; restored in the 19C), and Paradise, a Mannerist work of 1628–31, and, on the arch, the Apocalypse and Vision of St John, by the Zuccato brothers (1570–89; restored).

In the **right aisle** (E), is a frieze of five *mosaic rectangles with the single figures of the Madonna and the Prophets Isaiah, David, Solomon, and Ezekiel (c 1230; well restored in the 19C). On the wall above, ***Agony in the Garden**, a splendid large composition, the earliest 13C mosaic in the basilica. On either side of the windows, and in the arch above, lives of the Apostles (end of 12C, beginning of 13C). In the **left aisle** (F), is a frieze of five *mosaic rectangles with the single figures of a beardless Christ and the Prophets Hosea, Joel, Micah and Jeremiah. On the wall and arch above is a depiction of the Life of Christ and the Apostles, replaced in 1619–24 from cartoons by Tizianello, Padovanino, Aliense, and Palma Giovane.

Detail of the 12C pavement of the Basilica of San Marco

Right transept mosaics. The **Dome of St Leonard** (G) has just four lone figures of male saints: St Nicholas, St Clement, St Blaise, and St Leonard (early 13C); in the spandrels, four female saints: St Dorothea (13C), Saints Erasma and Euphemia (both 15C), and St Thecla (by Vincenzo Bastiani, 1512). In the arch towards the nave (H) are *scenes from the Life of Christ** (early 12C): the Entry into Jerusalem, Temptations of Christ, Last Supper, and the Washing of the Feet. The first narrow arch in front of the rose window is decorated with four saints (Anthony Abbot, Bernardino of Siena, Vincent Ferrer, and Paul the Hermit), fine works dating from 1458 (showing Tuscan influence). On the right wall (I): *prayers for and the miraculous rediscovery of the body of St Mark** (second half of the 13C, but restored), with interesting details of the interior of the basilica, and portraits of Doge Vitale Falier and Doge Ranier Zen (1253–68). In the vault (difficult to see), there are scenes from the Life of the Virgin (17C). On the arch above the Altar of the Sacrament (J) are the Parables and Miracles of Christ (end of 12C or beginning of 13C; restored). The mosaics on the end wall were renewed in the early 17C from cartoons by Pietro Vecchia (scenes from the Life of St Leonard).

Left transept mosaics. The *Dome of St John** (K) was decorated in the first half of the 12C. The Greek cross in the centre is surrounded by stories from the Life of St John the Evangelist. On the arch (L) towards the nave, 16C mosaics of the Miracles of Christ (cartoons by Jacopo Tintoretto, Giuseppe Salviati, and Veronese). Left wall (M): on the arch, scenes from the Life of the Virgin and the Infant Christ (end of 12C, beginning of 13C). The cycle was continued with the story of Susanna on the west wall in the 16C (from cartoons by Palma Giovane and Jacopo Tintoretto). In the archivolt; difficult to see above the marble wall of the Chapel of St Isidore), Miracles of Christ (end of 12C, beginning of 13C, restored), and, on the end wall, the huge Tree of Jesse (by Vincenzo and Domenico Bianchini, on a cartoon by Salviati, 1542). The arch (O) over the Altar of the Madonna of Nicopeia has Baroque mosaics of the Miracles of Christ by Pietro Vecchia (1641–52). The east wall of the transept has the Communion of the Apostles, and Christ at Emmaus from cartoons by Aliense and Leandro Bassano (1611–17).

The *Dome at the East End** of the church over the presbytery (P) is a superb work of the 12C showing the Religion of Christ as foretold by the prophets with the bust of Christ Emmanuel holding a half-revealed scroll (re-made c 1500), surrounded by the Virgin between Isaiah and Daniel and eleven other Prophets. In the spandrels, symbols of the Evangelists (St Matthew: angel, St Mark: winged lion, St Luke: winged bull, St John: eagle). In the arch above the rood-screen (Q) are 16C scenes from the Life of Christ (cartoons by Tintoretto). In the apse at the east end (R), Christ Pantocrator (Ruler of the universe), signed and dated 1506, but copied from its 12C prototype. Below, between the windows, are the four patron saints of Venice: **St Nicholas**, ***St Peter**, ***St Mark**, and **St Hermagorus**, among the earliest mosaics of the basilica (probably completed before 1100). The arches above the singing galleries to the left and right (S and T) are decorated with scenes from the life of Saints Mark and Peter (beginning of 12C, partly restored). The mosaics on the end walls are partly hidden by the organs; they represent scenes from the life of Saints Peter, Mark and Clement.

The little domes and arches at the piers forming the side aisles (marked U on the plan) are also beautifully decorated with mosaics of saints, etc (13C, but many of them restored or re-worked). Other important mosaics in the baptistery and the chapels of St Isidore and of the Mascoli are described below.

The lower part of the church
Right aisle. Stoup (1) of Oriental porphyry (the carved base is now in the Museo della Basilica, see below). On the south wall (2) is a Byzantine relief (12C) of Christ between Mary and St John the Baptist.

Right transept. On one of the corner piers (7) is a bas-relief of the Madonna and Child (known as the Madonna of the Kiss since it has been worn away by the kisses of the faithful), thought to date from the 12C. A small door (8) leads into the treasury, described on p 92. Above the main entrance (9) to the church from the Palazzo Ducale (now kept closed) is a 13C mosaic lunette of St Mark. Early 14C fresco fragments (including the Marys at the Tomb) have been uncovered in the passageway (no adm.). Above is a huge Gothic rose window inserted in the 15C. The altar (10) in this transept has a tabernacle borne by columns of porphyry and pavonazzetto. It is flanked by two bronze candelabra (by Maffeo Olivieri, 1527). On the two pilasters are rectangles of fine marble inlay; the one on the left marks the place where St Mark's body was hidden during reconstruction work on the church (see p 80), and miraculously rediscovered on 24 June 1094 (illustrated in the mosaic on the opposite wall, see above). On the wall to the right of the altar is a relief of St Peter enthroned (and two Bishop Saints in mosaic beneath the arch); to the left of the altar, Byzantine relief of the Madonna and Child. The mosaic pavement here bears early Christian motifs. On the nave pier (11) is the Altar of St James, a charming work with beautiful decorative details by Antonio Rizzo.

Here is the entrance to the sanctuary (see below). The doge traditionally showed himself to the people after his coronation in the sanctuary from the polygonal **pulpit** (12). Above the pulpit is a statue of the Madonna and Child, attributed to Giovanni Bon. The presbytery is raised above the crypt on a stylobate of sixteen little marble arches at the foot of the rood screen. The ***rood screen** (13) with eight columns of dark marble, bears the great rood, a work in silver and bronze by Jacopo di Marco Benato of Venice (1394), and marble ***statues** of the Virgin, St Mark the Evangelist, and the Apostles, signed by Jacobello and Pier Paolo Dalle Masegne (1394). The second **pulpit** (14) is really two pulpits one above the other, supported by precious marble columns and surrounded by parapets of verde antico. It is crowned by a little oriental cupola.

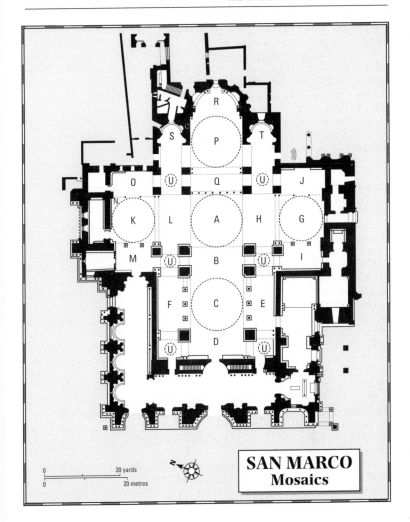

SAN MARCO
Mosaics

0 ___ 20 yards
0 ___ 20 metres

The fine stairway can be seen from the left transept. At the spring of the pendentives of the central cupola are four gilded marble *angels (Romanesque works
showing the influence of Antelami). In the pavement is a large rectangle of
veined Greek marble on the site of the old choir (11C–12C).

Left transept. On the nave pier (15) is the Altar of St Paul by Antonio Rizzo.
The **Chapel of the Madonna of Nicopeia** (16) contains a precious *icon, the
Virgin Nikopoios, representing the Virgin enthroned with the blessing Christ
Child. This type of icon, with a frontal view of the Child as Redeemer, was
known as the 'Victory-maker', since it was traditionally carried by the
Byzantine emperor into battle at the head of his army. A similar icon is known
to have hung in the apse of Hagia Sofia in Constantinople in 843. The San

Marco work, stolen by the Venetians from Constantinople in 1204, was traditionally considered to be the original icon, and became the protectress of Venice
and remains the most venerated image in the basilica. Most scholars now consider it to date from the 12C. It is surrounded by a fine enamelled frame
encrusted with jewels. Candelabra by Camillo Alberti (1520) flank the altar. On
the right is a Byzantine bas-relief of the Madonna and Child, and, on the left,
other Byzantine bas-reliefs.

At the end of the transept is the **Chapel of St Isidore** (17; officially reserved
for prayer, so usually difficult to visit) constructed by Doge Andrea Dandolo in
1354–55 (note the charming stoup near the door). Behind the altar, in a niche,
a sarcophagus bears a reclining statue of the saint (by the school of de' Santi,
14C), with an angel bearing a censor. The arch is richly carved; on the outside
are statuettes of the Annunciation. The upper part of the walls and the barrel
vault of the chapel are completely covered by mosaics in a beautiful decorative
scheme depicting the history of the saint.

The adjacent **Chapel of the Madonna dei Mascoli** (18; closed by a screen)
is so named because it became the chapel of a confraternity of male worshippers
('maschi') in 1618. Set into the end wall encased in splendid marbles is a carved
Gothic altar (1430), with statues of the Madonna and Child between Saints
Mark and John, by Bartolomeo Bon. The ***mosaics** (1430–50) on the barrel
vault depict the Life of the Virgin. They are one of the most important 15C
mosaic cycles, and one of the earliest examples of Renaissance art in Venice
(however they are usually unlit). They were carried out under the direction of
Michele Giambono, using cartoons by Andrea del Castagno and probably also
Jacopo Bellini. The Birth and Presentation of the Virgin (left wall) bear the sig-
nature of Giambono; on the right wall are the Visitation and Dormition of the
Virgin. On the wall outside the chapel (right) is a Byzantine relief of the
Madonna in prayer.

Above the door (19) leading out to the narthex is a pretty carved ogee arch
with a late 13C mosaic. The Greek marble stoup (20) has Romanesque carvings.
On the nave piers are a Byzantine Madonna in prayer, and a large bas-relief of
the Madonna and Child known as the Madonna dello schioppo because of the
gun placed here as an ex-voto.

In the **north aisle** the little ***Chapel of the Crucifix** (21) has a pyramidal
marble roof surmounted by a huge oriental agate and supported by six columns
of precious marble with gilded Byzantine capitals. It contains a painted wood
Crucifix thought to have been brought from the East in 1205. Nearer the west
door is a stoup made of bardiglio marble.

The entrance (22) to the **sanctuary** is from the right transept beneath a
transenna bearing Gothic statues of the Madonna and four female saints.
Ahead is the Chapel of St Clement (23) with sculptures by the Dalle Masegne
brothers. The upper part of the altar is by Antonio Rizzo. Below is a votive relief
of saints with Doge Andrea Gritti in adoration. Here tickets are bought for
admission (for times, see p 79) to the sanctuary and Pala d'Oro. On the side pier
is a fine Gothic tabernacle (24). The singing galleries in the chancel (25) have
bronze reliefs by Jacopo Sansovino (1537–44) of the Martyrdom and Miracles
of St Mark. The organ (1767), by Gaetano Callido, has recently been reconstructed.

The music school of San Marco

The music school of the Ducal Chapel of San Marco, founded in 1403, became famous towards the end of the 15C, when the first *Maestro di Cappella* was appointed. These distinguished *maestri* were usually well-known composers who acted as directors of religious music. Music was performed on all State occasions and every day at Vespers. The Flemish choirmaster Adrian Willaert (c 1490–1562) was appointed *Maestro di Cappella* in 1527 and remained here until the end of his life. Using the two organs, he experimented with double choirs. The composer Andrea Gabrieli first became organist in 1564, and then *Maestro di Cappella*, and his more famous nephew Giovanni, also a composer, succeeded him in 1585. Much of their choral and organ music was composed for the basilica with its unique acoustics and divided choirs, for example, *Selva morale* (1641), and *Messa a 4 Voci, et Salmi* (1650). Giovanni's fame attracted the German composer Heinrich Schutz as a pupil in 1609. Claudio Monteverdi directed the music at San Marco from 1613 until his death in 1643, and wrote some beautiful church music for Vespers during this period for small groups of solo voices and instruments. He was followed by Giovanni Rovetta (1596–1668). Monteverdi's pupil Pier Francesco Cavalli (1602–76), who came to Venice from Crema as a chorister, became organist at San Marco, and later followed his master's operatic lead, becoming *Maestro di Cappella* for the last nine years of his life. From 1748 until 1785 the position was held by Baldassare Galuppi (1706–85).

The baldacchino (26) of the high altar is borne by four *columns of eastern alabaster sculpted with New Testament scenes which are extremely interesting both from an artistic and from an historic point of view. It is still uncertain whether these are Byzantine works of the early 6C or even 5C, or Venetian works of c 1250. On the side walls of the sanctuary are six Gothic statues of saints. The sarcophagus of St Mark is preserved beneath the altar. On the marble balustrades are the four Evangelists by Jacopo Sansovino (c 1552) and four Patriarchs by Girolamo Paliari (1608–14). An altarpiece attributed to Michele Giambono has been placed over the altar (covering the back of the Pala d'Oro).

The Pala d'Oro

Behind the altar is the Pala d'Oro (27), an altarpiece glowing with precious stones, enamel, and old gold, the most precious work of art in the basilica. This is one of the most remarkable works ever produced by medieval goldsmiths, and incorporates some of the finest Byzantine enamels known. The first Pala was ordered in Constantinople by Doge Pietro Orseolo I. Embellished in 1105 (in Constantinople) for Doge Ordelafo Falier, it was enlarged by Doge Pietro Ziani in 1209, and finally re-set in 1345 by Gian Paolo Boninsegna, with a new gilded silver frame decorarted with busts and embossed patterns.

In the upper part, the Archangel Michael is surrounded by roundels with the busts of sixteen saints; on either side are six exquisite enamel scenes: Entry into Jerusalem, Descent into Limbo, Crucifixion, Ascension, Pentecost, and Dormition of the Virgin (these last perhaps from the church of the Pantocrator in

Constantinople). In the centre of the lower part, the Pantocrator (thought to be a 12C work also from Constantinople) is surrounded by 14C Venetian panels, with the four Evangelists in the tondoes. Above are two rectangles with angels, on either side of a lozenge depicting of the empty throne prepared for the Last Judgement.

Below the Pantocrator are three niches with the Virgin in prayer flanked by the empress Irene of Byzantium and Doge Ordelafo Falier. In this central lower section there are also two inscriptions on gilded plaques recording the work on the Pala carried out by the Falier doges in the 12C and 13C and by Andrea Dandolo in the 14C. The other 39 niches in three rows show the standing figures of Prophets, Apostles and angels with enamels from Constantinople.

In the border, the 27 rectangular scenes from the Life of Christ (at the top) and of St Mark (at the two sides), are thought to survive from the Pala of Doge Falier. The precious stones used to decorate the work include pearls, sapphires, emeralds, amethysts, rubies, and topaz. The enamels have been worked using the cloisonné technique, divided by narrow strips of metal. This is considered one of the most exquisite examples of this art, typical of Byzantine craftsmanship.

The **apse**, with two fine gilded capitals from Orseolo's basilica, has three niches. In the central one (28) is an altar with six precious columns, including two of unusually transparent alabaster. The gilded door of the tabernacle is by Jacopo Sansovino, and the statues of St Francis and St Bernardino by Lorenzo Bregno. The **sacristy door** in the left-hand niche (29) is also by Jacopo Sansovino, with bronze **'reliefs** (Entombment, Resurrection). The frame bears a self-portrait, as well as portraits of Pietro Aretino and Titian. Beyond a Gothic pier tabernacle (30), with sculptures by the Dalle Masegne, is the Chapel of St Peter (31), with a large 14C relief of St Peter with two small kneeling Procurators. The two columns have superb Byzantine capitals.

The treasury

In the south transept (see above) is the little door (8) which leads into the treasury, which has a pretty ogee arch with a 13C mosaic of two angels holding a reliquary of the True Cross, and a 14C statuette of the Risen Christ.

The treasury (adm. see p 79) contains a rich store of booty from the sack of Constantinople in 1204. Many of its most precious possessions were melted down in 1797 on the fall of the Republic, but it still retains one of the most important collections in existence of Byzantine goldsmiths' work of the 12C.

In the anteroom is a fine silver statuette of St Mark by Francesco Francesconi, 1804. The small marble **chair of St Mark** was a gift from the emperor Heraclius to the patriarch of Grado in 630. This was traditionally held to be the throne used by the Evangelist when he preached in Alexandria, but it is in fact a symbolic Egyptian throne made in Alexandria probably in the early 7C and subsequently decorated by Venetian craftsmen.

On the left is the sanctuary, with many precious reliquaries, mostly Byzantine. Above the altar frontal made of oriental alabaster is a relief of Christ among the Apostles, and, even higher, a tondo of Christ between two angels (13C).

On the right is the treasury proper, in a room with exceptionally thick walls thought to have once been a 9C tower of the Palazzo Ducale. Left wall: two elaborate silver-gilt altar frontals (13C and 14C), and two silver gilt 15C candelabra. Central case: Egyptian alabaster vase (500–300 BC); Roman ampulla in onyx, and a Roman lamp in rock crystal. **Four Byzantine *icons** (11C–13C), with gilding and enamels, two of them depicting St Michael Archangel, and two of them the Crucifixion. **Byzantine *chalices** and patens (10C–11C) in onyx, agate, alabaster, and other precious materials. The incense burner or ***coffer** in the shape of a Byzantine garden pavilion with five domes is a Romanesque-Byzantine work which comes from southern Italy (12C–13C).

Also here are displayed reliquary caskets, bowls made of precious stones including one in turquoise (a gift in 1472 from the Shah of Persia), one in alabaster, and one in rock crystal, and enamel, decorated with classical figures, which may be a Corinthian work; glass phial with incised decoration (Saracen, 10C); oriental vases; red onyx chalice with enamel panels (10C, Byzantine); two Roman situlae; ***paten** with Christ blessing, a Byzantine work thought to date from the 11C, richly decorated in oriental alabaster, cloisonné enamel, gold, silver gilt, rock crystal and pearls; a rare chalice which belonged to the 10C Byzantine Emperor Romanos (his name is inscribed in blue enamel letters on the base). Made of sardonyx it is possibly a reused Roman work of the 1C AD in agate-onyx, with a Byzantine silver gilt mount and cloisonné enamels, and gold. The chalice with a Eucharistic inscription made of sardonyx is also a Byzantine work of the 10C–11C in imitation of a classical work. On either side of the window: a marble monstrance (6C–7C) and the sword of Doge Francesco Morosini (a gift from Pope Alexander VIII). In the right wall cases: reliquary caskets, including a Gothic one which belonged to Charles VIII of France; ***gospel cover** in gilded silver (12C, from Aquileia); 16C paxes; and huge precious gems.

The **baptistery** and **Cappella Zen**, off the south aisle, are kept locked (but may be visited on request at the office of the Proto, see p 79). The font, designed by Jacopo Sansovino (c 1545), has a lid with bronze reliefs by his pupils Tiziano Minio and Desiderio da Firenze; the statue of St John the Baptist was executed by Francesco Segala (1575). The fine Gothic sarcophagus (4) of Doge Andrea Dandolo (d. 1354) is by Giovanni de' Santi. This doge, a friend of Petrarch, took a degree at Padua University and was a famous man of letters. He was the last doge to be buried in St Mark's. To the right (5), near a 13C relief of an angel, is the sarcophagus of Doge Giovanni Soranzo (d. 1328). A slab in the pavement marks the resting place of Jacopo Sansovino (d. 1570), one of the most prominent architects in Venice (see p 107). The huge block of granite (with an ancient inscription) is said to have been brought from Tyre in 1126. It has been raised to reveal traces (discovered at the end of the 20C) of a rectangular font, for total immersion, with fresco fragments, thought to have belonged to the first church. On the wall are three reliefs of the Baptism of Christ, and Saints George and Theodore on horseback (13C–14C). On the left wall are fresco fragments dating from the 13C. The ***baptistery mosaics**, carried out for Doge Andrea Dandolo (c 1343–54, see above) illustrate the life of St John the Baptist and the early Life of Christ. The ***Banquet of Herod**, above the door into the church, shows the influence of Paolo Veneziano.

The adjoining **Cappella Zen** (6) was built largely by Tullio Lombardo in 1504–22, in honour of Cardinal Giovanni Battista Zen who had left his patrimony to the Republic on the condition that he was buried in the basilica. Unfortunately the construction of the chapel blocked up the original entrance to the narthex from the piazzetta. The fine ***doorway** into the narthex remains:

beneath a mosaic of the Madonna between two Archangels (the Madonna dates from the 19C, but the two angels are 12C) are niches with mosaics (early 14C) alternating with fine statuettes of Prophets (by the school of Antelami). The remarkable bronze sculptures in the chapel include the tomb of Cardinal Zen (d. 1501), and the altar, which were started by Alessandro Leopardi and Antonio Lombardo and finished by Paolo Savin. The monumental statue of the Madonna 'of the Shoe' (so-called after a poor man offered a shoe to the statue which miraculously turned to gold) is a classical work by Antonio Lombardo (1506). Here, too, are some interesting bas-reliefs (11C–13C), and two red marble lions (Romanesque, thought to have been formerly outside the entrance to the basilica). The barrel vault mosaics (late 13C, restored) relate to the life of St Mark.

Museo della Basilica

From a small door to the right of the main west door (entered from the narthex; see Plan XIII) is access (by very steep stairs) to the **Museo della Basilica and the Loggia** (for admission see p 79). The museum has been in the process of rearrangment for many years: beyond two rooms which normally display 14C mosaic fragments from the baptistery, Persian carpets (16C–17C), and a lion of St Mark in gilded wood (16C), is the gallery above the narthex which provides a splendid view of the interior of the basilica and its mosaics. From here can be seen the walkways which encircle the upper part of the basilica: Jacopo Sansovino inserted iron girders here in an attempt to consolidate the structure of the church. A door leads out to the loggia on the façade with a spectacular view of the piazza. From here there is a good view of the Gothic sculpture on the upper part of the façade (described on p 81). The bronze horses are replicas (see below).

The last room displays (beneath a brick cupola) the original four famous **gilded bronze *horses**. After their restoration in 1979, the controversial decision was taken to exhibit them permanently here and place replicas on the façade of the basilica. The horses were brought to Venice from Constantinople (where they probably adorned the Hippodrome) at the time of the Fourth Crusade in 1204, and they were already in place on the façade of the basilica by the middle of the century. They remained a symbol of Venetian power throughout the Republic. Discussion continues about their origin; recent scholarship tends to assign them to the 2C AD, and therefore to a Roman rather than a Greek sculptor. They are the only quadriga known to survive from Classical times. Petrarch recorded his admiration for the horses when he sat beside the doge on the loggia in 1364 watching a tournament in the piazza.

In 1797 they were carried off to Paris by Napoleon where they remained until 1815 (the sculptor Canova being instrumental in their return). During the last two World Wars they were removed for safety (to Rome).

Also kept here are the magnificent cover for the Pala d'Oro, painted by Paolo Veneziano and his sons Luca and Giovanni (1345), and 16C illuminated choirbooks.

Another part of the Museum of the Basilica is to be opened in the Salone dei Banchetti (entered by lift from outside the basilica in the Piazzetta dei Leoncini, see p 108). This will contain the magnificent series of ten ***tapestries** (restored in 1982–94) depicting the Passion of Christ (c 1420), on cartoons attributed to the Venetian painter Niccolò di Pietro. They are the oldest complete series of tapestries to have survived in Italy.

The **crypt** of San Marco (restored and water-proofed in 1995; admission by appointment at the office of the Proto), which dates in part from the 9C, has an interesting plan with 50 ancient columns. Here the body of St Mark was placed in 1094. The pavement dates from the 19C.

The Renaissance **sacristy** by Giorgio Spavento and **Chapel of San Teodore**, with *organ shutters signed by Gentile Bellini (with *Saints Mark, Theodore, Jerome, and Francis*), are rarely open to the public.

Campanile of San Marco

In Piazza San Marco, at the corner of the Procuratie Nuove rises the Campanile of San Marco. It is normally open daily 09.00 to dusk (16.45 in winter, 19.00 in spring, and 21.00 in summer.

Over 98.5 metres high, it was first built in 888–912, and completed in 1156–73. It was later restored, the last time by Bartolomeo Bon the Younger in 1511–14. On 14 July 1902, it collapsed without warning causing little damage (except to the Loggetta, see below) and no human casualties. From the proceeds of a world-wide subscription an exact reproduction of the original was immediately begun and opened on 25 April 1912. At its base instruments record the level of the tides in the lagoon. The brick tower of the campanile is surmounted by a bell-chamber with four-light windows of Istrian stone, and a square storey decorated with two winged lions and two figures of Venice beneath the symbol of Justice; the spire at the top is crowned by an angel. The bell-chamber is reached by a lift from the Loggetta. Only one of the old bells survived the collapse of the tower; the others were presented by Pius X. Galileo experimented with his telescope from the top of the campanile in 1609. There is a magnificent *view of the town and the lagoon, and (on clear days of the Euganean hills, and the Alps).

Looking **north**, immediately below is the roof of San Marco and the Torre dell'Orologio. In the middle distance on the right is the huge flank of the basilica of Santi Giovanni e Paolo, with the cemetery island of San Michele with its cypresses behind, and behind that the island of Murano with its white lighthouse. Further to the right can be seen the smaller islands in the lagoon including Torcello marked by its campanile. Further to the left on the waterfront is the church of the Gesuiti and then the flank of the bare brick Scuola Grande della Misericordia and close by the church of the Madonna dell'Orto with its tall campanile. In the distance can be seen the mainland and the road and railbridge connecting it to Venice.

Looking **west** there is a good view of Piazza San Marco beyond which can be seen the building site of the Fenice theatre in the process of being reconstructed after fire. In the houses to the right can be seen the elaborate outside spiral staircase of Palazzo Contarini del Bovolo. To the left of the Fenice site is the marble façade of Santa Maria del Giglio, and, nearer at hand, the roof of the church of San Moisè. In the distance is the large red factory building of the Mulino Stucky on the Giudecca canal, and the mainland with the oil port of Marghera and the mountains in the far distance. On the left is the entrance to the Grand Canal, with the church of the Salute, the low Dogana building, and, beyond, the façade of the church of the Redentore on the island of the Giudecca.

Looking **south**, near at hand is the roof of the Libreria Sansoviniana and the two columns in the piazzetta. The island of San Giorgio Maggiore is prominent, with the Giudecca and the smaller islands of San Servolo and San Lazzaro degli Armeni. Beyond is the Lido facing the open sea.

Looking **east**, beyond the rooves and domes of Palazzo Ducale and the basilica of San Marco, is the tall façade of San Zaccaria, behind which are the shipyards of the Arsenal and the church and bell-tower of San Pietro di Castello. Further right is the long Riva degli Schiavoni, the quay on the edge of the lagoon. To the left can be seen the tall tower of San Francesco della Vigna (a copy of the campanile of San Marco) and further left the huge basilica of Santi Giovanni e Paolo.

At the base of the campanile is the **Loggetta**, in red Verona marble, by Jacopo Sansovino (1537–46), his first completed work in Venice. It was originally a meeting-place of the *nobili* or patricians during sessions of the Great Council (*Maggior Consiglio*) in Palazzo Ducale, see p 121. After 1569, owing to its strategic position, a military guard was posted here during the sessions of the Great Council.

The Loggetta was crushed by the fall of the campanile, but was carefully restored in 1912, and again in 1974. Its form is derived from the Roman triumphal arch and its sculptures celebrate the glory of the Republic. Three arches, flanked by twin columns, are surmounted by an ornate attic. White Carrara marble, Istrian stone, and verde antico have been used for the decorative details. Between the columns are niches with bronze statues of Pallas, Apollo, Mercury, and Peace, all by Jacopo Sansovino. The three reliefs in the attic show Venice (represented by the figure of Justice), Crete (represented by Jupiter), and Cyprus (represented by Venus). The two fine little bronze gates by Antonio Gai were added (1733–34). The sculpture inside of the Madonna and Child, also by Sansovino, was removed many years ago for restoration in the State laboratory in Florence. It is a charming work, recomposed (except for a young St John) from shattered fragments.

2 • Piazza San Marco and its museums

Piazza San Marco is one of the most beautiful squares in Europe. The adjoining piazzetta, overlooking the lagoon, is equally important to the historic townscape. The handsome buildings along one whole side of Piazza San Marco and overlooking the piazzetta opposite the Palazzo Ducale, designed by Jacopo Sansovino, are open to the public as they house the Museo Correr, the interesting city museum which illustrates the history of Venice, and includes a picture gallery, the Archaeological Museum (now entered directly from the Museo Correr), which has some masterpieces of Greek and Roman sculpture, and the Libreria Marciana, which preserves its 16C painted decorations, and houses the city's precious collection of books. The museums have splendid views of Piazza San Marco and the piazzetta.

Piazza San Marco

Piazza San Marco (Pl. 9; 5), is one of the most famous squares in the world. Laid out around the two most important buildings in Venice, the basilica of San Marco and the Doges' Palace, it had more or less reached its present vast dimensions by the 12C, although it was partly redesigned by Jacopo Sansovino in the 16C. It is the only square called *piazza* in the city. It is enclosed on three sides by the porticoes of the uniform façades of stately 16C palaces, built as the residence of the Procurators of San Marco who looked after the ducal basilica of San Marco. The colonnades open out towards the east end of the piazza and the fantastic façade of the Basilica of San Marco. On the left the decorative clock tower (Torre dell' Orologio) provides an entrance from the piazza to the Merceria, the main pedestrian thoroughfare of the city which leads to the Rialto. Opposite, beyond the tall isolated Campanile of San Marco, the piazzetta with the Palazzo Ducale opens on to the water-front, the entrance to the city in the days of the Republic.

Some of the most important events in the history of the Venetian Republic were celebrated in the piazza; it was always used for public ceremonies or religious festivals, when elaborate processions were held here (notably that of Corpus Christi), and it remains one of the centres of Venetian life. In the arcades (hung with draped curtains on sunny days) the elegant cafés have tables outside grouped around their orchestra podiums. Napoleon commented that it was 'the finest drawing room in Europe'. The present pavement in trachyte and Istrian stone was laid in 1722 by Andrea Tirali. The famous pigeons of St Mark still flock to the square, and the piazza is almost always crowded with tourists. In front of the basilica, between two standards of the Republic, the tricolour, bearing the winged lion of St Mark, is often flown from tall flagstaffs with elaborate pedestals (cast in bronze by Alessandro Leopardi in 1505). The flags are hoisted in a short military ceremony at 9 o'clock, and taken down at sunset.

On days when there is an *acqua alta* (an exceptionally high tide), the piazza is one of the first places in the city to be flooded; the duck-boards used on these occasions are usually stacked in readiness (the water first reaches the atrium of the basilica). The problem of flooding in the piazza is known to have existed since at least the 13C, and there has been a drainage system beneath the pavement for centuries which helps in part to channel away the water. However, since the frequency of the *acqua alta* has increased dramatically in the last few years, there is now a project to renew the drainage system below the pavement and introduce a waterproof lining beneath the layer of sand on which the pavement rests, so creating an *insulae* for this area (a solution which is also being experimented on other low-lying parts of the city).

Torre dell'Orologio

Above the entrance to the Merceria (Ch. 8) rises the Torre dell'Orologio, a tower built by Mauro Codussi to house a remarkable clock constructed in 1493–99 by Giampaolo Rainieri and his son Zuan Carlo Rainieri, celebrated clockmakers from Reggio Emilia. It was acclaimed at the time as the most complex astronomical clock in existence. It was restored by Bartolomeo Ferracina in the mid 18C, and its various parts were dismantled and restored in 1999 but the tower has still not been re-opened to the public.

The great **clock-face** shows the hours in Roman numerals (the hand of the clock is in the form of the sun); a moveable inner ring, brightly decorated with gilding and blue enamel, shows the signs of the zodiac and their constellations, and in the centre, on a dark blue sky filled with stars, is the earth with the moon, half gilded and half dark; as the moon turns its various phases are recorded. Above the clock is a tabernacle with the figure of the **Madonna**. Originally, every hour, figures of the Magi, accompanied by an angel, came out of the side doors and processed and bowed before her. This now only happens during

Ascension week and on special occasions because in 1858 two small drums which display the hour in Roman numerals and the minutes in Arabic numerals were inserted into the little doors (and lit from behind by gas lamps), in order to make the time easier to read from the piazza below, especially at night (these have to be removed temporarily when the 'procession' is reactivated).

Above the **lion of St Mark**, against an enamelled bronze background, hangs a great 15C **bell** which is struck every hour by two mechanical giant figures known as the **Mori** (or moors) in bronze, which date from 1497 and may be the work of Paolo Savin. In addition, another mechanism with two hammers strikes the bell 132 times at midday and midnight (the number represents the sum of the preceeding eleven hours).

The complicated mechanism of the entire clock was modified in 1753 by Bartolomeo Ferracina (when the wooden processional figures were remade) and again in 1866. The two wings of the tower, added in 1505 perhaps by Pietro Lombardo, were heightened in the mid 18C. There is another, simpler, clock-face on the other side of the tower overlooking the Merceria, where the hours are shown in Roman numerals and the hand is in the form of the sun fixed to a central 'sun' decorated with the lion of St Mark.

The Procuratie Vecchie

The rest of the north side of the piazza is occupied by the arcades of the Procuratie Vecchie reconstructed after a fire in 1512, perhaps by Mauro Codussi. After 1517 the work was continued by Guglielmo dei Grigi Bergamasco, and Bartolomeo Bon the Younger. Jacopo Sansovino added an upper storey in 1532. These were built as the residence and offices of the **Procurators of San Marco** in charge of the building and conservation of the basilica of San Marco, who were the highest officials in the Republic apart from the doge. They were the only patrician officers of the Republic (besides the doge) who were elected for life. By the 13C they had taken on a role of fundamental importance not only as guardians of the basilica but also as administrators of the conspicuous sums of money given by noble families to San Marco.

The buildings are fronted by three open galleries; the lowest has 50 arches, the upper two 100. Beneath the portico is the famous *Caffè Quadri*, which, together with the *Florian* opposite, is considered the most elegant café in Venice.

The upper storey of the Procuratie Vecchie is still used as offices. The church of San Geminiano, by Jacopo Sansovino, once stood at the west end of the piazza between the two Procuratie but was pulled down in 1807 by Napoleon. He replaced it by the so-called **Ala Napoleonica** of the Palazzo Reale, a building by Giuseppe Soli (1810). Its two lower floors copy the style of the Procuratie Nuove, while on top is a heavy attic fronted by statues of Roman emperors.

The Procuratie Nuove

The Procuratie Nuove, on the south side of the piazza, were planned by Jacopo Sansovino to continue the design of his Libreria Vecchia (see below) which faces the Doges' Palace. Up to the tenth arch from the left they are the work of Vincenzo Scamozzi (1582–86): they were completed by Baldassarre Longhena (c 1640). They were a later residence of the Procurators (see above), and became a royal palace under Napoleon.

In the portico beneath is one of the city's most celebrated cafés, the *Caffè*

Florian, named after its first proprietor in 1720, Floriano Francesconi. It retains a charming old-fashioned interior decorated in 1858 by Lodovico Cadorin.

Museo Corner

In 1920 the Procuratie Nuove were presented to the city by the Savoy royal family, and since 1923 they have been occupied by the Museo Correr (Pl. 8; 6), the city museum of art and history (open 09.00–17.00 or 19.00). The nucleus of the collection was left to Venice by the wealthy citizen Teodoro Correr (1750–1830). It was first opened to the public in 1836 in Correr's house on the Grand Canal, and moved here in 1922. Some of the exhibition space was designed by Carlo Scarpa in 1952–60.

The **entrance** is on the right of the central passage of the portico beneath the Ala Napoleonica. There is a small **café** in the museum.

From the central door in the Ala Napoleonica an imposing staircase leads to the first floor. The first rooms of the museum in the **Ala Napoleonica** retain their neo-Classical decoration from the Napoleonic era (1806–14), and they provide an appropriate setting for some important **works by Antonio Canova**. Some of these rooms are sometimes used for exhibitions, and the works by Canova are often changed around. The exquisite *bozzetti* (small models) by Canova for the funerary monuments of Francesco Pesaro and of Titian are usually displayed here. To the right is the ballroom, see p 104. The **Sala delle Belle Arti** has decorations attributed to Pietro Moro and Giuseppe Borsato. In another room is a huge bust of Clement XIII by Canova, and the cast of a self-portrait bust.

The **throne room** is decorated by Giuseppe Borsato and Giambattista Canal (1811). Fine neo-Classical *frescoes by Carlo Bevilacqua, detached from closed rooms in the Procuratie Nuove, hang here, along with panels with mythological scenes and dancers (early works by Francesco Hayez, 1817). There are two works by Canova here: *Daedalus and Icarus*, and a winged *Cupid*. The decoration of the **dining room** by Giovanni Carlo Bevilacqua and Giuseppe Borsato still survives. The early 19C French circular table has mythological scenes in Sèvres porcelain. A painting of *Amore and Psyche* and a portrait of *Amedeo Svajer*, a plaster cast of Venus Italica, and more clay models, all by Canova are displayed here.

The Historical Collections

Room 6. Painting of the *arrival of Caterina Cornaro, Queen of Cyprus, in Venice* (1489) by Aliense. On an easel, *portrait of Doge Francesco Foscari*, by Lazzaro Bastiani. Formal hats worn by the doges are also displayed here. **Room 7** contains an engraving by Matteo Pagan of a Procession in Piazza San Marco (1599), documents relating to the election of doges, medals, and paintings of state ceremonies. The **library (8)** has elaborately carved 17C bookcases (from the monastery of San Niccolò dei Tolentini) with a display of bookbindings. The 18C chandelier was made in Murano. **Room 9** has another fine chandelier, and 18C musical instruments and portraits. **Room 10** also has portraits of doges, including one by Alessandro Longhi, and more musical instruments.

Room 11 contains a very complete collection of coins, from the 9C to the fall of the Republic; and the huge standard from Doge Domenico Contarini's galley. The painting of *Santa Giustina with the treasurers*, is by Jacopo and Domenico Tintoretto. **Room 12** contains models of galleys, various navigational instruments, and lanterns. **Room 13** has exhibits relating to the Arsenal, with plans, engravings, models of boats, and a portrait by Alessandro Longhi of *Senator Angelo Memmo*. **Room 14** displays an inscribed edict in defence against the misuse of the 'public waters' of the city.

Rooms 15 & 16 display the armoury, and **Rooms 17 & 18** are devoted to Francesco Morosini who was doge in 1688–94. As an admiral he had conquered the Peloponnese, and during his siege of Athens in 1687 he all but reduced the Parthenon to ruins. Exhibits include the finely carved triple lantern from his galley, and Turkish banners; 17C Venetian and Turkish naval cannon; a replica of his bronze bust by Filippo Parodi in Palazzo Ducale; globes; an equestrian portrait by Giovanni Carboncino; Persian shields, oriental arms; Doge Morosini's cornu hat, his sword and prayer book (with a hidden dagger), and the standard from his galley painted by Vittore da Corfù.

From Room 18 or 19 access has recently been opened (with the same ticket) to the Museo Archeologico Nazionale and the Biblioteca Marciana. If you decide to visit them at this point, they are described on p 104; otherwise you can complete the visit to the Correr Museum, as described below, and then return here to visit these two museums.

Rooms 19 & 20 display small Renaissance bronzes of the late 15C and early 16C by Paduan and Venetian sculptors. **Rooms 21 & 22** continue the display with 16C and 17C Venetian works. At the foot of the stairs is a wood gilt statue, an 18C copy of one venerated in a temple in Canton (and thought to be an effigy of Marco Polo).

Picture gallery

The stairs lead up to the Quadreria, or picture gallery, on the second floor. This is arranged strictly chronologically. The rooms are now a little shabby. **Room 24**. Veneto-Byzantine period, including a late-13C painted coffin from a monastery on the Giudecca, and a relief of the Crucifixion. **Room 25**. Triptychs and polyptychs of the 14C, including works by Paolo Veneziano. **Room 26**. Lorenzo Veneziano. **Room 27**. Gothic fragments and frescoes; kneeling statuette of Doge Antonio Venier by Jacobello dalle Masegne. **Room 28**. Stefano Veneziano and Gothic painters of the 14C; Riminese school, *Madonna and Child between Saints Paul and John*. **Room 29**. International Gothic painters of the 15C: Stefano da Zevio (?), *Angel Musicians*; Francesco de' Franceschi, *Martyrdom of a Saint*; *Madonnas* by Michele Giambono and Jacobello del Fiore. The painted frontal of a marriage-chest by the Master of the Jarves marriage-chest illustrates a story from Boccaccio. **Room 30**. Cosimo Tura, **Pietà*; Ferrarese painter, c 1450, *Profile of a Man*. **Room 31** contains fine works by the Ferrarese school: Baldassarre Estense, *Portrait of a Man*; Angelo Maccagnino, *Profile of a Lady*; works by Leonardo Boldrini; Bartolomeo Vivarini, *Madonna and Child*, a particularly fine work.

Room 32 is one of the few rooms to have survived from the late 16C; it was decorated by Vincenzo Scamozzi. Here is displayed the famous **wood engraving of Venice in 1500** by Jacopo de' Barbari, together with the six original wood **blocks* which survive in excellent condition (the pear wood was carefully restored in 1999). De' Barbari invented the idea of the perspective view of a city, as seen from above: his work influenced a long series of maps and views of cities right up until the 18C. Very few representations of Venice had been made before this time, and this bird's-eye view, showing in detail how the city appeared in 1500, is of fundamental importance to historians of Venice. It is doubly remarkable as the wood blocks made by de' Barbari survive. It was originally attributed to Dürer, but in the

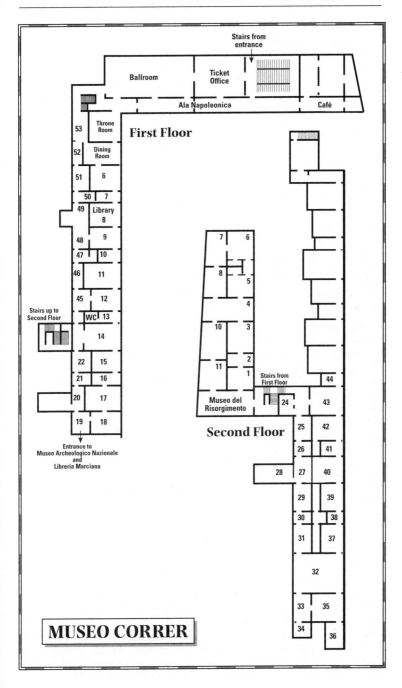

Stairs from
entrance

Ballroom

Ticket
Office

Ala Napoleonica

Café

First Floor

53

Throne
Room

52

Dining
Room

51

6

50

7

49

Library

8

48

9

47

10

46

11

45

12

Stairs up to
Second Floor

WC

13

14

22

15

21

16

20

17

19

18

Entrance to
Museo Archeologico Nazionale
and
Libreria Marciana

7

6

8

5

4

10

3

11

2

1

Stairs from
First Floor

44

24

43

Museo del
Risorgimento

Second Floor

25

42

26

41

28

27

40

29

39

30

38

31

37

32

33

35

34

36

MUSEO CORRER

19C recognised as the work of the otherwise little known artist de' Barbari, who left Venice for the court of the Habsburg Emperor Maximilian I. The engraving survives in three states and was first printed by a German merchant, Anton Kolb (the last time prints were made from the blocks was in the 19C).

Also displayed in this room is a Gothic altar frontal by Bartolomeo di Paolo and Caterino d'Andrea. The relief in stucco and papier mâché of the *Madonna and Child* is by Jacopo Sansovino. **Room 33**. Flemish painters: Pieter Bruegel, *Adoration of the Magi*. **Room 34** contains a very ruined painting of the *Pietà* by Antonello da Messina. Also here are displayed: Hugo van der Goes, *Crucifixion*; Dirk Bouts, *Madonna*.

Antonello da Messina

Antonello da Messina, born around 1430 in Messina, was one of the masters of the Italian Renaissance. He made a number of journeys from Sicily, including several to Naples and one to Venice in 1475, four years before his death, when he painted this work during a short stay in the city (the only painting by him in Venice). His work shows the influence of the Flemish school, particularly Jan van Eyck, in its attention to detail and particular sense of light. He was one of the earliest Italian painters to perfect the art of painting in oil, and it is probably through him that many Venetian artists decided to take up this medium. He had an important influence on Giovanni Bellini. His nephew Antonio da Saliba was also a painter (there are works by Antonio still in Venice in the Palazzo Ducale and the Galleria dell'Accademia). Some of his most beautiful works are in Sicily (including the *Virgin Annunciate* in the Galleria Regionale in Palermo and the *Portrait of a man* in the Museo Mandralisca in Cefalù) while other masterpieces are now in the National Gallery in London, the Metropolitan Museum in New York, the Louvre in Paris, and in museums in Berlin and Dresden.

Room 35 (with fine views of Piazza San Marco). Flemish and German painters: Herri met de Bles, *Temptations of St Anthony*; Jos Amman von Ravensburg *Saints*; Barthel Bruyn, *Portrait of a Woman*; Lucas Cranach (attributed), *Resurrection*. **Room 36** has important works by Giovanni Bellini and his brother Gentile. The *Transfiguration* is a remarkable early work by Giovanni painted c 1460, which shows Christ between Moses and Elijah on Mount Tabor, with the Apostles Peter, James and John below. The subject matter is particularly interesting as this is probably the first altarpiece to have been painted of the Transfiguration as the religious festival celebrating the event had only been introduced by Pope Calixtus III in 1457. The influence of Mantegna and Flemish painters such as Jan van Eyck can be seen here. The *Crucifixion*, also by Giovanni, probably dates from about the same time. Other works by him exhibited here: *Pietà*, *Madonna and Child* (the Madonna Frizzoni, damaged when it was transferred from panel to canvas), and *Portrait of a young Saint crowned with Laurel Leaves*. The other *Crucifixion* is attributed by some scholars to his father Jacopo. The portrait of *Doge Giovanni Mocenigo* is by Gentile Bellini.

Beyond room 32 is **room 37**. Alvise Vivarini, *St Anthony of Padua*, a lovely work in a fine frame; Cima da Conegliano, *Madonna and Child with Saints Nicholas and Laurence* (very ruined); Benedetto Diana (attributed), *Ecce Homo*; Bartolomeo

Montagna, *Holy Family and Donors*; Marco Basaiti, *Madonna and Child with Donor*; Bartolomeo Montagna, *St Giustina*. **Room 38** displays Vittore Carpaccio's famous painting of **Two Venetian Ladies*, probably painted around 1495 or later. For long thought to represent two courtesans, other critics, including Ruskin, thought it was simply the portrait of a mother and daughter with their pets. It may be a fragment, and is known to be the lower half of a painting; the other half depicting hunting scenes in the lagoon is now owned by the J. Paul Getty Museum in California. Some scholars think the panels decorated two doors of a cupboard. The two patrician ladies are shown deep in contemplation, and various symbols may represent allegories of Love (the dove and the orange) and Maternity (the lily and myrtle plants). Another painting by Carpaccio, *St Peter Martyr* is also displayed here.

Doge Giovanni Mocenigo, wearing the cornu hat

    Room 39 contains further works by Carpaccio, including the delightful *Portrait of a young Man in a red hat*. Also, Lazzaro Bastiani, *Annunciation*; Giovanni Mansueti, *St Martin and the Beggar*. **Room 40**. Works of the same period: Giovanni Dalmata, bust (Carlo Zen?); Il Riccio (attributed), *Bust of a young Man*; Boccaccio Boccaccino, *Madonnas*; Lorenzo Lotto, *Madonna crowned by two Angels*. Cases of ivories and enamels. **Room 41**. 16C–17C Greco-Venetian schools. **Room 42**. 15C–16C majolica (particularly from Venice and Urbino). **Room 43**. The library has 18C bookcases, an 18C Murano chandelier and a bust of Tommaso Rangone by Alessandro Vittoria. **Room 44** and the rooms beyond are used for exhibitions.

On the other side of the stairs up from the first floor is the **Museo del Risorgimento** which continues the history of Venice to the present day, with a well-arranged collection exhibited in eleven rooms. The first two rooms illustrate the first period of Austrian occupation (1798–1806). Room 3, the Napoleonic era (1806–14). Room 4, the second period of Austrian rule (1815–48). Rooms 5–7 and 9 the insurrection of Daniele Manin (1848), and room 8, the third period of Austrian rule (1849–66). Portraits of the time of Garibaldi and the Risorgimento are exhibited in these last two rooms.

The stairs lead back down to the first floor. **Room 45** commemorates the Bucintoro, with lanterns, and gilded wood fragments from the last Bucintoro, carved in 1729 by Antonio Corradini and his workshop. The portrait of the Dogaressa Morosini Grimani is by Palma Giovane, and the terracotta bust of Francesco Duodo by Alessandro Vittoria. **Rooms 46 & 47** contain paintings of festivals held in Venice, including three by Joseph Heintz the Younger (17C). **Rooms 48–50** contain a charming display illustrating the trades and crafts of Venice (shop signboards, household objects, lacemaking equipment, and ladies' apparel, including platform shoes), and materials (17C–18C lace, tapestries, embroideries and altar-frontals).

    Room 51 has sculptures: a relief in Istrian stone of St Mark between Saints Roch and Sebastian (as protectors from the plague) by Guglielmo dei Grigi Bergamasco (1525; from the entrance porch of the Lazzaretto Vecchio), and a high-relief of the 15C of the Madonna enthroned between a doge and magistrates from the island of Poveglia. **Rooms 52 and 53** illustrate the entertainments and games held during the Republic.

Beyond a room with a bust of Clement VIII by Canova and gesso reliefs is the entrance to the **ballroom**, designed by Lorenzo Santi in 1822 and decorated by Giuseppe Borsato. It contains two marble statues by Canova: Euridice (1775) and Orpheus (1777).

The **Correr Library**, with a fine collection of prints and drawings, and a photo archive, is open to scholars. The *drawings include many by Pietro Longhi and Palma Giovane.

Museo Archeologico Nazionale

Return to room 18 or 19 (see p 100) to visit the Museo Archeologico Nazionale (Pl. 9; 5). Open at the same times as the Museo Correr (see p 99), with a combined ticket. The entrance is from Room 18 or 19 of the Museo Correr. In summer it is sometimes open in the evenings, when you enter from the piazzetta, through its original main entrance at no. 17 in the portico of the Biblioteca Nazionale Marciana.

It was founded in 1523 from a bequest of Greek and Roman sculptures made by Cardinal Domenico Grimani to the Republic; in 1593 his nephew Giovanni Grimani, Patriarch of Aquileia, donated his collection from Palazzo Grimani (see Ch. 6). It is especially remarkable for its ancient Greek *sculpture, but some of the masterpieces have recently been moved to their original location in the vestibule of the Libreria Marciana (see p 106).

The recent opening of a door between Room 18 or 19 of the Museo Correr and Room XII of the archaeological museum has meant that it now has to be visited in reverse order, as described below. Since the room numbers have not been changed in situ, they have also been kept in the following description (but in the new order in which they have to be visited from the Correr Museum).

Room XII contains material from Zara, and Greek and Roman coins and gems. **Room XIII** displays reliefs, busts and statues related to Roman religious cults. **Room XIV**, the loggia, has a relief of vintage Scenes and Centaurs by Tiziano Aspetti (once thought to be a Roman work).

The two following rooms (**XVIII** and **XX**) contain the Correr collection including Greek and Roman heads and torsos; a black Romano-Egyptian head; a small Roman mosaic of a harbour scene (4C AD); the head of a boy of the Giulio-Claudian dynasty (1C AD); a statuette of Isis; and a mummy.

On the other side of room XIV is **room XV** which contains pre-Roman material, including Villanovan and Corinthian vases.

Room 1 has an original Greek inscription from Crete, and four busts, two Roman and two dating from the 16C. In **room II** is a well arranged numismatic collection, showing coins from the Roman to Byzantine periods. **Room III**. Roman copies of Greek works including Artemis. In **room IV** the fine series of female statues of 5C and 4C BC, includes Hera and Athena (modelled on the famous Parthenon Athena by Pheidias). **Room V** contains a series of heads and busts of Athena; funerary reliefs; and a Roman copy of the Apollo Lycius, perhaps after Praxiteles. (Here is the entrance to the great hall of the Libreria Marciana, descibed below.) In **room VI** is displayed the precious **Grimani altar** with Bacchic scenes (1C BC), as well as heads of satyrs, and the head of an athlete.

Room VII has two cases with precious small objects of varying date and provenence. In the left case: 5C Byzantine reliquary casket in ivory found near Pola with Christian motifs, restored in Vienna in the early 19C; 11C Byzantine ivory plaque of Saints John the Theologian and Paul; gems and cameos including the Zulian cameo of Jove, from Ephesus, variously dated between the 2C–3C BC and the 2C–3C AD; the head of a Hellenistic princess in rock crystal; and two heads of Jove, one of them the Chalcedon cameo (Pergamene art, 3C BC). Also here is an engraved cornelian, and a gem showing the Dioscuri from the Quirinal Hill in Rome, which is a neo-Classical work signed by Nathaniel Merchant.

In the right case: early bronzes, some dating from 1700 BC, and others Etruscan and Roman works, including the two most recent acquisitions, which are two Roman bronze statuettes found in the 20C in the lagoon near Malamocco dating from the 1C–3C AD.

Room VIII. Three Gallic *warriors found on Grimani property in Rome near the Quirinal Hill, copies of a group presented by Attalus of Pergamum to Athens; fragment of a Greek Hellenistic statue with good drapery; and heads of satyrs.
Room IX and X contain busts of Roman emperors including Trajan.

From room V (see above) is the entrance to the great hall of the famous library called the **Libreria Marciana** or **Sansoviniana** (its splendid façade on the piazzetta by Sansovino is described on p 107). Open at the same time as the Museo Correr (see p 99), with a combined ticket.

History of the Libreria Marciana

Petrarch gave his books to Venice in 1362, but it was not until Cardinal Bessarion, a native of Trebizond (in Armenia), presented his fine collection of Greek and Latin MSS in 1468 that the library was formally founded. Cardinal Pietro Bembo (1470–1547), the Venetian humanist, was appointed librarian and official historian of the Republic in 1530. Having been secretary to Leo X he was created a cardinal in 1539 by Paul III. He frequented Queen Caterina Cornaro's court at Asolo, and coined the term *asolare* from the town, meaning to amuse oneself at random. He used both Latin and Italian in his writings. This remarkable building was designed for the library by Jacopo Sansovino in 1537. Today the library contains about one million volumes and 13,500 MSS (many of them Greek). It is housed both in this building and in the adjoining building of the Zecca, also by Sansovino (see p 107).

The **Great Hall** has 21 **ceiling-medallions** with allegorical paintings by seven artists who each painted three tondoes. These are interesting examples of Venetian Mannerism (completed in 1557), and both Sansovino and Titian advised the Procurators on the choice of artists. Above the ticket desk are three works by Lo Schiavone; the next three are by Paolo Veronese; then come two by Giovanni Battista Zelotti (the third one by him was damaged and substituted in 1635 by Padovanino); then two by Giulio Licinio (the third one by him was damaged and substituted by Bernardo Strozzi in 1635); the next three are by Battista Franco; then three by Giuseppe Salviati; and the three at the far end (nearest to the door into the library Vestibule) are by Giovanni de Mio (called 'Fratina'; a painter who is not represented anywhere else in Venice). The painted architectural perspectives are by Battista Franco.

Around the walls are paintings of philosophers (1562–72): on the short wall by the ticket desk are two by Jacopo Tintoretto; on the right wall are four more by Tintoretto and two by Lo Schiavone; on the far wall, on either side of the door into the vestibule, are two by Paolo Veronese, and on the last wall are works by Benedetto Caliari, Giuseppe Salviati, Battista Franco, and the artist from the Netherlands Lamberto Sustris (only these last two formed part of the original decoration on this wall).

The floor was moved here from the Scuola Grande della Misericordia in 1815.

In the cases are displayed photocopies of some of the library's holdings. The most precious works include a late-14C *Divina Commedia* by Dante with illuminations, evangelisteries dating back to the 9C; a Byzantine book cover with Christ Pantokrator and the Virgin Orans dating from the late 10C or early 11C decorated with silver gilt, gold cloisonné enamel, gems and pearls; the exquisite *Grimani Breviary, illuminated by Flemish artists of c 1500; Fra Mauro's *map, a celebrated world-map of 1459 drawn on the island of San Michele; a map of Tunis by Hadji Mehemed (c 1560); Marco Polo's will; navigational charts; and a MS in Petrarch's hand.

The **vestibule** or **anteroom,** connected to the great hall by a monumental doorway, has a ceiling decorated with remarkable quadratura by Cristoforo Rosa framing a *fresco of the Allegory of Wisdom, by Titian. During restoration work in 1997 part of the public gallery of statues (which formerly numbered some 150 pieces) arranged here by the patriarch Giovanni Grimani in 1587 (and completed after his death by Vincenzo Scamozzi in 1596) was recomposed as far as possible on two of the walls. Although interesting from a historical point of view, this has meant that some of the masterpieces which had been moved to the Museo Archeologico in 1922 have been returned here and are less easy to see than they were in their museum setting. On the entrance wall the most important works include a Heracles of the Landau type, two original Greek female statues, and Eros bending the bow of Heracles, after Lysippus. On the opposite wall (on the floor by the door) is the *Kore, known as the **Abbondanza Grimani**, an Attic original of c 420 BC, the *base of a candelabra (Augustan period), a *bust thought to be of the Emperor Vitellius, a particularly fine Roman portrait of the early 2C AD, and, higher up, Aphrodite, Dionysus and a satyr (a Roman copy of a Greek original by Praxitiles), and Leda and the Swan.

The monumental **staircase** (which leads down to the original entrance), has a splendid stuccoed vault by Alessandro Vittoria.

Piazzetta di San Marco

The piazzetta (P1. 9; 5), with the Doge's Palace on the left, and the Old Library on the right, extends from St Mark's to the water-front on the Bacino di San Marco. Near the water's edge are two **huge monolithic granite columns** brought to Venice from the east by Doge Vitale Michiel II, and erected here at the end of the 12C. One bears a winged lion adapted as the symbol of St Mark. This is thought to be a Hellenistic work (4C–3C BC) and may have come from a tomb in Cilicia or Tarsus.

The other column is crowned with a statue of the first patron saint of Venice, St Theodore and his dragon. The torso is a fragment of a Roman statue of the time of Hadrian, and the head a fine Greek portrait in Parian marble (the original is now in the courtyard of Palazzo Ducale, see p 123). A scaffold used to be set up between the columns for capital executions, and the market stalls and booths here were removed by Jacopo Sansovino when he became *proto* of the procurators of San Marco.

The Libreria Sansoviniana

The Libreria Sansoviniana (Pl. 9; 5, Library of St Mark), opposite the Ducal Palace, is the masterpiece of Jacopo Sansovino, begun in 1537. Built of Istrian stone, its design is derived from Roman Classical architecture, with a Doric ground floor, and an Ionic *piano nobile* with an elaborate frieze beneath a balustrade crowned by obelisks and statues of gods and heroes by Tiziano Minio, Tommaso and Gerolamo Lombardo, Danese Cattaneo, Bartolomeo Ammannati, and Alessandro Vittoria. This ornate classical building was finished after Sansovino's death in 1570 by Vincenzo Scamozzi (1588–91). The great hall and vestibule and staircase are now open to the public, with access from the Museo Correr and Museo Archeologico, see pp 99 and 104 .

Jacopo Sansovino

Jacopo Sansovino (1486–1570), Tuscan architect and sculptor, left Rome (which had just been sacked) for Venice in 1527 at the age of 41 at the invitation of Doge Andrea Gritti, who later became a close friend. He was appointed *proto*, or chief architect in charge of the fabric of San Marco and the Piazza in the 1530s, and redesigned the Piazzetta, isolating the campanile of San Marco (and designing the Loggetta at its foot) and building the library. He helped to introduce a new Classical style of architecture into the city, based on his knowledge of Roman buildings, and the library was considered by Palladio to be the most beautiful building since the days of antiquity.

By the time of his death at the age of 84 he had built the Zecca (mint), the Fabbriche Nuove at the Rialto on the Grand Canal, the churches of San Francesco della Vigna, San Martino, and San Giuliano, and Palazzo Dolfin and Palazzo Corner both on the Grand Canal. His son, Francesco, wrote a remarkable guide to the city in 1581 called *Venetia città nobilissima et singolare*.

At the seaward end of the piazzetta is the **Molo** (Pl. 9; 5), the quay on the busy waterfront. Opposite stands the island of San Giorgio Maggiore, divided from the long Giudecca island by a narrow channel. On the Giudecca the Palladian façades of the Zitelle and Redentore churches can be seen. Nearer at hand is the promontory known as the Punta della Dogana with the church of the Salute. In the other direction (left) the quay extends along Riva degli Schiavoni to the public gardens.

To the right, beyond the end of the Libreria Sansoviniana, is the severe façade of the old **Zecca** or Mint (now part of the Biblioteca Nazionale Marciana, see above). This rusticated Doric building was finished in 1547 by Jacopo Sansovino on the site of the 13C mint. The first golden ducat was issued in 1284, and at the height of the Republic the Venetian *zecchini* were used as currency throughout the world.

Beyond a small bridge (with a Doric building recently attributed to Lorenzo Santi, c 1815) extend the **Giardinetti Reali**, public gardens laid out c 1814 after the demolition of the huge Gothic building which contained the Republican granaries. They contain, at the far end, an elaborate neo-Classical **coffee-house** (by Lorenzo Santi, c 1838), now a tourist information office. Across the next bridge is the Capitaneria di Porto (Port Authority office), once the seat of the Magistrato della Farina, the magistrates in charge of the distribution of bread and flour to the citizens of the Republic from the granaries. By the San Marco landing-stage is *Harry's Bar*, founded in the 1920s by Giuseppe Cipriani, which continues to flourish as one of the city's most celebrated restaurants and cocktail bars (entered from Calle Vallaresso).

To the left of the Basilica di San Marco is the **Piazzetta Giovanni XXIII** (formerly 'dei Leoncini' or 'di San Basso'), named after the former Patriarch of Venice who was pope from 1958 until 1963. It has a well head and two red marble lions presented by Doge Alvise Mocenigo in 1722. Here stands **Palazzo Patriarcale**, built in 1834–43 by Lorenzo Santi. In the corner a door gives access to the lift up to the Salone dei Banchetti, soon to be opened as part of the Museum of the Basilica (see above). The church of **San Basso**, with a façade by Longhena (1675), is sometimes open for exhibitions.

Calle di Canonica leads along the side of **Palazzo Patriarcale** (with interesting sculptural fragments in the courtyard) to Rio di Palazzo, across which rises the fine façade of the 16C Palazzo Trevisan-Cappello in poor condition, with good marble inlay. From Ponte della Canonica (rebuilt in 1755) there is a view of the Renaissance façade of Palazzo Ducale, and the Bridge of Sighs.

Museum of Diocesan Art

On the other side of the rio, at the end of the short fondamenta, is the entrance (at no. 4312) to the Museum of Diocesan Art (Pl. 9; 5), entered through the tiny **Cloister of Sant' Apollonia**. It dates from the early 14C, and is the only Romanesque cloister in the city, which retains its original brick paving. Here are displayed sculptural fragments (some dating from the 9C–11C) from the basilica.

On the far side is the entrance to the Museum of Diocesan Art. Admission weekdays 10.30–12.30; opened by volunteers. It contains a collection of sacred art (vestments, missals, church plate, crucifixes and reliquaries) as well as paintings and sculpture from churches either closed permanently or unable to provide safe keeping for their treasures. Works of art are added to the collection from time to time, so that the arrangement tends to change.

On the stairs is displayed a wood Crucifix of c 1300 from San Giovanni Nuovo. At the top of the stairs, in the gallery to the left, 17C lace vestments and illuminated choirbooks and *mariegole* (statute-books) from the city confraternities (14C–16C). Pope John XXIII's cardinal's beret; paintings from Sant'Antonin by Palma Giovane; two paintings by Luca Giordano from Sant'Aponal; 13C wood statue of the *Madonna and Child* from the church of San Francesco della Vigna; *Redeemer with Saints*, a ruined painting by Jacopo Tintoretto from San Gallo; and a number of paintings from Le Terese. The wood effigy of St John the Almsgiver from his sarcophagus by Leonardo Tedesco has been restored and may be returned to the church of San Giovanni in Bragora. Also here, and in the next room, are statues and busts (two by Juste Le Court), and paintings by Jacopo Marieschi, all recovered after their theft from the church on the island of San Clemente. A wooden model of the Fenice by Antonio Selva (1790) has also been placed here. In the room at the end (right), paintings from the Scuola del Crocifisso, by Giovanni Antonio Pellegrini, and a 16C lace altar cloth.

In the galleries on the other side of the stairs: portraits of the *Primiceri* (head chaplains) of San Marco; silver reliquaries; a rock crystal and gilt wood reliquary in the form of a domed tabernacle (17C, from San Martino di Murano); a reliquary with 12C enamels in a 15C setting from Santo Stefano; processional ***Crucifix** from San Pietro di Castello, with fine half-length figures in the terminals (late 15C); reliquary of St Tryphon, in the form of a leg (late 14C from Santa Maria del Giglio); chalice of 1460 from Sant'Eufemia; and two 19C ex votos from the Nicopeia chapel in San Marco. Also displayed here are forty pieces of church silver (14C–18C) donated to the museum in 1990 by Paolo Scarpa.

3 • Palazzo Ducale

This magnificent palace built for the doges is one of Venice's most famous buildings, with a remarkable Gothic exterior, which stands just out of Piazza San Marco. The visit to the vast interior with its numerous rooms decorated in the 16C and 17C, used by the various governing bodies of the Republic, takes several hours, and it gives a vivid idea of the glory of Venice at the height of her power. Although the palace is very well kept, it is often crowded with tour groups (except for the Museo dell'Opera on the ground floor where many of the beautiful original Gothic capitals from the exterior are displayed). If you have time it is also well worth booking the fascinating tour of the 'secret' rooms in the building, used by the adminstrators of the Republic.

The Palazzo Ducale, or Doges' Palace (Pl. 9; 5), the former official residence of the doges and the chief magistrates, was founded on this site in the 9C when it was transferred from Malamocco (see p 254). The present building dates from the 14C and the two façades overlooking the Bacino di San Marco and the Piazzetta are magnificent examples of florid Gothic architecture. The decoration of the interior by Venetian painters of the 16C–17C (after fires in 1574 and 1577) survives intact.

• Open 1 Apr–31 Oct 09.00–17.30 (the palace closes at 19.00) 1 Nov–31 Mar 09.00–15.30 (the palace closes at 17.00). For tickets and information see p 47. For the *itinerari segreti*, see p 123. For information, ☎ 041 522 4951.

The numbers in the text refer to the **plans** on pp 113, 116, 119. There is a **café** on the ground floor. The palace can be extremely cold in winter.

Building history

The palace was begun in the 9C and was rebuilt in the 12C under Doge Sebastiano Ziani; this in turn was destroyed by fire. In 1340 a large sum of money was voted by the *Maggior Consiglio* to build a room large enough to contain its 1212 members. This was built overlooking the Bacino di San Marco and was inaugurated in 1419. The building extended as far as the seventh column of the portico on the piazzetta. Shortly afterwards, in 1422, with the financial aid of Doge Tommaso Mocenigo, the *Maggior Consiglio* decided to demolish part of the 12C law courts on this site in order to extend the façade in exactly the same style towards the Basilica of San Marco. It is thought the building was constructed by a group of master-masons, including Filippo Calendario, under the direction of officials of the Republic. The exact role in the design of the palace of the obscure figure of Calendario, whose name is not connected with certainty to any other building work, is still not clear. All that is known is that he was beheaded in 1355, together with the Doge, because he had supported Doge Marin Falier in his treacherous conspiracy against the state, but sources as early as the 15C connect his name to Palazzo Ducale.

After another conflagration in 1483, Antonio Rizzo began the main interior façade and the Scala dei Giganti, and the work was continued by Pietro Lombardo, Giorgio Spavento, and Scarpagnino. Again burned in 1574 and 1577, it was decided to restore rather than rebuild the building under the direction of Antonio da Ponte. Paintings glorifying Venetian history were commissioned for the ceilings and walls of the main rooms. The courtyard and façade overlooking the Rio di Palazzo were then completed in the 17C on the old lines by Bartolomeo Monopola.

The **main façade** (overlooking the Bacino di San Marco) is a superb Gothic work. Each arcade of the portico supports two arches of the loggia decorated with quatrefoil roundels. This in turn is surmounted by a massive wall 12.5 metres high lightened by a delicate pattern of white Istrian stone and pink Verona marble. Marble ornamental crenellations crown the façade. The windows along this side belong to the immense Sala del Maggior Consiglio. In the centre is a balconied window built in 1404 by Pier Paolo di Jacopo Dalle Masegne, crowned with a statue of Justice. The high reliefs carved in the mid-14C on the three external corners of the building were inspired by the Old Testament and would have been seen as statements of the importance of the Christian faith. On the corner nearest to the Ponte della Paglia the relief depicts the **drunkenness of Noah**, and, in the loggia above, the Archangel Raphael.

On the corner nearest the piazzetta are **Adam and Eve**, separated by a fig-tree, with the Archangel Michael above. The third corner relief on the façade towards the piazzetta is described below. Restoration work began in 2000 on this façade. The level of the pavement used to be two steps lower so that the bases of the columns of the portico were exposed, altering the proportion of the lower façade.

The *capitals of the portico are superb examples of medieval carving dating from 1340–55. In a complicated series of allegories (mostly explained by inscriptions), they represent the virtues of wise government and the importance of justice (including scenes of childhood, birds, heads of men and women from various countries, emperors, Vices and Virtues, myths, animals, courtly love and famous men). The capital on the corner nearest to the piazzetta has particularly fine carvings of the signs of the zodiac. This, together with seven others capitals on this side of the building, were replaced by excellent copies in 1884–87, and the originals are now displayed in the Museo dell'Opera inside the palace (see below).

The **façade towards the piazzetta**. The original 14C building (see above) reached as far as the seventh column of the portico, above which is a **tondo of Justice** on the loggia above. This shows Justice (the personification of Venice) crowned sitting on a throne guarded by two lions with two Vices trampled under-

The Government of the Republic

The palace was the doge's residence as well as the seat of the government of the Republic, with a vast number of state offices, law courts and prisons. The Republican Constitution, at first democratic, gradually became oligarchic in the 14C, with power concentrated in the hands of just a few families. At the height of its power the government of the Republic was organised as follows: the *Serenissima Signoria* held executive power and consisted of the doge, six councillors, and three leaders of the *Quarantia* (a tribunal of 40 members); legislative power was vested in the *Maggior Consiglio*, the Senate, and the *Collegio*, a sort of Parliamentary committee; judicial power was managed by the Council of Ten, the *Inquisitori di Stato*, the *Avogadori del Comune*, the *Quarantia*, the *Signori di Notte*, and other officials. The elected officials usually held office for no more than a year or sixteen months at a time. Details of these governing bodies are given below in the various rooms where they met.

foot and the sea with fish below. In 1424 the palace was extended in the same style using the same building materials as far as the basilica, and the Porta della Carta was added in 1438. In the centre is a balconied window (1538), similar to that on the front of the building. During restoration work, necessitated by the deterioration of the Istrian stone and polychrome brick, which was completed in 1999, traces of colour were found, particularly on the earlier masonry and on the frames of the 14C windows.

In the ground level portico the first six **capitals** towards the lagoon, as on the main façade, were superbly carved in 1340–55 (three of them replaced by excellent copies in 1876–84). They represent sculptors, animals with their prey, craftsmen, astrology, and foreign nations. The seventh one beneath the tondo of Justice, which is slightly bigger than the others, has scenes of courtly love, and death. The last twelve capitals (two replaced in the 19C) were carved when the palace was enlarged in 1424 and are mostly copies of the earlier ones on the main façade. The most interesting is the last one, nearest the basilica, showing Justice surrounded by famous legislators and wise men, which was signed by two Florentine sculptors, Pietro di Niccolò Lamberti and Giovanni di Martino da Fiesole. On the corner above is a high relief illustrating the **Judgement of Solomon*, with the Archangel Gabriel in the loggia above, beautiful works attributed by some scholars to Jacopo della Quercia (c 1410).

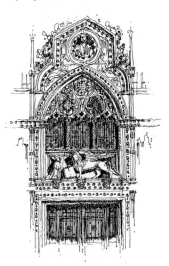

The **Porta della Carta* (1438–43) is an extremely graceful gateway in the florid Gothic style, by Giovanni and Bartolomeo Bon. It is thought to owe its name to the state archives or *cartae* (papers) which used to be kept near here. The fine **statues of Temperance, Fortitude, Prudence* and **Charity** are attributed to the Bon workshop. The gateway is crowned by a figure of Venice, symbolised by Justice, attributed to Bartolomeo Bon. The statues of Doge Francesco Foscari kneeling before the lion of St Mark are good reproductions (1885) of the originals destroyed in 1797.

The fine Renaissance façade on Rio di Palazzo, built of Istrian stone, can be seen from Ponte della Paglia or Ponte della Canonica. Begun by Antonio Rizzo, it was continued by the Lombardo family, by

Detail of the Porta della Carta

Scarpagnino, and finally completed in the 17C by Bartolomeo Monopola.

The quay extends in front of the Palazzo Ducale as far as the **Ponte della Paglia**, a bridge of Istrian stone, first constructed in 1360. It was widened in 1844 when the pretty balustrade of little columns with sculpted pine cones was added. It crosses Rio di Palazzo, with a view of the Renaissance east front of the palace (see above), and the famous **Bridge of Sighs** (or Ponte dei Sospiri) (Pl. 9; 5), a flying bridge in Istrian stone by Antonio Contino (1600). This elegant little bridge was constructed for the passage of the inquisitors of State between the prisons and the law courts. It received its popular name in the 19C when the idea of the sighing prisoners on their way to trial fired the imagination of the Romantics.

Ground floor

The entrance to the palace is through the **Porta del Frumento** at the centre of the main façade overlooking the Bacino di San Marco. The door gets its name *frumento* (wheat) from the offices here which used to be occupied by the government officials responsible for the distribution of grain in the city.

Museo dell'Opera

On the ground floor, in rooms which were once used as prisons, the Museo dell'Opera displays the **original *capitals** and **columns**, mostly dating from 1340–55 (restored), from the portico (see above), where they were replaced by fine copies in 1876–87. These six rooms are hardly ever visited by groups so they are one of the most peaceful areas of the palace. Diagrams in each room show where each capital was on the façade. In **room I** are six capitals from the main façade overlooking the lagoon dating from the 14C. They show *Solomon and wise men* (impersonating the Liberal Arts); *Birds with their prey; Heads of men from different latitudes* (each is shown with markedly different features and hats, but since the capital is without inscriptions it is difficult to identify them: one apparantly represents a Tartar and another, with a turban, a moor); *Kings of the ancient world and Roman emperors*: Titus, Trajan, King Priam of Troy, Nebuchadrezzar, Alexander of Macedonia, King Darius of the Persians, Julius Caesar, and Augustus (holding a globe with the inscription *Mondo di pace*); *Female heads* (representing Latin women of various ages in different costumes and head-dresses); and *Heads of Latin people*, including a soldier in armour decorated with two Crosses, and so usually identified as a crusader, women of various ages, and children (this capital is sometimes thought to represent a crusader's family). The model displayed here shows the wooden scaffolding used during the 19C when the capitals were removed.

Room II has four 14C capitals from the piazzetta façade. One of them illustrates the *Months of the year:* March is represented by a figure playing a musical instrument; June is shown with cherries; September is represented by a young man crushing grapes (signifying abundance) and December is represented by the butchering of a pig. The other months are shown in couples. There is also a capital with the heads of *Animals with their prey*. Another capital shows *Sculptors*, all of them intent on carving blocks of stone or sculpting figures, including the four patron saints of the Scuola dei Tagliapietra or stonemasons (identified by their haloes and crowns), and their four disciples. The fourth capital shows *Craftsmen* at work (a stonemason, a blacksmith, a notary, a peasant, a surveyor, a carpenter, a cobbler and a goldsmith).

In **room III** is displayed the famous capital from the corner of the palace between the piazzetta and the bacino which depicts the *Creation of Adam with the Planets* and *Signs of the Zodiac*. This is perhaps the most beautiful of all, greatly admired by Ruskin. Larger than the other capitals it represents the focal point of the carefully worked out narrative scheme which involved each capital as it introduces the history of the universe and the history of man. The *Creation of Adam*, shows God the Father seated on a throne and Adam as a boy. Saturn, depicted as an old man with a beard is shown sitting on Capricorn (a goat) holding Aquarias (a jug). Jove, wearing a doctorial head-dress, is seated on

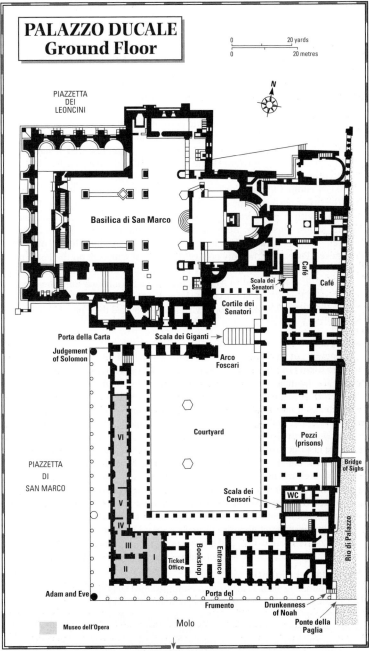

PALAZZO DUCALE
Ground Floor

0 — 20 yards
0 — 20 metres

N

PIAZZETTA DEI LEONCINI

Basilica di San Marco

Café

Café

Scala dei Senatori

Cortile dei Senatori

Porta della Carta

Scala dei Giganti

Arco Foscari

Judgement of Solomon

PIAZZETTA DI SAN MARCO

VI

Courtyard

Pozzi (prisons)

Bridge of Sighs

V

IV

Scala dei Censori

WC

III

I

Ticket Office

Bookshop

Entrance

II

Rio di Palazzo

Adam and Eve

Porta del Frumento

Drunkenness of Noah

Ponte della Paglia

Museo dell'Opera

Molo

BACINO DI SAN MARCO

Sagittarius (a centaur with a bow and arrow) and he indicates the sign of Pisces. Mars, a warrior in armour is seated on Aries, with Scorpio on his left. The Sun, personified by a young boy with rays around his head, is seated on Leo and he holds a disc carved with a face. Venus, holding a mirror, is seated on Taurus and holds the sign of Libra (the scales). Mercury, in a toga holding an open book, is shown between Virgo and Gemini (the twins). On the last side, the Moon, represented by a girl in a boat holding a crescent moon, is shown with Cancer. The movement in the sea and the girl's clothes symbolise the influence the moon has on tides and winds.

Also here are two 14C capitals, one decorated with baskets of fruit, and the other with allegories of the Seven Deadly Sins and Vanity (the deadly sins: Lust, Greed, Pride, Anger, Avarice, Envy, and Sloth, are all represented by female figures except for Pride). In **room IV** the massive wall of the old palace can be seen and in **room V** stonework from the tracery on the upper loggia.

The last **room VI**, a long gallery, has a splendid display of 14C–15C capitals from the upper portico, some of them with traces of gilding and paint. They are decorated with a great variety of motifs including foliage, acanthus leaves, flowers, shells, musicians, nuns, female heads, the lion of St Mark, animals, children, griffins and eagles, and warriors. The marble *head of Doge Francesco Foscari is the only part of the original sculpture on the Porta della Carta to have survived destruction in 1797. The doge kneels in front of the lion of St Mark. It is attributed to Antonio Bregno or Bartolomeo Bon; the original architrave of this door is preserved at the end of the room, with the signature of Bartolomeo Bon. The bust of Doge Cristoforo Moro used to be part of a group in the courtyard, also destroyed in 1797.

Courtyard

The magnificent east side of the courtyard was rebuilt after the fire in 1483 by Antonio Rizzo (1483–98). It consists of four storeys with richly carved decoration by the Lombardo family. The right-hand end was finished by Scarpagnino (1546–53). The lower storeys of the other two sides of the courtyard were completed in the same style by Bartolomeo Monopola in the 17C. In the centre are two splendid well-heads in bronze signed by Alfonso Alberghetti (1559) and Niccolò dei Conti (1556).

On the last side, towards the basilica, is a Baroque façade by Monopola incorporating a clock, and the side of the Arco Foscari which faces the Scala dei Giganti. This triumphal arch was begun in the 15C by the Bon family and completed by Antonio Bregno and Antonio Rizzo. On the side facing the main courtyard is a statue of the Condottiere Francesco Maria I della Rovere, Duke of Urbino (1490–1538) by Giovanni Bandini (1587), and (right) a Page attributed to Antonio Rizzo (both now replaced by copies; originals inside the palace, see p 121). The main front of the arch bears statues of the mid-15C, and bronze copies of two fine marble statues of Adam and Eve by Rizzo (originals inside the palace; see p 121).

The Scala dei Giganti

The ceremonial Scala dei Giganti was commissioned by Doge Marco Barbarigo in 1485 as a setting for the coronation ceremony of the doges (which, up to then, had not been held in public). The staircase was designed by Antonio Rizzo in Istrian limestone, and it is decorated with delicate marble reliefs and elaborate sculpture. On the wide landing at the top the doge was crowned (over a white skull cap) with the jewelled and peaked *cornu* or *berretta*, modelled on a Byzantine head-dress and always an important symbol of his position. The giant statues (from which the staircase gets its name) of Neptune and Mars symbolising the maritime and terrestial power of the Republic are late works (c 1554) by Jacopo Sansovino, added in order to diminish the figure of the doge during the ceremony.

The doge of Venice

The doge (or *dux*) of Venice was the symbol of the sovereignty of the Venetian State, but he was seldom more than a figurehead. Until 1172 he was elected by proclamation, but on that date Doge Sebastiano Ziani was elected by a group of *savi* (wisemen), their vote being ratified by a large popular assembly which became known as the *Maggior Consiglio* (see p 121). When, at the end of the 13C, this was restricted to patricians, an extremely complicated procedure was introduced for the election of the doge from among its members, partly by lot and partly by ballot in order to ensure that there was an element of chance in the choice of the candidate, and to prevent nepotism. From as early as the 12C every doge, on assuming office, had to make a *promissione ducale* which was a solemn vow that he would obey certain rules which restricted his authority. Councillors (6 nobles, one for each sestiere of the city, and the three judges who sat on the criminal tribunals) were appointed to assist and counsel the doge, and he was part of the *collegio* or cabinet of 26 officials. All this limited his power, and, interestingly enough, his importance as an individual diminished as the power of Venice grew to its greatest splendour in the 15C.

First floor ~ the Doges' Apartments

From the other end of the courtyard the Scala dei Censori leads up to the inner loggia. From here the **Scala d'Oro** (1), built in 1558–59, to Sansovino's design, and decorated with gilded stuccoes by Vittoria, continues up to the **first floor** (or **primo piano nobile**) and the **Doges' Apartments**, reconstructed after a fire in 1483.

The first room is the ***Sala degli Scarlatti** (18), or Robing Room (named from the scarlet robes worn by the magistrates), with a fine chimneypiece by Tullio and Antonio Lombardo (c 1501), and, over the door, a *bas-relief by Pietro Lombardo of Doge Leonardo Loredan at the Feet of the Virgin. Opposite is a Madonna in coloured stucco (attributed to Antonio Rizzo). The gilded ceiling is a fine work by Biagio and Pietro da Faenza (1506). The **Sala dello Scudo** (19), where the doge's guards were stationed, is named from the shield which was displayed here showing the arms of the doge who was in office. The walls are covered with maps and charts (16C, but repainted in 1762).

The **Sala Grimani** (20) has a chimneypiece is by Tullio and Antonio Lombardo and the ceiling (which bears the arms of Marino Grimani, doge from 1595–1605) is decorated with rosettes, above a frieze by Andrea Vicentino. Here there are four charming *paintings of the winged lion of St Mark, famous symbol of Venice (see p 80). The two opposite the fireplace are by Donato Veneziano (with two saints and a view of Venice), and Vittore Carpaccio (1516). Carpaccio's work shows the lion between the sea and the terraferma and has a very accurate view of Palazzo Ducale and the Campanile and domes of San Marco in the background, as well as a group of galleons setting sail from the Arsenal. Another lion here is by Jacobello del Fiore (1435). The **Sala Erizzo** (21),

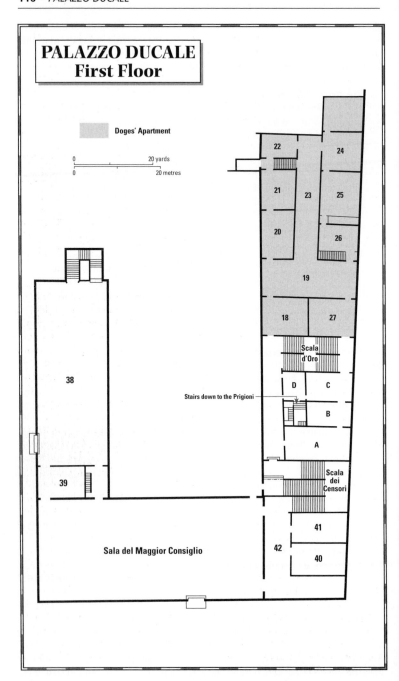

PALAZZO DUCALE
First Floor

Doges' Apartment

0   20 yards
0   20 metres

22

24

21

23

25

20

26

19

18

27

Scala d'Oro

D

C

Stairs down to the Prigioni

B

A

Scala dei Censori

38

39

41

Sala del Maggior Consiglio

42

40

beyond, has a similar chimneypiece (with the arms of Doge Francesco Erizzo, 1631–46), a good ceiling, and an interesting view of the Basilica. Three paintings attributed to Gerolamo Bassano have been hung here.

A passage with a Lombardesque ceiling leads to the **Sala degli Stucchi** (22), decorated with stuccoes at the end of the 16C and in the early 17C. From here there is a good view of the apse of the basilica. The gallery (23) is known as the **Sala dei Filosofi** since it housed for a time paintings of philosophers by Tintoretto and Veronese. On the staircase, above the door on the right is a fresco of *St Christopher* painted in three days in 1524 by Titian. There is a view of the Bacino di San Marco at his feet.

The rooms off the other side of the Sala dei Filosofi were the private rooms of the doge. The **Sale dei Leoni** (24) has been closed for a number of years. Beyond the **Sala Corner** (25) with a fine gilded ceiling (and a view across the rooftops towards San Zaccaria), is the **Sala dei Ritratti** (26), with a good fireplace by Antonio and Tullio Lombardo. The lunette of the *Dead Christ between the Madonna and St John the Evangelist* (and two kneeling saints) is almost certainly by Giovanni Bellini. Beyond the Sala dello Scudo (see above) is the **Sala degli Scudieri** (27; named after the doge's private guards) with two 16C portals with two large paintings of doges by Domenico Tintoretto.

Second floor

The Scala d'Oro continues up to the **secondo piano nobile**. The grand State rooms on this floor were restored after they were seriously damaged in fires in 1574 and 1577, and a new series of paintings glorifying Venice and her history were commissioned from the leading artists of the day on a scheme worked out by Giacomo Marcello, Giacomo Contarini, and Fra Girolamo Bardi. The subjects are mostly military and naval victories, the glorification of the doges, or allegories of wise government. At the top of the stairs is the **Atrio Quadrato** (29; square atrium), where the fine wooden ceiling has a painting by Jacopo Tintoretto with *Justice presenting the Sword and the Scales to Doge Girolamo Priuli*. On the right is the *Sala delle Quattro Porte* (30), named after its four doors, decorated together with the walls, for Doge Marino Grimani in 1595–1606. This waiting-room, used by ambassadors, was designed by Antonio da Ponte (1575), after a plan by Palladio and Rusconi. The rich ceiling, by Palladio, has frescoes by Jacopo Tintoretto, unfortunately spoilt by restoration. The fine stucco work is by Giovanni Cambi (1575). On the entrance wall (by the window): *Doge Marino Grimani before the Madonna and Saints* by Giovanni Contarini. In 1555 Titian was commissioned to paint *Doge Antonio Grimani kneeling before the Faith*; it was completed c 1600 by his nephew Marco Vecellio. The parts attributed to Titian's own hand are the figure of St Mark, the helmeted warrior, and the view of the Basin of St Mark's. On the opposite wall are two paintings by Carletto and Gabriele Caliari, and Andrea Vicentino. The other end of the room is described after room 33 (see below). The **Anticollegio** (31; another waiting-room which served as a vestibule to the Sala del Collegio) has a good ceiling by Marco del Moro with a ruined fresco by Veronese. The fireplace by Scamozzi has a relief of the Forge of Vulcan, an early work by Tiziano Aspetti and Girolamo Campagna. Opposite the window, *Rape of Europa* by Veronese; *Jacob's Return to Canaan* by Jacopo Bassano; on the other walls: *Vulcan's Forge*, *Mercury and the Graces*, *Bacchus and Ariadne*, and *Minerva dismissing Mars*, all by Jacopo Tintoretto.

The Sala del Collegio ~ room 32

It was here that the doge and the *Collegio*, or cabinet deliberated and received ambassadors. The *Collegio*, whose 26 members were known as *savii* (from 'wise') included the doge, six councillors, one for each sestiere of the city and the three judges of the criminal tribunals.

The room, decorated in 1575–81, is a treasure house of art. The chimneypiece is by Campagna. The ***ceiling**, by Francesco Bello, the finest in the palace, is doubly precious because of its wonderful paintings by Veronese. The most remarkable is that in the centre at the farther end: *Justice and Peace offering the Sword, the Scales, and the Olive-branch to triumphant Venice enthroned*. The other panels have allegorical figures of *Mars and Neptune, Faith and Religion*. Over the entrance, Jacopo Tintoretto's *Doge Andrea Gritti before the Virgin*; above the throne, **Doge Sebastiano Venier offering thanks to Christ for the Victory of Lepanto*, by Veronese. Facing the fireplace are three magnificent paintings by Jacopo Tintoretto: *Marriage of St Catherine, Doge Niccolò da Ponte invoking the Virgin, Doge Alvise Mocenigo adoring Christ*.

The Sala del Senato ~ room 33

This was where the Senate or legislative body of the Republic sat. The senators (also called *pregadi* because, when elected they were formally 'begged' or 'invited' by the doge to take part in sessions of the senate), whose number was increased from 60 to 120, were elected from among the patricians by the *Maggior Consiglio*, and held office for one year. At the centre of the political life of the Republic, they also nominated magistrates, ambassadors, bishops, and the patriarch. They treated with foreign courts, and only they could take the grave decision of declaring war.

Designed by Antonio da Ponte, the room has a fine ceiling by Cristoforo Sorte (1581), with *Venice exalted among the Gods*, by Jacopo Tintoretto in the central panal. Over the throne, **Descent from the Cross, with Doges Pietro Lando and Marcantonio Trevisan in adoration*, also by Tintoretto. Left wall. *Venice receiving the Homage of subject Cities presented by Doge Francesco Venier, Doge Pasquale Cicogna in prayer*, and an *Allegory of the League of Cambrai*, all by Palma Giovane; *Doge Pietro Loredan praying to the Virgin*, by Jacopo Tintoretto; and on the end wall *Doges Lorenzo and Girolamo Priuli praying to Christ*, by Palma Giovane.

In the **Sala delle Quattro Porte** (30; see above) is exhibited (on an easel), Giambattista Tiepolo's painting of **Venice receiving the Homage of Neptune* (it was removed from above the windows where it has been replaced by a photograph). The paintings on the walls here are by Giovanni Contarini (*Venice under Gattamelata conquering Verona*), and Gabriele Caliari (*Doge Pasquale Cicogna receiving Gifts from a Persian Ambassador*).

Sala del Consiglio dei Dieci ~ room 34

A corridor (with a view of the upper façade of San Zaccaria) leads into the Sala del Consiglio dei Dieci or the seat of the Council of Ten. This body was appointed after the rebellion of Bajamonte Tiepolo in 1310 against Doge Pietro Gradenigo. As a court which tried political crimes the consiglio became a notoriously severe organ of the government, particularly efficient in times of crises. It was this Council which ordered the execution of Doge Marin Falier in 1355, because he had tried to turn his elective office into a despotic seigniory. Judges held office for one year only, without the possibility of being re-elected in the succeeding year.

In the right-hand far corner of the ceiling is an **Old Man in Eastern Costume*

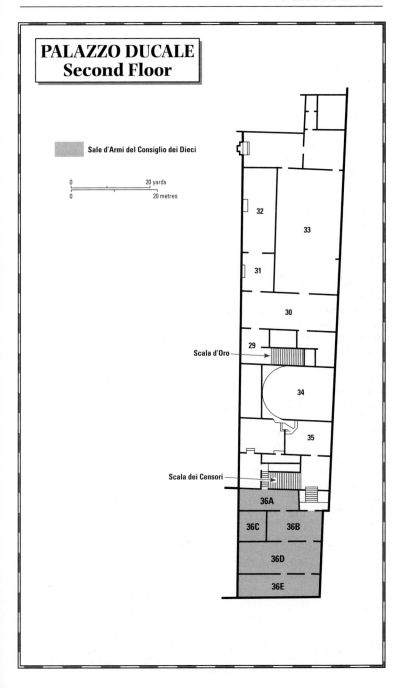

PALAZZO DUCALE
Second Floor

Sale d'Armi del Consiglio dei Dieci

0   20 yards
0   20 metres

32

33

31

30

29

Scala d'Oro

34

35

Scala dei Censori

36A

36C   36B

36D

36E

with a young Woman, by Veronese. In the centre of the left-hand side, *Juno offering Gifts to Venice*, also by Veronese, taken by Napoleon to Brussels in 1797 and only returned to Venice in 1920. The original of the oval ceiling painting (*Jupiter fulminating the Vices* by Veronese) was taken to Paris by Napoleon the same year and was not returned (it is now in the Louvre). On the right wall: *The meeting between Pope Alexander III and Doge Ziani*, by Francesco and Leandro Bassano; end wall: *Adoration of the Magi*, by Aliense; left wall: *Pope Clement VII and the Emperor Charles V*, by Marco Vecellio.

The **Sala della Bussola** (35) is named from the wooden screen which gives access to the Sala dei Tre Capi and the prisons. It has a marble chimney-piece. The original ceiling painting by Veronese of *St Mark in glory crowning the theological virtues* was also stolen by Napoleon and is now in the Louvre. On the right of the farther door is a **Bocca di Leone** (or 'mouth of truth'), a box in which secret denunciations were placed (posted from the outside). From the end of the 16C or early 17C a number of these were placed in various rooms of the palace (before then the practice had been to drop notes on the floor or give them to foreigners to deliver). The box could only be opened in the presence of all three head magistrates (*capi*) of the Council of Ten. There were notoriously severe punishments for false denunciations. The wall paintings are by Vecellio and Aliense. On the right is the Sala dei Tre Capi del Consiglio dei Dieci only open on the guided tours *itinerari segreti* of the palace (see below).

Sala d'Armi del Consiglio dei Dieci ~ room 36

From the landing outside the Sala della Bussola is the approach upstairs (right) to the Sale d'Armi del Consiglio dei Dieci, the Council's private armoury, in which the state arms and armour were stored until the fall of the Republic. **Room 36A**. Various suits of armour, including one traditionally supposed to have belonged to the condottiere and protector of the Venetian Republic, Gattamelata, and one belonging to a page, found on the field of Marignano (1515). In a case: a display of 16C–17C helmets (Northern Italian); a unique visored helmet of the 14C, shaped like a bird's beak and made of a single piece; and tournament armour (c 1510–20). A long case contains swords (the earliest dating from the 15C), and halberds made by Giovanni Maria Bergamini (Venice, c 1620–25). Cross-bows are hung on the walls.

Room 36B (right). In a niche is a suit of armour which belonged to Henry IV of France, presented by him to the Serenissima in 1603. Also lances, swords, falchions (short, sickle-shaped swords); suits of armour; Persian arms; horses' battle frontlets (15C–16C) and painted shields. There is a Turkish standard on the ceiling, a trophy from the Battle of Lepanto. On the right, **Room 36C** (formerly a prison, reserved for important prisoners) has another fine display of shields and swords. **Room 36D**, with the bust of Doge Morosini, has a superb collection of swords, lances and shields beautifully displayed in old show-cases. In the centre are two early quick-firing guns, one with 20 barrels, the other with a revolver mechanism, a fuse-case holding a hundred and six fuses made of perforated and embossed copper, signed by Giovanni Antonio Comino, and a culverin (an early type of cannon) complete with its carriage and fittings (16C German?). The lantern belonged to a dismantled Turkish galleon. **Room 36E** has a superb view of the basin of St Mark and island of San Giorgio Maggiore. In the cases: 16C–17C pistols; muskets and arquebuses; various instruments of torture and a 16C cuirass (or breastplate). Steps descend to the Scala dei Censori.

The Scala dei Censori takes you back to the **Primo Piano Nobile** (or first floor). On the left is the **Liagò** or **Andito del Maggior Consiglio** (42), the corridor where the patricians would gather during intervals in the session of the *Maggior Consiglio*. It has a good 16C ceiling and works by Domenico Tintoretto. In the **Sala della Quarantia Civil Vecchia** (41), the tribunal of forty members met, who tried civil cases regarding the city. There is a painting (right wall) of *Moses* by Andrea Celesti, and (left wall), a painting by Pietro Malombra, and a 15C panel of the *Virgin and Child*. A fragment of mural painting has been revealed behind the panelling. The adjoining **Sala del Guariento** (40) contains the remains of a huge fresco of the **Coronation of the Virgin* by Guariento (1365–67) which used to adorn the Sala del Maggior Consiglio. This famous work was ruined by the fire of 1577 and was discovered in 1903 beneath Tintoretto's painting. In the veranda at the end are exhibited three statues removed from the Arco Foscari in the courtyard (see above): **Adam and **Eve, the masterpieces of Antonio Rizzo (c 1470) and Francesco Maria I della Rovere, Duke of Urbino (and a condottiere who served the Venetian Republic) by Giovanni Bandini.

Sala del Maggior Consiglio ~ room 37

This vast hall was the seat of the governing body of the Republic. It was first built on this scale in 1340, and was large enough to hold the assembly of Venetian patricians (which reached a maximum of 1700 members). Here laws were ratified and the highest officials of the Republic were elected.

The Maggior Consiglio

The *Maggior Consiglio*, or Great Council, when first formed in 1172–73, was an assembly of nearly 500 Venetians who held office for one year only and were responsible for electing the doge, and all the chief officials who controlled the judicial, adminstrative, and legislative offices of the State.

The *Serrata del Maggior Consiglio* (1297), literally the locking of the Great Council, restricted membership to those families only who had already been represented in the *Maggior Consiglio*. These 'patricians' included both nobles and merchants, and they inherited the right to sit on the *Maggior Consiglio* for life on reaching the age of 25. This signified the introduction of an oligarchic form of government. At the beginning of the 16C the members were formally registered in the *Libro d'Oro* (or Golden Book). The size of the Council varied; the greatest number it reached was 1700.

The hall is 52m long, 24m wide and 11m high. The 14C–15C frescoes by leading artists of the time and the magnificent ceiling were all destroyed in the disastrous fire of 1577. The paintings which replaced these in 1578–95, all by Venetian artists, record three important events in the history of the Republic: the meeting in Venice between Barbarossa and Pope Alexander III in 1177; the capture and sack of Constantinople during the Fourth Crusade in 1202; and the triumph of Doge Contarini after the victory at the Battle of Chioggia in 1379. The paintings and carved wood ceiling have all been recently restored.

On the entrance wall is *Paradise by Domenico Tintoretto and assistants (1588–c 1592), a huge painting (7 x 24m). The **ceiling is divided into 35 compartments of which the most noteworthy are the three central panels: **Venice *surrounded by Gods and crowned by Victory*, a masterpiece of light and colour by Veronese (painted just before he died in 1588); *Venice surrounded by Gods gives an Olive-branch to Doge Niccolò da Ponte*, by Jacopo Tintoretto; and (at the far end) *Venice welcoming the conquered Nations around her Throne*, by Palma Giovane.

The walls are covered with large historical canvases: right wall, *Episodes from the Life of Barbarossa* by Benedetto and Carletto Caliari, Leandro and Francesco Bassano, Jacopo Tintoretto, Paolo dei Franceschi, Andrea Vicentino, Palma Giovane, Federico Zuccari, Girolamo Gambarato, and Giulio del Moro. On the left wall (with a fine *view from the balcony over the Bacino di San Marco): *History of the Fourth Crusade* by Carlo Saraceni, Jean Leclerc, Andrea Vicentino, Palma Giovane, Domenico Tintoretto, and Aliense. On the end wall, between the windows overlooking the piazzetta, *Triumph of Doge Andrea Contarini after the Victory at the Battle of Chioggia* by Paolo Veronese and assistants.

The **frieze of the first 76 Doges** (from Obelario degli Antenori, c 804, to Francesco Venier, d. 1556) begins in the middle of the wall overlooking the courtyard and runs left to right. It is the work of Domenico Tintoretto and assistants. The space blacked in on the wall overlooking the piazzetta takes the place of the portrait of Marin Falier; an inscription records his execution for treason in 1355 after his famous conspiracy against the state. The frieze is continued in the Sala dello Scrutinio.

The last door on the right admits to the **Sala della Quarantia Civil Nuova** (39; now occupied by a bookshop), used by the high court of forty magistrates, set up in 1492 to act in civil cases for Venetian citizens in the new territories on the *terraferma*. The **Sala dello Scrutinio** (38), which is usually closed, was used after 1532 to record the votes of the Great Council for the new doge and other officials of the Republic. It has 16C paintings of Venetian battles and a triumphal arch erected in honour of Francesco Morosini by Antonio Gaspari in 1694.

A small door to the left of the throne in the Sala del Maggior Consiglio leads out to the Scala dei Censori and a loggia overlooking the courtyard and into the **Sala del Quarantia Criminale** (A), seat of a criminal tribunal. Beyond another room (B), the **Sala al Magistrato alle Legge** (C) contains *works by Hieronymus Bosch owned by Cardinal Domenico Grimani in 1521 (probably aquired in Anversa). The *Paradise* and *Hell* formerly flanked a *Last Judgement* which has been lost. Also by Bosch and Herri met de Bles (known as 'Il Civetta') are the *Martyrdom of Santa Liberata*, and *Triptych of the Hermits*. The painting by Quentin Metsys of the *Derision of Christ* (or *Ecce Homo*), which may also have belonged to Cardinal Grimani, is anyway known to have been in Venice by the end of the 16C and has been kept in Palazzo Ducale since 1664.

From the adjoining room (D) stairs lead down to a prison corridor and the passage across the **Bridge of Sighs** (by Antonio Contino, 1600) a flying bridge across the Rio di Palazzo which was constructed so that the inquisitors of State could reach the new prisons built on the other side of the canal from the law courts in Palazzo Ducale. At the end of the corridor beyond the bridge there is a choice of two itineraries: the one on the right is shorter and passes a few prison cells before returning across the Bridge of Sighs.

Otherwise you can continue downstairs (signposted Prigioni Nuovi) to visit the 'new' **prisons** built between 1560 and 1614 to replace the old ones (known as the 'Pozzi', described on p 124). They were begun by Giovanni Antonio Rusconi

(1560), continued by Antonio da Ponte (1589), and completed by Antonio and Tommaso Contino (1614). Their façade overlooks the Riva degli Schiavoni. A labyrinth of corridors passes numerous prison cells to emerge in a grim court-yard with a well surrounded by barred windows. On the opposite side of the couryard, stairs lead back up to a room with a display of Venetian ceramics found in the 20C (including excavations in the 1990s) from various periods (those from San Lorenzo date from the 9C; those from San Francesco del Deserto from the 14C, and those found when the Campanile of San Marco collapsed from the 15C). Beyond a series of more corridors and cells (some with graffiti made by the prisoners) the Bridge of Sighs is recrossed.

The exit from Palazzo Ducale is through some rooms of the **Avogaria**, used by a branch of the judiciary elected to be public prosecutors in criminal trials, and as supervisors during council meetings. There is a good view of the side of the new prisons on the canal. The **Sala dei Censori** has portraits of censors (who controlled electoral procedures after 1517) by Domenico Tintoretto, and the **Sala dei Notai**, similar portraits of Avogadori and Notaries, by Leandro Bassano, and others.

The exit is along the loggia past the top of the Scala dei Giganti (described above) to the Scala dei Senatori which descends to the **Cortile dei Senatori**, a charming Renaissance work by Spavento and Scarpagnino. From here there is a fine view of the exterior of the Basilica of San Marco, with the original brick-work visible (restored). Beneath the portico is displayed the original statue of St Theodore with his dragon which was set up on one of the columns in the piazzetta in 1329 (see p 106). The head is a Hellenistic portrait, the Roman torso dates from the period of Hadrian, and the arms, legs, shield and dragon were made by an early 14C Venetian sculptor.

The Itinerari Segreti of Palazzo Ducale

The *Itinerari Segreti*, literally 'secret tours' around the Palazzo Ducale are actually guided tours of the lesser known parts of the palace. The guide is particularly well-informed, and the tour lasts about an hour and a half. It is highly recommended as it gives a unique insight into the way the Republic was run. The rooms have been well-restored where necessary and furnished with period furniture. Tours take place daily in English at 10.00 and 11.30 (by appointment at the ticket office); Lire 24,000, c €12 (students, Lire 14,000, c €7, and children (6–14 years old), Lire 8000, c €4.

From the **Atrio Quadrato** (29, see p 117) a door gives access to the tiny administrative offices used by the bureaucrats of the Republic. These were constructed in wood making optimum use of the space available. Often two floors have been created in one storey of the building.

The well-lit **Ducal Chancellery**, where documents were transcribed, retains its original 18C furnishings and is decorated with the coats of arms of all the Chancellors from 1268 onwards. The Grand Chancellor was responsible for keeping all the government records and registering the decisions made by the various councils of state. He was elected for life from the middle classes (he could not be a patrician) and he held an extremely important position within the hierarchy of state officials.

The area of the law courts and judiciary offices of the Council of Ten includes the macabre **Torture Room** (with four cells for prisoners who had to wait their turn), and the **Sala dei Tre Capi del Consiglio dei Dieci**. This contains a chimneypiece by Jacopo Sansovino with statues by Danese Cattaneo and Pietro da Salò, and ceiling paintings by Paolo Veronese, Giovanni Battista Zelotti, and Giovanni Battista Ponchino. It also has a lovely floor. The *Descent from the Cross*, derived from Antonello da Messina's painting in the Museo Correr, is by Antonello da Saliba. The little **Sala dei Tre Inquisitori** was used by the three members of the special commission of enquiry used by the Council of Ten. These officials also examined the conduct of each doge after his death. The ceiling has a painting of the *Return of the Prodigal Son* by Jacopo Tintoretto (in excellent condition). A *Madonna and Child* by Boccaccio Boccaccino has been hung here.

From the Sala dei Tre Capi del Consiglio dei Dieci a staircase leads up to the top floor and the seven prison cells called the **Piombi**, so named because of their position beneath the leaden roof. They were built in wood, and have been reconstructed. Prisoners were only kept here for brief periods. Casanova's cell is shown.

Giacomo Casanova was arrested in 1755 and sentenced to five years imprisonment. The charges against him concerned his lifestyle: he was accused of being a mason, a gambler and a cheat, of frequenting people from every walk of life, of practising alchemy and magic, of showing little respect for Christians, and of writing irreverent and satirical verse and reading it in public. He escaped in 1756, with his fellow inmate, Father Marino Balbi, via the roof. His colourful description of the miseries he suffered here and his courageous escape in *Storia della mia fuga dalle prigioni della Repubblica di Venezia che si chiamono Piombi* ('Story of my flight from the prisons of the Venetian Republic which are called the Piombi') was published in 1788 and widely acclaimed throughout Europe. Silvio Pellico later described his imprisonment here by the Austrians in 1822 in *Le Mie Prigioni*.

The remarkable structure of the *roof of the Sala del Maggior Consiglio, built in 1577, can also be seen here. A small collection of sculptural fragments includes a 'Bocca di Leone' for secret denunciations (see p 120) found in the palace. At the end of the tour the **kitchens** are sometimes shown. The **Pozzi**, eighteen dark dungeons on the two lowest storeys have been closed to the public. These were reserved for the most dangerous criminals. Even the lowest of them, however, was above ground-level and they were less terrible than many medieval prisons.

4 • The Grand Canal

This chapter describes the Grand Canal from the water: the right bank is described from San Marco to the station, and the opposite bank from the station back to San Marco. The canal is remarkable for its splendid palaces, but it is also always busy with numerous types of boats which give a vivid idea of the way the city works, based on water transport. The comfortable vaporetto no. 1 travels slowly along the canal, giving time to enjoy the scene.

The Grand Canal (Canal Grande), over 3km long, is the main thoroughfare of Venice. This splendid waterway, winding like an inverted S through the city, is filled with every kind of boat, from waterbuses (*vaporetti*) to motorboats, barges, and gondolas. It is lined on either side with a continuous row of beautiful old buildings, including more than 100 palaces, mostly dating from the 14C–18C, though a few date back to the 12C. The canal follows the old course of a branch of the Brenta as far as the Rialto, and is 30–70 metres wide, with an average depth of 5 metres. The coloured posts or *pali* in front of the palaces show the livery or *divisa* of their proprietors.

The best way to see the Grand Canal is by the slow vaporetto no. **1** (map pp 42–43).

San Marco to the station ~ the right bank

San Zaccaria From Riva degli Schiavoni the boat steers out into the Bacino di San Marco (to avoid disturbing the gondolas), providing a wonderful view of the buildings on the waterfront: beyond the Prigioni can be seen the rio crossed by the Bridge of Sighs, Palazzo Ducale, the piazzetta with its two columns and the Libreria Sansoviniana, the Zecca, and the Giardinetti. Across Rio della Luna is the low Capitaneria di Porto.

San Marco Behind the landing-stage of San Marco (Calle Vallaresso) is the building (with blue awnings) which houses Harry's Bar (see Ch. 2). Beyond the *Hotel Monaco* is the 15C Gothic **Palazzo Giustinian**, with the municipal tourist offices, and the Biennale headquarters. It was a noted hotel in the 19C; Giuseppe Verdi, Théophile Gautier, Ruskin and Marcel Proust all stayed here.

It is followed by the Hotel Bauer, with a modern extension. Across Rio di San Moisè is the plain classical façade of the 17C Palazzo Treves de' Bonfili, attributed to Bartolomeo Monopola. Palazzo Tiepolo (also 17C) is now occupied by the Europa and Regina Hotel. There follow Palazzo Gaggia with its tall chimney-pots, and the 15C Palazzo Contarini. Next to it is the tiny ***Palazzo Contarini-Fasan**, with just three windows on the piano nobile and two on the floor above. The charming 15C decoration includes a balcony with wheel tracery. It is traditionally called the House of Desdemona because it was believed she had lived there. Palazzo Manolesso-Ferro (15C Gothic) has been converted into offices for the Regional administration. Palazzo Flangini-Fini is attributed to Alessandro Tremignon (1688). Beyond the rio is the 15C Palazzo Pisani, now the *Gritti Palace Hotel* with a terrace restaurant on the canal. John and Effie Ruskin stayed here in 1851.

> ### John Ruskin
> Ruskin, one of the most scrupulous observers of the monuments of Venice, visited the city on numerous occasions betwen 1835 and 1888. He considered the most important period of Venetian architecture to have been between 1180 and 1480 before the influence of the 'pestilent art of the Renaissance', and the beginning of the decline of Venice. He went up ladders to examine the buildings of Venice, including the tombs of the doges in Santi Giovanni e Paolo and the capitals of the portico of San Marco. He made numerous accurate sketches and described his findings in his most famous work *The Stones of Venice* (1851).

A gondola ferry operates from Campo Santa Maria del Giglio, at the end of which can just be seen the Baroque façade of the church.

Santa Maria del Giglio The 17C Palazzo Venier Contarini is by the landing-stage. Across the rio, the 17C Palazzo Barbarigo adjoins the 15C Gothic Palazzo Minotto. Next rises the huge ***Palazzo Corner** called Ca' Grande, a dignified edifice in the full Renaissance style by Jacopo Sansovino (begun after 1545). Above the rusticated ground floor are the Ionic and Corinthian upper storeys. It is now occupied by the Prefecture. Behind the little garden can be glimpsed the Casetta delle Rose, where Canova had his studio, and d'Annunzio lived during the First World War.

There follow a series of less distinguished palaces; beyond a narrow rio and two more houses are the two Palazzi Barbaro, one 17C, the other, on Rio dell'Orso, 15C Gothic decorated with marbles and carvings. This is still owned by the Curtis family who in the 19C entertained John Singer Sargent, Henry James (who took this palace as a model for the Palazzo Leporelli in which Milly Theale stayed in *The Wings of the Dove*), James Whistler, Robert Browning, and Monet here. Across the rio is Palazzo Cavalli-Franchetti, a sumptuous building, restored (and a wing added) in 1878–1922 in neo-Medieval style (see p 158). It is adjoined by its 19C garden, behind which rises the brick campanile of San Vitale.

The wooden **Ponte dell'Accademia** was built in 1932–33 by Eugenio Miozzi to replace an elaborate 19C iron bridge. The present structure, partly in iron, is an exact replica made in 1986 of Miozzi's bridge. Beyond Casa Civran-Badoer, with a small garden, stands Palazzo Giustiniani-Lolin (marked by its two pinnacles), an early work by Longhena (1623). It is now owned by the Fondazione Levi, a music study centre. Next comes the 15C Gothic Palazzetto Falier with two protruding loggie (or *liagò*), rare survivals of what used to be a characteristic feature of Venetian houses. Across the rio is a palace which incorporates the rusticated corner in Istrian stone of the **Ca' del Duca**, a remarkable building begun by Bartolomeo Bon in the mid-15C, but never completed. It takes its name from Francesco Sforza, Duke of Milan who bought it in 1461 from Andrea Corner. Steps lead down to the water from the adjoining campo. Beyond is the garden, with statuary, of Palazzo Cappello Malipiero, rebuilt in 1622. In the Campo di San Samuele can be seen the 12C campanile of the church (the San Samuele landing-stage is not used by vaporetto no. **1**).

The vast ***Palazzo Grassi** was begun in 1748 by Giorgio Massari. It is now a cultural centre owned by the *Fiat* organisation, which has restored it and holds important exhibitions here (see Ch. 10). Beyond a narrow calle is the 17C Palazzo Moro-Lin with a long balcony above the portico on the waterfront. The Palazzi da Lezze and Erizzo-Nani-Mocenigo, on the bend of the canal, have been altered from their original Gothic form. Palazzo Contarini delle Figure is a graceful 16C Lombardesque building (in poor condition) by Scarpagnino decorated with heraldic trophies and marbles. It is thought to have been named after the two figures (difficult to see) beneath the balcony. The four **Palazzi Mocenigo** (with blue and white *pali* in the water) consist of two palaces on either side of a long double façade. In the first Emanuele Filiberto of Savoy, one of the most able rulers of the House of Savoy, was a guest in 1575, and Giordano Bruno in 1592 (when he was betrayed by his host to the Inquisition); in the third (plaque) Byron wrote the beginning of *Don Juan* (1818) and entertained his close friend the Irish poet Thomas Moore (1779–1852). The fourth has blue awnings. They are adjoined by the 16C Palazzo Corner Gheltof. By the San Tomà ferry stands an old one-storeyed house. Next comes the 15C Palazzo Garzoni (now owned by Venice University), with two putti high up on the façade.

Sant'Angelo 🛥 Beyond a wide rio next to the modern brick-coloured administrative offices of *ACTV* (*Azienda del Consorzio Trasporti Veneziano*; the Venetian transport headquarters) is the Sant'Angelo landing-stage. ***Palazzo Lando Corner-Spinelli**, by Mauro Codussi (1490–1510) is a particularly successful Renaissance palace, with a rusticated ground floor and attractive balconies. The two-light windows beneath an oculus within an arch are typical of his architecture. Beyond two more rii is the buff-coloured Palazzo Benzon, which, in the time of the Countess Marina Benzon (c 1818) was the rendezvous of Venetian fashionable society and was visited by Byron, Moore, Canova and others. Next to the 16C Palazzo Martinengo, with two coats of arms (the façade once had frescoes by Pordenone), are Palazzo and Palazzetto Tron (15C restored). On Rio di San Luca stands Palazzo Corner Contarini dei Cavalli, an elegant Gothic work of c 1450 with two coats of arms and a fine central six-light window.

Palazzo Corner-Spinelli

Across the rio rises ***Palazzo Grimani**, a masterpiece designed by Sanmicheli just before his death in 1559 and built by Gian Giacomo dei Grigi. It is now the seat of the Court of Appeal. Next to the rust-coloured façade decorated with marbles of the Casa Corner Valmarana, is the Casa Corner-Martinengo-Ravà. It was owned by the distinguished Morosini family who were visited here in the 16C–17C by Paolo Sarpi (a fierce opponent of Church involvement in politics, see p 215), the astronomer Galileo Galilei, and the philosopher and scientist Giordano Bruno, among others. In the 19C it was a well-known hotel and the novelist James Fenimore Cooper stayed here in 1838. The Fondamenta del Carbon now skirts the Grand Canal as far as the Rialto bridge.

The 13C Veneto-Byzantine ***Palazzi Farsetti** and **Loredan** are occupied by the town hall. Palazzo Farsetti, built by Doge Enrico Dandolo, was heavily restored in the 19C. Palazzo Loredan has a double row of arches and statues of Venice and Justice beneath Gothic canopies and bears the arms of the distinguished Corner family. Elena Corner Piscopia (1646–84), who lived here, was the first woman to receive a degree (in philosophy from Padua University in 1678). In the middle of the next group of houses is the tiny Gothic Palazzetto Dandolo, with a double row of four-light windows.

Rialto Just beyond is Ponte Manin (on the site of a bridge built in stone before the 15C by the Dolfin family) across Rio di San Salvador. The large Palazzo Bembo was the probable birthplace of the scholar Pietro Bembo (1470–1547; see Ch. 2). Across the rio stands the white façade of Palazzo Dolfin-Manin, by Jacopo Sansovino, begun in 1538 for a Venetian merchant, Zuanne Dolfin. It is now an office of the Banca d'Italia. The portico on the ground floor extends over the fondamenta.

The **Ponte di Rialto** is a famous Venetian landmark, and was the only bridge across the Grand Canal throughout the long history of the Republic. There was a bridge of boats at this point from the earliest days of the city's history. This was replaced by a wooden bridge in the mid-13C which was destroyed in 1310 by supporters of Bajamonte Tiepolo after their retreat from Piazza San Marco and the failure of their rebellion against the Venetian State. After the restored bridge collapsed in 1444 under the weight of a large crowd, it was rebuilt on a larger scale and as a drawbridge. We have a detailed picture of this bridge in Carpaccio's painting of the *Cure of a Lunatic by the Patriarch of Grado*, commissioned by the Scuola di San Giovanni Evangelista, and now in room 20 of the Galleria dell'Accademia (see Ch. 11).

Antonio da Ponte won the commission to rebuild the bridge in stone in 1588: other contenders whose designs were rejected included Palladio, Sansovino, Vignola, and possibly also Michelangelo. Its single arch, 48 metres in span and 7.5 metres high, carries a thoroughfare divided into three lanes by two rows of shops. It bears high reliefs of the Annunciation by Agostino Rubini (16C).

Just beyond the bridge is the **Fondaco dei Tedeschi**, the German trading-centre from the mid 13C onwards (see p 189). In the next group of houses are Palazzo Civran, with a mask over the door, and the 19C Palazzo Sernagiotto, with a columned portico. Beyond the pretty Campiello del Remer (the 13C Palazzo Lion-Morosini here has an external staircase), is Rio San Giovanni Crisostomo, followed by three small palaces. Next comes Ca' da Mosto, a 13C Veneto-Byzantine building decorated with *paterae* above the windows. This was the birthplace of Alvise da Mosto (1432–88), discoverer of the Cape Verde Islands. From the 15C–18C it was a famous inn (the Albergo del Leon Bianco). Across Rio dei Santi Apostoli stands Palazzo Mangilli-Valmarana, a classical building to a design by Antonio Visentini for the distinguished English consul Joseph Smith (1682–1779), patron of Canaletto and other Venetian artists. Smith's remarkable art collection and library were acquired by George III. The palace was completed by 1751. The name of the adjoining Palazzo Michiel dal Brusà is a reminder of the great fire of 1774 (*brusà*, meaning burnt) which destroyed the previous Gothic palace on this site. The Palazzo Michiel dalle Colonne has a tall columned portico (remodelled by Antonio Gaspari in the 17C). Just before the busy *traghetto* or ferry station (which serves the Rialto markets), in Campo Santo Sofia, is Palazzo Foscari (a fine 15C window has colourful marble columns). On the other side of the campo is the 14C red-painted Palazzo Morosini-Sagredo with a pretty balconied Gothic window and a variety of windows on its partly Byzantine façade. It is adjoined by the 15C Gothic brick Palazzo Pesaro-Ravà.

Ca' d'Oro ⚓ The **'Ca' d'Oro** has the most elaborate Gothic façade in Venice (1425–c 1440), famous for its tracery (it is described, together with the Galleria Franchetti, in Ch. 16). Beyond the green façade of the 18C Palazzo Duodo (with statues), now also part of the Galleria Franchetti, is the 16C Palazzo Fontana, birthplace of Clement XIII who became pope in 1758 (Carlo Rezzonico, 1693–1769). Across Rio di San Felice is a house with a garden, then Palazzo Contarini-Pisani, with a plain 17C façade above a portico; Palazzo Boldù (also 17C, with a rusticated ground floor) and Palazzo da Lezze, with its little garden on the canal. Across the rio stands the handsome Palazzo Gussoni Grimani della Vida, attributed to Sanmicheli (1548–56), formerly decorated with frescoes by Tintoretto. Sir Henry Wotton, sent as English ambassador to Venice by James I on three occasions (1604–10, 1616–19 and 1621–23), lived here during his second embassy.

Sir Henry Wotton

Sir Henry Wotton was a poet and art collector (with a particular interest in drawings by Palladio), and one of the most cultivated Englishmen of his time. He had a profound knowledge of Italy and the Italian language, and his famous letters provide a vivid picture of 17C Venetian society.

In a letter dated 1622 from Venice ('this watery seat') he remarks: 'We are newly here out of our Carnival. Never was there in the licensing of public masks a more indulgent decemvirate [Council of Ten], never fewer mischiefs and acts of private revenge; as if restrained passions were indeed the most dangerous. Now, after these anniversary follies have had their course and perhaps their use likewise, in diverting men from talking of greater matters, we begin to discourse in every corner of our new league. . .'

For a time he was dismissed by James I for his contention that an ambassador was an honest man sent to lie abroad for the good of his country. He was a friend of Fra' Paolo Sarpi and gave Venice the support of the English King in the Republic's famous quarrel with the Pope in 1606 (see p 215). At the end of his life he was Provost of Eton and went fishing with Izaak Walton. He was probably the first person to recognise the great qualities in the writings of Milton, who asked him for his advice before starting out on a journey to Italy.

There follow two 17C palaces, and, on Rio della Maddalena, the 16C Palazzo Barbarigo which has almost lost its façade frescoes by Camillo Ballini. Across the rio are the 17C Palazzi Molin and Emo on the bend of the canal, and then Palazzo Soranzo with a fine façade probably by Sante Lombardo. Palazzo Erizzo alla Maddalena is a red 15C Gothic building with a good window. This is adjoined by Palazzo Marcello (rebuilt in the 18C), the birthplace of Benedetto Marcello which was acquired by the State in 1981 and is to house the Oriental Museum (at present in the Ca' Pesaro, see Ch. 19).

The imposing building in Istrian stone beyond its garden is *Palazzo Loredan Vendramin Calergi*, almost certainly Mauro Codussi's, last work, built in the first decade of the 16C. The façade is a masterpiece of Renaissance architecture

Benedetto Marcello

Benedetto Marcello (1686–1739) was a famous Venetian composer (and rival of Vivaldi). He studied in Venice under Francesco Antonio Calegari, and Francesco Gasparini. He wrote numerous compositions for the church of Santa Sofia, but his most famous work is L'estro poetico armonico (1724–27), based on the liturgical music he had heard in the ghetto. He also wrote some 500 secular vocal works, and music for recorders, keyboard, 'cello, and violin. In 1720 he published anonymously the Teatro alla Moda, a satire on Venetian opera at the Teatro di Sant' Angelo where Vivaldi was director of music. As a patrician he became a member of the Maggior Consiglio in 1707, and was elected to the Quarantia tribunal in 1716. When standing at a window of this palace he heard a young girl, Rosanna Scalfi, singing from a gondola. He went down to meet her and they fell in love; she became his pupil and secret wife (noblemen were forbidden to marry beneath their class).

in Istrian stone and marble with Corinthian columns and pilasters dividing the three storeys beneath a classical cornice with a finely carved frieze. Wagner died here on 13 February 1883 (the rooms where he died can sometimes be seen by appointment on Saturday mornings, see p 215). It is now the winter home of the Casinò, and in summer is often open for art exhibitions. Beyond the rio, Casa Gatti-Casazza, with a roof garden (the typical Venetian altane), was restored in the 18C style.

San Marcuola ⚓ This landing stage is in front of the unfinished façade of the church. On the other side of a garden is Palazzo Martinengo Mandelli, reconstructed in the 18C. There follow several 17C palaces, including Palazzo Correr-Contarini. Shortly after the Campiello del Remer, the Cannaregio canal, the second largest in Venice, diverges right. Palazzo Labia (described in Ch. 21) can be seen on the canal next to the church of San Geremia. Beyond the church, on the Grand Canal, is the little Scuola dei Morti (rebuilt after 1849), and the stone façade of Palazzo Flangini, left unfinished by Giuseppe Sardi (c 1682). After a group of modern houses, and just before the bridge, is the long Palazzo Soranzo Calbo Crotta, a 15C building enlarged and altered in later centuries. The bridge which serves the railway station was built by Eugenio Miozzi in 1932–1934 (who also designed the Accademia Bridge).

Ferrovia ⚓ Just before this is the Baroque façade of the church of the **Scalzi** by Giuseppe Sardi. The railway station was built in 1955. Beyond it rise the huge modern office blocks of the State railways. The last landing-stage is at **Piazzale Roma**, the terminus of the road from the mainland (with a multistorey garage built in 1931–34 by Eugenio Miozzi.

Piazzale Roma to San Marco ~ the right bank

Piazzale Roma ⚓ From here the boat steers out into the Grand Canal and soon passes the mouth of the Rio Nuovo, a canal cut in 1933 as a short route from the station to Piazza San Marco. Beyond the Giardino Papadopoli (public gardens) a bridge crosses Rio della Croce (at the end of which stands the campanile of the church of San Niccolò da Tolentino). The next important building on this side of the canal is the 18C church of **San Simeone Piccolo**, with a lofty green dome and Corinthian portico. Just before the station bridge (see above) is Palazzo Foscari Contarini, a Renaissance building. The boat passes beneath the bridge. Beyond Rio Marin and a pretty garden opens Campo San Simeone Grande with trees and a well. At the far end is a portico along the flank of the church. There follow a group of simple palaces before the landing-stage of Riva di Biasio.

Riva di Biasio ⚓ On the corner of the next rio, just beyond a pretty garden, stands the 15C Gothic Palazzo Giovanelli. Beyond two more houses is the plain façade of Casa Correr, which was the home of Teodoro Correr whose collection forms part of the Museo Correr (see Ch. 2). The **Fondaco dei Turchi** is an impressive Veneto-Byzantine building, over restored in the 19C. It was the Turkish warehouse from 1621–1838, and is now the Natural History Museum (see Ch. 19). Beneath the portico are several sarcophagi; one is that of Doge Marin Falier, beheaded for treason in 1355 (see p 118). Across the rio is the plain brick façade of the **Granaries** of the Republic. This 15C battlemented edifice bears a relief of the lion of St Mark (a modern replacement of one destroyed at the fall of the Republic). Palazzo Belloni-Battagià was built by Baldassarre Longhena in 1647–63 for Girolamo Belloni whose coat of arms with a star and crescent motif appears on the façade. In the late 17C ownership passed to the Battagià family, one of whom was an admiral. The fine water-gate is flanked by iron grilles. Across the rio stand Palazzo Tron (1590) and Palazzo Duodo (Gothic). Beyond a garden is Palazzo Priuli Bon, with 13C Veneto-Byzantine traces on the ground floor.

San Stae ⚓ This is next to the church of **San Stae**, whose rich Baroque façade (c 1709) is by Domenico Rossi. It is adjoined by the charming little Scuola dei Battiloro e Tiraoro (goldsmiths), attributed to Giacomo Gaspari (1711). Next comes Palazzo Foscarini-Giovanelli (17C) where Doge Marco Foscarini was born in 1695. Across the rio stands the bright clean façade of *Ca' Pésaro, a grand Baroque palace by Baldassarre Longhena decorated with grotesque masks. It was completed after Longhena's death in 1682 by Antonio Gaspari, who was responsible for the façade on the rio. It now contains the Museum of Modern Art and the Oriental Museum (see Ch. 19). Beyond two smaller palaces rises **Palazzo Corner della Regina**, by Domenico Rossi (1724), now the Biennale archive of contemporary art. It stands on the site of the birthplace of Caterina Cornaro, queen of Cyprus (1454–1510). The lower part of the façade is rusticated and bears masks. A plaque on Casa Bragadin Favretto records the studio here of the painter Giacomo Favretto (d. 1887). Beyond two more palaces is the Gothic Palazzo Morosini Brandolin. A bridge connects Fondamenta dell'Olio with the Pescheria, a graceful neo-Gothic market hall built in 1907 by Cesare Laurenti and Domenico Rupolo on the site of the 14C fish-market.

Here begin the **Rialto markets** (see Ch. 15), the busy wholesale markets of the city, the buildings of which continue right up to the Rialto bridge. The waterfront is colourful in the early morning when boats put in laden with fruit and vegetables. A gondola ferry (*traghetto*) is particularly active here. On the other side of the campo is the long arcaded **Fabbriche Nuove di Rialto**, a serviceable market building which follows the curve of the Grand Canal, begun by Jacopo Sansovino in 1554. It is now the seat of the Assize Court. Behind the Erberia, the fruit and vegetable market, can be seen the Fabbriche Vecchie di Rialto, by Scarpagnino. The building at the foot of the Rialto bridge is *Palazzo dei Camerlenghi**, restored by Guglielmo dei Grigi (Il Bergamasco) in 1523–25. The ornate Renaissance façade is curiously angled. This was once the seat of the Lords of the Exchequer; the name of the fondamenta here—Fondamenta dei Prigioni—is a reminder that the ground floor of the palace was conveniently used as a prison.

The boat passes beneath the **Rialto bridge** (described on p 127). The reliefs of St Mark and St Theodore on this side of the bridge are by Tiziano Aspetti. At its foot (and partly concealed by it) is Palazzo dei Dieci Savi, a building of the early 16C by Scarpagnino. A tondo bears a modern lion, and on the corner stands a figure of Justice (late 16C). This was used by the financial ministers of the Republic. The view down the Grand Canal is closed in the distance by Ca' Foscari and Palazzo Balbi with its prominent obelisks (see below). Fondamenta del Vin runs in front of a modest row of houses. At the end, behind a garden, is the rust-coloured façade of Palazzo Ravà, a successful neo-Gothic building (1906), thought to occupy the site of the palace of the patriarchs of Grado.

San Silvestro ⚓ Beyond is San Silvestro landing-stage. Palazzo Barzizza bears remarkable reliefs on its façade (12C Veneto-Byzantine). Palazzo Businello (formerly Giustinian), on the corner of Rio dei Meloni, was rebuilt in the 17C but preserves some Veneto-Byzantine elements. On the opposite corner stands **Palazzo Coccina-Tiepolo Papadopoli**, with its two obelisks. This is a work built in the best Renaissance tradition by Gian Giacomo Grigi of Bergamo in the early 1560s. Beyond the garden is Palazzo Donà, with a fine 12C–13C window. This is adjoined by the smaller Palazzo Donà della Madonnetta, named after a 15C relief of the Madonna and Child set into the façade. It has an interesting arched window with good capitals and *paterae*. Across the rio stands ***Palazzo Bernardo**, with a lovely Gothic façade (c 1442) especially notable for the tracery on the upper piano nobile. **Palazzo Grimani** (now Sorlini) has an Istrian stone façade decorated with marbles. It is an elegant Lombardesque building of the early 16C. Beyond is the plain façade of Palazzo Cappello-Layard, on the corner of Rio San Polo. This was once the residence of the English diplomat Sir Henry Layard (1817–94), the discoverer of Nineveh (his fine collection of paintings was left to the National Gallery of London in 1916). Across the rio stands Palazzo Barbarigo della Terrazza, named after its balconied terrace on the Grand Canal (now used by the German Institute). Dating from 1568–69 it is attributed to Bernardo Contino. Next comes Palazzo Pisani della Moretta, with graceful Gothic tracery of the second half of the 15C. Beyond the 16C Palazzo Tiepolo is the smaller 15C Palazzo Tiepoletto. There follow two smaller houses and the rust-coloured Palazzo Giustinian Persico, a 16C work.

San Tomà (Frari) ⚓ Palazzo Civran-Grimani, on the corner of the rio, dates from the 17C. Just before the Rio Nuovo rises the grand **Palazzo Balbi**, with its two obelisks, probably by Alessandro Vittoria (1582–90); this is the seat of the Regional Government. Next to it is the plain brick façade (and handsome large chimneys) of the Fondazione Angelo Masieri for which Frank Lloyd Wright designed a small palace in the 1950s; it was never built since planning permission was refused. This spot on the Grand Canal is known as the Volta del Canal since it is situated on a sharp bend. Here stands the beautifully proportioned ***Ca' Foscari** (1428–37; it has been covered for restoration for a number of years), a grand residence built for Francesco Foscari, doge for 34 years. It has notable tracery, fine marble columns, and a frieze of putti bearing the Foscari arms. It is now the seat of the University Institute of Economics and Commerce. There follows the double façade of the ***Palazzi Giustinian**, begun c 1452 by Bartolomeo Bon. Wagner wrote the second act of *Tristan* here in 1858–59. After two small palaces rises **Ca' Rezzonico** by Longhena (begun c 1667), with a storey added by Giorgio Massari in 1745. It now houses the city's collection of 18C works of art (Ch. 13).

Ca' Rezzonico ⚓ Behind the landing-stage is the 17C Lombardesque Palazzo Contarini-Michiel. Next comes Palazzetto di Madame Stern, a reproduction of a Venetian Gothic palace, built by Giuseppe Berti in 1909–12 with a garden on the canal. Beyond the plain façade of Palazzo Moro stands Palazzo dell'Ambasciatore, so named because it was the Austrian embassy in the 18C. It is a Gothic building of the 15C with two shield-bearing pages, fine Lombard works by the school of Antonio Rizzo. Beyond Rio San Trovaso stand the Palazzi Contarini Corfù and Contarini degli Scrigni. The former is 15C Gothic with vari-coloured marbles, while the second was built in 1609 by Vincenzo Scamozzi.

Accademia ⚓ Just before the Accademia landing-stage is the British Vice-Consulate at Palazzo Querini. Across the campo can be seen the 18C façade (by Giorgio Massari) of the Scuola della Carità, and the bare flank (with Gothic windows) of the former church of Santa Maria della Carità (both now used by the Academy of Fine Arts and the Accademia Galleries, see Ch. 11).

Beyond the **Accademia bridge** (described above), is Palazzo Contarini dal Zaffo (Polignac), a graceful Lombardesque building with fine marble roundels and garden. Next comes Palazzo Molin Balbi-Valier, with a handsome ground floor, followed by the 16C Palazzo Loredan (now Cini). Beyond the pretty Campo San Vio, planted with trees, stands Palazzo Barbarigo, with a harshly coloured mosaic façade by Giulio Carlini (d. 1887). Next door is the 15C Gothic Palazzo da Mula. The portrait painter and miniaturist Rosalba Carriera died in 1757 in the red Casa Biondetti. **Palazzo Venier dei Leoni** was begun in 1749 and only the ground-floor was completed. The wall on the Canal has a frieze of colossal lions' heads at water level, and the building is surrounded by a luxuriant garden. It was owned by Mrs Peggy Guggenheim from 1949 until her death in 1979 and houses her remarkable collection of modern art (see Ch. 12). Beyond is *Palazzo Dario*, whose outside walls incline noticeably. This is a charming Lombardesque building of 1487 in varicoloured marble, highly decorated with motifs taken from classical, Byzantine and Gothic architecture. It has numerous delightful chimney-pots.

Palazzo Dario

Next to it is the 15C Palazzo Barbaro (Wolkoff). Palazzo Salviati was built in 1924 by Giovanni dall'Olivo with an overbright mosaic on its façade. It is the headquarters of the Salviati glasshouse, founded in 1866, and still one of the leading Venetian glass companies. Palazzo Orio Semitecolo has fine Gothic windows. A gondola ferry (*traghetto*) operates from the end of a calle here to Campo Santa Maria del Giglio. The last big palace on this side of the Canal is Palazzo Genovese, a successful imitation of the Gothic style built in 1892. Beside it are the low buildings of the ex-abbey of San Gregorio, with a delightful water-gate crowned by a large relief of the saint (which gives on to the cloister; see Ch. 12). Behind (on the rio) can be seen the fine apse of San Gregorio.

Salute A marble pavement opens out before the grandiose church of *Santa Maria della Salute** (see Ch. 12), a masterpiece of Baroque architecture by Longhena which dominates this part of the Canal. It is adjoined by the 17C Seminario Patriarcale. The **Dogana di Mare**, the ex-customs house, soon to be restored, is a Doric construction by Giuseppe Benoni (1676–82), extending to the end of the promontory. The picturesque turret has two telamones supporting a golden globe on which is balanced a weathervane depicting Fortune. The boat re-crosses the Grand Canal (with a fine view of the island of San Giorgio Maggiore) to the **San Marco (Vallaresso)** .

5 • The Riva degli Schiavoni and San Zaccaria

This chapter describes the attractive promenade called the Riva degli Schiavoni which lines the lagoon, always busy with Venetians and tourists. Off it a calle leads to the important church of San Zaccaria, with a splendid 15C façade. In the interior is a superb altarpiece by Giovanni Bellini, and the Chapel of St Tarasius, for which you have to pay an entrance fee, which contains fine Venetian altarpieces and Tuscan frescoes. On Riva degli Schiavoni is the lovely oval church of La Pietà, built for concerts in the 18C, where Vivaldi was choir-master. The church of San Giovanni in Bragora, in a quiet campo just off the Riva, has important works by artists from Venice and the Veneto, including a very fine altarpiece by Cima da Conegliano. From here this walk continues away from the waterfront to the Scuola di San Giorgio degli Schiavoni, typical of the buildings of the Venetian lay confraternities (or *scuole*), well known for its charming cycle of paintings by Vittore Carpaccio. On the parallel Rio dei Greci are the church and *scuola* built in the 16C–17C by the Greek colony in Venice where there is now a Museum of Icons. Nearby is the interesting church of San Lorenzo where excavations are in progress, and which will one day be opened to visitors.

Riva degli Schiavoni (Pl. 9; 5, 6) is a wide and busy quay on the basin of St Mark's, with landing-stages for vaporetti, and numerous moorings for gondolas, boats and tourist launches. It was called Schiavoni from the inhabitants of Schiavonia (now Dalmatia) because the waterfront here was used as a mooring for the trading vessels from Dalmatia and other Slavonic ports.

Between Palazzo Ducale and the Prigioni, the new prisons built in the 16C–17C (see p 122), is the Rio di Palazzo: the two buildings are connected by the famous Bridge of Sighs (see p 122). The **Danieli**, which has been a hotel since 1822, occupies the Gothic Palazzo Dandolo. Its ugly extension was built in 1948 near the place where Doge Vitale Michiel II was killed in 1172. The decree of the same year that no stone building should ever be built on the spot was observed until this century. Across **Ponte del Vin** (with pretty colonnades) towers the **Monument to Vittorio Emanuele II** by Ettore Ferrari (1887). At a house on the quay here (no. 4161) Henry James finished *The Portrait of a Lady* in 1881.

Sottoportico San Zaccaria leads under an arch away from the riva into the peaceful **Campo San Zaccaria**, with its fine church. Behind the little garden with two elms and architectural fragments is the brick façade of the earlier church which was used as an entrance to the Benedictine convent (with two fine cloisters, now occupied by a police station) and the 13C brick campanile. Along one side of the square the 16C portico of the former cloister is incorporated into the house-fronts.

San Zaccaria

The church of San Zaccaria (Pl. 9; 6; open 10.00–12.00, 16.00–18.00; fest. 16.00–18.00) is built in a remarkably successful mixture of Gothic and Renaissance styles (1444–1515), begun by Antonio Gambello, and finished after 1483 by Mauro Codussi. The church is dedicated to Zacharias, the father of St John the Baptist, whose relics are preserved here. It was founded by Doge Giustiniano Particiaco in the 9C. The famous Benedictine convent was visited annually by the doge at Easter in gratitude for the donation of part of the convent orchard to the Signoria in the 12C, so that Piazza San Marco could be enlarged.

The ceremony included the presentation to the doge of the ducal cap (or *cornu*). Eight doges of the early Republic were buried in the first church.

The tall **façade** is particularly handsome in a transitional style, with the lower part by Gambello and the upper storey by Codussi. Over the doorway, by Giovanni Buora and Domenico Duca (1483), is a statue of the patron saint, by Alessandro Vittoria.

The elegant **interior** has a high aisled nave; the columns on fine raised bases have good capitals. The multiple apse with an ambulatory and coronet of chapels lit by long windows, typical of Northern European Gothic architecture, is unique in Venice. The aisle walls are entirely covered with 17C–18C paintings. The statues of the Baptist and of St Zacharias on the stoups are by Alessandro Vittoria.

At the beginning of the **north aisle** there is a painting of the *Visitation* by Angelo Trevisani, and on the first altar, the *Saviour and Saints* by Giuseppe Salviati. The beautiful second altarpiece of the **Madonna enthroned and four Saints* is one of Giovanni Bellini's greatest works, signed and dated 1505. It is the last of a series of altarpieces with similar subjects painted for the churches of Venice which included the triptych still in the Frari and that painted for San Giobbe, now in the Galleria dell'Accademia. The architectural setting is classical, but its apse mosaic also recalls the Basilica of San Marco. The monumental figures of San Pietro, Santa Caterina, Santa Lucia, and San Gerolamo are enveloped in a remarkable atmosphere of calm, while the angel plays a melody at the foot of the throne.

At the end of the aisle is the tomb of the sculptor and architect Alessandro Vittoria (1528–1608), with a bust of the artist by himself (1595). Other remarkable portrait busts by Vittoria of his Venetian contemporaries can be seen in the Ca' d'Oro and Seminario Patriarcale, and many Venetian churches have monuments, statues, and altars by him. At the end of the **south aisle** is an *Adoration of the Shepherds* by Antonio Balestra.

Off the south aisle is the entrance (fee) to the **Chapels of St Anthanasius and St Tarasius**. The **Chapel of St Athanasius**, contains stalls by Francesco and Marco Cozzi. The *Birth of St John the Baptist* over the altar is an early work by Jacopo Tintoretto. The other paintings here include a *Flight into Egypt* by Gian Domenico Tiepolo (right of the altar), a *Madonna and Saints* attributed to Palma Vecchio (right wall) and a small *Crucifixion* attributed to Van Dyck (above the entrance). The five gilded chairs here (three of them dating from the 17C) were used for the annual visit of the doge (see above). Beyond, a small room displays the church treasury. The 10C **crypt**, with three aisles divided by low columns, can be seen below. The adjoining **Chapel of St Tarasius** has three fine **altar-paintings* by Antonio Vivarini and his brother-in-law Giovanni d'Alemagna (1443), with extraordinarily ornate gilded Gothic frames. The central polyptych incorporates an earlier *Madonna and Child and two Saints* signed by Stefano di Sant'Agnese in 1385. These three polyptychs are typical of the late florid Gothic style of these painters from Murano totally at odds with the new Renaissance period of art produced the year before, which can be seen above in the fan vault (the early 15C chancel of the previous church). These frescoes by Andrea del Castagno and Francesco da Faenza (signed and dated 1442; damaged) are one of the earliest known works by Tuscan Renaissance painters in Venice. In front of the altar has been placed a predella recently attributed to Paolo Veneziano. Also here are two 15C wood statues of St Benedict and

St Zacharius. Beneath is a fragment of mosaic pavement, thought to date from the 12C (glass in the floor reveals another fragment which may date from the 9C).

Opposite the church a calle leads under an arch, the outer face of which is decorated with a large marble relief of the Madonna and Child between St John the Baptist and St Mark, dating from the first half of the 15C.

La Pietà

On Riva degli Schiavoni, beyond Rio dei Greci (the bridge, with a stone balustrade was first built in the 14C), is the church of La Pietà (Pl. 9; 6; open in summer 10.00–13.00, 15.30–19.30 except Tues; in winter it can usually only be seen from the doorway; concerts are held here regularly). This belonged to an orphanage and hospital (*ospedale*) founded in 1346 (see below). The 18C façade by Giorgio Massari was only completed in 1906.

The bright **interior** was sumptuously rebuilt in the present oval plan (particularly adapted for musical performances) by Giorgio Massari (1745–60) with galleries for choir and musicians, and an oblong vestibule. The contemporary decorations remain intact, with a fine ceiling fresco of the *Triumph of Faith* by Giovanni Battista Tiepolo (1755), and altarpieces by Francesco Daggiù, called Il Cappella (*Madonna and Child with four Saints*); Domenico Maggiotto (*Miracle of St Spiridion*); (on the high altar) Giovanni Battista Piazzetta (*Visitation*; finished by his pupil Giuseppe Angeli); Giuseppe Angeli, *St Peter Orseolo*; Andrea Marinetti, called Il Chiozzotto, *Crucifixion*. The organ is by Nacchini (1759). Above the west door is a painting of the *Supper in the House of Simon*, by Moretto da Brescia (1548).

Music at La Pietà and the hospitals of Venice

There were four main hospitals in Venice (the Ospedaletto, the Incurabili, the Mendicanti, and the Pietà) where music was taught and performed. These institutions attained a remarkably high reputation for music in the 18C, overshadowing even the music school of the Basilica di San Marco. The Pietà achieved European fame for its music in the 17C–18C through the choral and orchestral performances given by the girls. The hospitals were unique in that they were the only places in Italy where women were allowed to sing in church (although they were concealed behind grilles). Here they were even allowed to play instruments normally considered unsuitable for them (such as the oboe, bassoon, trumpet and horn). Some of the girls went on to become directors of the orchestra. The institute of the Pietà still operates as an orphanage from offices in the Calle behind the church.

Beyond the next bridge, with a stone balustrade (rebuilt in 1871), a plaque on no. 4145 records Petrarch's house. He came to Venice in 1362 to escape the plague in Padua and lived here with his daughter and her family until 1367. The house was given to him by the Republic in return for his promise to leave his library to the city of Venice (see Ch. 2). Calle del Dose leads away from the waterfront into the peaceful Campo Bandiera e Moro.

Antonio Vivaldi

Antonio Vivaldi (1678–1741) taught at the Pietà on and off for most of his life. He was violin-master in 1704–18, and concert-master in 1735–38, and many of his best compositions were written for the hospital, including numerous concertoes which were first performed here. His father was a violinist and barber. Vivaldi took orders in 1703, but obtained permission not to serve as a priest, apparently because of ill-health. Goldoni, who praised him as a violinist but not as a composer, relates that he was nick-named *Il Prete Rosso* (the red priest), either because of his red hair or from the red robes worn at La Pietà. Vivaldi also wrote some 50 operas and directed the opera house of Sant'Angelo in Venice from 1713–39. The *Quattro Stagioni* (Four Seasons) was published in Amsterdam in 1725. He travelled extensively in Italy and Europe, but died in poverty in Vienna, and was forgotten after his death. Although Bach transcribed many of his con-certoes for the keyboard, Vivaldi was not 'rediscovered' until the late 19C.

San Giovanni in Bragora

The church (Pl. 10; 5) was rebuilt in 1475. The **interior** (open 09.00–11.00, 17.00–19.00; Sat and Sun 09.00–11.00) contains some remarkable works from various periods of Venetian art. On the west wall, *Christ before Caiaphas*, by Palma Giovane. **South aisle.** Over the side door is a late Byzantine *Madonna and Child*. On the right, *Saints Andrew, Jerome, and Martin* by Francesco Bissolo, and on the left, triptych of the *Madonna enthroned between Saints John the Baptist and Andrea*, signed and dated 1478 by Bartolomeo Vivarini. The second chapel is dedicated to St John the Almsgiver whose relics were brought from Alexandria in 1247. The front of the sarcophagus, with an effigy of the saint, is carved in wood by a northern European artist usually identified with Leonardo Tedesco, and it was subsequently painted and gilded in Venice (it is at present in the Museo Diocesano). Above the sacristy door, Byzantine relief of the *Madonna and Child*. To the right of the door, painting of *Constantine and St Helena* (1502; with a predella showing the *Finding of the True Cross*), by Cima da Conegliano; to the left, the *Risen Christ* by Alvise Vivarini (1498).

In the **sanctuary** a great marble frame encloses the *Baptism of Christ*, a superb work by Cima da Conegliano (1494). This is one of the most beautiful works by Cima in Venice, whose master was Alvise Vivarini. Born at Conegliano, this deeply religious painter carried out numerous altarpieces in the Veneto, but is also well represented in Venice with superb altarpieces in the Carmini, Madonna dell'Orto, and Galleria dell'Accademia. On the walls, *Washing of the Feet*, by Palma Giovane, and *Last Supper* by Paris Bordone. On the Baroque high altar are two statues of saints by Heinrich Meyring (c 1688). On the wall right of the sanctuary there is a beautiful painting of the *Deposition* by Lazzaro Bastiani from the church of Sant'Antonin. In the chapel to the left of the sanctuary is a carved wood Crucifix by Leonardo Tedesco and Leonardo Boldrini (1491).

North aisle. *Head of the Redeemer*, and *Madonna and Child* by Alvise Vivarini on either side of *Christ and St Veronica* by the school of Titian (in a pretty frame). The second chapel has three works by 16C artists from Crete who worked in Venice in the Byzantine style. On the north wall are four **saints** by a painter in the circle of Jacobello del Fiore (removed for restoration). Vivaldi, who was born in the campo, was baptised in the lovely 15C font in 1678. The cover (by Giorgio Massari) and the niche date from the 18C. Outside the church is a little 18C building, the Scoletta della Bragora, which housed a confraternity.

From the north corner of the Campo, Salizzada Sant'Antonin leads to the church of **Sant'Antonin**, traditionally founded in the 7C. The 13C church was reconstructed in 1636–82 under the direction of Baldassarre Longhena, who also designed the unfinished façade. The campanile dates from the mid 18C. The exterior has been restored, but the interior is closed. A fondamenta follows Rio della Pietà to the little Scuola di San Giorgio degli Schiavoni.

The Venetian Scuole

The *scuole* of Venice were lay confraternities dedicated to charitable works. Their members, elected mostly from the middle classes, attended to each others needs and administered public charity throughout the city, as well as offering medical assistance, and visiting prisoners. They often were associations of people in a particular trade or of a certain nationality. No priest or patrician could hold a position of responsibility in a *scuola*. The five most important *scuole*, known as the *Scuole Grandi*, were those of San Marco, San Rocco, Santa Maria della Carità, the Misericordia, and San Giovanni Evangelista (and San Teodoro also became a *Scuola Grande* in the 16C). The other *scuole* probably numbered around 100. Many of them became rich through legacies and donations, and were an important source of patronage as they commissioned numerous works of art for their headquarters. They held a particularly prestigious place in Venetian life from the 14C to the 16C.

The Scuola di San Giorgio degli Schiavoni

The Scuola di San Giorgio degli Schiavoni (Pl. 10; 3; open 10.00–12.30, 15.30–18.00; Sun 10.00–12.30; closed Mon) was founded in 1451 by the Dalmations (many of them sailors) in Venice.

The **façade** of 1551 by Giovanni de Zan bears a relief of St George and the Dragon by Pietro da Salò, and a 14C Madonna and Child. The dimly-lit **interior** is one of the most evocative places in the city. The walls of the little room are entirely decorated with a delightful series of *paintings by Vittore Carpaccio (carried out between 1502 and 1508), relating to the lives of the three Dalmatian patron saints, Jerome, Tryphone, and George. On the left wall: *St George and the Dragon*, justly one of his best known paintings, and the *Triumph of St George*. On the end wall: *St George baptising the Gentiles*; altarpiece of the *Madonna and Child* attributed to Benedetto Carpaccio, Vittore's son; the *Miracle of St Tryphone* (the boy saint is freeing the daughter of the Emperor from a demon, in the form of a basilisk). On the right wall: *Agony in the Garden*; *Calling of St Matthew; the Lion led by St Jerome into the Monastery* (putting the terrified monks to flight); *Funeral of St Jerome*; *St Augustine in his Study having a Vision of St Jerome's Death*. This last panel depicts the story of St Augustine who wrote a letter to St Jerome asking him his advice because he wanted to write a book on the saints in Paradise. But St Jerome's death occurred at the same moment, and Augustine's studio was filled with light and he heard a voice reproaching him for daring to describe Paradise before his own death.

Vittore Carpaccio

Vittore Carpaccio (1460/65–1525/6), the greatest Venetian narrative painter between the 15C and 16C, here produced his masterpiece. He also worked for other scuole in the city, including that of Sant'Orsola (his nine paintings illustrating the *Legend of St Ursula* are now in the Galleria dell'Accademia), and San Giovanni Evangelista (the *Miracle at Ponte di Rialto* is also now in the Accademia). Although influenced by the Bellini family (with whom he worked in Palazzo Ducale on paintings subsequently lost in a fire), he had a remarkable sense of colour and architectural detail, as well as an atmosphere of calm, all his own. In the Museo Correr are two portraits by him, one an early work of a *Man in a red hat*, and the other of *Two Venetian ladies on a balcony*. Carpaccio was the earliest Italian master of genre painting, and numerous details in his paintings give a particularly vivid picture of Venice and the Venetians at the end of the 15C.

The room upstairs (from which the Carpaccio paintings were moved after 1551) has 17C decorations, including a prettily carved wood ceiling incorporating paintings attributed to Andrea Vicentino. The Treasury of the Guild (including a 15C processional Cross) is kept in the little sacristy on the ground floor.

Across the bridge Calle Lion leads to Rio dei Greci where the Fondamenta di San Lorenzo leads south to **Ponte dei Greci** (Pl. 9; 4), named after the Greeks who settled in this area in the 15C after the Fall of Constantinople and subsequent invasion of Greece by the Turks. Together with the Jewish community this became the largest foreign community in Renaissance Venice, reaching around 6000 members by the 16C. Venice became the most important centre of Greek culture in the west, and the community is still active in the city. Houses were built in the area for the Greek inhabitants, as well as a hospital, archive, and cemetery. At the end of the 15C they were given permission to found a *scuola* and a Greek Orthodox church seen across the canal in a charming courtyard planted with trees, behind a decorative wall (by Longhena). They can be reached through a gateway beside of the Greek Collegio Flangini, founded in the 17C by Girolamo Flangini (and now the seat of the Hellenic Institute for Byzantine and post-Byzantine Studies), also by Longhena.

The church of **San Giorgio dei Greci** (09.00–13.00, 14.00–16.30; closed Sun) was the most important in Europe for the Greek Orthodox rite. Its construction was begun in 1539 on a design by Sante Lombardo. The cupola and graceful leaning campanile were added in the late 16C. It contains an iconostasis with late Byzantine figures, a Byzantine *Madonna* (12C–13C), and early 14C *Christ Pantocrator*, brought to Venice before the fall of Constantinople.

In the **Scuola di San Nicolò dei Greci**, by Longhena (1678) is the **Museo dei Dipinti Sacri Bizantini**, a Museum of Icons (Pl. 9; 4, open 09.00–12.30, 13.30–16.30; fest. 10.00–17.00) with a good, well-labelled collection (mostly 16C–17C), including products from the workshop of the *madoneri di Rialto*, where artists from Crete, who worked in Venice from the 15C–18C, combined Byzantine traditions with the local school of painting.

On the other side of Rio dei Greci is Fondamenta dell'Osmarin, crossed by two pretty bridges. The first one, Ponte del Diavolo, was well reconstructed in 1983, and the second one, Ponte dei Carmini, dates from 1793. Palazzo Priuli, on the corner of another rio, is a fine Venetian Gothic palace, probably dating from the late 14C, with an attractive corner window.

From Ponte dei Greci, Fondamenta San Lorenzo returns north along the pretty canal. By the first bridge, on the corner, is the Gothic Ca'Zorzi (recently restored). The second bridge leads across to the campo in front of the huge deconsecrated church of **San Lorenzo** (Pl. 9; 4). The first church, on a basilican plan, was founded by the Particiaco doges in the 9C. It was rebuilt by Simone Sorella in 1592, on a remarkable light design on a grand scale. Marco Polo (1256–1324) was buried here but his sarcophagus was lost during the rebuilding. The church was damaged in the First World War, but is at last being restored. Excavations are in progress here down to a depth of c 1.60m below the level of the lagoon: three distinct periods will be visible of the earlier churches: the earliest 9C foundations built directly on piles driven into the bed of the lagoon supporting a mosaic pavement in opus sectile; 10C–11C fragments, and remains of the 12C church of the Benedictine convent, part of the buildings of which are now used as a hospice. Roman fragments have also been found here. A museum illustrating the techniques of construction used in Venetian buildings is to be opened here.

6 • Santa Maria Formosa

In the large Campo Santa Maria Formosa, a short way north of Piazza San Marco, Santa Maria Formosa is interesting for its unusual Renaissance interior and its very fine altarpiece by Palma Vecchia, as well as a charming triptych by Bartolomeo Vivarini. In the same campo is the Galleria Querini Stampalia, with Venetian paintings from all periods, collected by the Querini Stampalia family from the 16C onwards. Artists well represented include Caterino Veneziano, Giovanni Bellini, Vincenzo Catena, Palma Vecchia, and Giovanni Battista Tiepolo, and there are 18C Venetian scenes by Gabriel Bella. However the gallery has lost some of its atmosphere during recent alterations to the building. The exterior of some important Venetian palaces in the district of the campo are also described.

Campo Santa Maria Formosa (Pl. 9; 3), around the church of the same name, is one of the most lively campi near San Marco. It has a few market stalls and lies in an area abounding in canals. At the end bordered by a canal with four small bridges (mostly private) is the 16C Ca'Malipiero Trevisan (no. 5250), attributed to Sante Lombardo. On the side opposite the apse of the church, Palazzo Vitturi (no. 5246) has Veneto-Byzantine decorations. A small house (no. 6129) was the home of Sebastiano Venier, commander of the victorious fleet at the battle of Lepanto in 1571 (plaque). Palazzo Donà (no. 6125–26) has a pretty doorway and Gothic windows, and at the far end of the Campo, Palazzo Priuli is a classical work by Bartolomeo Monopola (c 1580).

Santa Maria Formosa

The church of Santa Maria Formosa (Pl. 9; 3), rebuilt by Mauro Codussi in 1492 with a dome was restored in 1916. The name of the church is derived from the tradition that the Madonna appeared to its founder San Magno (in the 7C) in the form of a buxom ('*formosa*') matron.

Of the **two façades**, that towards the campo, crowned by five 17C statues, dates from 1604; the other (1542), at the main west entrance, overlooks a canal and a statue commemorates Vincenzo Cappello, Admiral of the Venetian fleet in the 16C. The Baroque **campanile**, designed by the priest Francesco Zucconi, has a grotesque mask at its foot. The local lore suggests it was put here to scare away the devil in case he tried to enter the bell tower and ring the bells at the wrong time.

In the **interio**r (open 10.00–18.00, 15.00–18.00) the Greek-cross plan of the original church, derived from Byzantine models, was preserved by Codussi when he gave it its beautiful Renaissance form in the 15C. Its complex design includes double open arches between the chapels, and domes over the bays in the aisles.

South aisle. Over the baptistery, the tondo of the *Circumcision* is attributed to Vincenzo Catena. In the first chapel there is a charming triptych of the *Madonna of the Misericordia*, by Bartolomeo Vivarini (1473), restored in 1998, and (over the door), *Holy Father and four angels* attributed to Lazzaro Bastiani.

In the **south transept** (with a *Last Supper* by Leandro Bassano) is the **Chapel of the Bombardieri**. The composite *altarpiece is by Palma Vecchio (1522–24), notable especially for the colourful and majestic figure of St Barbara in the centre, typical of the Giorgionesque style of Venetian beauty. On the right wall of the **Chapel of the Sacrament** (in the **north transept**) is a *Circumcision* (much darkened) by a follower of Cima da Conegliano. The oratory (admission on request) contains a fine *Madonna and Child* by Sassoferrato, in a beautiful frame, and another by Pietro de Saliba.

In front of the earlier façade of the church, Fondamenta dei Preti runs along the canal across a bridge (note the Roman tabernacle with a Latin inscription, set into the corner of a house here) to the short Fondamenta del Dose where at no. 5878 Vivaldi lived in 1722–30 and wrote the *Quattro Stagioni*. Ponte del Paradiso, a 17C bridge, was well reconstructed in 1901. Here the calle has a fine overhead arch, the **Arco del Paradiso** with a 14C relief of the Madonna and a donor and the coats of arms of the Foscari and Mocenigo families. The calle preserves its wooden eaves for the whole of its length. The bridge, archway and calle get their name Paradiso from their appearance on Good Friday, when numerous lanterns once illuminated this district of the city.

Palazzo Querini-Stampalia

From Campo Santa Maria Formosa a bridge leads across a small canal to the 16C Palazzo Querini-Stampalia (Pl. 9; 3), now occupied by the Museo Querini-Stampalia and the Fondazione Scientifico Querini-Stampalia, the bequest to the city of Count Giovanni Querini (1869). The Querini were among the earliest settlers in Venice and by the 13C one of the five richest families in the city. They acquired their second name, Stampalia, from the Greek island where some members of the family decided to live after their exile from Venice in the 14C as a result of their participation in the Bajamonte Tiepolo conspiracy (see p 118). The collection of paintings was begun by the family in the 16C when they built the present palace. It was used from 1807–50 as the residence of the patriarchs of Venice. Open 10.00–13.00, 15.00–18.00; Fri & Sat 10.00–13.00, 15.00–22.00; closed Mon. There is a shop and café on the ground floor.

The **second floor** (lift) is occupied by the museum which has some important paintings and good Venetian furniture (mostly 18C and 19C). The entrance has recently been changed so that the approach is no longer the logical one from the *portego* (see below) but through a secondary room of the palace. The rooms have no numbers in situ, and the arrangement is subject to change.

Room 1 has Pompeian style furniture by Giuseppe Jappelli, a case of 18C Sèvres porcelain, and a clay model by Canova of Letizia Ramolino Bonaparte. The **second room** has three allegorical ceiling paintings by Sebastiano Ricci. **Room 3**. *St Sebastian* by Luca Giordano and a self portrait by Palma Giovane. **Room 4** has 18C Venetian furniture and genre scenes by Pietro Longhi (one of the most interesting of which is *The Geography Lesson*). **Room 5** has more 18C furniture and portraits by Sebastiano Bombelli (1635–1719). **Room 6** displays the **Presentation of Christ in the Temple*, a very fine work attributed by most scholars to Giovanni Bellini (apparently a copy made c 1469 of a painting by his brother-in-law Andrea Mantegna now in Berlin). Beyond is the **portego (7)**, the large central hall on the piano nobile, which is decorated with stuccoes and frescoes by Jacopo and Vincenzo Guarana (1790), and a colourful 18C Murano chandelier. **Room 8** (to the left, off the *portego*) is filled with charming views of Venetian life in the 18C by Gabriel Bella; the paintings provide a valuable documentation of the city at that period. On the other side of the portego **Room 9** contains a Venetian scene with the Bucintoro by Antonio Stom and a case of 17C–18C musical instruments.

To the right **room 10** exhibits the masterpieces of the collection: *Madonna and Child* in the style of Giovanni Bellini; **Francesco Querini* and **Paola Priuli Querini*, two portraits by Palma Vecchio, commissioned by the family to celebrate the engagement of Francesco and Paola, but not finished in time for their marriage in 1528 since the artist died in the same year; a tondo of the *Adoration of the Virgin* by Lorenzo di Credi; **Judith*, by Vincenzo Catena; **Coronation of the Virgin*, by Catarino Veneziano and Donato Veneziano (1372); and a *Crucifixion* attributed to Michele Giambono.

Room 11 has four large portraits of officials of the Republic including (left of the far door) the **Procurator Daniele IV Dolfin* by Giovanni Battista Tiepolo. **Room 12** displays a portrait of *Andrea Querini* by Bernardino Castelli.

The **ground floor** is in the process of radical restoration which has altered the character of this historic palace. Innovations in questionable taste have included neon 'mottoes' on the façade, a huge new staircase, and a carpeted courtyard. Carlo Scarpa began reconstruction of the ground floor in 1961–63 and his elegant intervention includes the atrium of the main palace and the wood and metal bridge across the rio to the Campiello Querini, a lecture hall, and the little walled garden, in which water is a prominent feature.

The **library** has over 275,000 volumes and 1200 manuscripts. The third floor has also been totally modernised for exhibitions and lectures.

From Campiello Querini, Ponte Avogadro and Ponte Pasqualigo lead to the attractive Rio del Rimedio, which has interesting water-gates, and a series of little private bridges with pretty iron balustrades. At the far end a passageway leads into a stark campo with the church of **San Giovanni Nuovo** (or San Giovanni in Oleo; closed). A church of ancient foundation, it was rebuilt in the 18C by Matteo Lucchesi on a Palladian design (but the façade was left half-finished).

Ruga Giuffa (Pl. 9; 3, 4), a busy street with a number of shops, leads out of the southeast side of Campo Santa Maria Formosa. In Ramo Grimani (left) is the monumental entrance (with three Roman busts) to the huge **Palazzo Grimani**, attributed to Sanmicheli. The palace was acquired by the State in 1981 and is being restored. Some of the rooms are decorated by Giovanni da Udine and Francesco Salviati. The famous Grimani collection of antique sculpture used to be housed here: it was left to the Republic in 1593 and now forms the nucleus of the Archaeological Museum (see Ch. 2; there are long-term plans to move the museum here). Its classical 16C façade, with its monumental water-gate on Rio di San Severo can be seen by taking the next calle left (Calle di Mezzo) off Ruga Giuffa. There are several fine palaces and their water-gates on this rio.

The bridge leads across the Rio to Fondamenta di San Severo in a secluded part of the town. To the left this passes Borgoloco San Lorenzo, with two pretty wellheads, and ends by a house on the corner (no. 5136) which incorporates two ancient columns into its façade. In Calle Larga San Lorenzo (with a view of the church of San Lorenzo, see p 140), no. 5123 is the Gothic Palazzo Dolfin, which has a handsome doorway. Calle della Madonnetta leads north past Ramo I della Madonnetta, with a garden, an oasis for birds, and a picturesque palace.

Fondamenta di San Severo (see above) leads in the other direction along the rio from which can be seen two Zorzi palaces: the Gothic Palazzo Zorzi-Bon, with two water-gates, and **Palazzo Zorzi**, by Mauro Codussi (c 1480), with three water-gates. The latter is being restored as the new seat of ROSTE, the Unesco Regional office for Science and Technology for Europe. A bridge crosses the canal beside the palace, which has an entrance on the *salizzada* beneath a long balcony. The tiny Campiello del Tagliapietro has a fine well-head. Calle della Corona is a local shopping centre. Ruga Giuffa leads back (right) to Campo Santa Maria Formosa.

7 • Santi Giovanni e Paolo

The huge church of Santi Giovanni e Paolo, easily reached from Campo Santa Maria Formosa (Ch. 6) is one of the most important in Venice, with a superb light interior filled with numerous splendid Gothic and Renaissance monuments to doges and heroes of the Republic, including many by the Lombardo family. It also contains important stained glass, and a polyptych by Giovanni Bellini. Beside the church is the 15C façade of the Scuola di San Marco, at present being restored. The equestrian statue of Colleoni in the campo is a Renaissance masterpiece by Verrocchio. The church of the Ospedaletto, just out of the campo, with its charming 18C Sala della Musica are also worth a visit. A short way east, in a remote part of the city, is the church of San Francesco della Vigna, with a façade by Palladio and works from all periods of Venetian art in the interior, including a delightful painting by Antonio da Negroponte in florid Gothic style.

Campo Santi Giovanni e Paolo

Campo Santi Giovanni e Paolo (San Zanipolo; Pl. 9; 1) is historically one of the most important campi in the city. Its simple houses are dominated by the huge Dominican church.

The statue of Bartolomeo Colleoni

On a fine high pedestal rises the superb equestrian bronze statue of Colleoni, particularly well seen as it is silhouetted against the sky. This splendid monument, a masterpiece of the Renaissance, was designed by the Florentine sculptor Verrocchio. He made a full-scale model for it which he sent to Venice in 1481, but by the time of his death in 1488 the statue had still not been cast. The casting was eventually entrusted to the Venetian, Alessandro Leopardi in 1490, who signed his name prominently on the horse's girth. Leopardi also designed the pedestal.

The horse, which owes much to Classical works including the horses of St Mark and the Marcus Aurelius monument in Rome, is particularly fine, and technically more advanced than Donatello's charger which supports his famous equestrian statue of Gattamelata in Padua, since its front hoof is raised off the ground, without the need for a support. The feeling of movement in the whole statue is further emphasised by the turn of the rider's body. Colleoni is shown as a warrior, in an idealised portrait.

Colleoni (c 1400–75), a native of Bergamo, was one of the most successful military leaders of his time. As a brilliant captain-general he served both the Visconti and the Venetians at different periods of his career and he accumulated a huge personal fortune. When he died, he left a legacy to the Republic on condition that an equestrian monument be erected in his honour in front of San Marco. Since this would have been extremely out of place in Piazza San Marco, after four years of discussion the Signoria decided they were justified in interpreting the language of his will to mean the campo in front of the Scuola di San Marco instead. During the First World War the statue accompanied the horses of St Mark to Rome for safe keeping.

Santi Giovanni e Paolo

The church of Santi Giovanni e Paolo (San Zanipolo; Pl. 9; 1) is a huge Gothic brick church, founded by the Dominicans in 1234. The present church was begun around 1315, and continued in 1373–85, but only completed in 1430 (and restored in 1921–26). It is the burial place of twenty-five doges, and after the 15C the funerals of all doges were held here. Open 07.30–12.30, 15.00–19.15; Sat 07.30–12.30, 15.00–18.00; fest. 15.00–18.00. The Dominican friars are well-informed about their church. The numbers in the text refer to the plan.

The fine **façade** was never finished; against it are the tombs of three doges including (second on the left) the donor of the site, Jacopo Tiepolo. The delicately carved *main portal, attributed to Bartolomeo Bon (1460) incorporates six Greek marble columns from Torcello. It is flanked by Byzantine reliefs of the Madonna and Angel Gabriel. On the corner facing the campo is an interesting early relief of Daniel in the Lion's Den. From the campo, beyond the fine 16C well-head decorated with garlanded putti, the Gothic exterior (the brick pavement of the campo has been revealed here below ground level) can be seen, and the huge stained glass window of the south transept. The Gothic apse (seen from the calle behind) is particularly fine.

The vast light **interior** is 101m long and 46m across the transepts. It has tall aisles separated from the nave by ten columns of Istrian stone blocks, with slender arches and a beautiful luminous choir. Wooden tie-beams help to stabilise the structure of the building (an architectural feature of several Venetian churches). Among the impressive series of funerary monuments to doges and heroes of the Republic are some masterpieces of Gothic and Renaissance sculpture.

West wall. Around the doorway is the colossal tomb of Doge Alvise Mocenigo (d. 1577) and his wife. In niches below are two saints by Pietro Lombardo. The monument (**1**) to Doge Giovanni Mocenigo (d. 1485) is by Tullio Lombardo. The **monument to Doge Pietro Mocenigo** (d. 1476; **2**) is a masterpiece by Pietro Lombardo, with the help of his two sons, Tullio and Antonio (1476–81). Inside a triumphal arch flanked with niches containing statues of warriors, the doge depicted as a general stands on his sarcophagus, borne by three warriors representing the Three Ages of Man. The sarcophagus bears reliefs of his most famous victories at Scutari and Famagusta (Cyprus) and the inscription is a reminder that the monument was funded by war booty. The religious element (introduced at the top of the monument with a relief of the Marys at the sepulchre) takes second place to the explicit intention to glorify the doge as a hero of the Republic.

South aisle. Tomb (**3**) of Doge Ranier Zeno (d. 1268), with a Veneto-Byzantine relief of Christ enthroned in Glory between two angels. The first altar (**4**) was designed by Pietro Lombardo; it contains an early 16C *Madonna and Saints*. The monument (**5**) to Marcantonio Bragadin, the defender of Famagusta (1571) flayed alive by the Turks, has his bust above an urn, behind which a niche contains his skin. Second altar (**6**), *polyptych of St Vincent Ferrer*, with a *Pietà* and *Annunciation* above, usually attributed to Giovanni Bellini as an early work, with the possible help of assistants. The figure of St Christopher crossing a river is particularly remarkable. The predella appears to be by another hand. The fine frame dates from c 1523.

In the pavement in front of the next chapel, the 15C tombstone of Alvise Diedo, is a masterpiece of niello work by Pietro Lombardo. The Chapel of the Scuola del Santissimo Nome di Dio (**7**) was given its Baroque decoration c 1639. The richly ornamented ceiling contains paintings by Giovanni Battista Lorenzetti. The huge **Valier monument** to Bertucci (who became doge in 1656) and his son Silvestro (doge in 1694) is a splendid theatrical Baroque work designed by Andrea Tirali (1708; restored in 1999). In front of a huge yellow marble drape stand the figures of Bertucci Valier (by Pietro Baratta) in the centre flanked by his son Silvestro Valier with his wife, Elisabetta Querini Stampalia, the last doge's wife to be crowned as 'dogaressa'. The statue of Silvestro is by Antonio Tarsia, and of Elisabetta by Giovanni Bonazza.

Beneath the Valier monument is the entrance to the Chapel of the Madonna della Pace (**8**), with a Byzantine Madonna brought to Venice in 1349, and (right wall) a *Flagellation* by Aliense. The Chapel of St Dominic (**9**) has six large bronze reliefs by the Bolognese sculptor Giuseppe Mazza (1716–35) and a ceiling painting of *St Dominic in Glory* by Giovanni Battista Piazzetta (1727).

South transept. *Coronation of the Virgin*, by Giovanni Martini da Udine or Cima da Conegliano. The monument (**10**) above to Niccolò Orsini (d. 1509), Count of Pitigliano, Prince of Nola, defender of Padua in 1588, has an equestrian statue in gilded wood. The *stained glass* (1473) in the great window was made in Murano from cartoons by Bartolomeo Vivarini and Girolamo Mocetto, and possibly also Cima da Conegliano. On the altars below: *St Antonine* by Lorenzo Lotto (1542), and *Christ between Saints Peter and Andrew*, one of the best works of Rocco Marconi. Surrounding the door there is a monument (**11**) to the condottiere Brisighella (d. 1510), by Antonio Minello.

Choir chapels. First chapel (**12**). On the black marble altar are two bronze statues from a Crucifixion group by Alessandro Vittoria. On the right, tomb of Sir Edward Windsor (d. 1574) attributed to Vittoria, and on the left, sarcophagus with the figure of a warrior thought to be Paolo Loredan. Second chapel (**13**). High up in the fan vault are frescoes attributed to Palma Giovane. The Lombardesque altar bears a statue of St Mary Magdalen by Bartolomeo di Francesco da Bergamo (1524). On the right wall is a modern reconstruction of the monument to the condottiere Vettor Pisani (d. 1380), which incorporates the original framework and the statue. Pisani was the popular victor over the Genoese at the battle of Chioggia (1380), decisive to the survival of the Republic. To the left is the sarcophagus of Marco Giustiniani della Bragora (d. 1346).

The **choir** (**14**) is closed by a polygonal apse, lit by fine Gothic windows. The Baroque high altar, begun in 1619 (and attributed to Longhena) blends surprisingly well into the Gothic setting. On the right wall (**15**) is the Gothic *tomb of Doge Michele Morosini (d. 1382), with an elaborate tabernacle with statuettes in niches flanking the effigy of the doge. The carving is attributed to the Dalle Masegne school, and the mosaic of the Crucifixion to 15C Tuscan artists. Beyond is the Renaissance tomb (**16**) of Doge Leonardo Loredan (d. 1520; wrongly dated) designed by Grapiglia, with his statue signed by Girolamo Campagna and allegorical figures by Danese Cattaneo (restored in 1998). This doge was one of the most important in the history of the Republic since he was an extremely able diplomat at a time when Venice had very few allies.

On the left wall, monumental *tomb of Doge Andrea Vendramin** (**17**) (d. 1478), a masterpiece of the Renaissance designed by Tullio Lombardo, with the help of Antonio. The architectural design of the monument takes the form of a Roman triumphal arch above the effigy of the doge surrounded by allegorical figures and warriors, all beautifully carved, some from classical models, others in the late-Gothic style. To the right are traces of 14C frescoes. The Gothic tomb of Doge Marco Corner (d. 1368) (**18**) was moved in the 19C to make room for the Vendramin monument. The *Madonna is signed by Nino Pisano.

The third choir chapel (**19**) has paintings by Leandro Bassano, and the fourth choir chapel (**20**), two hanging sarcophagi, of Jacopo Cavalli (d. 1384), with an effigy by Paolo Dalle Masegne, and of Doge Giovanni Dolfin (d. 1361).

North transept. The bronze statue (**21**) of Doge Sebastiano Venier (d. 1578), who commanded the fleet at Lepanto, is by Antonio dal Zotto (1907). Above the door of the Chapel of the Rosary is the tomb of Doge Antonio Venier (d. 1400), and, left, the monument to his wife and daughter, Agnese and Orsola Venier (d. 1411), both sumptuous works in the style of the Dalle Masegne brothers. The tomb (**22**) of the condottiere Leonardo da Prato (d. 1511) bears a gilded wood equestrian statue attributed to Lorenzo Bregno or Antonio Minello.

The **Chapel of the Rosary** (**23**), erected in memory of the battle of Lepanto at the end of the 16C from the designs of Vittoria, was gutted in 1867 by a fire. All its paintings perished, including an important painting by Titian of *St Peter Martyr* and a *Madonna and Saints* by Giovanni Bellini, which had been placed here temporarily. The ceiling paintings (coin operated light) by Paolo Veronese of the *Annunciation, Assumption*, and *Adoration of the Shepherds*, were brought here from the ex-church of the Umiltà. The wooden benches are finely carved by

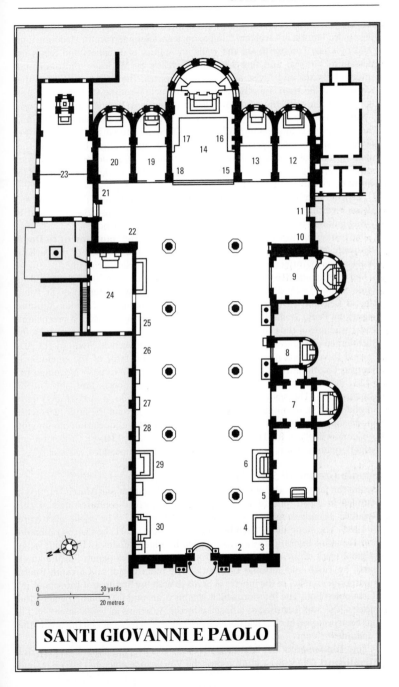

SANTI GIOVANNI E PAOLO

Giacomo Piazzetta (1698). In the choir the altar tabernacle is attributed to Alessandro Vittoria or Girolamo Campagna; it encloses a terracotta Madonna and Child by Carlo Lorenzetti. On the walls are statues of Prophets and Sibyls by Alessandro Vittoria, and fine 18C marble reliefs by Morleiter, Giovanni and Antonio Bonazza, and Alvise and Carlo Tagliapietra. The ceiling painting of the *Adoration of the Magi* is another good work by Paolo Veronese. On the west wall of the chapel is the *Adoration of the Shepherds* also by Paolo Veronese and his *bottega*.

North aisle. *Three Saints* (fragments of a polyptych) by Bartolomeo Vivarini. The fine organ is by Gaetano Callido (1790), was restored in 1999. Over the sacristy door, the busts of Titian and of the elder and younger Palma form the funerary monument designed by Palma Giovane (d. 1628) for himself. He was one of the most prolific of the Venetian painters, and his works are to be found in almost every church in the city.

The 16C **sacristy** (**24**) has paintings by Andrea Vicentino, Palma Giovane, Alvise Vivarini (*Christ carrying the Cross*, 1476), Leandro Bassano, and a ceiling painting by Marco Vecellio. It also has fine carved benches.

The rest of the north aisle is crowded with tombs. The *monument to Doge Pasquale Malipiero* (d. 1462) by Pietro Lombardo (**25**) is one of the earliest Renaissance monuments in Venice, a masterpiece of delicate carving.

The monument (**26**) to senator Gianbattista Bonzi (d. 1508), attributed to Paolo Stella (1525–26), is above two blind arches with statues of St Peter Martyr (left), an early work by Antonio Lombardo, and St Thomas Aquinas (right), by Paolo Stella. Below are the effigies of Alvise Trevisan, a precocious undergraduate of the University of Padua who died in 1528 at the age of 23, by Bartolomeo di Francesco Bergamasco, and of Doge Michele Steno (d. 1413). Beyond the classical monument with an equestrian statue of the condottiere Pompeo Giustiniani (d. 1616) is the *tomb of Doge Tommaso Mocenigo (d. 1423) in a transitional style by Piero di Niccolò Lamberti, and Giovanni di Martino (**27**). The *monument to Doge Nicolò Marcello (d. 1474), by Pietro Lombardo (**28**), is another fine Renaissance work. Beyond the altar (**29**) with an old copy of Titian's *St Peter Martyr* (see above) is the equestrian monument of General Baglioni (d. 1617). On a Renaissance altar (**30**) by Guglielmo dei Grigi Bergamasco, is a statue of St Jerome signed by Alessandro Vittoria.

Scuola Grande di San Marco

Beside the façade of the church is the Scuola Grande di San Marco (Pl. 9; 1), founded in 1260, one of the six great philanthropic confraternities of the Republic. The *scuola* moved to this site in 1437 and had to be rebuilt after a fire in 1485. The sumptuous *façade (to be restored in 2001) by Pietro Lombardo and Giovanni Buora (1489), was finished by Mauro Codussi (1495). It is an original work of great charm with unusual trompe l'oeil panels (on the lower part), by Tullio and Antonio Lombardo. The main portal by Giovanni Buora incorporates a relief in the lunette of St Mark with the Brethren of the school, by Bartolomeo Bon. The interior, which retains a ground-floor hall typical of the other *scuole*, was first used as a hospital by the Austrians in 1809; since 1819 it has been occupied by the civic hospital of Venice which extends all the way to the Fondamente Nuove on the lagoon.

The Fondamenta dei Mendicanti leads north past **San Lazzaro dei Mendicanti** (Pl. 5; 8), a church built by Vincenzo Scamozzi (1601–31), and now used as the hospital chapel. The Ospedale of San Lazzaro dei Mendicanti was one of the four most important hospitals in Venice, transferred here from the island of San Lazzaro (see p 260) in 1595. It had been founded during the crusades to help care for lepers, and later looked after the city's destitute. It included two large cloisters, also designed by Scamozzi. Attached to the Mendicanti was an orphanage for girls. The church **façade** was completed by Giuseppe Sardi in 1673. Between the vestibule and the **interior** is the huge funerary monument in sumptuous marble of the procurator Tommaso Alvise Mocenigo (d. 1654) also by Sardi, with two classical statues signed by Juste Le Court on the side facing the church. The architecture is interesting and includes two singing galleries for the girls from the orphanage where music was taught and performed (Baldassare Galuppi was choir master 1740–1751). The organ is by Callido (1772). The paintings include a good early work, *St Ursula and the eleven thousand Virgins*, by Jacopo Tintoretto, and a *Crucifixion with the Madonna and St John* by Veronese.

The fondamenta ends on the lagoon opposite the cemetery island of San Michele with its dark cypresses. Some way along the Fondamente Nuove, which skirt the waterfront, on the right behind a high wall, is the octagonal church of Santa Maria del Pianto built by Francesco Contino in 1647–59. It has been abandoned and closed indefinitely.

Ospedaletto

Beyond the south side of Santi Giovanni e Paolo the salizzada continues to the church of the Ospedaletto (Pl. 9; 2), otherwise known as Santa Maria dei Derelitti with an extremely elaborate façade by Baldassarre Longhena (1674). Open Thurs, Fri & Sat, Oct–March 15.00–18.00; April–Sept 16.00–19.00.

The church and Sala della Musica were part of the Ospedaletto, one of the four great Venetian hospitals (see Ch. 5). Founded in 1528 it included a hospice and orphanage, and is still an old peoples' home. The Palladian **interior** of the church (1575) contains a very fine organ by Pietro Nacchini (1751) above the high altar designed by Palladio, flanked by the *Birth of the Virgin*, the *Visitation*, and small paintings of the *Annunciation*, attributed to Antonio Molinari. The fine painted 18C spandrels high up along the walls include (between the second and third altars on the south side) a *Sacrifice of Isaac*, by Giovanni Battista Tiepolo. The two apostles in the spandrels above the first north altar are also now attributed to Tiepolo, as his earliest works (1715–16). The first altarpiece on the south side is by Johann Karl Loth.

The **Sala della Musica** is shown on request (same opening hours as the church; fee). It is reached by a beautiful spiral oval staircase by Antonio and Giuseppe Sardi. The elegant little oval music room, with four doors and a pretty pavement in the Venetian style, was designed by Matteo Lucchesi in 1777. The orphanage for girls here had a good musical reputation, particularly in the 18C when its last director was Domenico Cimarosa (1749–1801). The children sang behind the three screens (those at the far end are trompe l'oeil). The charming frescoes are by Jacopo Guarana, with quadrature by Agostino Mengozzi-Colonna. On the end wall *Apollo and the Muses* includes portraits of some of the girls of the Ospedaletto with their master of music at a concert; on the ceiling is the *Triumph of Music*. The room was beautifully restored in 1991, and it is sometimes possible to visit (on request) the charming gallery above where the children sang. Concerts are still given here and in the church. The courtyard below was designed by Longhena.

Barbarie de la Tole continues east to Campo di Barbarie, with a recently restored little chapel. Calle Zen continues to a bridge over Rio di Santa Giustina by the former church of **Santa Giustina** now used by a school. The façade by Longhena (1640) was altered in 1841 by Giovanni Casoni when it became a school for the education of sailors. In the campo is the 18C Palazzo Gradenigo. Calle San Francesco continues right to the campo in front of San Francesco della Vigna.

San Francesco della Vigna

The name of this church (Pl. 10; 1, 3) recalls the vineyard bequeathed to the Franciscan order for a convent in 1253 by Marco Ziani, son of Doge Pietro Ziani. On this site, in 1534, Doge Andrea Gritti laid the foundation stone of the present church built by his friend Jacopo Sansovino. The humanist friar Francesco Zorzi was involved in the design of the church which is based on a complicated harmony of the progression of the number 3. In 1562 the brothers Giovanni and Vettor Grimani paid for the Istrian stone **façade** to be added by Palladio. It bears two bronze statues of Moses and St Paul by Tiziano Aspetti. The tall campanile is by Bernardo Ongarin (1581).

The dignified **interior** (open 07.30–12.30, 15.30–19.30) has a broad nave with five side chapels between Doric pilasters and a long chancel (with the monks'choir behind the altar). On the west wall, is a 13C Byzantine relief of the Madonna and Child, and a triptych attributed to Antonio Vivarini.

South side. First chapel (left wall), *Resurrection*, a 16C Venetian work; third chapel, *Madonna and Child with Saints*, by Palma Giovane; fourth chapel, *Resurrection* attributed to Paolo Veronese. **South transept**. *Madonna and Child enthroned*, by Antonio da Negroponte (c 1465). This is the only work known by this artist, and it represents one of the last great paintings in the florid Gothic style which had persisted in Venice under the influence of Antonio Vivarini. It is a large painting with a charming Madonna in a rich brocade robe sitting on an intricately carved throne beneath a garland of fruit and in front of a dark wood of pomagranate trees with a great variety of birds on the lawn at her feet.

In the nave, beneath the crossing, is the huge tombstone of Doge Marcantonio Trevisan (d. 1554). In the **sanctuary**, in front of the modern altar, is the carved pavement tomb of Andrea Bragadin (d. 1487). On the left wall is the funerary monument of Doge Andrea Gritti (d. 1538; see above). On the left of the sanctuary arch hangs an early-15C painting of the *Madonna of Humility* (restored in 1999).

The **Badoer-Giustiniani Chapel** (on the left; restored in 1998) which belonged to the Procurator Lorenzo Giustiniani and his brother Antonio, was designed in the 1530s by Jacopo Sansovino. He decorated it with very fine 15C sculpted *reliefs (removed from the earlier church where they were probably part of the choirscreen) by Pietro Lombardo and his two sons Antonio and Tullio. Over the sacristy door, monument to Doge Trevisan with a 16C relief of the doge. In the niche to the right is an alabaster statue of a Bishop Saint (16C?).

North transept. The Cappella Santa has a *Madonna and Saints John the Baptist, Francis, Sebastian, and Jerome, with a donor*, attributed to Giovanni Bellini and his *bottega* (signed and dated 1507). From outside the chapel one of the three surviving 15C cloisters of the convent can be seen.

North side. In the fifth chapel is the *Pala Giustiniani* (the *Holy Family with the young St John the Baptist, with Saints Anthony Abbot and Catherine of Alexandria)* by Veronese, his first Venetian commission, from the Giustiniani brothers Lorenzo and Antonio (see above). The Cappella Sagredo (the third chapel) was beautifully decorated in the 18C with grey sculpture by Antonio Gai and monochrome frescoes (including the four Evangelists, and two medallions of the Virtues) by Giovanni Battista Tiepolo. The elaborate sculpted garlands are by Temanza. The only colour in the chapel is provided by the frescoes in the cupola by Girolamo Pellegrini and the altar frontal in pietre dure.

The altar in the second chapel has three good statues of saints, a good work by Vittoria. The grandiose **Grimani chapel** was decorated c 1560 with ceiling paintings by Battista Franco and an altarpiece by Federico Zuccari. The bronze statues of Justice and Temperance are by Tiziano Aspetti (1592).

8 • The Merceria

The Merceria is a narrow calle, usually very crowded with both Venetians hurrying between Piazza San Marco and the Rialto, and with tourists. On its winding course it passes some interesting churches, notably San Giuliano with a fine 16C façade and interior, and San Salvatore, with a Renaissance interior and two paintings by Titian.

The narrow **Merceria** (Pl. 9; 5, 3 and Pl. 8; 4) is the shortest route from Piazza San Marco to the Rialto. Its name comes from *merce* (goods) since from earliest days, most of the shops in the city were concentrated here. As the busiest thoroughfare of the city it is always crowded, and many of its well-stocked shops cater for tourists. On the way to the Rialto it changes name five times: Merceria dell'Orologio, Merceria di San Zulian, Merceria del Capitello, Merceria di San Salvador, and Merceria 2 Aprile.

A passage leads away from Piazza San Marco under the Torre dell'Orologio (see Ch. 2). Just beyond the arch of the clock tower, above the Sottoportego del Cappello (left), a relief of an old woman is a reminder of Bajamonte Tiepolo's conspiracy against Doge Pietro Gradenigo in 1310 (see p 118) which was foiled when his standard-bearer was killed by a mortar which an old lady let fall (apparently by accident) from the window-sill here.

San Giuliano
At the first bend (right) in the Merceria stands the church of San Giuliano (San Zulian; Pl. 9; 3), a church rebuilt in 1553 by Jacopo Sansovino (and completed after his death by Alessandro Vittoria). A careful restoration programme of the church was carried out in 1990–98 financed by the Venice in Peril Fund. The **façade**, well-suited to this unusually cramped site, bears a seated bronze *statue of Tommaso Rangone, the wealthy physician and scholar from Ravenna, who paid for the rebuilding of the church, and is buried in the chancel. The statue is attributed to Vittoria. Between the columns on the façade are inscriptions in Greek and Hebrew praising Rangone's own munificence and learning.

The charming **interior** (open 08.45–12.00, 16.00–18.30) has a simple rectangular plan with two side chapels flanking the sanctuary. The fine ceiling

(1585) has a painting of *St Julian in glory* by Palma Giovane and assistants. **South side**, first altar, *Pietà*, with three *Saints* below, by Paolo Veronese; above the side door, *St Jerome*, by Leandro Bassano; second altar, statues of St Catherine of Alexandria and Daniel, by Alessandro Vittoria and *Assumption* by Palma Giovane. The high altar by Giuseppe Sardi (1667) encloses a *Coronation of the Virgin with three Saints* by Girolamo da Santacroce (c 1544). On the sanctuary walls hang two huge paintings by Antonio Zanchi. The chapel of the Scuola del Santissmo Sacramento (left of the sanctuary) has good stuccoes in the vault by Francesco Smeraldi (1582), and on the altar is a relief of the Pietà by Girolamo Campagna. **North side**. First altar, *Madonna enthroned with Saints* by Boccaccio Boccaccino. On the west wall, *St Roch curing the plague-stricken in a lazzaretto* (isolation hospital), by Sante Peranda. The organ is one of the first works by the great organ-maker from the Veneto, Gaetano Callido (1764).

From the Merceria in front of the church a short detour can be made down Calle Fiubera which leads across a bridge: the first calle on the right, Calle dei Armeni, leads to the lovely old Sottoportico degli Armeni, where there is the entrance to the inconspicuous little church of **Santa Croce degli Armeni** (Pl. 8; 4, open fest. at 11.00 for a service in Armenian). The church dates from 1496 and was rebuilt in the 17C, and the little cupola with a lantern and small bell-tower can be seen on the rio. It contains 17C paintings by Andrea Celesti, Gregorio Lazzarini, Alberto Calvetti and Pietro Liberi. The Armenian community in Venice lived in this charming district from the late 12C onwards, and they were allowed to build a small fontego on the rio dei Ferai. The calle ends on Rio terrà de le Colonne, named after its portico with wooden eaves and stone columns. In the courtyard of the nearby police station there is a delightful well-head in imitation basket-work.

The Merceria continues from San Giuliano (signposted for the Rialto) across Ponte dei Barettari, one of the widest in the city, rebuilt in 1771 with an Istrian stone balustrade. To the right beneath the portico (no. 4939) is the entrance to the **Ridotto Venier**, famous in the 18C as the meeting place of elegant Venetian society (see p 153), when it was the home of Elena, wife of the Procurator Federico Venier. The delightful small rooms preserve their original stuccoes and frescoes intact. It is now the seat of the *Associazione Italo-Francese* and is sometimes open for exhibitions. Farther on, the apse and flank of the church are skirted before emerging in Campo San Salvatore, laid out in the 17C.

San Salvatore

The rebuilding of the church of San Salvatore (also called San Salvador; Pl. 8; 4) was begun by Giorgio Spavento in 1508, and, after his death, continued by Tullio Lombardo. It was finished by Vincenzo Scamozzi. The Baroque façade, to a design of Giuseppe Sardi, was added in 1663.

The plan of the *interior (open 09.00–12.00, 16.00–19.00; fest. 09.00–12.30, 17.00–19.30), with its five domes and barrel vaults is one of the best examples in Venice of the way in which the problems of light and construction were solved at the height of the Renaissance. The Corinthian columns have figured capitals.

South aisle. Between the first two altars is a monument to Andrea Dolfin by Giulio del Moro (1602) with two busts by Campagna. Beyond is the monument to Doge Francesco Venier (d. 1556), with statues of Charity and *Hope, sculpted by Jacopo Sansovino when nearly 80 years old. The second altar has a Madonna and Child by Campagna. Over the third altar (attributed to Jacopo Sansovino) is Titian's splendid *Annunciation*, painted in 1566.

South transept. The tomb of Caterina Cornaro (Corner), queen of Cyprus (died 1510) is by Bernardino Contino. Over the high altar is a *Transfiguration* by Titian. The silver reredos (which formerly covered Titian's painting) is only shown on special religious festivals; it is a masterpiece of Venetian goldsmith's work (14C). The original silver gilt panels folded up for easy transportation; the upper and lower rows of sculpture are later additions. Beneath the floor is the tomb of a merchant with worn frescoes attributed to Francesco Vecellio, Titian's brother.

In the chapel to the left of the sanctuary, *Supper at Emmaus* a painting which has had various attributions in the past including Carpaccio. It was commissioned by Girolamo Priuli whose portrait is included (shown in black sitting next to Christ). It is now thought that the cartone is by Giovanni Bellini (who painted another painting of the same subject) but it was probably painted by his workshop. In the chapel to the right, *Martyrdom of St Theodore*, attributed to Paris Bordone. **North aisle**. The third altar is designed by Alessandro Vittoria, with statues of St Roch and St Sebastian. The organ, designed by Jacopo Sansovino, has doors painted by Francesco Vecellio, and a statuette beneath of St Jerome by Danese Cattaneo (1530). The second altar bears a statue of St Jerome by Tommaso di Lugano. Between the second and first altars is the dark classical monument of the Doges Lorenzo and Gerolamo Priuli by Cesare Franco (1567). The **sacristy** has a fine Renaissance interior which is to be restored. The frescoes at the side entrance of the *Transfiguration* are attributed to Francesco Vecellio.

The column outside the church commemorates Manin's defence of Venice in 1848–49 (see p 161). The former Scuola di San Teodoro has a façade by Giuseppe Sardi (1655).

9 • The Fenice and Santa Maria del Giglio

This chapter describes the busy area immediately to the west of Piazza San Marco. Both the churches of San Moisè and Santa Maria del Giglio have Baroque façades—that of Santa Maria del Giglio is one of the best in Venice, while that of San Moisè is much less successful. Between the two churches a calle leads right to the site of the Fenice, the famous 18C opera house, which is being rebuilt after it was gutted by fire in 1996. In the same campo are the *scuola* and Renaissance church of San Fantin.

Beyond the colonnade at the end of Piazza San Marco beneath the Ala Napoleonica with the entrance to the Museo Correr (see Ch. 2) is the wide Calle dell'Ascension. At the end on the right Calle Salvadego leads to the **Bacino Orseolo** (Pl. 8; 6), a pool usually filled with moored gondolas. The *Hotel Cavalletto* here is on the site of the Ospizio delle Orsoline, founded as a hospice for pilgrims in 977 by Doge Pietro Orseolo. To the left of the post office, Calle Seconda dell'Ascension (signposted for the Accademia) continues past Calle Vallaresso which leads down to the San Marco landing-stage on the Grand Canal.

At no. 1332, with tall windows on the piano nobile, is the **Ridotto**, a famous gambling house opened, with the approval of the Council of Ten, in 1638. It was in an annexe (or *ridotto*) of Marco Dandolo's house, attached to the private theatre of San Moisè. There were two 'sitting out' rooms where savouries and wine as well as coffee, hot chocolate and tea were served, and ten gaming rooms where the croupier was always a patrician. If you were not a nobleman you had to be masked and ladies were welcome. Francesco Guardi's painting, of the crowded interior around 1745 is preserved in Room 20 of the Ca' Rezzonico (see Ch. 13). Although the Ridotto was enlarged in 1768 and another gambling house opened next to the San Cassian theatre, both were closed by order of the *Maggior Consiglio* in 1774 in an attempt to heal the decadence in Venetian society, but gambling continued in private houses throughout the city (such as the Ridotto Venier, see p 152), and Venice today has one of the few official casinòs in Italy.

San Moisè

The Salizzada San Moisè leads to the campo and church of San Moisè (Pl. 8; 6). Built by the brother of the priest of the church Alessandro Tremignon (1668) it has an over-elaborate Baroque **façade** with good relief sculpture (restored in 2000). Its brick campanile can be seen to the right.

The **interior** (open to visitors 15.30–19.00) contains some good 17C–18C paintings, including (right and left of the organ by Gaetano Callido, 1801), *Crucifixion* by Girolamo Brusaferro, and the *Stoning of St Stephen*, by Sante Piatti. **South side**: first altar, *Adoration of the Magi* by Giuseppe Diamantini; second altar, *Invention of the True Cross* by Pietro Liberi. The **sacristy** contains a remarkable bronze altar frontal of the Deposition, by Niccolò and Sebastiano Roccatagliata (1633). The prettily framed small paintings (all labelled) include works by Morleiter, Giuseppe Angeli, Giambattista Canal and Vincenzo Guarana. An extraordinary sculpted altarpiece fills the apse. Inside the entrance, one of the white marble paving stones has an inscription which marks the grave—transferred from the church of San Geminiano in 1808—of John Law (1671–1729), originator of the Mississippi Scheme.

The charming Rio San Moisè is used as a mooring for gondolas. The *Bauer Hotel* here was built in 1949–54. To the left the side façade of Palazzo Trevès de' Bonfili (Ch. 4) can be seen, and, across the Grand Canal, the low Dogana building. Beyond is the broad Calle Larga 22 Marzo, recording the date of Manin's rebellion in 1848 (see below). It was enlarged in 1880 (a number of banks have their head offices here). Half-way along, Calle e Corte del Teatro di San Moisè recall the theatre founded here in 1620 and demolished after 1906. Claudio Monteverdi's *Arianna* was performed at the inauguration in 1639.

On the other side of Calle Larga 22 Marzo, Calle del Sartor da Veste diverges right and crosses a canal before reaching **Campo San Fantin**. The charming Renaissance church of San Fantin, probably by Scarpagnino (1507–49) almost fills the campo. It has a beautiful domed sanctuary and apse, attributed to Jacopo Sansovino (1549–63). Nearby is the **Scuola di San Fantin** (the seat of the Ateneo Veneto since 1811), with an Istrian stone façade by collaborators of Alessandro Vittoria; ring at the entrance in the calle to the left.) The *scuola* contains paintings by Paolo Veronese and his school, and a bronze portrait bust of Tommaso Rangone by Vittoria. Members of this confraternity comforted those condemned to death and accompanied them in black hoods in a solemn procession to the scaffold.

The Fenice

La Fenice (Pl. 8; 5), one of the most important opera-houses in Italy, was gutted by fire (two electricians have been charged with arson) in 1996, and it was immediately decided to build a replica. However, because of irregularities in the terms of the tender (disputed with success by the losing construction company) reconstruction work has sadly been delayed. Work was finally re-started in mid 1999 and it is possible the theatre will be reopened in 2003. The fine neo-Classical building was begun by Giovanni Antonio Selva in 1786 for the Venier family and inaugurated in 1792 with *I Giuochi d'Agrigento* by Giovanni Paisiello. It was rebuilt after a fire in 1836 on the same lines by Giovanni Battista Meduna. For the time being concerts and operas are performed in a temporary pavilion called the Palafenice on the Tronchetto, and in the Teatro Malibran, reopened after restoration in 2001.

The **Fenice** (the name means phoenix) is famous in the history of operatic art. Domenico Cimarosa's *Gli Orazi e i Curiazi* was performed here in 1796 (the composer died in exile in Venice in 1801). The première of Rossini's *Tancredi* took place here in 1813 and many of Verdi's operas had their opening nights here: *Rigoletto* was received with great enthusiasm in 1851 but *La Traviata* had a disastrous reception in 1853. Other historic performances included Vincenzo Bellini's *I Capuleti e i Montecchi* (1830), and works by Gaetano Donizetti, and Richard Wagner (including *Rienzi* in 1874).

In the 20C Igor Stravinsky's *The Rake's Progress* (1951) and Benjamin Britten's *The Turn of the Screw* both had their first nights here. Britten also composed *Curlew river* (1964) and much of *The Prodigal Son* (1968) during stays in Venice. The first performance in Italy of a work by the Venetian composer Luigi Nono (1924–90) was given here in 1961 (*Intolleranza 1960*). Other composers whose works had first performances here in the 20C include Gian Francesco Malipiero, Alban Berg, Sergej Prokofiev, Luciano Berio, and Paul Hindemith.

The Fenice also became the centre of the political life of the city after the fall of the Republic in 1797. During Manin's rebellion in 1848 the royal box which had been erected for Napoleon in 1807, was hastily demolished. Verdi became a symbol in the struggle against the Austrians who in 1851 attempted to censor his *Rigoletto*. From 1859–66 the theatre was closed by popular request since no one felt like enjoying themselves at the opera under the oppressive regime. When Verdi's name was acclaimed at performances it was understood to signify support for the King: the letters of his name spelt 'Vittorio Emanuele Re d'Italia'.

Between San Fantin and the Scuola di San Fantin a calle leads down to a rio crossed by the Ponte dei Barcaroli overlooking which is a little palace where Mozart stayed during the carnival of 1771, aged 15.

In the campiello to the left of the Fenice is the 15C **Casa Molin**, with an outside staircase and Veneto-Byzantine fragments. Calle della Fenice now skirts the huge charred building of the opera-house, emerging beneath a portico. Ponte Cristoforo crosses the rio and a fondamenta continues to Ponte Storto, a crooked bridge, well designed in 1767 to fit this awkward site. Across the bridge, Ramo I dei Calegheri leads to a campiello with a pretty well, and another asymmetrical bridge leads over the Rio di Santa Maria Zobenigo. Beyond the water-gate is a handsome stone bridge, built as the main entrance to the Fenice.

Calle del Piovan (or Gritti) leads back to Campo Santa Maria Zobenigo which opens on to the Grand Canal (with a gondola ferry).

Santa Maria del Giglio

The church of Santa Maria del Giglio (or Santa Maria Zobenigo; Pl. 8; 7) is dedicated to the Madonna of the Lily; its second name comes from Jubanico, the name of a family who lived in this district before the 12C. The fine **façade**, one of the best examples of the Venetian Baroque style, was built in Istrian stone and Carrara marble by Giuseppe Sardi in 1678–81 as a monument to the Barbaro family who paid for the rebuilding of the church. It bears portraits of them, and plans of Zara, Crete, Padua, Rome, Corfu, and Spalato (Split) record the victories of various members of the family in the service of the Republic.

In the light **interior** (open 10.00–18.00, fest. 15.00–18.00), the 17C–18C paintings above the cornice of the nave and on the ceiling are by Giovanni Battista Volpato and Antonio Zanchi. The 18C *Stations of the Cross* include paintings by Francesco Fontebasso, Giovanni Battista Crosato, Jacopo Marieschi, Gaspare Diziani, and Domenico Maggiotto. The 16C paintings on the west wall include a *Last Supper* by Giulio del Moro, and four *Sibyls* by Giuseppe Salviati.

South side. On the first altar, *Virgin and St Anthony of Padua and Martyrdom of St Eugene*, by Loth. The **Cappella Molin** displays the contents of the treasury, and a *Madonna and Child with the young St John*, attributed to Rubens. The ceiling painting of the *Madonna* is attributed to Domenico Tintoretto, and the paintings round the walls are by Giovanni Antonio Pellegrini. The second south chapel has a statue of St Gregorio Barbarigo by Giovanni Maria Morleiter; and the third chapel, a *Visitation* by Palma Giovane.

The **sacristy** is an interesting little 17C room (open 10.00–11.30 exc. fest.). It contains a Tuscan sculpted head of the young St John the Baptist, a small *Annunciation* by Andrea Schiavone, and *Abraham* by Antonio Zanchi. Above the altar, *Two angels in Adoration* by Giulio del Moro, and below it, a bas-relief with the head of St John the Baptist. The *Adoration of the Magi* is by Pietro Muttoni. Beneath the organ in the sanctuary are two paintings of the *Evangelists* by Jacopo Tintoretto. The fine 18C high altar has sculptures by Meyring.

North side. Third chapel: *Christ with two Saints* by Jacopo Tintoretto (damaged by restoration); second chapel: *Immaculate Conception* by Morleiter.

The calle continues (signposted Accademia) across two more bridges, the first one in the form of a semi-arch in order that boats can pass beneath it. There is a view from the second bridge to the right of the pretty Ponte de la Malvasia Vecchia, with a wrought-iron parapet decorated with marine monsters (1858), and to the left of the side façade of Palazzo Corner, now the Prefecture (see p 125). The calle ends in Campo San Maurizio (see Ch. 10).

10 • Campo Santo Stefano

This busy large campo is soon reached from Santa Maria del Giglio, described in Ch. 9, and it is also at the foot of the Accademia bridge over the Grand Canal. It takes its name from the church of Santo Stefano with a Gothic interior and a wooden ship's keel roof. It has some interesting paintings and sculptures in the sacristy. At the other end of the campo, in the church of San Vitale, there is a delightful painting by Carpaccio. Nearby is the 18C Palazzo Grassi where important exhibitions are held. North west of Campo Stefano is a palace which wa sonce the home and studio of the designer of fabrics and stage sets Mariano Fortuny who died in 1949. However, at present the Museo Fortuny, which preserves many of his works, is closed for long-term restoration and the palace is only open for exhibitions. Near Campo Manin is Palazzo Contarini del Bovolo, famous for its delightful outside spiral staircase which can be climbed for the view.

The huge Campo Santo Stefano (or Campo Morosini; Pl. 8; 5) is one of the most pleasant squares in the city. The statue of Nicolo Tommaseo (1802–74), an eminent man of letters and leading figure in the Risorgimento, is by Francesco Barzaghi. On the left (no. 2802–3) is the 17C **Palazzo Morosini**, home of Doge Francesco Morosini (1688–94). On the opposite side of the campo is the long **Palazzo Loredan** (no. 1945). The Gothic structure was remodelled after 1536 by Lo Scarpagnino (the fine door-knocker with Neptune is by Alessandro Vittoria). The Palladian façade on the north end was added by Giovanni Grapiglia. It is now occupied by the Istituto Veneto di Scienze, Lettere ed Arti, an acadamy of arts and sciences founded by Ferdinando I of Austria in 1838, which has an important library. It also owns Palazzo Franchetti, nearby (see below).

The corner of the campo is filled by the imposing **Palazzo Pisani**. Since the beginning of this century this has housed the Conservatory of Music, named after the composer Benedetto Marcello (1686–1739; see p 129). This remarkable building, one of the largest private palaces in Venice, was begun by Bartolomeo Monopola (1614) and continued by the Paduan, Girolamo Frigimelica (1728). The two interior courtyards are divided by a huge open-arched loggia.

Santo Stefano

The other end of the campo is occupied by the early Gothic church of Santo Stefano (Pl. 8; 5), rebuilt in the 14C and altered in the 15C. The fine brick façade bears a portal in the florid Gothic style. The Gothic **interior** (open 10.00–17.00; fest. 13.00–17.00), with three apses, has tall pillars alternately of Greek and red Veronese marble. The fine wood tricuspid *roof in the form of a ship's keel, is thought to have been built by the same architect, Fra Giovanni degli Eremitani, who built the church of the Eremitani in Padua.

South side. First altar, *Birth of the Virgin*, by Niccolò Bambini (1709); third altar, *Immaculate Conception*, by Jacopo Marieschi (1752–55).

In the **sacristy** are some interesting paintings and sculptures (the light can be turned on). On the entrance wall are four paintings by Gaspare Diziani (1733). On the right wall, *Washing of the Feet*, and *Prayer in the Garden* by Jacopo Tintoretto, and a *Holy Family with Saints* by Bonifacio de' Pitati. On the bench are displayed two very beautiful marble statuettes, including a female Virtue, attributed to Tullio Lombardo. On the altar wall is a large unfinished *Martyrdom of St Stephen* (c 1630) by Sante Peranda, and two small paintings of saints by Bartolomeo Vivarini. Above the altar is a *Crucifixion* by Giuseppe Angeli and a very fine high relief of the head of St Sebastian by Tullio Lombardo. The other statuettes of St John the Baptist and St Anthony of Padua are by Jacopo and Pier Paolo dalle Masegne. Displayed on a bench is a beautiful Byzantine icon of the Madonna dating from the 12C, with a Byzantine frame (12C–13C). Another frame (now exhibited separately) was added in 1541 by Venetian craftsmen. On the last wall is a *Last Supper* and a small *Resurrection* both by Jacopo Tintoretto and paintings by Antonio Triva.

On the wall to the right of the sanctuary is a painted *Crucifix* by Paolo Veneziano. On the walls of the **sanctuary** are two 15C carved marble screens, fine Renaissance works, and in the choir in the apse are elaborate wooden stalls by Leonardo Scalamanzo and Marco and Francesco Cozzi (1488).

North side. In the baptistery is the funeral stele of Giovanni Falier, by Canova, c 1808. The cloister (usually closed) of 1532 contains the tomb of Doge Andrea Contarini (d. 1382). The tomb of Giacomo Surian (1493) on the west wall of the church is a graceful Renaissance composition, with an equestrian statue. The sepulchral seal of Francesco Morosini, in the pavement of the nave, was cast by Filippo Parodi in 1694.

At the other end of the campo is the church of **San Vitale** (or San Vidal) (open 11.00–16.00 exc. fest.), founded in the 11C and rebuilt in the 12C: the charac-teristic campanile, which incorporates an antique Roman inscription, survives from this time. The monumental **façade** by Andrea Tirali dates from 1734–37. The **interior** decorarated in 1696 contains a delightful painting of **San Vitale on horseback with six Saints* by Carpaccio, with a splendid grey charger, signed and dated 1514. On the third south altar Archangel Raphael, St Louis Gonzaga, and St Anthony of Padua by Giovanni Battista Piazzetta and on the third north altar *Immacolata* by Sebastiano Ricci with a dragon at the feet of the Madonna, and on the second north altar, *Crucifix and Apostles* by Giulia Lama, one of the few women painters known to have worked in Venice (a pupil of Piazzetta).

Opposite the church is **Palazzo Cavalli-Franchetti**, remodelled in the 17C. It was owned by Archduke Frederick of Austria in 1840, and after his death in 1847 by the Conte di Chambord (heir to Charles X) who lived here until 1866. He entrusted Giambattista Meduna to restore it and create the garden on the Grand Canal. In 1878 the palace was acquired by Baron Raimondo Franchetti and it remained in the Franchetti family until 1922. In this period it was remodelled in the neo-Medieval style by Camillo Boito, including the Gothic façade and new wing and interior staircase. Since 1999 it has been the property of the Istituto Veneto di Scienze, Lettere ed Arti (see above).

To the right of the façade of San Vitale, from Campiello Loredan, a bridge leads across to Calle del Fruttarol. Beyond a school, Rame Calle del Teatro diverges left. The school occupies the site of the Teatro di San Samuele (which is recalled in the name of the calle) built by the Grimani in 1655 and demolished in 1894. Goldoni collaborated with opera productions here in 1734–43 (when works by Antonio Vivaldi and Baldassarre Galuppi were performed). In 1746 Giacomo Casanova was a violinist in the orchestra. Four fables by Carlo Gozzi were produced here in 1761–62.

The Corte del Duca Sforza, with a tree, has an archway on the Grand Canal, from which there is a view (left) to the Accademia, and (right) to Ca' Rezzonico. **Palazzo del Duca** has a private museum of 18C porcelain.

A series of narrow calli continue more or less straight on (signposted for Palazzo Grassi) to emerge (by a house with a plaque recording Giacomo Casanova's birth in this calle, in 1725) at **Campo San Samuele** (Pl. 7; 6) which opens onto the Grand Canal (and has a landing-stage and a gondola ferry). There is a good view of Ca' Rezzonico (Ch. 13) across the canal. The ancient church of **San Samuele** (closed to worship, but sometimes used for concerts and lectures) preserves its quaint 12C campanile, and contains frescoes by the 15C Paduan school which are to be restored.

Palazzo Grassi (Pl. 7; 6) was built by Giorgio Massari in 1748 for Angelo Grassi, son of Paolo, who had contributed a huge sum of money to support the Venetian war against the Turks in the Morea. The family was one of the richest in Venice by the end of the century. The palace was acquired by the *Fiat* organisation in 1984 and restored. It is now used for important art exhibitions. The interior contains a staircase frescoed with carnival scenes, attributed to Alessandro Longhi. The small theatre in the garden has also been restored.

Calle delle Carozze leads up to Salizzada San Samuele, with the house (plaque) where Paolo Veronese died in 1588. Calle Corner is surmounted high up by a Gothic arch. Ramo di Piscina continues to the curiously shaped Piscina San Samuele, its wide, oblong space unique in Venice. To the left, Calle del Traghetto leads down to the gondola ferry across the Grand Canal to San Tomà, while this route continues over two iron bridges to Calle del Pestrin which leads back past the raised Campiello Nuovo to Santo Stefano.

Calle del Spezier leads out of the east side of Campo Santo Stefano and crosses the Rio Santissima, so named because it runs beneath the east end of Santo Stefano. To the left can be seen a low bridge surmounted by two windows which once connected two wings of the convent of Santo Stefano; a few metres beyond (only visible from a boat) is another large low arch, c 15m wide, which supports the apse of Santo Stefano. Calle del Piovan leads on past (no. 2762) the little building which used to house the **Scuola degli Albanesi** (1531), the meeting-place of the Albanian community who were established in this area by the end of the 15C. There are Lombardesque reliefs on the façade. In Campo San Maurizio is the church of **San Maurizio**, begun in 1806 by Giovanni Antonio Selva and Antonio Diedo (closed to worship). The attractive well-proportioned interior has a fine domed tabernacle and two angels on the high altar. The leaning brick campanile which can be seen behind belongs to Santo Stefano (see below). No. 2667 is the Gothic Palazzo Zaguri (now a school). The Calle continues to Santa Maria del Giglio, described in Ch. 9.

Campo Sant'Angelo (Pl. 8; 5), which adjoins Campo Santo Stefano, is reached from the church of Santo Stefano across a wide bridge with a beautiful wrought-iron balustrade (beside another fine bridge in Istrian stone). The former convent of Santo Stefano fills one side of the campo, its door surmounted by a lunette with a relief of St Augustine and monks (15C Paduan school). Here there is a view of the fine tower of Santo Stefano—the most oblique of the many leaning towers of Venice—and the vault supporting the east end of the church of Santo Stefano can also be seen here above a canal. The little oratory contains a large wooden Crucifix (16C), surrounded with ex votos, and an *Annunciation* attributed to Antonio Triva (1626–99, formerly thought to be by Palma Giovane). Among the fine palaces here is the Gothic **Palazzo Duodo** (no. 3584), once the Tre Stelle inn, in which the composer Domenico Cimarosa died in 1801. It faces the Gothic Palazzo Gritti (no. 3832). Calle del Spezier (probably named from the spices which used to be sold here), signposted for the Rialto, is a busy shopping street which leads out of the campo.

The first turning on the left (signposted for Palazzo Fortuny) leads along Rio terra della Mandola. Beneath the arch (by the entrance to a hotel) at the end (right) is the grand 15C **Palazzo Pesaro degli Orfei**, now the **Museo Fortuny** (Pl. 8; 5). At present only open for exhibitions 10.00–18.00; ☎ 041 520 0995. This was the home of the Spanish painter Mariano Fortuny (1871–1949) who designed the famous Fortuny fabrics here. His gorgeous silks and velvets were derived from ancient Venetian designs, and he set up a factory on the Giudecca (near the Mulino Stucky) which is still in operation. He was also a pioneer in costume design, stage sets, and lighting for the theatre. The additional name of the palace, *degli Orfei*, was added in 1786 when the palace became the seat of the Philharmonic Society called *L'Apollinea*. The house was left to the city in 1956 by Fortuny's widow, and preserves a fine old wooden staircase and loggia in the picturesque courtyard. The interior which has a remarkable fin de siècle atmosphere, and is filled with curios and the artist's own works was closed in 1999 for long-term restoration (expected to take until 2004), and the main room transformed into an exhibition space.

The splendid main façade of the palace faces the small Campo San Benedetto where the church of **San Benedetto** (or San Beneto) is closed to worship (it contains works by Bernardo Strozzi; Carlo Maratta, Sebastiano Mazzoni and Giambattista Tiepolo.

Salizzada della Chiesa leads towards the high bare wall of the Rossini theatre; just before it Calle Sant'Andrea diverges left and Sottoportico delle Muneghe emerges on Rio San Luca. From the iron bridge the view towards the Grand Canal includes the back and side of Palazzo Grimani (now the Court of Appeal, see Ch. 4). The church of **San Luca** contains a damaged high altarpiece by Veronese, and a 15C high relief of the Madonna and Child enthroned, in terracotta. Pietro Aretino (d. 1556) was buried here.

Behind the church is Campiello San Luca where Palazzo Magno (no. 4038) has a fine 13C brick doorway.

From here Ramo della Salizzada leads on to the **Campo Manin** (Pl. 8; 4, 6) dominated by a disappointing building designed in 1964 by Pier Luigi Nervi and Angelo Scattolin. Here is a 19C monument to Daniele Manin by Luigi Borro.

Palazzo Contarini del Bovolo

Calle della Vida leads out of the piazza towards **Palazzo Contarini del Bovolo** (Pl. 8; 6; signposted), celebrated for its graceful **spiral staircase* (open daily April–Oct 10.00–18.00) and loggia by Giovanni Candi (c 1499). It has a picturesque little garden with seven well-heads, one of them Byzantine. There are traces of painted decoration on the stairs, and a wooden dome over the circular loggia at the top, from which there is a delightful view over the roof tops of Venice which takes in most of her bell-towers. The shell of the Fenice theatre, the church of the Salute, and the basilica and campanile of San Marco are particularly prominent, even though the lagoon and the city's numerous canals are invisible.

Daniele Manin

Daniele Manin was a Venetian lawyer and descendent of Ludovico, the last doge of the Republic. Having been imprisoned by the Austrians (who had ruled Venice since 1815), he became the leader of a successful rebellion in 1848 against Austrian rule, in which patriots, intellectuals, professional people and the populace of the city joined. They proclaimed a Republic, with Manin as President, and heroically resisted the Austrians for more than a year, being subjected to the first air raid in history when bombs were dropped from balloons by means of pre-set fuses. Manin was defeated in August 1849, and Venice had to wait until 1866 before it was finally reunited to Italy. Although Manin died in poverty in Paris in 1857, his tomb is on the north façade of San Marco, and he is also commemorated in this piazza, in the name of the Calle Larga 22 Marzo (the date of his rebellion in 1848), and in a commemorative column outside San Salvatore.

---

11 • The Galleria dell' Accademia

At the foot of the Accademia bridge (Pl. 7; 8; see Ch. 4) Campo della Carità is dominated by the flank of the former church and ex-convent of Santa Maria della Carità, its Gothic doorway surrounded by large reliefs dating from 1377. This and the **Scuola Grande della Carità** (with a Baroque façade by Giorgio Massari) are now occupied by the **Galleria dell'Accademia** (Pl. 7; 8), one of the most important art galleries in Italy which contains paintings covering all periods of Venetian art from the 14C, through the 15C with masterpieces by Giovanni Bellini, and the wonderful era of Titian, Jacopo Tintoretto, and Veronese, down to Giovanni Battista Tiepolo and the 18C. Open 08.15–19.15; Mon 08.15–14.00.

As the paintings are well labelled and all the works are of the highest quality, only a selection of the paintings is given below, and asterisks—to indicate the highlights—have been used sparingly. Some rooms are kept closed when there is a shortage of custodians (especially on Sundays and Mondays). Because of the restricted space available, less than half the collection is at present on view here, but work is under way to expand the exhibition space since the Accademia di Belle Arti, which occupies part of the building, is to move to new premises on the Giudecca canal (see p 176). The **Quadreria** (reserve collection) is open by appointment on Tues 15.00–17.30, ☎ 041 522 2247.

The Scuola Grande della Carità, founded in 1260, was the oldest of the six Scuole Grandi (see p 138) in Venice, and two of its rooms survive with some of their original decorations inside the gallery. The gallery was first opened to the public in 1817, and includes numerous works from suppressed or demolished churches in the city. The present arrangment was designed by Carlo Scarpa in 1950. The works are arranged chronologically.

Stairs lead up to **room 1**, the former **chapter house of the Scuola della Carità**, with a superb gilded wooden *ceiling, by Marco Cozzi (1461–84) with carved cherubs and paintings of the *Holy Father* attributed to Pier Maria

Pennacchi) and of four *Prophets* attributed to Domenico Campagnola.

The earliest works in the collection are exhibited here, including two works by Paolo Veneziano: a splendid polyptych of the *Coronation of the Virgin* flanked by *Stories from the Life of Christ and St Francis*, and a *Madonna enthroned with Angels and two donors*. Paolo was the first truly Venetian painter born in the last years of the 13C and his works show the influence of Byzantine art (it is thought that he may even have visited Constantinople) but also provided a prelude to the great Venetian school of painting. Lorenzo Veneziano, who was no relation to Paolo but succeeded him as an important artistic personality in Venice in the mid 14C, is also well represented here by a large polyptych with the *Annunciation* in the central panel with the tiny kneeling figure of the donor Domenico Lion, surrounded by numerous saints and prophets. His masterly use of colour is also evident in the later *Annunciation with Saints*, signed and dated 1371. Another important artist who was at work later in the century is Niccolò di Pietro whose *Madonna and Child* exhibited here is signed and dated 1394 (with the addition of the address of his studio at the foot of Ponte del Paradiso).

Venetian art of the early 15C is also well illustrated in this room by artists such as Jacobello del Fiore and Giambono, working in the International Gothic style.

At the top of the stairs is Jacobello del Fiore's *Justice enthroned and the two archangels Michael and Gabriel*, a work commissioned for a law court in Palazzo Ducale, showing Venice personified as Justice. At the other end of the room is his *Coronation of the Virgin in Paradise* surrounded by a huge crowd of saints and angels: there is another painting of the same subject here by Michele Giambono. The *Madonna della Misericordia with Saints John the Baptist and John the Evangelist* is also by Jacobello, and *St James the Greater between four other Saints* is a late work (c 1450) by Giambono.

Also here are late-14C works by Jacobello Alberegno, including an unusual polyptych illustrating the *Apocalypse*, particularly interesting for its iconography, and early 15C works by Michele di Matteo, Antonio Vivarini, and Jacopo Moranzone. In the centre of the room is displayed the *Cross of St Theodore* made from rock crystal and gilded silver in the 15C by Venetian goldsmiths.

A superb group of large altarpieces by leading artists of the Venetian school painted for churches in the city (three of them for San Giobbe), mostly dating from the early 16C, are displayed in **room 2**. The *Crucifixion and the Ten Thousand Martyrs of Mount Ararat* (also interesting for its complex iconography) and *Presentation of Christ in the Temple*, with three charming little angels, by Vittore Carpaccio were both painted in the second decade of the 16C. The *Prayer in the Garden and Saints* and *Calling of the sons of Zebedee* (1510) are by Marco Basaiti. The latter has a remarkably intense atmosphere and the two brothers indicate clearly their willingness to devote their lives to Christ. The Pala of San Giobbe, which depicts the *Madonna enthroned with Saints*, is a very beautiful work by Giovanni Bellini, with the magisterial figure of the Madonna holding the Child looking towards the future, beneath a golden apse decorated with mosaics which recalls the basilica of San Marco. The classical details of the throne and architecture are also exquisitely painted and were repeated in the architecture of the altar itself in San Giobbe. The St Sebastian is a superb nude figure study, and at the foot of the throne are three delightful angels playing musical instruments. Probably painted in 1478 it had a profound influence on

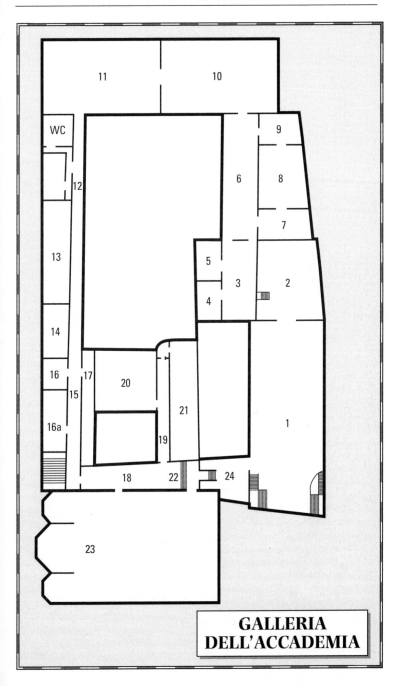

**GALLERIA
DELL'ACCADEMIA**

Bellini's contemporaries as can be seen from the altarpieces in this room by Carpaccio and Cima. The *Pietà* is also by Giovanni, with the help of assistants. There are also three works by Cima da Conegliano: a *Madonna enthroned with Saints*, the *Incredulity of St Thomas*, and the *Madonna of the Orange tree*, a lovely painting with delightful botanical details.

Room 3. Displayed here are the painted organ doors from San Bartolomeo and Santa Maria dei Miracoli: those with *Four Saints* are early works by Sebastiano del Piombo, and those with the *Annunciation*, are by Giovanni Bellini. The two small works are by Cima da Conegliano

The two small **rooms 4 and 5**, with exquisite small paintings, provide one of the most vivid insights into Venetian art at its height. They contain a remarkable group of deeply religious paintings by **Giovanni Bellini**, the greatest Venetian master of the 15C. Son of the painter Jacopo Bellini, he was born c 1433 and throughout his long life (he lived to be over eighty) he had a profound influence on Venetian painting. He was an innovator whose works reveal all the qualities of the Venetian Renaissance. In 1482 he was made official painter of the Republic. He is especially noted for his beautiful paintings of Madonnas, more than eighty of which survive by his hand or by one of his many pupils who worked in his important *bottega* (workshop). His brother Gentile was also a painter. Some of his most delightful small paintings can be seen in these two rooms, all of which were restored in the 1990s. Those in **room 4** depict the *Madonna and Child between Saints Paul and George* (possibly with the help of assistants), the **Madonna and Child between Saints Catherine and Mary Magdalene*, against a dark background with remarkable light effects on the heads, and the **Madonna and Child blessing*, an early work with the half length figure of the Madonna with exquisitely painted hands, holding the standing Child who is playing with the Madonna's left thumb. The **Madonna enthroned* in the act of prayer with the sleeping Child fast asleep on her lap is one of Bellini's most moving works and the abandoned figure of the Child has echoes of the figure of the Dead Christ in a Pietà. Also here are two **Madonnas* by Giovanni's father Jacopo and **St George* by Andrea Mantegna, Giovanni's brother-in-law. The other small works in this room are by non Venetian artists: an exquisite *Portrait of a Young Man* by Hans Memling painted around 1480 but of unknown provenence; a *Madonna and Child* by the Ferrarese painter Cosmè Tura; and **St Jerome in the Desert* by Piero della Francesca, with a kneeling donor and a view of Borgo San Sepolcro, the painter's Umbrian birthplace, in the background. Piero's signature is on the tree trunk which supports the Crucifix, but the painting is damaged since the green pigment has turned brown.

    Room 5 has more lovely works by **Giovanni Bellini**: another **Madonna and Child*, with the blessing Child standing, and the **Madonna degli Alberelli*, named after the two unusual trees present in the painting. This is arguably the most beautiful of all the Madonnas in these two rooms with an extraordinary expressive energy in the movement of the Madonna's head with her eyes downcast. The **Madonna dei Cherubini rossi*, receives its name from the red cherubims in the sky: again the Virgin's hands are superbly painted and the tender expression of the Madonna contrasts with the chubby curly haired Child who is shown in a far from idealised portrait. There is also a *Madonna and Child* *between St John the Baptist an d a female Saint*, and a *Pietà*, in a landscape with depictions of Vicenza and Ravenna in the background. In these works Giovanni was apparently influenced by German Gothic sculptures of the same subject. The *Head of the Redeemer* is a fragment, and the five *allegories* were probably made for the doors of a cupboard.

Also here are two famous paintings by **Giorgione**: *La Tempesta*, and *Old Woman*. Giorgio da Castelfranco became known as Giorgione as his fame as a painter increased. He was born around 1476, and despite the fact that very little is known about his life and very few paintings can be attributed with certainty to his hand, he has always been one of the best known Venetian painters. A pupil of Giovanni Bellini and influenced by Flemish and Dutch masters, he had an innovative technique of painting on canvas, applying a rich impasto and a broad range of colours. He was particularly interested in landscape as can be seen here from the remarkable depiction of the outbreak of a storm in a pastoral landscape in his late masterpiece *La Tempesta*, and in the other paintings he produced for his private Venetian patrons which are full of mystery with an atmosphere derived from the spirit of Venetian Humanism. The famous *La Tempesta*, known to have been owned by the patrician Gabriele Vendramin, is a painting of uncertain subject-matter, but one the few paintings attributed with certainty to Giorgione. He died young (of the plague) in 1510, and some of his works have also been attributed to Titian, including, in the past, the portrait of an *Old Woman*, which is now dated c 1508–09 and probably preserves its original frame. It shows the influence of Dürer, and is an allegory of old age rather than a portrait. Giorgione is also known to have frescoed numerous palace façades in Venice, but only one fragment survives: the exterior decoration of the Fondaco dei Tedeschi (now in the Ca' d'Oro).

Room 6 exhibits *St John the Baptist* by Titian, the *Creation of the Animals, Temptation of Adam and Eve*, and *Cain and Abel* by Jacopo Tintoretto, and *Venice receiving the Homage of Hercules and Ceres* (from a ceiling in Palazzo Ducale) and *St Francis receiving the stigmata* (from a church ceiling), both by Paolo Veronese.

Room 7 contains some remarkable portraits including two female portraits by Bernardino Licinio, Giovanni Cariani's *Portrait of a Man*, and Lorenzo Lotto's, *Gentleman in his Study*, one of his best portraits, painted around 1530.

Room 8. The *Visitation* is a fine 16C Venetian painting which has received many attributions in the past but whose author remains unknown. The two works by Bonifacio de' Pitati are interesting for their Venetian elements; *God the Father above Piazza San Marco* provides a detailed documentation of the piazza in the 1540s including Sansovino's recently completed Loggetta at the foot of the Campanile, and the *Madonna' dei Sartori' with Saints Omobono and Barbara* painted for the tailors' confraternity shows their patron saint in Venetian garb and the scissors, symbol of the *scuola*, at the foot of the throne. This is the only work known to be signed and dated (1533) by this artist. The *Archangel Raphael with Tobias* is now generally considered to be the work of Titian, who also painted *St John the Almsgiver* (removed from the high altar of the closed church of San Giovanni Elemosinaro). The two works by Palma Vecchio depict the *Assumption* and the *Holy Family with Saints*, one of his best works which was left unfinished at his death in 1528. It is now thought that Titian completed the head of St Catherine and the landscape in the background. Also here are works by Andrea Previtali and Romanino.

Room 10 is dominated by Paolo Veronese's huge painting of *Christ at the Banquet in the House of Levi*, a splendid Venetian banquet-scene framed in a Palladian loggia; the man in the foreground against the pillar on the left is said to be the painter himself. Some fifty figures animate the scene with everyone busy enjoying themselves, dressed in splendid colourful costumes, and including servants, clowns, and dogs. In the background are extravagant buildings against a twilight sky. The secular character of this painting dating from 1573 brought Veronese into conflict with the Inquisition, and the name had to be changed from *The Last Supper to Christ at the Banquet in the House of Levi* before it was allowed to be hung in the refectory of Santi Giovanni e Paolo.

There are five other works in this room by Veronese: a *Madonna and Child with Saints*, painted around 1564 for the church of San Zaccaria; an *Allegory of the Battle of Lepanto*, which he painted shortly after the battle in 1571 probably as an ex-voto for a Venetian who had taken part in this celebrated defeat of the Turks at the hand of a Christian fleet; the *Marriage of St Catherine* (dated around 1575), an *Annunciation*, with beautiful architectural details, and a late *Crucifixion*.

Also in this room are four masterpieces by Jacopo Tintoretto painted for the chapter hall of the Scuola Grande di San Marco (1562–66) illustrating Miracles related to St Mark, all of which show the painter's remakable imagination. The *Transport of the Body of St Mark* illustrates the story of the Venetian merchants who stole the body of St Mark from Alexandria in 828 and had it transported to Venice. The splendid camel adds an exotic Arab element to the setting, and the extraordinary ephemeral ghost-like figures in the background conjure up a miraculous atmosphere. The nude figure of St Mark is painted with great skill. *St Mark liberating a Slave* is another dramatic scene on which the saint descends in flight from above our heads while the astonished crowd observe the nude figure of the slave who has just been freed from his shackles. The painter's remarkable technique can be observed in the few brush strokes which indicate with an extraordinary freshness of touch the details in the foreground of the hatchet and splinters of wood and severed ropes. These two works were paid for by the rich scholar Tommaso Rangone whose portrait can be seen at the extreme left, and, in the first work, beside the camel. In *St Mark saving a Saracen from shipwreck* a tempest at sea rages while the saint effortlessly lifts the hand-some figure of a saracen out of a sinking boat to safety. The *Dream of St Mark* shows a night scene on board ship with St Mark (who dreams of the angel in the sky) and his three companions warmly wrapt up in blankets, indicated by large abstract patches of colour. This is arguably one of his most innovative works.

The moving *Pietà* is one of the last works by Titian painted for his burial chapel in the Frari the year before his death at the age of 86 or 88 in 1576 when Venice was devasted by a plague. The muted tones produce a strikingly dramatic and tragic effect, and the kneeling figure of the old man is a self-portrait.

Room 11 displays frescoes and ceiling paintings by Giovanni Battista Tiepolo including a ruined frieze with the *Miracle of the bronze Serpent*, fresco frag-ments from the Scalzi, and the circular *Exaltation of the True Cross*. *Dives and Lazarus the Beggar* is the best work of Bonifacio de' Pitati, the scene set in a villa in the Veneto. Artists from the Veneto and Liguria born outside Venice but with strong connections with the Venetian school are also represented here including Leandro Bassano (*Resurrection of Lazarus*), Bernardo Strozzi (*Portrait of the Procurator Grimani*, and *Dinner in the House of the Pharisee*), and Pordenone (*St Lorenzo Giustiniani and Saints*). There are two more works by Tintoretto, here: a *Crucifixion*, and the *Madonna dei Camerlenghi*, commissioned by the treasurers of the Republic who are shown here in front of a beautiful sunset, magnificently robed, followed by their secretaries bearing gifts for the Madonna.

The **corridor** (**room 12**) exhibits 18C landscapes, bacchanals and hunting-scenes by Francesco Zuccarelli, Giuseppe Zais, and Marco Ricci. **Room 13** contains works by Jacopo Bassano, portraits by Jacopo Tintoretto, including *Doge Alvise Mocenigo*, and a *Madonna and Child* by Titian. **Room 14** contains late 16C and early 17C works including paintings by Domenico Fetti (notably *David* and *Meditation*), Annibale Carracci, and Johann Liss.

Room 16 has amusing mythological scenes by Giambattista Tiepolo and Sebastiano Ricci. **Room 16a** exhibits Giambattista Piazzetta's, *Fortune-teller, and works by Giuseppe Nogari (*Head of an old Woman*); portraits by Alessandro Longhi, and *Portrait of Count Vailetti* by Vittore Ghislandi (Fra Galgario). **Room 17** has *capricci* by Canaletto and Francesco Guardi, and a view of Venice by Bernardo Bellotto. In the other part of the room are works by Giovanni Battista Pittoni, Sebastiano Ricci and Giovanni Battista Tiepolo, portraits in pastel by Rosalba Carriera and typical Venetian interior scenes by Pietro Longhi. **Room 18** contains more 18C works by members of the Accademia di Belle Arti in Venice.

Off this corridor is an entrance to the upper part of the large **Church of the Carità (23)** built in 1441–52, with a fine wooden roof, but divided into two floors in 1811 by Giannantonio Selva. In the central polygonal apse are displayed four early triptychs painted for this church attributed to Giovanni Bellini and his *bottega*. The four kneeling sculptured angels date from the 15C. In the left apse is **The Blessed Lorenzo Giustiniani*, signed by Gentile Bellini (probably a processional standard which accounts for its ruined condition) and *Saints Matthew and John the Baptist* by Alvise Vivarini. On the window wall is a carved and gilded Gothic wooden 15C ancona by Bartolomeo Giolfino; a **Madonna and Child with Saints Andrew, John the Baptist, Domenic, and Peter* by Bartolomeo Vivarini, *Saints Claire and Margaret* by Alvise Vivarini, and *Saints Jerome, Augustine, Peter and Paul* by Carlo Crivelli.

At the end of the room are large canvases from the Sala dell'Albergo of the Scuola Grande di San Marco with *Scenes from the life of St Mark*. The works were commissioned in 1492 first from Gentile and Giovanni Bellini and then after their death from Giovanni Mansueti (who had worked in Gentile's studio). When he died in about 1527 Paris Bordone and Palma Vecchio were chosen to complete the cycle. The *Martyrdom of St Mark* is by Giovanni Bellini (finished after his death in 1516 by Vittore Belliniano, and the Miracle of St Mark healing the cobbler Ananias is by Giovanni Mansueti, who also painted the *Episodes from the Life of St Mark*. The two later works are *St Mark in a storm at sea* by Palma Vecchio (with the intervention of Paris Bordone) and **The Fisherman presenting St Mark's Ring to the Doge*, by Paris Bordone, with a fine architectural background. Members of the *scuola* are depicted presenting the fisherman to the doge. On the wall opposite the windows is a *Triptych* from the church of San Pietro Martire in Murano by Andrea da Murano.

In a corridor (**room 19**) are small 15C works. Marco Marziale, *Supper at*

Emmaus; Bartolomeo Montagna, *St Peter and a donor*; Marco Basaiti, *Dead Christ*; Pietro de Saliba (attributed), *Christ at the Column*; Antonello de Saliba, *Virgin Annunciate* (copy from a work by Antonella da Messina, now in Palermo); Giovanni Agostino da Lodi, *Washing of the Feet*.

On the left is **room 20**, with charming **paintings from the Scuola di San Giovanni Evangelista** (end of 15C and beginning of 16C), relating especially to the *Miracles of the Relic of the Cross* which were given to the *scuola* in 1369 by Filippo de' Masseri on his return from Jerusalem. The paintings are particularly remarkable for their depiction of Venice, including the old Rialto bridge and the brightly painted Gothic palace façades, and also give a vivid picture of 16C Venetian dress. Carpaccio, *Cure of a Lunatic by the Patriarch of Grado*; Giovanni Mansueti, *Healing of a sick Child*, showing details of a Venetian interior; Gentile Bellini, *Recovery of the Relic from the Canal of San Lorenzo*, the first of the ladies on the left is Caterina Cornaro; *Healing of Pietro de' Ludovici by touching a candle in contact with the Relic*; *Procession of the Relic* showing the piazza as it was in 1496; Benedetto Diana, *A Child fallen from a Ladder is miraculously saved*; Lazzaro Bastiani, *Filippo de' Masseri offers the Relic to the chief guardian of the Scuola di San Giovanni Evangelista*; Giovanni Mansueti, *The Brothers fail in their attempt to carry the Relic inside the Church of San Lio, at the Funeral of a companion who had disparaged it*.

Room 21 (beyond room 19) contains the *Legend of St Ursula* by **Carpaccio**, painted for the **Scuola di Sant'Orsola** (1490–96). It is a delightful cycle of paintings, with charming details and a remarkably Venetian atmosphere. *Glory of St Ursula and her 11,000 Virgins*; *The Ambassadors of England demand the hand of Ursula, daughter of King Maurus of Brittany, for Hereus, son of their King Conon*. On the right, *Ursula's answer: Dictating the conditions of the marriage* (a delay of three years for Ursula to make a pilgrimage to Rome and the conversion of Hereus to Christianity); *Departure of the Ambassadors to England and the reading of the conditions to Conon*; *Hereus meets Ursula and Ursula leaves for Rome*; *Dream of Ursula; an Angel foretells her Martyrdom*; *Ursula, with Hereus and the 11,000 meets Pope Cyriac at Rome*, with a view of Castel Sant'Angelo; *The Pilgrims and the Pope reach Cologne*; *The Huns, besieging Cologne, massacre the Pilgrims; Funeral of St Ursula*.

Room 24 is the former **Sala dell'Albergo of the Scuola della Carità** (with benches and a fine 15C ceiling). Here is Titian's, *Presentation of the Virgin*, painted in 1534–39 for its present position. The solitary figure of the infant St Mary is charmingly graceful and the distant view of the mountains is a reminder of the artist's alpine home. The details such as the man dressed in red above at the window, and the old woman seated at the foot of the steps beside her basket of eggs are particularly beautiful, as well as the two splendid female figures in the centre of the picture observing Mary. The *large triptych of the Madonna enthroned between Doctors of the Church* by Antonio Vivarini and his brother-in-law Giovanni d'Alemagna was also painted (in 1446) for this room, although it was formerly on the wall in front of the *Presentation* (it was moved when the door was opened and steps installed in 1811 by Giannantonio Selva). One of the first works in Venice to be painted on canvas it was beautifully restored in 1999. The Byzantine *reliquary of Cardinal Bessarion was made in the 14C–15C (nearby is displayed a painting of c 1540 showing the cardinal holding the reliquary).

The Reserve Collection

Part of the Quadreria or reserve collection of the Accademia is kept in the buildings which belonged to Santa Maria della Carità, part of which were begun by Palladio, but later mostly destroyed by fire. His fine oval spiral staircase survives, as well as the long corridor in which the paintings are hung. Only some of the more interesting paintings are mentioned below. Admission by appointment only, Tues 15.00–17.30, ☎ 713498. A handlist is lent to visitors.

Left wall: Giovanni Bellini and assistants, *St Peter*; Marco Marco (attributed), *Christ and four Saints*; Bartolomeo Montagna, *Madonna enthroned with Saints Sebastian and Jerome*; Marescalco, *Three Saints*; Giovanni Mansueti, *Five Saints*; Marco Basaiti (attributed), *Portrait of a man*; Francesco Bissolo, *Presentation of Christ with Saints and donor*; Pier Maria Pennacchi, *Death of the Virgin*; Vittore Carpaccio, *Meeting of Joachim and Anne*; Cima da Conegliano, *Archangel Raphael with Tobias and Saints*; Marco Basaiti, *St George and the princess*; Titian and his workshop, *Symbols of the Evangelists, cherubs*, and other fragments from the ceiling of the Sala dell'Albergo in the Scuola di San Giovanni Evangelista; Paris Bordone, a small panel with winged putti; two small panels with *Saints Peter and Paul* by Jacopo Tintoretto; and another small work (*Christ on the Cross between the two thieves*) by Giambattista Piazzetta; Gian Domenico Tiepolo, *Institution of the Eucharist*; Michele Marieschi, *Capriccio*.

Right wall: Padovanino, frieze with *putti*; Pietro da Cortona, *Daniel in the lions' den*; Luca Giordano, *Deposition*, Jacopo Tintoretto, **Deposition*; a copy of Carpaccio's *Ten Thousand Martyrs of Mount Ararat*, and **Presentation of Christ at the temple*. Niccolò di Pietro, *Madonna and Child with two Saints*; Lazzaro Bastiani, *St Anthony of Padua in a walnut tree*.

12 • Dorsoduro and the Zattere

This walk follows a winding route from the Accademia (described in Ch. 11) through Dorsoduro, the charming quiet district of Venice on the other side of the Grand Canal from the crowded area of Piazza San Marco. It passes the Galleria di Palazzo Cini, open only at certain times of the year, with a fine collection of Tuscan paintings, and the Peggy Guggenheim Collection, famous for its works of modern art, mostly dating from the first half of the 20C. The important 17C church of Santa Maria della Salute by Baldassarre Longhena stands at the end of the Grand Canal. In the great sacristy are paintings by Jacopo Tintoretto and Titian. Next door is the Manfrediniana gallery (which can only be seen by appointment) with a collection of paintings and sculpture. The walk then follows the pleasant Fondamenta delle Zattere which overlooks the wide Giudecca canal. It passes several interesting buildings and churches, including the Gesuati with works by Giovanni Battista Tiepolo. The walk ends at the church of San Trovaso, with works by Michele Giambono and Jacopo Tintoretto, as well as an interesting bas relief, in its well kept interior. Close by is the picturesque Squero di San Trovaso, a boat yard where gondolas are made and repaired.

At the foot of the Accademia bridge, and to the left of the Academy buildings (see Pl. 7; 8), the wide Rio terra di Sant'Agnese leads away from the Grand Canal towards the Giudecca canal (which can just be seen in the distance, beyond a clump of trees). Calle Nova a Sant'Agnese (a shopping street) diverges left to cross the picturesque Rio di San Vio.

Galleria di Palazzo Cini

The Palazzo Cini (no. 864; left) on the canal houses the Vittorio Cini Collection (Pl. 7; 8) of Tuscan paintings and decorative arts. This was the home of Vittorio Cini (1884–1977), patron of the arts, collector, philanthropist and politician. The collection now belongs to the Giorgio Cini Foundation, which he founded in memory of his son (see Ch. 22). Usually open in Sept and Oct and March–June 10.00–13.00, 14.00–18.00 exc. Mon, but the opening times often vary according to exhibitions in progress (☎ 041 521 0755).

The paintings are arranged on the **first floor** (lift). In the entrance hall there is an 18C Neapolitan sedan chair, and some very fine 13C and 14C ivories, and a case of 15C–17C Venetian ceramics. **Room I**. Giunta Pisano, processional *Cross*; Bernardo Daddi, **Crucifixion**; Taddeo Gaddi, two small predella scenes from the *Life of St John the Evangelist*; Guariento, *Ascension*; Maestro di Badia a Isola, *Maestà (c 1315); Maestro del Trittico Horne, **Madonna enthroned and two Saints*. The Tuscan dower chest has relief decoration dating from 1340–60. In the **main hall**: Lorenzo di Niccolò, **polyptych**; Sassetta, *Madonna of Humility*; Maestro dell'Osservanza, **Redeemer**; Vecchietta, *St Peter Martyr*; Maestro Francesco dell'Orcagna (second half of the 14C), *St Paul enthroned with Saints*. In a stuccoed **alcove** is displayed a set of Venetian porcelain from the Cozzi manufactory (1785–95).

Room III. Botticelli and pupils, **Judgment of Paris*; Piero di Cosimo, **Madonna and Child with two Angels*, a beautiful composition, perhaps the painter's masterpiece; Piero della Francesca (attributed), **Madonna and Child*. **Room IV**. Pontormo, double **Portrait of two Friends* (unfinished); Filippo Lippi, *Madonna and Child with Saints, angels, and a donor*, a small painting in an interesting setting. There is a bust in polychrome terracotta here by Francesco Messina of Yana Cini Alliata di Montereale (1924–89), Vittorio Cini's daughter who donated these two floors of the palace to the Fondazione Giorgio Cini in 1984.

A charming little spiral staircase leads up to the **second floor** usually reserved for exhibitions, but where sometimes the important Cini collection of Renaissance paintings by the Ferrara school is displayed. This includes works by Ercole de' Roberti, Cosmè Tura, Ludovico Mazzolino, Battista and Dosso Dossi, and Baldassare d'Este. The collection also includes illuminated manuscripts, miniatures, books, Venetian and Bolognese drawings, and prints.

On the other side of the bridge, Campiello San Vio opens on to the Grand Canal. Here a little votive chapel incorporates reliefs from the church of San Vio (demolished in 1813). The Anglican church of **St George** (normally open for services on Sunday), once the showroom for the Venice-Murano Glass Company, was given to the English community in Venice in 1892 by Sir Henry Layard (1817–94), the English politician and archaeologist who carried out excavations at Nineveh. It contains the tombstone of consul Joseph Smith (1682–1770), art collector and diplomat, removed from the cemetery on the Lido in 1974. The narrow Calle della Chiesa continues to a bend in the Rio delle Torreselle.

Peggy Guggenheim Collection

The fondamenta on the left side of the Rio de le Torreselle continues to Calle San Cristoforo which leads to the main entrance (at no. 701; Pl. 8; 7) of Palazzo Venier dei Leoni (the palace façade on the Grand Canal is described on p 133). A secondary entrance is also often open on the rio (at no. 708) beside the museum bookshop. Here the Peggy Guggenheim Collection provides one of the most representative displays of modern art (after 1910) in Europe. There is a café/restaurant in the garden. Open 10.00–18.00; 1 April–31 Oct 10.00–22.00; closed Tues. Exhibitions of modern art are frequently held here.

Peggy Guggenheim

Peggy Guggenheim (1898–1979) was the flamboyant daugher of one of the seven Guggenheim brothers who became rich at the end of the 19C thanks to copper mines. Her father, Benjamin Guggenheim, was drowned on the SS *Titanic* in April 1912. Though born in New York, Peggy spent most of her life in Europe. In 1939 she decided to create a contemporary art museum in London with the help of the art critic Herbert Read. Her plans were frustrated by the Second World War and she returned to New York to open (in 1942) a sensational museum-gallery called *Art of This Century*. Here, up until 1947, she exhibited European works from her own collection as well as giving exhibitions to then unknown American artists—Jackson Pollock among them. Her patronage helped to launch the careers of several of the artists who were later to form the New York school of abstract Expressionism. Her first husband was the American collage artist Laurence Vail, and her second (whom she subsequently divorced) the Surrealist Max Ernst.

Her own collection made its European debut at the first post-war Venice Biennale (1948) in the otherwise empty Greek pavilion. In 1949 she bought Palazzo Venier dei Leoni (from the heirs of Doris, Viscountess Castlerosse) where she lived for the rest of her life. Here in 1951 she founded her contemporary art museum, and opened it every summer to visitors. Today the Collection is owned and operated by the New York Foundation named after one of her uncles, Solomon R. Guggenheim, who founded the famous museum in New York.

In the Nasher Sculpture Garden there is a Byzantine-style bishop's throne, and sculptures by Arp, Moore, Giacometti, Ernst, as well as works loaned from the Raymond and Patsy Nasher Collection. In the corner, beyond the gazebo, an inscription on the wall marks the place where Peggy Guggenheim's ashes are preserved, next to the place where her pet dogs were buried. The entrance hall of the palazzo leads on to the terrace fronting the Grand Canal with Marino Marini's equestrian statue, *Angel of the Citadel*.

Important Cubist paintings include works by Picasso (**The Poet**, **The Studio**), Braque (**The Clarinet**), Léger (**Men in the City**), Duchamp, Gris, Gleizes, Metzinger and Delaunay. Early Italian Modernism is represented by Futurist paintings by Balla and Severini, as well as a sculpture by Boccioni (**Dynamism of a Speeding Horse** and **Houses**), and Metaphysical paintings by De Chirico (**The Red Tower**). Works by Kupka, Kandinsky (**Landscape with Red Spot**), Mondrian,

Van Doesburg, Malevich, Pevsner, Lissitzky and Hélion represent European Abstraction and Non-Objective art in the period from 1910 to the 1930s. Works by Arp, Picabia, Schwitters and Ernst belong to the Dada movement, while elements of fantasy in works by Chagall (*Rain*) and Klee (*Magic Garden*) relate these artists to Surrealism, which is particularly well represented: Ernst (*The Kiss*, *Attirement of the Bride* and *Anti-Pope*), Miró (*Dutch Interior II* and *Seated Woman II*), Magritte (*Empire of Light*), Delvaux, Dalí (*Birth of Liquid Desires*), Tanguy, Cornell, Brauner, Matta and others. Peggy Guggenheim's support of young American artists in the 1940s is manifest in the paintings by Jackson Pollock (*Moon Woman*, *Circumcision*, and *Alchemy*, among others) and early works by Motherwell, Still, Rothko and Baziotes. There is also an important painting by Gorky. Post-War European art is represented by Dubuffet, Vedova, Appel, Jorn, Alechinsky, Bacon, Davie, Fontana, Nicholson, Tancredi and Bacci.

The sculpture collection includes two bronzes by Brancusi (*Maiastra* and *Bird in Space*). Alberto Giacometti is represented by early Surrealist works (**Woman with her Throat Cut** and *Walking Woman*) as well as later works (*Piazza* and *'Leoni' Woman*). There are also works by Pevsner and Gonzalez (*Cactus Man*). Two mobiles and a silver bedhead were made for Peggy Guggenheim by Alexander Calder.

The new wing of the collection (opened 1993) includes a sculpture garden, a café-restaurant, a museum shop and galleries for temporary exhibitions. In the garden wing, or *barchessa*, is exhibited, on long-term loan, the Gianni Mattioli Collection, one of the last great private collections of early 20C Italian art. Six early paintings by Morandi include his first masterpiece, **Bottles and a Fruit Bowl**. There are also paintings by Modigliani (*Frank Haviland*) and exponents of the Metaphysical school (Carrà and Sironi). The collection is dominated by Italian Futurism, with works by Boccioni (*Materia and Dynamism of a Cyclist*), Severini (*Blue Dancer*), Balla (*Mercury passing before the Sun*), as well as Carrà (*Interventionist Demonstration*), Russolo, Rosai, Soffici, and Depero.

The calle ends at a pretty little 18C bridge, and steps lead down into the attractive Campiello Barbaro with four trees and a fountain. From here Calle and Ramo Barbaro continue (with a view from the first bend of the cupola of Santa Maria della Salute) across Ponte San Gregorio (1772), its 19C iron balustrade equipped with iron flagstaff holders. Rio della Fornace (with double fondamenta) connects the Grand Canal and the canal of the Giudecca. Its name recalls the brick ovens which were formerly here. The calle continues beyond several glass-blowing works (visitors are admitted) and a passageway which leads to the gondola ferry on the Grand Canal for Campo Santa Maria del Giglio. The next campo is dominated by the Gothic façade of the church of **San Gregorio** (closed). The calle tunnels beneath the former monastic buildings (with the entrance at no. 172 to the charming cloister on the left, now part of a private house) to emerge beside (right) the fine triple apse (1342) of San Gregorio.

Santa Maria della Salute

Santa Maria della Salute (Pl. 8; 8) was built in 1631–81 in thanksgiving for the deliverance of Venice from the plague of 1630–31 which had left 46,000 dead, some thirty per cent of the city's population. It is a beautiful octagonal church, the masterpiece of Baldassare Longhena, and the most important edifice built in

Venice in the 17C. The water is reflected on its bright surface, built partly of Istrian stone and partly of *marmorino* (brick covered with marble dust). It rests on more than a million piles of oak, larch and elm. A unique building, and particularly well adapted to its impressive site at the entrance to the city, it dominates the view of the Grand Canal from the lagoon. Open 09.00–12.00, 15.00–17.30 (18.30 in summer).

The church was built on the site of the church of the Trinità which can still be seen in the Seminario Patriarcale (see below). The doge visited the church annually on 21 November in a procession across a pontoon of boats from San Marco: this Venetian festival is still celebrated by a bridge of boats across the Grand Canal at the Dogana. On this occasion a *Madonna and Child* attributed to Gentile Bellini is exhibited behind the high altar.

Santa Maria della Salute

Exterior. The church is built on a central plan with six lateral façades; you enter by a monumental flight of steps. Huge volutes surmounted by statues support the drum of the fine dome crowned by a lantern; a smaller cupola covers the east end. The sculptural decoration is attributed to Francesco Cavrioli, Michele Ongaro, Tommaso Ruer, Juste Le Court and Francesco Cabianca.

Interior. The high dome, its drum pierced by large windows, sheds a beautiful light on the central area of the church, which has a circular aisle (enhanced when the central door is open on to the Grand Canal). The polychrome marble floor is extremely fine. The large sanctuary, with the high altar beneath a second dome is, in contrast, dimly lit. In the chapels to the right are three fine altarpieces of the *Life of the Virgin* by Luca Giordano. On the left side, the first altar has an *Annunciation* by Pietro Liberi, and on the third altar is the *Pentecost*, by Titian.

In the **sanctuary** designed by Longhena the arch has four columns from the Roman theatre at Pola. On the high altar is a 12C–13C Byzantine icon of the *Madonna and Child* (the *Mesopanditissa*) brought from the cathedral of Herakleion in Crete by Francesco Morosini in 1669. The altar is crowned with a remarkable sculptural group (1670) of the **Virgin casting out the Plague* by Juste Le Court (or Josse de Corte), unfortunately rather too small for its setting. It shows a kneeling figure representing Venice interceding with the Virgin and Child, and the ugly female figure, an allegory of the plague, being frightened away with the help of cherubims. Also part of the group are the statues at the sides of St Mark and St Lorenzo Giustinian, both patron saints of Venice. The bronze paschal **candalabrum* is by Andrea Bresciano (1570), friend of Vittoria, and the roundels in the ceiling behind the altar are by Giuseppe Salviati.

The **great sacristy** (usually open daily 10.00–12.00, 15.00–17.00, but often closed in the mornings and when Mass is being held) is entered either by a little door on the left of the high altar or from the chapel in the circular aisle with the painting of the *Pentecost* by Titian. It has an important collection of works of art (all well labelled). Over the altar *St Mark enthroned between Saints Cosmas and Damian, and Saints Roch and Sebastian*, a votive painting for the liberation of Venice from the plague (probably that of 1510), an early work by Titian. It was commissioned by the monastery of Santo Spirito in Isola and moved to the Salute by the order of the Senate in 1656. It shows St Mark (representing Venice) enthroned above and between the two doctor saints (Cosmas and Damian) and the two saints traditionally associated with the plague, St Roch and St Sebastian. The 15C tapestry which forms the altar frontal is of exquisite workmanship (note the charming landscapes). On either side of the altar are eight tondi of the *Evangelists and doctors of the church*, by Titian (from the ceiling of Santo Spirito in Isola, see below). To the right of the altar is another votive painting, the *Madonna, with Angels holding a model of the Salute*, by Il Padovanino. On the wall opposite the entrance, *Madonna, donors, and an angel*, by the school of Palma Vecchio; *Marriage at Cana*, a splendid work by Tintoretto, with remarkable perspective and light effects; and *St Sebastian*, attributed to Marco Basaiti. On the wall to the right of the entrance: *Madonna and Child in clouds*, by Pier Maria Pennacchi, and *St Roch between Saints Sebastian and Jerome*, by Girolamo da Treviso. On the last wall, four *Madonnas* by Sassoferrato. In the ceiling are three *canvases (*Cain and Abel, Sacrifice of Isaac, David and Goliath*), in remarkable perspective, by Titian, removed from Santo Spirito in Isola.

The **small sacristy** (kept locked) contains a kneeling figure of Doge Agostino Barbarigo, from the family tomb in the church of the Carità, attributed to Antonio Rizzo; and a frieze of *Patriarchs* by the school of Carpaccio.

From Campo della Salute, with its fine pavement in front of the church, there is a splendid view: directly opposite the vaporetto landing-stage is the tiny Gothic façade of Palazzo Contarini-Fasan (see p 125), and to the left, towards the Accademia bridge, Palazzo Corner rises in the distance. In the other direction, the tip of the campanile of San Marco can be seen near the half-hidden façade of Palazzo Ducale, and, in the far distance, the tall campanile and dome of San Pietro di Castello.

Seminario Patriarcale and Manfrediniana Picture Gallery
In the campo by the church is the entrance to the Seminario Patriarcale (Pl. 8; 8; admission by previous appointment; ☎ 041 522 5558).

The **cloister** (in need of restoration) contains tombs and inscriptions, and a collection of sculpture (a beautifully carved sarcophagus has been restored but all the rest is in poor condition and uncatalogued), and the oratory has a Lombardesque altar. The grand **staircase** by Longhena (with a ceiling painting by Antonio Zanchi) overlooks a charming garden on the Giudecca canal with some fine old trees.

The **Manfrediniana Picture Gallery** was left to the seminary by Federico Manfredini of Rovigo (1743–1829). The **entrance hall** contains sculpture by the Dalle Masegne, a relief of the *Nativity* thought to be by Pietro Lombardo or Antonio Rossellino, and very fine Greek head of a poet (1C AD).

Room I. Triptych by Temporello (one of the few works known by this artist, a follower of Giovanni Bellini); *Madonna and Child, St Joseph*, and one of the *Magi*, a sculptural group of c 1250 (the *St Joseph* is close in style to Benedetto Antelami); (above) painted frieze of six *Bishops of Olivolo* (a fragment by the *bottega* of Carpaccio, another part of which is in the small sacristy in Santa Maria della Salute, see p 174); *Holy Family*, by a follower of Leonardo, perhaps Giovanni Antonio Boltraffio (harshly restored in 1999); Antonio Vivarini, lovely half figures of *Saints Nicholas and Ambrose* on either side of the *Death of the Virgin* attributed to Maestro Pfenning or Conrad Laib (c 1450). Filippino Lippi, tiny panels of *Christ and the Woman of Samaria*, and *Christ and Mary Magdalen*, with charming landscapes. The small *Madonna and Child* by Mariotto Albertinelli is another lovely work. The profile of San Lorenzo Giustiniani is by Gentile Bellini or his *bottega*. In the centre, Gerard David, *St Veronica*; Cima da Conegliano, *Madonna and Child*. The fine *Madonna and Child crowning Santa Eularia* (in need of restoration) is by Juan Matas of the late 14C Catalan school.

Room II contains five terracotta *busts* by Alessandro Vittoria (recently restored); they are portraits of Girolamo Grimani, Apollonio Massa, a famous doctor, Nicolò da Ponte, Pietro Zen, and a condottiere. The detached *fresco* above is by Paolo Veronese. The paintings include: Titian, *Apollo and Daphne* (in very poor condition); an exquisite small *Deposition* attributed to Bachiacca; Beccafumi, *Penelope*. The busts of cardinal Agostino and cardinal Pietro Valier are early works by Gian Lorenzo Bernini.

Room III. Terracotta bust of Gian Matteo Amadei by Canova, two monochrome sketches by Pittoni, and a collection of small paintings of the Dutch and Italian schools. The **library** is a fine room with has a central ceiling painting by Sebastiano Ricci, flanked by two others by Antonio Zanchi and Niccolò Bambini. It contains some 20,000 volumes (out of the 100,000 owned by the seminary). The gilded lion of St Mark dates from the 15C and the two globes from the 18C. Also here is preserved a wooden model of the dome of the Salute which may have been begun by Longhena himself (in urgent need of restoration). Outside are two alabaster *roundels* with reliefs of galleons in full sale (second half of the 16C).

In the **refectory** is a *Last Supper* by Giovanni Laudis, and two paintings by Aliense. In the corridor, a portrait of Benedict XIV by Subleyras. Off the cloister is the oratory or **church of the Trinità**, which predates the church of the Salute. It contains a very interesting relief of *God the Father blessing* by Tullio Lombardo, and a relief tabernacle from San Niccolò di Castello with the Maries kneeling at the Tomb, also by him. The 16C carved altar from Murano is by the Lombardo *bottega*. In a little room off the cloister there is a bust of Beranrdo Mocenigo by Juste Le Court, from the island of San Clemente.

A mosaic *Madonna*, a rare Byzantine work made for Santa Sophia in Constantinople in 1115, is also kept here.

The narrow fondamenta continues past a little wooden hut in the water, where gauges measure the tides, to the **Dogana di Mare**, the ex-customs house on the canal (recently acquired by the Comune and to be restored). The low Doric façade is by Giuseppe Benoni (1676–82). At the extreme end of the promontory is a little turret surmounted by a golden ball with a weathervane supported by two telamones. The superb *view* embraces the whole Basin of St Mark's: the campanile of San Marco, the domes of the basilica, the mint, the end of Sansovino's Library, and the Palazzo Ducale; then the long Riva degli Schiavoni as far as the Giardini. Opposite lies the island of San Giorgio Maggiore with its church by Palladio. Facing the Giudecca canal, the long line of house-fronts is broken by the white façades of the Palladian churches of the Zitelle and the Redentore.

The Fondamenta delle Zattere

The Fondamenta delle Zattere (Pl. 14; 2, 3, 4), first paved in 1520 is named after the Zattere or cargo boats which used to pull in here and unload into various warehouses along the quay. In centuries past there were also brickworks and boat building yards in the area. The fondamenta skirts the wide Giudecca canal, still busy with shipping including the large ocean-going vessels bound for the industrial port and oil refinery of Marghera, and with the car ferries which ply to and from the Lido. Beyond the Dogana and the garden wall of the seminary (see above), and a short way beyond the first bridge, Rio terrà dei Catecumeni opens out onto a characteristic Venetian court with a single row of trees and two houses above a low portico. The school here succeeds an institution founded in 1571 for the conversion of slaves and prisoners of war to Christianity.

Next come the huge **Magazzini del Sale** (salt warehouses). One of the richest resources of the Republic in the 11C–15C was the salt monopoly. The exterior was reconstructed in a neo-Classical style by Giovanni Alvise Pigazzi (c 1835–40). Part of the splendid 15C interior is sometimes opened for exhibitions in connection with the Biennale, and boat-houses occupy the rest of the building. From here there is a good view of the Palladian façade of the church of the Redentore across the Giudecca canal (see Ch. 23).

Across Rio della Fornace (which extends to the Grand Canal) is the church of **Spirito Santo** (Pl. 14; 3, usually open 15.00–18.00, Sun 09.00–11.00), founded in 1483 with a Renaissance façade. The interior, remodelled in the 18C, contains a painting of the *Redeemer and Saints* (first south altar) by Giovanni Buonconsiglio, and (third north altar), *Marriage of the Virgin* by Palma Giovane. The upper nuns' chapel (opened on request) contains an 18C cycle of paintings of the *Mysteries of the Rosary*, including an *Assumption* by Francesco Fontebasso. On either side of the church are the former Scuola del Spirito Santo, founded in 1506, with a façade by Alessandro Tremignon (1680; now a private house), and a building of 1958 by Ignazio Gardella. From here there is a distant view, beyond a conspicuous 19C factory (the Mulino Stucky), of the industrial port of Marghera.

The huge classical building by Antonio da Ponte (with a fine colossal stone head on either end of the façade) of the **Incurabili** (Pl. 14; 3), was once one of the four main hospitals of the city. It was founded in 1522 by Gaetano Thiene, and in 1537 the founder of the Jesuit order, Ignatius Loyola was a visitor here. At the end of the 16C the orphanage attached to the hospital became famous for its girls' choir and Jacopo Sansovino designed an oval church in 1567 in the courtyard, particularly adapted to these concerts (demolished in 1831). It later became an institute for children but is now being restored as the seat of the Accademia di Belle Arti which is soon to be moved here from its former premises which it shared with the Galleria dell'Accademia (see p 161). Founded in 1750, its first director was Battista Piazzetta; he was succeeded by Giovanni Battista Tiepolo.

Beyond a pretty, walled garden on the corner of Rio San Vio, the Zattere becomes more animated. The house on the corner (now a hotel) is where John Ruskin stayed in 1877 (plaque).

Beyond a mooring for barges, is the church of the **Gesuati** (Pl. 13; 4; Santa Maria del Rosario; open 09.00–18.00; fest. 13.00–18.00; Lire 3000, c €2 and coin-operated lights), a fine building by Giorgio Massari (1726–43). The Rococo **interior** has a remarkably successful design, with the dark high altar lit from behind. The ceiling of the *Instutution of the Rosary* was frescoed in 1737–39 by Giambattista Tiepolo, who also painted (first south altar) the *Virgin in Glory with Saints Rosa, Catherine of Siena, and Agnes of Montepulciano* (1739). First north altar, *Three Saints*, by Sebastiano Ricci (SS Pius V, Thomas Aquinas and Peter Martyr); third north altar, *Crucifixion*, by Jacopo Tintoretto (c 1570); third south altar, *Saints Ludovico Bertrando, Vincent Ferrer and Giacinto*, by Giambattista Piazzetta. The statues and reliefs in the nave are by Gian Maria Morleiter. The elaborate tabernacle on the high altar is encased in lapis lazuli and has precious marble columns.

On the Zattere is the Renaissance church of **Santa Maria della Visitazione** (1494–1524) with a handsome Lombardesque façade and portal. The interior was restored in 1995. It contains a charming wooden roof filled with fifty-eight panels of *Saints and prophets*, and a central tondo of the *Visitation* painted in the 16C by a Tuscan or northern Italian artist. In the sanctuary are four large painted tondi of the *Evangelists* and two 16C monochrome figures of bishops. In the choir, *Pentecost* by Padovanino, and a 15C bas-relief of the *Trinity*.

The next bridge crosses Rio San Trovaso, which has a picturesque boat-building yard, the **Squero di San Trovaso** (Pl. 13; 1) which dates from the 17C (restored). The living quarters above have a long wooden balcony usually decorated with plants. It was in yards such as this (another survives nearby in Rio della Avogaria) that the great Venetian fleet of warships and merchant ships were built before the end of the 15C; after that date boat building, along with repair work, was concentrated in the Arsenal.

This *squero* specialises in the construction and repair of **gondolas**,

The squero *at San Trovaso*

whose remarkable design has been perfected over the centuries. Although some 11 metres long, they are particularly light and easy to manoeuvre by a single standing oarsman with just one oar. Their asymmetrical shape compensates for the weight of the oarsman and the fact they are rowed only at one side. As the numerous ferries across the Grand Canal still demonstrate, they are able to transport a great number of passengers in respect of their weight and size. They are constructed with 280 pieces of seven different types of wood, and have a peculiarly shaped crutch (*forcola*), sculpted out of walnut, where the oar rests (it can be angled in three different positions). Another feature is the long prow which rises proudly up above the water.

The quay of the Zattere, lined with trees, provides a mooring for large ships; and the offices of several shipping companies are here. Sottoportico Fioravante leads away from the water-front along a narrow alley and over a bridge into the peaceful **Campo San Trovaso**, occupied by a raised cistern around its well-head. In the second campo on Rio di San Trovaso, with two more well-heads, a house bears a Byzantine relief of St Peter and the 15C Palazzo Nani can be seen across the canal.

San Trovaso

The church of San Trovaso (Pl. 13; 1), founded before 1000 (in 731 or 931) was once one of the most important churches in Venice. It was dedicated to Santi Gervasio e Protasio, but its name is always 'shortened' to San Trovaso. The relics of St Chrysogonus were preserved here: after his beheading in Aquileia under Diocletian his relics were taken to Zara in Dalmatia, but during the Fourth Crusade in 1202 they were seized by the Venetians. However, in 1240 they were given back to Zara and only in the 16C returned to Italy, but to the church of San Crisogono in Rome. San Trovaso had to be reconstructed the year after it collapsed in 1584, and the architect appears to have been a pupil of Palladio. It is unusual in having two similar **façades**.

In the **interior** (open 08.30–11.00, 15.30–18.00) the altarpieces in the chapels on the north side are by Palma Giovane, including (third altar), *Birth of the Virgin*, a very well composed painting. The two paintings in the choir (*Adoration of the Magi* and *Expulsion from the Temple*) are by Domenico Tintoretto. In the chapel to the left of the sanctuary, *Temptation of St Anthony*, by Jacopo Tintoretto (c 1577, restored in 1996), commissioned by Antonio Milledonne, a wealthy citizen who took an active part in government administration and who is shown here in the guise of the saint. The charming decorative painting of *St Chrysogonus on horseback*, by Michele Giambono (in a 17C frame), comes from the earlier church (see above). Although painted in the 15C this shows a flowery archaic Gothic style. The adjacent chapel of the Scuola del Santissimo Sacramento (which survived when the rest of the church collapsed in 1584), preserves its charming furnishings including four little lamps (kept permanently alight), a gilded tabernacle, and an altar of Carrara marble. It contains a *Last Supper*, by Jacopo Tintoretto, one of a number of paintings of this subject by him still in Venice (the painting of the *Washing of the Feet*, opposite, is a copy of a painting by Jacopo formerly here but bought by the National Gallery in London in 1882). This is one of many such chapels in Venetian parish churches founded during the Counter Reformation and dedicated to the Eucharist, and often decorated with paintings by Tintoretto. Their members tended to be from the lower artisan classes and their activities were controlled by the Church rather than the Council of Ten (who, instead, oversaw the building activities of the other Scuole in the city).

Over the south door is the *Wedding at Cana* signed by Andrea Vicentino. In the Cappella Clary, to the right of the door, the altar bears a lovely very low *bas-relief* in Greek marble of angels holding signs of the Passion or playing musical instruments, one of the most interesting products of the Venetian Renaissance thought to date from c 1470 but of unknown provenence and by an unknown master, known as the Maestro di San Trovaso (in the past identified with Antonio Rizzo, Pietro Lombardo, Agostino di Duccio or even Donatello). The organ is by Callido (1765).

In the sacristy is a *Madonna in Adoration* which has been attributed to Jacobello del Fiore. The church also owns a *Madonna* donated to the church by Rosalba Carriera who lived in the parish (it is probably, in fact, a self portrait or portrait of a Venetian lady).

Fondamenta Bonlini continues along Rio di Ognissanti, crossed by two handsome 18C bridges; opposite rises Ca' Michiel (now the French Consulate), with its two protruding wings, famous for its garden in the 16C. Ponte Trevisan (1772, redesigned in 1861) crosses the particularly pretty Rio degli Eremite lined on either side by fondamente. The little church of the **Eremite** here dates from 1694 (admission on request at the convent of the Canossiane nuns next door). It contains two marble altars with sculptures by Tommaso Ruer and Antonio Corradini (the ceiling paintings by Niccolò Bambini have been removed for restoration). Behind the altar is an unusual early-15C polychrome wood relief of the *Madonna of the Misericordia*. Fondamenta Ognissanti continues past the hospital and church of **Ognissanti**, and (no. 1461) a house with reliefs and lions' heads. The boat-yard (*squero*) on Rio della Avogaria has belonged to the Tramontin, a family of boat-builders, since 1809.

13 • Ca' Rezzonico

The water entrance to Ca' Rezzonico (Pl. 7; 6), one of the most important 17C–18C palaces in Venice, can be reached by a graceful little wooden bridge built a few years ago over the Rio di San Barnaba directly from the landing-stage of Ca' Rezzonico on the Grand Canal, and the land entrance by Calle del Traghetto from Campo San Barnaba (see p 182).

The palace was begun by Baldassare Longhena (c 1667) and completed by Giorgio Massari (1756); its grandiose façade is seen from the Grand Canal (described in Ch. 4). It was bought by the Rezzonico family in 1751, a few years before Carlo Rezzonico became Pope Clement XIII. They employed Giorgio Massari to modify the building, which was decorated for them by Giambattista Tiepolo, Giovanni Battista Crosato, and Jacopo Guarana. The last member of the Rezzonico family died in 1810, and the palace changed hands frequently in the 19C. Whistler occupied a room here in 1879–80. In 1888 it was purchased by Robert Browning's son, Pen, and the great poet died here in 1889 (in a small apartment on the first floor, which will eventually be restored). A plaque on the side canal records 'Roberto'.

It is expected to reopen after restoration in 2001. The room numbers follow the plan on p 181. In the following description the arrangement is given as it was before its closure.

The palace has been owned by the Comune since 1934, and was opened to the public in 1936. It contains the Museo del Settecento Veneziano, the city's collection of 18C art, displayed in rooms decorated in the most sumptuous 18C style with superb views over the Grand Canal.

Off the fine courtyard and atrium are the ticket office, bookshop, cloakroom, and café. On the **grand staircase** (by Giorgio Massari) one of the putti (winter) on the banister is signed by Juste Le Court.

First floor The **Ballroom** (**room 1**), with 18C chandeliers, is covered with sumptuous frescoes by Giovanni Battista Crosato and Pietro Visconti. The remarkable set of *furniture was carved in the early 18C by Andrea Brustolon; other pieces by him are displayed in the following rooms (especially room 12). These ceremonial pieces, made from boxwood and ebony, include a vase stand with Hercules and the moors, an extraordinarily elaborate Baroque scene.

Room 2 has a ceiling fresco of the *Allegory of the Marriage of Ludovico Rezzonico* by Giambattista Tiepolo (1758), with the help of his son Gian Domenico, and quadratura by Gerolamo Mengozzi Colonna), and a stuccoed alcove.

Room 4 contains pastels and miniatures by Rosalba Carriera, and a *Portrait of Cecilia Guardi Tiepolo*, painted by her son, Lorenzo, in 1757.

In **room 5**, with an 18C lacquer-work door, are 17C Flemish tapestries. On the ceiling, the *Allegory of Virtue* is by Jacopo Guarana.

The sumptuous **Throne Room** (**room 6**) overlooks the Grand Canal. The ceiling *fresco of the *Allegory of Merit* is by Giambattista Tiepolo. An elaborate frame (c 1730) surrounds the *Portrait of Pietro Barbarigo* by Bernardino Castelli. The furniture is attributed to Antonio Corradini. The **portego** (**room 7**), with a balcony on the Grand Canal, is decorated with 18C busts, and has two statues of atlantes by Alessandro Vittoria.

Room 8 has another fine ceiling *fresco (*Strength and Wisdom*) by Giambattista Tiepolo. The four *heads of old men* are by Gian Domenico and Lorenzo Tiepolo, and the *Portrait of Bartolomeo Ferracina* by Alessandro Longhi. The **library** (**room 10**) has ceiling paintings by Francesco Maffei and a Murano chandelier. The 18C books on display were published in Venice. **Room 11** has two large paintings by Gregorio Lazzarini, and one by Antonio Molinari. **Room 12** has more elaborate furniture by Brustolon and a ceiling by Francesco Maffei. The paintings include: *Rape of Europa* attributed to Gregorio Lazzarini and *Judith and Holofernes* and *Jael killing Sisera* by Jacopo Amigoni. From the *portego* stairs continue up to the second floor.

Second floor The **portego** (**room 13**), on this floor, displays paintings (all labelled) by Giuseppe Zais, Johann Lys, Gian Antonio Pellegrini, Giovanni Battista Piazzetta, Giuseppe Angeli, and Canaletto (two Venetian views acquired in 1983). In **room 14** are frescoes by Gian Antonio Guardi.

Room 15 is a charming (reconstructed) bedroom with the bed in an alcove, and a fine bureau. The adjoining closet (**room 16**) has an oval ceiling fresco of a hawk swooping on a flock of sparrows by Gian Domenico Tiepolo (detached from Villa Zianigo, see below). **Room 17**, the **boudoir**, has graceful 18C stucco decoration, and a ceiling fresco by Jacopo Guarana. From room 14 there is access to the **Green Drawing Room (room 18)** with fine lacquer furniture, views of Venice, and a ceiling fresco by Gian Antonio Guardi. **Room 19**, the **Longhi Room**, has another ceiling by Giambattista Tiepolo, and an interesting series of 34 small genre paintings by Pietro Longhi with contemporary scenes of Venetian life (including one with a rhinoceros). To the right of the door into the next room, the *Painter's Studio* shows Longhi at work. The life-size *Portrait of Francesco Guardi* is also by Longhi. On the other side of the Portego, **room 20** has two paintings by Francesco Guardi: the *Sala del Ridotto* and the *Parlatorio delle Monache*, delightful Venetian interior scenes. The first shows the famous gambling house called the Ridotto (see p 153), and the second the visitors' room at the Convent of San Zaccaria.

A passageway (**room 21**), with a rosary-maker's signboard attributed to Francesco Guardi, leads down to **room 22**, with an early 18C spinet.

There follow a charming series of rooms (**23–29**) reconstructed from the simple little Villa di Zianigo, near Mira, bought by Giambattista Tiepolo at the end of the 18C, and decorated with *frescoes by his son, Gian Domenico Tiepolo. Beyond **room 23**, with a fresco of Rinaldo leaving the garden of Armida, is the tiny **room 24**, with a frescoed statue of *Abundance* in a niche. **Room 25** has a delightful scene, called *The New World* (1791), showing a crowd, with a splendid miscellany of hats, seen from behind. They are waiting to see a magic

CA' REZZONICO

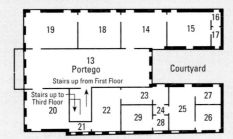

Second Floor

First Floor

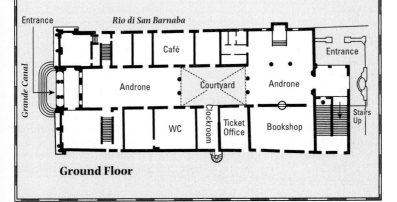

Ground Floor

lantern show at a fairground. Opposite are two satirical scenes of court life. **Room 26** has carnival scenes with Pulcinella (the Punch of 17C Neapolitan comedy), and acrobats (also on the ceiling). The chapel (**room 27**) has suitable grisaille frescoes. The last two rooms (**28** and **29**), also in grisaille, except for a brightly painted parrot, have amusing satyrs.

Third floor an attic, with low ceilings. In the first room are paintings, including a *Portrait of Giovanni Battista Piazzetta* by Alessandro Longhi, and two *Battle Scenes* by Matteo Stom. The second room has works by the *bottega* of Pietro Longhi, including a delightful *Banquet Scene*. The large painting of the *Sagra di Santa Marta* is by Gaspare Diziani. The charming Farmacia ai do San Marchi, an 18C pharmacy, and laboratory, with its original panelling, furniture, and pharmacy jars, has been carefully reconstructed here (seen through its windows). In the last room there is an 18C puppet theatre.

14 • The Carmini and San Sebastiano

This walk covers a lovely part of Dorsoduro, reached from the Galleria dell'Accademia (Ch. 11). It includes the characteristic Campo Santa Margherita with a little daily market and the peaceful district around San Nicolò dei Mendicoli. The Scuola Grande dei Carmini, with fine ceiling paintings by Giovanni Battista Tiepolo is next to the church of the Carmini, with a pleasant interior and good paintings by Lorenzo Lotto and Cima da Conegliano. The church of San Sebastiano is famous for its splendid paintings by Paolo Veronese. The remote little church of San Nicolò dei Mendicoli, of ancient foundation, has a lovely interior.

Outside the Galleria dell'Accademia (see p 161) a calle (on the line of the façade) leads west to the Campiello Gambara; beyond, the pretty Rio di San Trovaso is soon reached. The first bridge leads across to the Calle and Fondamenta della Toletta, a local shopping area—no. 1169 has a wooden *altane*, a characteristic Venetian balcony on its roof. Beyond the next bridge a passageway with two arches leads on to the campo in front of the church of **San Barnaba** (Pl. 7; 5; open in the morning until 12.00), by Lorenzo Boschetti (1749–76), with a 14C campanile (seen to the left). The ceiling fresco is by Costantino Cedini. On the second south altar, *Three Saints*, attributed to Francesco Beccaruzzi; second north altar, *Two Saints* and the *Pietà*, attributed to Giovanni and Bernardo d'Asola.

Ponte San Barnaba (reconstructed in 1873) has an elegant iron balustrade. A fondamenta leads down the peaceful Rio di San Barnaba (where a picturesque greengrocer's barge is always moored). The first bridge (rebuilt in the mid-19C), **Ponte dei Pugni**, has white marble footprints which recall the traditional fist fights which took place in the 14C–18C on the bridge (formerly without a parapet) between the inhabitants of two rival factions of the city (the Nicolotti from San Nicolò dei Mendicoli in Dorsoduro and the Castellani from San Pietro di Castello). At the end of the canal the 17C campanile of the church of the Carmini (see below) is conspicuous. On the opposite side of the canal is the house where Ermanno Wolf-Ferrari (1876–1948), composer of operas, choral and chamber music and keyboard works, was born (plaque).

From Ponte dei Pugni the wide Rio terrà Canàl leads to the spacious pleasant

Campo di Santa Margherita (Pl. 7; 5) surrounded by simple low houses, some of them dating from the 14C–15C. At the end, beyond the market stalls, the domed campanile of San Pantalon (see below) and the square tower of the Frari (see Ch. 18) can be seen in the distance. The isolated building is the Scuola dei Varotari (tanners), which bears a worn relief of the Virgin amidst the brothers of the *scuola* (1501). At the far end of the campo, an old house and the stump of a campanile bear interesting sculptural fragments from the former church of St Margaret whose decayed façade is just out of the campo, next to the campanile.

Scuola Grande dei Carmini

At the bottom end of Campo di Santa Margherita Rio Terrà della Scoazzera leads past the Scuola Grande dei Carmini (Pl. 7; 5), founded in 1597, beside the church of the Carmini, attributed to Baldassarre Longhena (1668). Open 09.00–16.00 or 18.00; fest. 09.00–16.00.

In the delightful interior the 18C decoration of the **chapel**, on the ground floor, includes monochrome paintings by Niccolò Bambini and an altarpiece by Sante Piatti. On the right of the stairs is the charming little 18C **sacristy**, with a stuccoed barrel vault. An elaborate double **staircase**, to a design by Longhena, with stucco decoration by Alvise Bassi (1728–29), leads to the **upper floor**.

The **salone** was probably designed by Longhena and built by his pupil Antonio Gaspari. The nine *paintings in the ceiling are by Giambattista Tiepolo (1739–49), with allegories of the Virtues around the central *Virgin in Glory* (*the Apparition of the Madonna del Carmelo to the Beato Simone Stock*). Beautifully restored in the last few years, they are among his masterpieces.

Giovanni Battista Tiepolo

Giovanni Battista Tiepolo, who lived from 1696 to 1770, was the most important fresco painter in Venice in the 18C and received numerous commissions from the Venetian aristocracy and the church. His Rococo decorative style with numerous charming details, particularly well suited to ceilings, had a great influence on European painting and made Venice a centre of European art. A follower of Veronese, he worked in numerous palaces and churches in Venice, and in villas in the Veneto, as well as in Germany and Madrid (where he died). The huge fresco on the staircase of the Residenz of Würzburg (1753) is considered his masterpiece. He was famous both in Italy and abroad during his lifetime. In 1719 he married Cecilia Guardi, sister of the painter Francesco. His son, Gian Domenico, worked with him, and later developed his own style to depict delightful scenes of Venetian social life.

On the walls are works by Antonio Zanchi and Gregorio Lazzarini. In the **Sala dell'Albergo** is a ceiling painting of the *Assumption* by Padovanino, and around the walls, 17C paintings including works by Antonio Balestra. The **Sala dell'Archivio**, was decorated in 1748 by Giustino Menescardi and Gaetano Zompini. By the door into the Sala dell'Albergo, the painting of *Judith and Holofernes* was added by Giovanni Battista Piazzetta. The **treasury** contains 15C–17C ceramic fragments, a statute book (1611), and an 18C cope.

Santa Maria dei Carmini

Next to the Scuola dei Carmini is a fine Romanesque porch decorated with Byzantine reliefs. To the right is the campo on a rio in front of the church of the Carmini (Pl. 7; 5; Santa Maria del Carmelo). The 16C **façade** is attributed to Sebastiano Mariani da Lugano, with statues by Giovanni Buora.

The most striking feature of the spacious basilican **interior** (open 07.30–12.00, 15.00–19.00; fest. 07.30–12.00, 16.30–19.00) is the gilded wooden sculptural decoration in the nave beneath a frieze of 17C–18C paintings. On the **west wall** is a monument to Jacopo Foscarini (d. 1602) by the school of Sansovino. Foscarini was a Procuratore of San Marco and took an active part in the government of the Republic, but just failed to become doge.

South aisle. On the second altar is a beautiful painting of the *Nativity*, by Cima da Conegliano (c 1509). The vault above the third altar (being restored) is frescoed by Sebastiano Ricci. The altarpiece is by Pase Pace, and on the balustrade, the two bronze angels are by Girolamo Campagna. On either side of the altar are statues by (right) Antonio Corradini, and (left) by Giuseppe Torretti. On the fourth altar, *Circumcision*, attributed to Polidoro da Lanciano.

In the chapel to the right of the main altar, a small bronze plaque with a *relief* of the *Deposition* is ascribed to Francesco di Giorgio Martini; it includes portraits (right) of Federico da Montefeltro and Battista Sforza (c 1474). Also here is a charming small painting of the *Holy Family* by Paolo Veronese, from the church of San Barnaba. The singing-galleries are decorated with paintings by Andrea Schiavone. The chancel walls are covered with four large paintings by Palma Giovane (1613), Gaspare Diziani (1749), and Marco Vicentino (1613). Above the high altar hangs a 14C gilded wood Crucifix.

North aisle, second altar, *Saint Nicholas in Glory, with St John the Baptist and St Lucy*, by Lorenzo Lotto, painted for the church in 1529 (and still in its original Istrian stone frame). This is one of Lotto's masterpieces, with a remarkable coastal landscape beneath, showing the influence of northern painters. Using a bird's eye perspective it illustrates St Nicholas' protection of navigators and his help in times of famine and pestilence. On the wall near the west door is a vast canvas by Padovanino.

From the campo in front of the church Fondamenta del Soccorso leads along the rio past the huge **Palazzo Zenobio**, now an Armenian college (undergoing a lengthy restoration; admission sometimes granted on request). Built at the end of the 17C to a design by Antonio Gaspari, it contains a fine ballroom. On the other side of the rio is the Gothic **Palazzo Arian** (no. 2376; now a school), opposite the end of Rio San Sebastiano. The remarkable six-light window has a double row of superimposed quatrefoils with fine tracery and two plutei.

San Sebastiano

Fondamenta San Sebastiano leads down to Ponte San Sebastiano, dated 1698, beside the church of San Sebastiano (open 10.00–18.00; fest. 10.00–15.00. Pl. 6; 8), rebuilt after 1506 by Scarpagnino, and decorated in 1555–70 by Paolo Veronese for Fra Bernardo Torlioni.

Interior. In the panels of the beautiful ceiling is the *Story of Esther* (1555–56) by Veronese, and *Prophets, Apostles, and Evangelists*, with charming decoration by his brother Benedetto Caliari. Over the altar beneath the gallery,

St Nicholas of Bari, by Titian (1563), painted when he was in his mid-seventies.

In the church proper: **south side**, second altar, Tommaso Lombardo, *Madonna and Child with the young St John*, a marble group; beyond the third altar, the huge tomb of archbishop Podocattaro of Cyprus (d. 1555) by Sansovino. In the **choir** are more *paintings by Veronese; over the altar, also designed by Veronese, *Madonna and Child with St Sebastian* (c 1570); left wall, *St Sebastian encourages Saints Mark and Marcellian to Martyrdom* (c 1565); right wall, *Second Martyrdom of St Sebastian*. The **Lando Chapel** to the north of the choir has a rare majolica faience pavement of c 1510. The tomb of Paolo Veronese (d. 1588) and his brother Benedetto Caliari (d. 1598) is set in the floor in front. There is also a bust of Paolo on the wall. The organ, by Francesco Fiorentino and Domenico da Treviso (1558), was designed by Veronese who painted the panels. Beneath it a door admits to the **sacristy** (closed for restoration), with a panelled and painted ceiling, one of the earliest of Veronese's works in Venice (1555). The fine series of paintings (including a *Resurrection*) are by Brusasorci and Bonifacio Veronese.

The **nuns' choir** (at present closed) has frescoes of the *Trial and Martyrdom of St Sebastian* by Veronese and his brother. On the **north side**, third altar; Veronese, *Madonna, St Catherine, and the friar Michele Spaventi*, a small work dating from c 1560–70 (and restored in 1996). The chapel also contains fine sculpture by Alessandro Vittoria (bust of Marcantonio Grimani, and statuettes of St Mark, and St Anthony Abbot).

Paolo Veronese

Paolo Veronese, born in Verona in 1528, was one of the great painters of the 16C and he decorated numerous villas in the Veneto. He moved to Venice in 1555 where he carried out many works for Palazzo Ducale, although his art is perhaps best understood here in his local parish church (he lived in the neighbouring salizzada), where he is also buried. Although a devout Catholic, he was particularly interested in profane subjects and his elegant colourful figures are often sumptuously dressed. The atmosphere in his works is usually serene, in contrast to the more dramatic scenes produced by his contemporary Tintoretto. He influenced a great many artists, including Giambattista Tiepolo.

A short way farther north, across two campi, is the church of the **Angelo Raffaele** (Pl. 6; 8). Over the door is a sculptured Tobias, Angel and dog attributed to Sebastiano Mariani da Lugano. The dark **interior** (closed for restoration) was designed on a Greek-cross plan in 1618, by Francesco Contino. The organ bears paintings of *Tobias and the Angel* by Francesco or Giovanni Antonio Guardi. On the west wall are two paintings of the *Last Supper*, one by Bonifazio Veronese.

Behind the church, in Campo dell'Angelo Raffaele is a well-head in Istrian stone dated 1349. A merchant called Marco Arian left funds in his will for its erection to provide fresh water for the district. He died in 1348 of the plague, believing that the outbreak of the epidemic could have been caused by contaminated water.

On the oppostie side of the rio, Fondamenta Barbarigo leads through an area traditionally inhabited by fishermen and sailors towards the church of **San Nicolò dei Mendicoli** (Pl. 6; 7; open 10.00–12.00, 16.00–18.00). Founded in the 7C, it was subsequently rebuilt and restored. It has a well preserved detached 12C campanile, and a little 15C porch (entrance on the north side). The charming **interior** retains its 12C Veneto-Byzantine plan, with fine columns (the capitals were replaced in the 14C). In the **nave**, the interesting gilded wooden sculptural decoration was added in the late 16C, and the fine series of paintings commissioned in 1553 from Alvise dal Friso and other pupils of Paolo Veronese. In the apse is a wooden statue of the titular saint, by the school of Bon. A tondo of *St Nicholas in Glory* by Francesco Montemezzano, is in the ceiling and, on either side, *Miracles of St Nicholas*, by Leonardo Corona. Outside is the little Oratorio di San Filippo Neri.

On the other side of the canal, a former cotton factory has been converted into lecture halls by the department of architecture at Venice University (IUAV). On its roof, conspicuous from the Giudecca canal, is a sculpture (huge wooden wings) by Massimo Scolari (1991). The university may also use the nearby disused church of **Le Terese** and its ex-convent (facing Rio delle Terese), when they have been restored. The church was completed in 1688 on a design by Andrea Cominelli.

The huge **Stazione Marittima**, or maritime station at **San Basilio**, has been closed for decades by the Port Authority, but this area is due to become more accessible to the public. Old warehouses on the waterfront are to be demolished and a new building erected, designed by the Catalan architect Enric Miralles Moya (who died in 2000), for Venice University.

At present, in order to leave this remote part of the city, it is best to return to San Sebastiano (see above), and follow the fondamenta along the rio and out to the Zattere and the Giudecca canal on the waterfront. The ex-Scuola dei Luganegheri (grocers' confraternity) is on the Zattere. Restored in 1683, it has a charming statue of St Anthony Abbot, with his pig, on the façade.

15 • The Rialto and Santa Maria dei Miracoli

The district around the famous Rialto bridge is always very busy with Venetians and tourists, much as it was in the time of the Republic. The Rialto markets, where most Venetians seem to do their food shopping, are extremely colourful and the produce particularly good (especially the fish). Behind the market stalls are two churches, San Giacomo di Rialto, which preserves its ancient Byzantine plan, and San Giovanni Elemosinario, which has, however, been closed for many years. On the other side of the bridge near the crowded Campo San Bartolomeo the two little churches of San Lio and Santa Maria della Fava are well worth a visit for their Venetian works.

Also near Campo San Bartolomeo, in a district where Marco Polo lived, is the little Renaissance church of San Giovanni Crisostomo, which contains good works by Sebastiano del Piombo and Giovanni Bellini. The church of Santi Apostoli has an interesting interior. The little church of Santa Maria dei Miracoli is one of the most beautiful buildings in Venice. Built beside a canal in the late 15C by Pietro Lombardo it is an exquisite architectural work with superb marble decoration, inlay and carving both on the exterior and interior, recently carefully restored.

The **Rialto bridge** (Pl. 8; 2; see Ch. 4) stands at the topographical centre of the city. A bridge has existed at this point since earliest times, and it remained the only bridge across the Grand Canal throughout the Republic. The area known as the Rialto (*rivo alto*, high bank) is thought to have been one of the first places to be settled by the earliest inhabitants of the lagoon because it was one of the highest points and the best protected. Since the beginning of the Republic it has been the commercial and economic centre of Venice. The markets, established here as early as 1097, were reconstructed by Scarpagnino along the lines of the medieval buildings, after a disastrous fire in 1514. Remains of the quay of the 14C market were discovered beneath the present markets during maintenance work in 1999 (since covered over).

The walkways of the Rialto bridge descend past the 16C Palazzo dei Camerlenghi (see p 131) and the east end of San Giacomo di Rialto (see below), with a 12C inscription exhorting merchants to honesty. The busy **Ruga degli Orefici**, where the goldsmiths had their workshops, leads through the colourful market in front of the porticoed **Fabbriche Vecchie**, by Scarpagnino. These buildings also extend around the Campo San Giacomo.

Here, amidst the stalls and barrows, is the little church of **San Giacomo di Rialto** (San Giacometto; Pl. 8; 2; open 09.00–12.00, 16.00–18.00), once thought to have been founded in the year 421 and so considered to be the oldest church in Venice. It is, instead, first documented in 1152 and so probably dates from that century. It is preceded by a Gothic entrance portico; above is a large clock of 1410. The domed Greek-cross plan on a tiny scale, derived from Byzantine models, was faithfully preserved in the rebuilding of 1601. The interior retains its six ancient reused Greek marble columns with finely carved 11C Corinthian capitals and pulvins, also in Greek marble. Over the high altar, statues of *St James and angels* by Alessandro Vittoria (1602), and on the right, *Annunciation*, by Marco Vecellio.

Across the campo is the 16C **Gobbo di Rialto** by Pietro da Salò, a crouching figure which supports a flight of steps leading to a rostrum of Egyptian granite from which the laws of the Republic were proclaimed. Behind the Fabbriche Vecchie, the **Erberia**, the wholesale market for fruit and vegetables, opens onto the Grand Canal, adjoined by Sansovino's Fabbriche Nuove (see p 131) and the markets which extend along the canal to the fish market (see below).

At the end of Ruga degli Orefici, in the broad Ruga Vecchia San Giovanni (left), an archway forms the inconspicuous entrance to **San Giovanni Elemosinario** (Pl. 8; 1, 2), the first church to be built in the Rialto area (mentioned as early as 1051), which still has its campanile of 1398–1410. After the Rialto fire of 1514 it was rebuilt by Scarpagnino in 1527–29. It has been closed for years for restoration.

In the **interior**, on a Greek-cross plan, the frescoes on the cupola by Pordenone were discovered under a thin layer of plaster in 1985. More frescoes have been found in the porch. The high altarpiece of *St John the Almsgiver* was painted for the church by Titian (c 1545). In the chapel to the right of the main chapel, *Saints Catherine, Sebastian, and Roch*, by Pordenone; on the left wall of the church, *Doge Leonardo Donà receiving the Holy Water from the parish priest of the church*, by Marco Vecellio. The church also contains various works by Leonardo Corona and Palma Giovane (including a lunette of *St Roch healing the Plague-stricken*). During work on the pavement some 15C painted tombs have been discovered, including that of the philosopher Paolo della Pergola (d. 1455).

Ruga dei Spezieri (where spices were sold), continues the line of Ruga degli Orefici into Campo delle Beccarie with the arcaded hall of the neo-Gothic

Pescheria (see p 131), scene of the busy daily fish market. From here, across a bridge set at an angle, and beneath a covered passageway, the wide Calle dei Botteri is soon reached and the market area left behind.

On the other side of the Rialto bridge (see above) steps descend to the Salizzada Pio X. In the calle on the right is the inconspicuous entrance to the church of **San Bartolomeo** (Pl. 8; 4; rebuilt in 1723 by Giovanni Scalfarotto; closed to worship). It is now used by a musical society which gives concerts here and charge an entrance fee to see its relatively uninteresting private museum of musical instruments. The concerts are heavily adverstised but are not of the standard of the other concerts held all over the city (see p 53). This was formerly the church of the German community in Venice, and Dürer painted his famous *Madonna of the Rosary* (now in Prague) for the church when he was in the city in 1506, and it shows the influence of Paolo Veneziano and Giovanni Bellini. He made two visits to Venice, the first in 1494–95, and the second in 1505–07, and from his letters we know that he was struck by the great respect shown to him and other artists at work in the city at that time. At the foot of the campanile is an amusing grotesque mask. The Salizzada ends in **Campo San Bartolomeo** (Pl. 8; 4), the crowded business centre of Venice. It is at the crossroads of the city. The spirited statue of Goldoni, the dramatist of Venetian life, is by Antonio dal Zotto (1883).

Behind and to the right of the statue, Sottoportego della Bissa leads across a wide bridge to the church of **San Lio** (Pl. 9; 3; usually opened by a custodian 09.00–12.00, exc. fest., or ☎ 041 520 5355), dedicated to Pope Leo IX (1049–54).

In the rectangular **interior** the ceiling *painting (in good condition, restored in 1983) of *St Leo in Glory* surrounded by *Angels* and the *Cardinal Virtues* in monochrome is by Gian Domenico Tiepolo. The organ (above the west door) bears paintings by the 18C Venetian school. High up at the end of the **right wall** (difficult to see) is a *Pietà*, attributed to Liberale da Verona, in an elaborate sculpted frame. The domed **Gussoni Chapel** (right of the high altar; being restored), with lovely sculptural details (including a marble relief of the *Pietà*), is thought to be an early work by Pietro Lombardo (possibly with the help of Tullio Lombardo). On the left wall of the pretty **sanctuary** there is a large *Crucifixion* by Pietro Muttoni, which was an ex voto for the plague of 1630. The early 17C silver high altar is to be restored, and the high altarpiece of the *Deposition* is by Palma Giovane. On the left pilaster of the sanctuary is a Byzantine *Madonna and Child*. Over the first left altar is a painting of *St James Major* by Titian.

Calle della Fava leads south to the church of **Santa Maria della Fava** (or Santa Maria della Consolazione; Pl. 9; 3), begun in 1705 by Antonio Gaspari, and completed by Giorgio Massari. In the delightful **interior** the nave is decorated with statues in niches by Giuseppe Torretto, Canova's master. On the first altar on the south wall is an early work (1732) by Giambattista Tiepolo, the *Education of the Virgin*, and on the second altar on the north wall is the *Madonna and St Philip Neri*, by Giovanni Battista Piazzetta.

From the bridge over Rio della Fava can be seen (left) the Gothic façade of Palazzo Giustinian-Faccanon, which faces Palazzo Gussoni, a building by the school of the Lombardo family (late 15C). Calle dei Stagneri leads directly back to Campo San Bartolomeo and the Rialto.

The salizzada behind the statue of Goldoni skirts the back of the huge

Fondaco dei Tedeschi (Pl. 8; 2) which faces the Grand Canal. This was the most important of the trading centres on the Grand Canal leased by the Venetians to foreign merchants. By the mid-13C the Germans, Austrians, Bohemians, and Hungarians had their warehouses, shops, offices, and lodgings here. The severe commercial building, devoid of marble or carved decorations, was reconstructed after the fire of 1505 by Giorgio Spavento and completed by Scarpagnino from the designs of Girolamo Tedesco. Giorgione was commissioned to fresco the main façade, and Titian the side façade (on Calle del Fontego): the frescoes have entirely disappeared, although fragments survive in the Ca' d'Oro. The building is now the central post office.

There is a good view (left) of the arch of the Rialto bridge at the end of a calle. As you cross the Ponte dell'Olio (rebuilt in 1899), with its marble columns and iron balustrade, you leave the Sestiere di San Marco and enter that of Cannaregio. From the bridge there are views (left), across the Grand Canal, to the corner of Palazzo dei Camerlenghi, the brick tower of San Giacomo, and the beginning of the Rialto markets.

San Giovanni Crisostomo

The busy salizzada soon reaches San Giovanni Crisostomo (Pl. 8; 2), which almost fills its small campo. It was rebuilt after serious damage by fire and is dedicated to St John Chrysostom, a famous 4C preacher who became Patriarch of Constantinople and revised the Greek Liturgy. A book which supposedly belonged to him was brought to Venice from Constantinople as a holy relic to be preserved in San Marco. The church is the last work of Mauro Codussi (1497–1504), a masterpiece of Venetian Renaissance architecture.

The **interior** (open 08.15–12.15, 15.00–19.00; fest. 10.00–12.30, 15.30–19.00) of the church, much visited by worshippers, is on a Greek-cross plan of Byzantine inspiration. Over the high altar, *San Giovanni Crisostomo with six Saints* (1510–11), by Sebastiano del Piombo.

South side. Above the side door are four small paintings from the old organ, attributed to Girolamo da Santacroce. The marble bust of the **Madonna delle Grazie** is highly venerated (the church became the Santuario della Madonna delle Grazie in 1977). First altar, *Saints Christopher, Jerome, and Louis of Toulouse*, a beautiful painting by Giovanni Bellini. Second altar, **Death of St Joseph**, by Johann Karl Loth.

North side. Second altar, classical bas-relief of the **Coronation of the Virgin** by Tullio Lombardo, and (above) a Veneto-Byzantine relief of the **Madonna in prayer**. First altar, **St Anthony of Padua**, by a follower of Vivarini. Above the west door, four organ doors by Giovanni Mansueti.

Calle Dolfin begins across the bridge; beyond a campiello it continues (with a view at the end of the campanile of Santi Apostoli) to a rio with a huge stone bearing a long 18C inscription set up by the Bakers' Guild, forbidding the making or selling of bread in the city by anyone who was not a member of the guild. To the left the portico of Palazzo Falier leads on to Ponte Santi Apostoli. The Veneto-Byzantine palace (seen from the bridge) dates from the end of the 13C and is a characteristic merchant's house of the period. It is traditionally thought to be home of Doge Marin Falier, executed in 1355 for treason, by order of the Council of Ten.

Santi Apostoli

In the pleasant campo is the church of Santi Apostoli (Pl. 4; 8), much rebuilt, which has a tall campanile of 1672 (the bell was restored in 1998). In the **interior** (open 07.30–12.00, 17.00–19.00), the ceiling paintings are by Fabio Canal and Carlo Gaspari (1748). **South side**. The Cappella Corner is an interesting Lombardesque work (late 15C) attributed to Mauro Codussi. Over the altar is the *Communion of St Lucy*, by Giambattista Tiepolo (c 1748), and to the right and left are the tombs of Marco Corner (attributed to Tullio Lombardo) and Giorgio Corner (school of the Lombardi).

The **sanctuary** has an early 19C altar by Francesco Lazzari, which incorporates statues of Saints Peter and Paul by Il Torretto (1711). The two large paintings here are by the school of Veronese (*Fall of Manna*), and Cesare da Conegliano (*Last Supper*, 1583). Interesting remains of early 14C frescoes (*Deposition* and *Entombment*), showing Byzantine influence, have been removed for restoration. The marble relief of the head of *St Sebastian* is by Tullio Lombardo. In the chapel to the left of the sanctuary, Francesco Maffei, *Guardian Angel*, and a high relief of the *Madonna and Child*, a charming 15C work (attributed to Niccolò di Pietro Lamberti). The first altarpiece on the **north side** of *St Jerome and Saints* is by Domenico Maggiotto.

In the wide, busy shopping street, **Strada Nuova** (Pl. 4; 8; opened in 1871) is the former Scuola dell'Angelo Custode (now the Lutheran Evangelical Church), with a façade by Andrea Tirali (1714). Campo Santa Sofia opens out on to the Grand Canal with the gondola ferry over to the Rialto markets. The church of **Santa Sofia** (open 09.00–12.00), with a squat brick campanile, is hidden behind the house fronts. It contains four statues of saints (on the west wall and on the high altar), by Antonio Rizzo. The Ca' d'Oro on the other side of the Strada Nova is described in Ch. 16.

Behind the church of Santi Apostoli (see above) Calle Manganer leads out of the Campiello della Chiesa into the Campiello della Cason (where Agnello Particiaco lived as doge in 811–827). Calle della Malvasia leads to a bridge with an iron parapet. At the end of the canal (right) stands Palazzo Falier (see above). Beyond is the church of **San Canciano**, of ancient foundation, rebuilt in the 18C. By the brick campanile is an old house with a low portico. Adjacent is Campiello Santa Maria Nova where Palazzo Bembo-Boldu, with tall Gothic windows, bears a relief of a bearded figure holding a solar disc.

Santa Maria dei Miracoli

To the left opens a larger campo bordered by a canal with the church of Santa Maria dei Miracoli (Pl. 9; 1), a masterpiece of the Renaissance by Pietro Lombardo (1481–89), sumptuously decorated with splendid marble inlay both inside and out, and beautifully restored in 1987–98.

It was built in this confined site, with its north side set directly on a canal, because there was a shrine here in the 15C with a painting of the Madonna which was held to be miraculous. It has a single, unusually tall, nave and barrel-vaulted roof, with a high domed apse and tiny attached campanile. A great variety of marble, including *pavonazzetto*, red Verona marble, white Carrara marble, and *cipollino* was used in the elegant polychrome inlay in geometric designs. The exquisite carved friezes are decorated with shields, helmets, arms, griffins, and marine creatures, as well as numerous classical motifs. The **exterior** is divided in two orders, with pilasters below and, above an architrave, a blind arcade. At the top of the well proportioned façade is a semi-circular gable which follows the curve of the roof and is decorated with a rose window, smaller oculi, and marble tondi. In the lunette above the door is a 16C Madonna by Giorgio Lascaris.

The **interior** (open daily 10.00–18.00; fest. 15.00–18.00) is as beautiful as the exterior, with marble walls and a raised choir and domed apse. The nuns' choir at the west end is supported by beautifully carved pillars. The nave barrel vault is adorned with fifty panels bearing heads of prophets and saints painted by Pier Maria Pennacchi (1528). Preceded by a pretty marble balustrade, with fine half-length figures probably by Tullio Lombardo, is the *choir, with more exquisite carving by Pietro and his son Tullio Lombardo. On the high altar is a charming *Madonna* by Niccolò di Pietro Paradisi (1409), the painting for which the church was built.

Calle Castelli leads away from the church and emerges on Fondamenta Sanudo (named after the famous 16C Venetian diarist). To the left is the fine Gothic door-way of **Palazzo Vanier Sanudo Van Axel**, with Gothic and Veneto-Byzantine elements on its handsome canal façade. One of the most important late-Gothic palaces in the city, it was built for Marco and Agostino Soranzo in 1479, and was owned by the Van Axel in the 17C and restored by Dino Barozzi in 1920. Across the wide Ponte delle Erbe it is a short distance to Santi Giovanni e Paolo (see p 144). Ponte del Cristo stands at the junction of three canals. On the left is the white façade of Palazzo Marcello-Papadopoli, attributed to Longhena; and to the right is the 15C Gothic façade of Palazzo Pisani, with fine balconies.

Calle del Cristo leads into Campo Santa Marina where a high archway connects the symmetrical wings of a former palace. From the end of the campo (right), Sottoportego and Calle Scaletta lead to Ponte Marco Polo. Opposite, on the curve of the canal, is the Gothic Palazzo Bragadin Carabba. A plaque records that Marco Polo lived in this area. Here is the side entrance to the **Teatro Malibran** (Pl. 9; 1), the successor to the theatre of San Giovanni Crisostomo, built in 1677 and the largest and most famous theatre in Europe for music in the 17C and early 18C. In 1707 two operas by Alessandro Scarlatti were put on here and in 1709 Handel's *Agrippina* had its première here (in the presence of the composer); it was a major success. After restoration, the theatre was reopened in 1819 with Gioachino Rossini's *La Gazza Ladra*. In 1835 Maria Malibran, the Spanish mezzo-soprano sang here in Vincenzo Bellini's *Sonnambula* the year before her death (aged 28) and the theatre was subsequently named after her. It was reopened in 2001 and is used by the Fenice.

A sottoportico leads into two courtyards; they bear Marco Polo's nickname which is derived from the fact that his contemporaries thought he always talked in 'millions' and exaggerated in his description of his travels in the East. The **Corte Seconda del Milion** is surrounded by ancient houses which bear 12C–15C elements, and a Byzantine *arch (possibly 12C), richly carved with animals and birds.

Beyond Corte Prima del Milion lies San Giovanni Crisostomo and the salizzada which returns across Ponte dell'Olio to the Rialto bridge.

Marco Polo

Marco Polo (1254–1324) came from a merchant family; his father was one of three brothers who travelled regularly to the East. Marco accompanied his father and uncle in 1271 on an overland journey which took four years from Trebizond on the Black Sea, through Persia, Tibet, and the Gobi desert to Peking. He was employed at the court of the Mongol ruler, Kublai Khan, grandson of Genghis Khan for 17 years, being sent as envoy throughout the Empire from Siberia to Southern India and Japan. He returned to Venice by sea along the coast of China and India. In 1298 he was taken prisoner by the Genoese in the Battle of Cursola, and during a year's imprisonment he dictated to a fellow prisoner, Rusticello di Pisa, a superb description of the world he had seen on his travels. This was probably the first description of Asia ever to reach the west and remained the most accurate for many centuries. His book was well known in Europe in the Middle Ages.

16 • The Ca' d'Oro and the Gesuiti

The Ca' d'Oro has a landing-stage on the Grand Canal and can be reached by foot in a few minutes from the Rialto. This splendid Gothic palace houses one of the most important musuems in the city, extremely well kept. It has a very fine ollection of Venetian sculpture (15C and early 16C), a masterpiece by Mantegna, and a large collection of paintings, detached frescoes, small bronzes and ceramics. The views of the Grand Canal from the palace windows are superb.

The church of the Gesuiti is in a remote part of the city close to the Fondamenta Nuove, from which there is a view across the lagoon: opposite is the island of Murano, and (right) the cemetery island of San Michele. On the extreme right can be seen the campanile and dome of San Pietro di Castello and the Arsenal buildings. The landing-stages here (to the left, and to the right across Rio dei Gesuiti) are served by vaporetto nos. 51, 52, 41 and 42, and the services for Burano, and Torcello. The Baroque church of the Gesuiti has elaborate Venetian marble decorations and the paintings include the Martyrdom of St Lawrence by Titian. Close by is the Oratorio dei Crociferi (closed in winter) with a cycle of paintings by Palma Giovane.

Ca' d'Oro

From the Strada Nova (see p 190) the inconspicuous Calle della Ca' d'Oro leads to the Ca' d'Oro (Pl. 4; 7). Open 08.15–19.15; Mon 08.15–14.00. The rooms are not numbered, but the description below follows the plan on p 195.

Famous as the most beautiful Gothic palace in Venice, it was built between 1420 and 1434 for the procurator of San Marco, Marino Contarini, who pre-served elements of the previous Veneto-Byzantine Palazzo Zeno on this site. It is the work of Matteo Raverti and Lombard collaborators, and of Giovanni and Bartolomeo Bon. It received its name (the 'Golden House') from the bright polychrome and gilded decoration carried out in 1431 by the French painter Jean Charlier, which used to adorn the sculptural details of its façade (best seen from the Grand Canal, see Ch. 4). The façade was restored in 1996.

Having been poorly renovated in 1840, the palace was carefully restored by Baron Giorgio Franchetti in 1894, who presented it to the State in 1916, together with his collection of paintings and antiquities which constitute the Galleria Franchetti. It was first opened to the public in 1927 and works from the Accademia and other state collections are also housed here. The collection of Venetian sculpture is particularly beautiful. Palazzo Duodo, which adjoins the palace on the Grand Canal, has been restored to house part of the collection.

Ca' d'Oro

A small door beside the main gateway gives access to the **ticket office**. Beyond is a charming little **entrance court** with a 15C well. Adjoining is the lovely **portico** (closed in winter), through which the house was approached from the canal, with the water-gate and an outside stair. The Greek marble columns have beautiful Veneto-Byzantine and Romanesque capitals. The mosaic pavement was added by Franchetti. The *well-head, by Bartolomeo Bon (1427) is decorated with figures of Charity, Justice, and Fortitude. The other sculptures here include 16C and classical works. The museum is beautifully maintained.

First floor

This consists of an anteroom with an alcove, and a *portego*, extending towards the canal, with rooms on either side. **Anteroom** (1) Veneto-Byzantine sculptural fragments; an interesting fragmentary sculpted group of the *Massacre of the Innocents*, thought to be the work of the Veneto school c 1350; Antonio Vivarini (and his school), polyptych from the convent of Corpus Domini; alabaster scenes of the *Life of St Catherine* (English, 16C); seated statue in terracotta of the *Madonna* attributed to Andrea Briosco (Il Riccio). The **alcove**, or chapel (2) with a richly decorated 15C ceiling, was created by Franchetti for the most precious piece in his collection, *St Sebastian, by Mantegna, one of the last works by this remarkable painter (1506). The **portego** (3) has a very fine collection of *Venetian sculpture: Antonio Rizzo (?), female statuette, called *Rhetoric* (but perhaps representing an angel); Tullio Lombardo, double *portrait bust of a young couple*. There follows a series of very fine bronze reliefs: Andrea Briosco, *St Martin and the Beggar*, four scenes of the *Legend of the True Cross*, and a door of a tabernacle, all from the church of Santa Maria dei Servi; *Assumption* and *Coronation of the Virgin*, early 16C works from the funerary monument of the Doges Marco and Agostino Barbarigo in Santa Maria della Carità; Vittore Gambello, two *Battle Scenes* (also from Santa Maria della Carità). On the pedestal: *bust of a boy* attributed to Gian Cristoforo Romano. On the wall: 15C marble relief of the *Death of Portia* by Giovanni Maria Mosca; and a life-like marble bust of Matteo dai Letti, a parish priest of San Gemignano (d. 1523) attributed to Bartolomeo di Francesco Bergamasco. On the opposite wall, *Last Supper* (unfinished) attributed to Tullio Lombardo (formerly in the crypt of Santa Maria dei Miracoli), a copy of Leonardo's work; Girolamo Campagna, bronze andirons with Venus and Adonis;

school of Jacopo Sansovino, lunette of the Madonna and Child from the Zitelle.

To the right of the *portego* are three smaller rooms. **Room 4** has painted *Madonnas* by Michele Giambono, Francesco dei Franceschi (attibuted), and Alvise Vivarini (attributed). In the case: bronze statuette of **Apollo* by l'Antico. The *Madonna dagli occhi belli* is by Giovanni Bellini or Lazzaro Bastiani, and the *Madonna and Child* in a landscape is by the 16C Venetian school. The *Christ between the Virgin and St John* has recently been attributed to Francesco Bonsignori. In a case **medals* by l'Antico, Gentile Bellini, Vittore Gambello, Leone Leoni, Pisanello, Matteo de' Pasti, and Bertoldo di Giovanni (attributed) are displayed. These double-sided small medallions in bronze, were cast to celebrate rulers, military leaders, Humanists, important buildings or events. Modelled on Roman coins, they often have a portrait head in profile. Italian Renaissance medals are particularly famous for their exquisite workmanship.

Room 5 has three cases of small bronzes, including Paduan and Florentine works, and paintings by Benedetto Diana and Carpaccio (including the *Annunciation*, which was one of six scenes from the *Life of the Virgin* which once decorated the Scuola degli Albanesi). **Room 6**. Small bronzes, andirons by Roccatagliata; two 16C Venetian tondi in bronze with portraits of Agostino Angeli da Pesaro and his son, the scientist, Girolamo. There is a striking bronze bust of Giampietro Mantova Benavides (d. 1520) by an unknown Paduan sculptor, based on his death mask. On the loggia overlooking the Grand Canal there is a 13C lion. A small room dedicated to Franchetti, illustrates the history of the palace and its restoration.

Off the left side of the *portego* is **room 7** with non-Venetian paintings of the 14C–16C by Carlo Braccesco, Andrea di Bartolo, Francesco Botticini, Raffaellino del Garbo (**Madonna in Adoration of the Child and two Angels*), Biagio d'Antonio and Antoniazzo Romano. The tiny **Flagellation* is by Luca Signorelli. The front of a 15C Florentine dower-chest shows the *Victory of Alexander*, and the *Construction of Alexandria*.

In **room 8,** with a *Madonna and Child and two Angel musicians* probably by Bernardino Zaganelli; there is a splendid 15C carved wooden staircase.

Second floor

In **room 9**, at the top of the stairs are works attributed to Giuliano Bugiardini, Girolamo Macchietti, and Pontormo (*Young Girl with a dog*). The *Young Man with a letter* is by Franciabigio. **Room 10** is a large room hung with 16C Flemish tapestries. Jacopo Tintoretto, *Portrait of the Procurator Nicolò Priuli*; Alessandro Vittoria, busts of the *Procurator Giovanni Donà*, of **Benedetto Manzini*, the parish priest of San Gemignano, the Procurator *Marino Grimani*, the Procurator *Domenico Duodo*, and *Francesco Duodo*. Titian, *Venus;* Van Dyck, **Portrait of a Gentleman*; Paris Bordone, *Sleeping Venus and Cupid*.

In the **portego** (11) are detached **frescoes* (very damaged) from the cloister of Santo Stefano by Pordenone (c 1532: *Expulsion from Paradise, Christ appearing to Mary Magdalen*, and *Christ and the Samaritan*). Among the frescoes attributed to Domenico Campagnola, particularly interesting are the three figures in niches of *Hope, Temperance*, and *Charity*, and nudes and putti.

Two rooms in **Palazzo Duodo** (reached from the loggia) contain a well displayed collection of ceramics. The **first room (16)** has finds from recent excavations in the lagoon, including local ceramics of the 13C–14C (the pieces from Malamocco are particularly interesting). The **second room (18)** contains the Luigi Conton

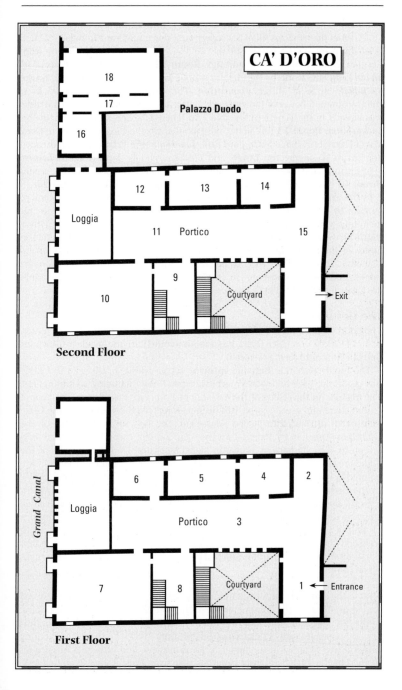

CA' D'ORO

Palazzo Duodo

18
17
16

Loggia

12   13   14

11   Portico   15

9

10   Courtyard   → Exit

Second Floor

Grand Canal

Loggia

6   5   4   2

Portico   3

7   8   Courtyard   1   ← Entrance

First Floor

collection, with more ceramics (mostly 15C–17C) from the lagoon, acquired in 1978. From the windows there is a superb view down the Grand Canal.

To the right of the *portego* in the Ca'd'Oro are three smaller rooms with German, Dutch and Flemish paintings. **Room 12**. Antonio Mor (?), *Portrait of an old Lady*, and works by the Flemish school. Jan van Scorel (attributed), *Tower of Babel*; circle of Dürer, *Deposition*. The *Crucifixion* is attributed to a collaborator or follower of Jan van Eyck. It was painted some time after 1430 and was already in the Veneto by the mid 15C. There is a view of Jerusalem in the background. **Room 13** has a charming painted wood ceiling attributed to Gian Maria Falconetto (15C–16C). Paul Brill, *Jonah and the Whale*, and landscapes and genre scenes by the Dutch and Flemish schools. Jan Steen, *Alchemist* (1668). In a case, Gabriel Metsu, *Sleeping Woman*; Jan Steen, *Interior scene*. **Room 14** has more Flemish works, and a *Seascape* by Willem II Van de Velde.

In the **anteroom (15)** at the end of the *portego* are interesting fragments of frescoes by Giorgione and Titian from the façade of the Fondaco dei Tedeschi, including a *Female nude* by Giorgione, and, by Titian, two fragments with a *Battle between giants and monsters* (from a frieze along the side façade), and the figure of *Judith* (or Justice?). A case contains terracotta models (*bozzetti*) by Giacomo Piazzetta, Gian Lorenzo Bernini (for his fountain in Piazza Navona in Rome), and Stefano Maderno. The two Venetian views of the Piazzetta and Molo are generally attributed to Francesco Guardi.

The Gesuiti

The church of the Gesuiti (Santa Maria Assunta; Pl. 5; 5), rebuilt for the Jesuits in 1714–29 by Domenico Rossi, has a monumental Baroque façade by Giovanni Battista Fattoretto (being restored).

The highly elaborate Baroque **interior** (open 10.00–12.00, 17.00–19.00) has decorative grey and white marble intarsia (inlay) imitating wall hangings. The frescoes on the ceiling of the nave are by Francesco Fontebasso. The floor of Istrian stone and green marble has been restored. On the west wall is the Lezze monument attributed to Jacopo Sansovino. The first south altarpiece of the *Guardian Angel* is by Palma Giovane, and on the second south altar is a sculpture of St Barbara by Giovanni Maria Morleiter. On the four piers of the dome are statues of archangels by Giuseppe Torretto; the tondi in the vault are painted by Ludovico Dorigny. The fantastic high altar is by Giuseppe Pozzo (18C). In the chapel to the right of the sanctuary, *St Francis Xavier*, by Pietro Liberi. Over the door into the sacristy, monument to Doge Pasquale Cicogna, with a fine effigy by Girolamo Campagna. The sacristy is entirely decorated with paintings by Palma Giovane in celebration of the Eucharist (1589–90). In the north transept, the *Assumption* is an early work by Jacopo Tintoretto. On the first north altar is the *Martyrdom of St Lawrence*, by Titian, a remarkable night scene (1548–59).

Next to the church is the former monastery (with a good cloister), being restored for use as offices by the Comune. Some of the houses were built at the beginning of the 20C. Opposite, with four tall chimneys, is the little **Oratorio dei Crociferi** (Pl. 5; 5; open 1 April–31 Oct Thur, Fri, Sat only 10.00–13.00). The adjoining hospital was founded in the mid-12C for crusaders, and became a hospice for women in the 14C. It received generous help from Doge Ranier Zeno in 1268.

The chapel, dating from 1582, with a relief of the Madonna and Child enthroned over the door, contains an interesting cycle of *paintings by Palma Giovane (1583–92), illustrating the history of the hospital.

From Campo dei Gesuiti a bridge leads over Rio di Santa Caterina to the Salizzada Seriman where the fine 15C Palazzo Contarini Seriman (no. 4851) is now a convent school. The interior (admission on request) contains a staircase with a fresco by the school of Tiepolo and an alcove with stuccoes by Tencala.

From Campo dei Gesuiti Fondamenta Zen leads along the attractive Rio di Santa Caterina in a peaceful area of the city past the huge Palazzo Zen (nos 4922–4924) with its balconies (in poor repair), designed by Francesco Zen (d. 1538). The Zen family included Nicolò and Antonio, famous seafarers in the 15C. Fondamenta Santa Caterina continues to the church of **Santa Caterina** (Pl. 4; 6), now deconsecrated and used as a store; the ship's keel roof, destroyed by fire in 1977, has been rebuilt. From the bridge the Campo dell'Abbazia can be seen to the left (see Ch. 20).

17 • Campo San Polo

This chapter describes the district near the large and peaceful Campo San Polo. Here the church is interesting especially for its painting of the *Last Supper* by Jacopo Tintoretto and the works by Gian Domenico Tiepolo in the Oratory of the Crucifix. Close by is the Casa Goldoni where Carlo Goldoni lived, normally open to the public but at present closed. In Campo San Tomà can be seen a charming little relief above the former entrance to the Scuola dei Calegheri.

From the foot of the Rialto bridge (see Ch. 15) Fondamenta del Vin (Pl. 8; 4) skirts the Grand Canal as far as Rio terrà San Silvestro which leads away from the water-front.

The *rio terrà* passes a column with an 11C capital (set in to the wall of a house) before reaching (left) the church of **San Silvestro** (Pl. 8; 3), with a façade completed in 1909. The neo-Classical interior (open 08.00–11.30, 15.30–18.30) is by Lorenzo Santi. The apse (with the organ on the east wall) is divided from the nave by Corinthian columns. On the right side, the first altar has a *Baptism of Christ* by Jacopo Tintoretto, and the second altar a *Holy Family* by Johann Karl Loth. The first altar on the left side has *St Thomas Becket enthroned* (interesting for its iconography) by Girolamo da Santacroce. On the left wall is a Gothic polyptych in an elaborate 14C frame.

Opposite the church is Palazzo Valier (no. 1022), with a Doric doorway, where Giorgione died in 1510. In the peaceful Campo San Silvestro the fine brick campanile has a stone bas-relief. Calle del Luganegher leads from here to the busy Campo Sant'Aponal with eight calli leading into it. Here is the deconsecrated church of **Sant'Aponal** (Sant'Apollinare; Pl. 8; 1). Founded in the 11C, it was rebuilt in the 15C. On the Gothic façade, above a round window, is a badly worn relief of the Crucifix (14C); below, in a tabernacle, are reliefs of the Crucifixion and episodes from the Life of Christ (1294). It has been closed to worship since 1970 and the interior is used as an archive. To the left, in Calle del Campanile, is the Romanesque campanile.

Calle del Ponte Storto leads to the bridge of the same name; on the right (no.

1280) is the birthplace of Bianca Cappello (c 1560–87), the 'daughter of the Republic' and wife of Francesco de' Medici. Across the canal, the sottoportico continues past an unusually narrow calle to the next bridge which re-crosses the canal. Calle Cavalli soon diverges right and over another bridge, emerging in **Campo San Polo** (Pl. 7; 4). This is one of the largest and most attractive squares in the city and its shape makes it a favourite playground for children. Among the interesting palaces which follow the curved side of the campo (once bordered by a canal) are (no. 1957) the well-proportioned Baroque Palazzo Tiepolo, attributed to Giorgio Massari, and (no. 2169) Palazzo Soranzo, with its marble windows with good capitals.

San Polo

The church of San Polo (Pl. 7; 4) bears interesting reliefs (the earliest dating from the 13C) on the exterior of the east end. The south doorway is a fine Gothic work attributed to Bartolomeo Bon with two angels holding an inscription and crowned by the half-figure of St Paul (removed). Outside the isolated campanile (1362) has two fine Romanesque lions carved at its base.

The **interior**, with a ships' keel roof, is open 10.00–18.00; fest. 15.00–18.00. It was altered in 1804 by Davide Rossi and given a neo-Classical arcade. On the left of the west door, **Last Supper*, by Jacopo Tintoretto (light; fee), one of his best paintings of this subject. On the left side of the south entrance door is an interesting sculptural fragment. Above the high altar is an early 15C Venetian Crucifix, and in the sanctuary are paintings by Palma Giovane. In the left apse chapel, *Marriage of the Virgin*, by Paolo Veronese (light; fee). Left side: third altar, *Preaching of St Paul*, by Paolo Piazza; second altar, *Virgin appearing to a Saint* by Giambattista Tiepolo (1754).

At the west end, beneath the organ by Gaetano Callido (1763) is the entrance to the **Oratory of the Crucifix** (fee; to be restored). The chapel, with an attractive east end, lit by a dome with four columns, has an extraordinary series of **paintings* by Gian Domenico Tiepolo. On the right of the altar, *Miracle of the True Cross*, and *St Joseph*. On the right wall of the nave begins the series of fourteen small paintings of the *Stations of the Cross* (1749), remarkable for their portraits of Venetian 18C society with turbaned oriental figures in colourful robes and elegantly dressed ladies. To the left of the altar, two paintings of *Saints*. In the ceiling have been hung a *Glory of Angels* and *Resurrection*, also fine works by Gian Domenico Tiepolo.

From the north side of the campo, Rio terrà Sant'Antonio and Calle Bernardo lead towards Rio terrà Secondo, where a small Gothic palace (no. 2311) is the traditional site of the Aldine Press set up in 1490 by the Roman scholar and celebrated printer **Aldus Manutius** (1450–1516) on his arrival in Venice in the same year. The first dated book issued from the press is 1494, which became famous for its publication of the Greek classics. Manutius designed the Italic type in 1501, and took advice from his friend Erasmus. Numerous other presses were set up in the city in quick succession, and about a quarter of the 1821 books published in Europe between 1495–97 were produced in Venice. Manuzio's work was carried on at the Press by his son and grandson, and it has been estimated that during the 16C three new books were printed every week in Venice.

From the pretty Ponte San Polo (1775) the main façade, Sanmicheli, of Palazzo

Corner Mocenigo (begun after 1545) can be seen on the canal (right). The writer, Frederick Rolfe, author of *The Desire and Pursuit of the Whole* was an eccentric who lived his last years in Venice, in an apartment here (1909–10), calling himself Baron Corvo. Calle dei Saoneri continues to Rio terrà dei Nomboli. At the end on the left the dark and narrow Ramo Pisani diverges towards the Grand Canal and Palazzo Pisani della Moretta. The fine 18C interior (no admission) has been beautifully restored. The calle ends before reaching Palazzo Barbarigo della Terrazza (with the German Institute) on the Grand Canal. Calle dei Nomboli continues to (no. 2793) Palazzo Centani (15C), known as the **Casa Goldoni** (Pl. 7; 4); the famous playwright, Carlo Goldoni was born here. It has a picturesque Gothic courtyard with a charming staircase and a pretty well-head. The interior (closed for restoration) contains Goldoni memorabilia and the Institute of Theatrical Studies (which has a library and an archive).

Carlo Goldoni

Carlo Goldoni (1707–93) was a prolific writer who produced numerous superb comedies which give a vivid idea of social life in 18C Venice. Not only did he satirise the old Venetian aristocracy, but he described with brilliance the ordinary people of the city. He marked an important stage in the development of theatrical production which up to his time had been dominated by the *Commedia dell'Arte*, improvised drama by professional masked actors. Goldoni worked in several theatres in the city: at San Samuele in 1734–43; and at Sant'Angelo from 1748–53, where he first produced his famous *La Bottega del Caffè* and *La Locandiera*. From 1753 he collaborated with the Teatro San Luca (now called Teatro Goldoni) where he put on other comedies, including *Le Baruffe Chiozzotte*. In 1562 he was invited to Paris where he remained for the rest of his life.

The recently restored canal façade of Casa Goldoni and another picturesque old palace with reliefs and an ancient watergate can be seen from Ponte San Tomà. Beyond Campiello San Tomà (with a relief of the Madonna of the Misericordia) **Campo di San Tomà** (Pl. 7; 4) is soon reached. The church has been closed for restoration of years. Calle del Traghetto leads down to the gondola ferry which crosses the Grand Canal diagonally to the calle near Santo Stefano (see Ch. 10). In Campo San Tomà the 15C **Scuola dei Calegheri** (shoemakers) bears a charming relief of St Mark healing the Cobbler Ananias from the East, attributed to Pietro Lombardo or Antonio Rizzo (1478), and a Madonna of the Misericordia. The building has been restored, and is used as a library.

A calle leads down to the Grand Canal and a vaporetto landing-stage.

18 • The Frari and Scuola Grande di San Rocco

This walk describes two of the most important buildings in Venice, the huge Gothic church of the Frari which contains numerous masterpieces of painting and sculpture and the Scuola Grande di San Rocco, famous for its remarkable paintings on the walls and ceilings by Jacopo Tintoretto. The Frari contains Titian's huge *Assumption*, as well as his Pesaro altarpiece, and, in the sacristy, one of Giovanni Bellini's most beautiful works. It has numerous important doges' tombs, a statue by Donatello, and a 15C choir. Next to the Scuola Grande di San Rocco, the church of San Rocco is worth visiting, and close to the Frari the Scuola Grande di San Giovanni Evangelista has a carved screen by Pietro Lombardo in its courtyard, but its interesting interior is not at present open regularly to the public. The church of San Pantalon is also of interest.

Many hours are needed to do justice to the superb works of art described in this chapter.

Santa Maria Gloriosa dei Frari

Santa Maria Gloriosa dei Frari, commonly known as the Frari (Pl. 7; 4), is dedicated to the Assumption. It rivals Santi Giovanni e Paolo in size, and it

contains remarkable sculptures and paintings. The original Franciscan church was founded c 1250. The present brick Gothic church was begun c 1330 but not finished until after 1443. Open from 10.00–18.00; fest. 15.00–18.00; an entrance fee is charged to cover the expense of the lighting.

Santa Maria Gloriosa dei Frari

The majestic **campanile** (the tallest in the city after St Mark's) dates from the second half of the 14C. On the severe **west front** the Gothic doorway has sculptures attributed to Alessandro Vittoria (the *Risen Christ*), and the workshop of Bartolomeo Bon. The usual entrance is on the **north side** near another doorway with a statue of St Peter; another door on this side has a fine relief of the *Madonna and Child with angels* (15C).

The imposing *****interior**, 90m long, is cruciform with an aisled nave of eight bays joined by wooden tie-beams. Titian's magnificent *****Assumption** in the apse, is framed by the arch of the monks' choir. Many of the most interesting monuments in the church are high up and difficult to see, but a number of them have recently been cleaned. Although the church faces southwest, it is described here as though it had the altar at the east end. The letters in the text refer to the plan.

On the right of the main door, tomb (**A**) of the senator Pietro Bernardo (d. 1538), thought to be a late work by Tullio Lombardo; to the left of the door, tomb (**B**) of the procurator Alvise Pasqualigo (d. 1528), attributed to Lorenzo Bregno.

South aisle

Near the first column, stoup with a bronze statuette of *St Agnes* by Girolamo Campagna, forming a pair with the one opposite, bearing a statuette of *St Anthony of Padua* (1609). Above the place where Titian was traditionally believed to have been buried (**C**) is a huge monument to him in Carrara marble commissioned by the Austrian emperor Ferdinand I from Luigi Zandomeneghi, and his son Pietro in 1843, and inaugurated in 1852. The monument was

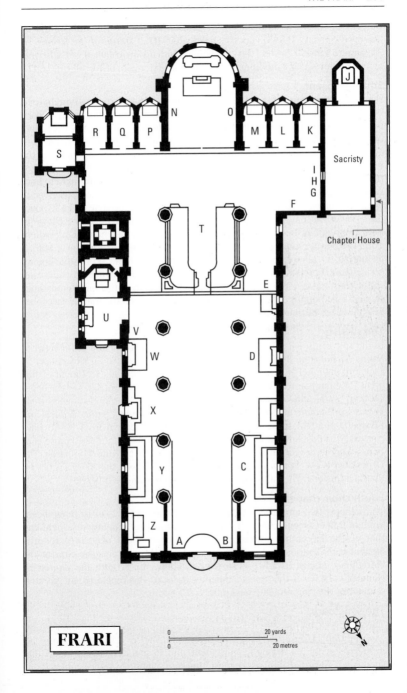

FRARI

0   20 yards
0   20 metres

restored in 1996. Second altar, *Purification of the Virgin and Saints*, by Giuseppe Salviati (1548); on the third altar (**D**), *statue of St Jerome* by Alessandro Vittoria. Beyond the fourth altar (with a *Martyrdom of St Catherine*, by Palma Giovane) is a monument (**E**) to Bishop Marco Zen, of Torcello (d. 1641).

South transept

Here is the *monument (**F**) to Jacopo Marcello (d. 1484), formerly thought to be by Pietro Lombardo, but recently attributed to Giovanni Buora, with a worn fresco high up of the *Triumph of Jacopo Marcello* by a 15C artist of the school of Mantegna. The monument is unique in that it does not follow the usual form of niches and statues but has an oval frame and three free-standing statues at the top of a double sarcophagus. On the right of the sacristy door is the sarcophagus (**G**) of 'Beato Pacifico' (Scipione Bon, a friar of the church who is thought to have supervised part of the building work), beneath an elaborate canopy, ascribed to Nanni di Bartolo and Michele da Firenze, in a florid Gothic style of 1437. Over the door is the fine tomb (**H**), beautifully restored, by Lorenzo or Giovanni Battista Bregno of Benedetto Pesaro, the Venetian general who died in Corfu in 1503 (with interesting reliefs of battleships and fortresses). The statue of Mars is by Baccio da Montelupo (1537). On the left is the tomb (**I**) of the Roman condottiere Paolo Savelli (c 1406), the first in Venice to include an equestrian statue (restored in 1994). The tomb, which shows both Gothic and Renaissance elements, is thought to be a Tuscan work. The statues on the marble sarcophagus have been attributed to Jacopo della Quercia.

The sacristy

In the apse of the sacristy is a *triptych (**J**) of the *Madonna and Child between Saints Nicholas of Bari, Peter, Mark, and Benedict*, painted for this chapel by Giovanni Bellini (1488), a perfect expression of the religious sentiment of this great Venetian painter. The splendid frame is by Jacopo da Faenza. On the opposite wall is a lunette signed and dated 1339 by Paolo Veneziano showing *Doge Francesco Dandolo and his wife presented to the Virgin by Saints Francis and Elizabeth*, thought to be the earliest ducal portrait drawn from life to have survived (the doge's sarcophagus is in the chapter house). The sacristy also contains a Lombardesque lavabo and a marble tabernacle by Tullio Lombardo. The *Deposition* is by Niccolò Frangipane, and the 17C clock signed by Francesco Pianta il Giovane. The Palladian cloister has an elaborate well-head.

South choir chapels

Third chapel (**K**), altarpiece by Bartolomeo Vivarini (1482) in its magnificent original frame; second chapel (**L**), two Gothic funerary monuments, including that of the Florentine ambassador, Duccio degli Uberti (d. 1336) recently attributed to Andriolo de'Santi. The first chapel (**M**) contains the altar of the Florentines erected in 1436. The wooden statue of *St John the Baptist* by Donatello (1438) is the first documented work in the Veneto by the greatest sculptor of the Florentine Renaissance.

The sanctuary

The apse is lit by fine stained glass windows and is filled with Titian's huge *Assumption* (1518), the largest altarpiece in Venice, celebrated among his masterpieces for its dramatic movement and its amazing colouring. Titian succeeded Giovanni Bellini as the most important painter in Venice, and was one of the greatest Italian painters of all time. He was born around 1490 and died in 1576 so he was painting at a time when Venice was flourishing at the height of her power. The *Assumption*, commissioned by the Franciscans in 1516, is an early work showing the influence of Raphael and Michelangelo. It was widely acclaimed by the Venetians, and he soon became the favourite portrait painter of the nobility. His other masterpiece in the Frari, the *Pala Pesaro* (1526) includes excellent portraits of the Pesaro family. Although there are numerous paintings by Titian in Venice, he also worked for the most important Italian courts, as well as for the Pope, the Habsburg emperors, and Philip II of Spain.

The high altar dates from 1516. The *tomb of Doge Niccolò Tron (d. 1473) (N), by Antonio Rizzo, is one of the most sublime examples of Renaissance funerary art in Venice. Opposite is the fine tomb (O) of Francesco Foscari, who died in 1457 after thirty-four years as doge. The late Gothic mausoleum may be the work of Niccolò di Giovanni Fiorentino. The painted 13C *Crucifix* is attributed to the Maestro del Crocifisso dei Frari, probably of the Tuscan school.

North choir chapels
First chapel (P), *Madonna and Saints* by Bernardino Licinio; second chapel (Q), on the right wall, tomb, perhaps by Lorenzo Bregno, of Melchiorre Trevisan (d. 1500) a Venetian commander who donated the reliquary of the Holy Blood to the church (taken from Constantinople, 1480); third chapel (R), *St Ambrose and eight Saints*, begun by Alvise Vivarini (1503) and finished by Marco Basaiti. A plain slab on the floor marks the grave of the great composer Claudio Monteverdi who directed the music at the basilica di San Marco for the last thirty years of his life (he died in 1643). His date of birth given here is incorrect: he was born in 1567. The fourth chapel (S) contains the tomb of Federico Corner, an unusual but graceful work (of Tuscan provenance) with an angel in a niche holding an inscription recording his generosity in paying for the war against the Genoese at Chioggia. The font bears a statue of St John, exquisitely carved in marble by Jacopo Sansovino (1554). On the altar, *St Mark enthroned and four other Saints*, by Bartolomeo Vivarini (1474), in a fine frame. The stained glass dates from the 15C. In 1990 some interesting and rare frescoes dating from around 1361 were discovered between the vault of the chapel and the roof.

North transept
This contains a delicately carved 15C bench-back attributed to Lorenzo and Cristoforo Canozzi da Lendinara. The pretty circular monument to Genorosa degli Orsini and San Maffeo Zen is by the Lombardesque school.

The ritual choir
The ritual choir (T) extends into the nave as in many cathedrals in England and France, a rare survival for Italian church interiors. It contains three tiers of *choir stalls carved by Marco Cozzi (1468), with beautifully detailed intarsia decoration by Lorenzo and Cristoforo Canozzi. The *choir-screen (1475) by Bartolomeo Bon and Pietro Lombardo is faced with Carrara marble and decorated with figures in Istrian stone of saints and prophets in relief; above are ten apostles and a Crucifixion between the Virgin and St John the Evangelist, with angels as lecterns. The organs are by Gaetano Callido (1795) and Giovanni Battista Piaggia (1732).

North aisle

The Cappella Emiliani (**U**) has a marble altarpiece with ten statues in niches by the school of Jacobello dalle Masegne (15C), and the tomb of Bishop Miani, with five similar statues. Next comes the monument (**V**) to Bishop Jacopo Pesaro (d. 1547) with a fine effigy. Over the Pesaro altar (**W**) is the *Madonna di Ca' Pesaro*, by Titian (completed in 1526; recently restored), a marvel of composition and colour. Commissioned by Bishop Pesaro in 1519, it shows the *Madonna and Child with Saints before members of the Pesaro family* (Bishop Pesaro is to the left, and his brother to the right, both kneeling). The huge mausoleum (**X**) of Doge Giovanni Pesaro (d. 1659), a bizarre Baroque work (being restored), and one of the most elaborate funerary monuments in Venice, is attributed to Longhena, with sculptures by the German sculptor Malchior Berthel. The mausoleum (**Y**) of Canova (1827), by his pupils, including Bartolomeo Ferrari, and Luigi Zandomeneghi, reproduces Canova's design for a monument to Titian. The altar of the Crucifix (**Z**) designed by Longhena, has sculptures by Juste Le Court.

The adjoining conventual buildings, with the Palladian cloister (see above) and another in the style of Sansovino, contain the **State Archives**, restructured c 1815–20 by Lorenzo Santi. Among the most famous in the world, they fill some 300 rooms, and provide a remarkable documentation of the Venetian Republic. The 15C summer refectory is used as a reading room.

San Rocco

Close to the Frari are the church and *scuola* (Pl. 7; 3) dedicated to San Rocco (St Roch), born in Montpellier in 1295. He caught the plague when he came to Italy to help cure victims of this contagious disease, but he retired alone to a wood where he was miraculously saved by an angel. He was particularly venerated in Venice in the 15C when the Scuola di San Rocco was founded and his relics were brought to the church. Members of the confraternity offered their services especially during the frequent plagues which broke out in the city, the worst of which (after the Black Death of 1348) occurred in 1575–77 and 1630. After the plague of 1576 St Roch was declared a patron saint of the city and the doge made a pilgrimage to the church and *scuola* every year on his feast-day (16 August) which is still celebrated here (when the treasury of the *scuola* is exhibited). There are paintings of St Roch and plague victims in the church and the *scuola* (St Roch is usually depicted as a young man with a sore on his leg).

The church was designed by Bartolomeo Bon the Younger (1489) but almost entirely rebuilt in 1725 (façade of 1765–71). Open 07.30–12.30; Sat, Sun 08.00–12.30, 14.00–16.00.

Interior. Two statues flank the west door: *David with the head of Goliath*, and *St Cecilia* by Giovanni Marchiori (1743). To the left and right, *Annunciation and St Roch presented to the pope*, by Jacopo Tintoretto. In the centre of the nave ceiling, *Charity of St Roch*, by Gian Antonio Fumiani. **South side**. First altar, *Miracle of San Francesco di Paola*, by Sebastiano Ricci. Between the first and second altars, two large paintings: (above) *St Roch taken to Prison*, attributed to Jacopo Tintoretto, and (below) *Pool of Bethesda*, by Jacopo Tintoretto.

In the sanctuary (covered for restoration) the altar has marble statues of Saints Sebastian, John the Baptist, Roch, and Francis by Giovanni Maria Mosca; the remaining figures are by Bartolomeo di Francesco Bergamasco. On either side are putti frescoed by Pordenone. The carved dossals are attributed to Giovanni

Marchiori. On the walls are four paintings by Jacopo Tintoretto: on the left wall: *St Roch in prison comforted by an Angel*, and (above) *St Roch healing the Animals*. On the right wall: *St Roch cures victims of the plague*, the first Venetian painting to show the saint inside a hospital (1549), and (above), *St Roch in Solitude*.

North side. Second altar, *Annunciation* and *God the Father with Angels*, by Francesco Solimena. Between the first and second altars, *Christ expelling the Money-changers from the Temple*, by Gian Antonio Fumiani, and (above) *St Martin on Horseback and St Christopher*, by Pordenone (formerly cupboard doors, restored in 1999). First altar, *St Helena and the Discovery of the True Cross*, by Sebastiano Ricci.

Scuola Grande di San Rocco

Beside the church is the Scuola Grande di San Rocco (Pl. 7; 3). The numbers in the text below refer to the plans on p 207. It was built for the important confraternity of St Roch (founded in 1478; see above) by Bartolomeo Bon the Younger (1515) and finished by Scarpagnino (1549), who added the extravagant main façade. The less imposing canal façade is also by Scarpagnino. The interior is famous for its *paintings by Jacopo Tintoretto, who produced over fifty works here; it is one of the most remarkable pictorial cycles in existence. Open April–Oct 09.00–17.30; Nov–March 10.00–16.00. Concerts of Baroque music are usually given here on Tues & Sat throughout the year.

In 1564 a competition was held for the decoration of Scarpagnino's recently completed building. Jacopo Tintoretto was the winner, having entered a finished work (rather than a preparatory sketch) of *St Roch in Glory*, which he had installed already in the Sala dell'Albergo. A year later he was elected a brother of the confraternity, and spent the next twenty-three years working on the paintings (largely without the help of collaborators). In return he received a modest pension from the brotherhood. When Ruskin saw the *scuola* in 1845 he commented 'As for painting, I think I didn't know what it was until today' and his visit inspired him to pursue his study of the city and her art.

Tintoretto

Jacopo Robusti, born in Venice c 1519, was called Tintoretto because his family were *tintori* (dyers). Throughout his long life (he died at the age of about 76) he worked exclusively in Venice, producing a remarkable number of superb paintings in the *scuole* and churches commissioned from him by the Venetian middle classes, as well as official works for Palazzo Ducale. Influenced by the Mannerists, he is famous for his use of light and his dramatic scenes often in humble settings, and his style of painting was transmitted to his large bottega as well as his son Domenico. A member of several *scuole*, he was a deeply religious man as well as a brilliant artist.

Ground floor. In the entrance passageway is a statue of St Roch by Giovanni Buora (c 1494). The columned **hall**, where religious ceremonies were held, was the last to be painted in the *scuola* by Tintoretto (1582–87). The superb cycle of paintings illustrating the *Life of the Virgin Mary* begins on the left wall near the entrance: (1) *Annunciation*; (2) *Adoration of the Magi*; (3) *Flight into Egypt*; with a splendid landscape; (4) *Massacre of the Innocents*; and (5) *Mary Magdalen reading* in a charming twilight landscape. Right wall (opposite): the matching panel (6) represents *St Mary of Egypt*, also reading in a landscape. (7) *The Circumcision* appears to have been painted partly by the *bottega* of Tintoretto and by his son Domenico. The last painting (8), the *Assumption*, has suffered from poor restorations in the past. The statue of St Roch on the altar is by Girolamo Campagna (1587).

Part of a collection of Islamic, Hispano-Moresque, and European majolica and porcelain, left to the *scuola* in the 1960s, is also displayed here. The precious treasury of the confraternity is only exhibited on 16 August, the Feast of San Rocco.

The grand **staircase**, by Scarpagnino (1544–46) has two huge paintings commemorating the end of the plague of 1630, the one on the right by Antonio Zanchi (1666), and the one opposite by Pietro Negri (1673). The horror of the suffering caused by the plague is depicted with great realism.

Upper floor. The huge **chapter house** is a splendid hall by Scarpagnino. The paintings here by Tintoretto (1576–81) represent Old Testament subjects on the ceiling, and New Testament subjects on the walls, chosen in a careful iconographical scheme related to the teaching of St Roch and his efforts to relieve thirst, hunger, and sickness. **Ceiling**: the huge central painting (9) shows *Moses erecting the brazen serpent to save those bitten by fiery serpents sent by God as a punishment*. The subjects of the other remarkable paintings are as follows: (10) *Moses striking water from the rock to quench the people's thirst*; (11) *The miraculous fall of Manna from Heaven*; (12) *Adam and Eve* (the *Fall of Man*); (13) *God the Father appearing to Moses*; (14) *Moses led into the desert by the Pillar of Fire*; (15) *Jonah issuing from the belly of the whale*; (16) *Vision of Ezekiel of the Resurrection*; (17) *Jacob's ladder*; (18) *Sacrifice of Isaac*; (19) *Elisha's miracle of the loaves of bread* (restored by Giuseppe Angeli in 1777); (20) *Elijah fed by an angel*; (21) *The Jewish Passover*.

The eight smaller panels in chiaroscuro are replacements of works by Tintoretto by Giuseppe Angeli (1777).

The paintings on the **walls** represent New Testament subjects: (22) *Adoration of the Shepherds*; (23) *Baptism of Christ*; (24) *Resurrection of Christ*; (25) *Agony in the Garden*; (26) *The Last Supper*; (27) *Miracle of the Loaves and Fishes*; (28) *Resurrection of Lazarus*; (29) *Ascension*; (30) *Miracle of Christ at the pool of Bethesda* (damaged by poor restorations); (31) *Temptation of Christ*. End walls: (32) and (33) *Saints Roch and Sebastian*; and, on the altar, *Vision of St Roch* (with the help of his son Domenico). The late 17C carved wooden benches around the great hall by Francesco Pianta il Giovane incorporate bizarre figures including (near the altar) a caricature of Tintoretto and a self-portrait. The processional lanterns (*fanaloni*) date from the 18C.

The walls of the **presbytery** have carved wooden reliefs of the *Life of St Roch* by Giovanni Marchiori. The two statues on the altar of St John the Baptist and St Sebastian are late works by Girolamo Campagna. The *Annunciation* by Titian was acquired by the *scuola* in 1555 and the *Visitation* is by Jacopo Tintoretto. *Christ carrying the Cross* is a greatly venerated painting which hung in the church of San Rocco from around 1510 until 1955. Painted c 1508, and now in poor condition, it has been attributed in the past to Giorgione, but most scholars now consider it to be a late work by Titian. In contrast, the *Christ in Pietà*, formerly thought to be an early work by Titian, is now generally attributed to the circle of Giorgione instead. The *Portrait of a Man* by Tintoretto was once considered to be a self-portrait. The charming little **Sala della Cancelleria** preserves its

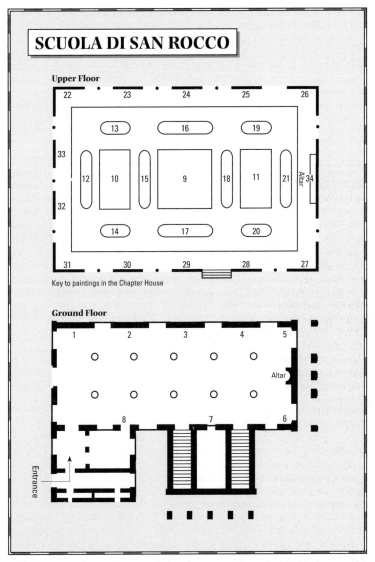

SCUOLA DI SAN ROCCO

Upper Floor

Key to paintings in the Chapter House

Ground Floor

Altar

Entrance

original 18C furnishings. Outside the entrance to the Sala dell'Albergo are two easel paintings acquired by the *scuola* in 1785 by Giambattista Tiepolo: *Hagar and Ishmael comforted by an Angel*, and *Abraham visited by an Angel*.

The **Sala dell' Albergo** was the first room to be decorated by Tintoretto (1564–67). On the carved and gilded ceiling is *St Roch in Glory* (see above) and twenty smaller panels with heads of *putti*, *the four seasons*, *allegories of the Scuole Grande of Venice*, and the *Cardinal Virtues*. The vast **Crucifixion* is generally considered to be his masterpiece. On the opposite wall, *Christ before Pilate*, *Crowning of*

Thorns, and the *Way to Calvary*. Here also is displayed a fragment of a frieze from the ceiling of three apples, showing Tintoretto's remarkable painting technique. From Campo San Rocco, Calle della Scuola on the left side of the Scuola Grande, leads down to a bridge over a rio and continues to the busy Crosera. Here you can make a detour to the left to see two palaces on Rio Foscari beside a bridge designed in 1933 by Eugenio Miozzi. Beside the crenellated brick wall of Ca' Foscari is the main entrance gate to the university which occupies the palace (its main façade on the Grand Canal is described in Ch. 4). On the right is Palazzo Dolfin, also owned by the university (the ballroom has interesting frescoes). In Corte Foscari is the fire station built in 1932–34 by Brenno Del Giudice. Beyond is Campiello dei Squellini with a clump of plane trees.

From the Crosera (see above) Calle San Pantalon continues to the the campo in front of the bare unfinished façade of the church of **San Pantalon** (Pl. 7; 3; open 16.00–18.00 exc. Sat). In the **interior** the nave roof is covered by a huge *painting** (1680–1704) on canvas by Gian Antonio Fumiani. He was killed in a fall from the scaffolding at the end of the work and is buried in the church. It describes, in remarkable perspective, events in the life of the titular saint, and his martyrdom under Diocletian. In the second south chapel, *San Pantaleone healing a Child* was commissioned from Veronese for the high altar of the church by the parish priest in 1587. In the third south chapel the altarpiece of *San Bernardino* is attributed to Alvise dal Friso. The high altar and tabernacle were designed by Giuseppe Sardi in 1668–71. In the chapel to the left of the high altar (seen through a grille; unlocked on request) is an elaborately carved Gothic tabernacle. Also displayed here: *Coronation of the Virgin* by Giovanni d'Alemagna and Antonio Vivarini (1444); *Madonna and Child* and four stories from the *Life of the Virgin*, by Paolo Veneziano; and a 13C statuette of the Madonna and Child in alabaster.

On the right of the façade the Campiello de Ca' Angaran has a remarkable large sculpted roundel of a Byzantine Emperor (late 12C). A bridge (redesigned by Eugenio Miozzi in 1932) leads over the Rio Nuovo to Campo Santa Margherita (see Ch. 14).

Scuola Grande di San Giovanni Evangelista

In front of the church of the Frari Ponte dei Frari, with a marble balustrade of 1858, crosses a rio, and Fondamenta dei Frari leads left to another bridge and (left) Rio terrà San Tomà (in front of the Archivio di Stato, see above). Calle del Magazen and its continuation leads to the fine courtyard (left) in front of the Scuola Grande di San Giovanni Evangelista (Pl. 7; 1), one of the six chief confraternities in Venice, founded in 1261. By 1301 the *scuola* had a chapel in San Giovanni Evangelista under the protection of the Badoer family, and in 1349 it moved to its own premises on the site of the present building. The eagle, symbol of John the Evangelist, recurrs frequently in the decoration of the building.

The **first court** has a beautiful marble screen and portal by Pietro Lombardo (1481). In the **second court** is the wall of the *scuola* (right), with Gothic windows, dating from 1454. The relief shows the brothers of the *scuola* kneeling in front of St John the Evangelist, and the inscription below (copy of the original preserved inside) records the acquisition of this site in 1349 for the *scuola*. Ahead is the former entrance (1512, by Mauro Codussi) to the *scuola*; the double windows above are typical of the work of this architect. To the left is the church, or oratory (described below), with its campanile.

The **interior** of the *scuola* is at present only open by appointment (☎ 041 718

234; important concerts are also often held here, as well as lectures). In the entrance hall is a relief of the *Resurrection of Christ*, by the workshop of Rizzo. The handsome hall has a fine row of columns with Gothic capitals (decorated with the kneeling figures of members of the confraternity) and sculpture including a 14C relief of St Martin with Doge Andrea Contarini and a monk.

The double *staircase, a work of great skill and elegance by Mauro Codussi (1498), leads up to the **salone**, transformed in 1727–57 by Giorgio Massari. On the walls is a 16C cycle of paintings with scenes from the *Life of Christ* and *St John the Evangelist* by Domenico Tintoretto; Sante Peranda; Andrea Vicentino and Giovanni Battista Cignaroli (18C). On the altar wall are tondi by Jacopo Guarana and paintings by Jacopo Marieschi.

The **ceiling** (1760) has scenes from the *Apocalypse*: the central painting is by Giuseppe Angeli; it is surrounded by four works by Gaspare Diziani. The three paintings towards the altar are by Jacopo Marieschi, and at the opposite end of the ceiling is a painting by Jacopo Guarana flanked by two interesting smaller works by Gian Domenico Tiepolo. On the altar is a statue of St John and above the door into the oratory is a relief showing the donation of the relic of the Holy Cross, both attributed to Giovanni Maria Morleiter.

The **Oratorio della Croce** contains an exquisite gilded silver reliquary made by Venetian goldsmiths in 1379 to preserve a relic of the True Cross brought from Cyprus and donated to the school in the 14C. The famous cycle of paintings illustrating the Miracle of this relic by Giovanni Bellini, Vittore Carpaccio and others (now in the Galleria dell'Accademia) was painted for this room (a model shows how the paintings were arranged). The **Sala dell'Albergo Nuovo**, now used as an office by the confraternity, contains four paintings by Palma Giovane. The 14C Venetian icon of the *Madonna and Saints* was formerly in the church of San Giovanni Evangelista.

Opposite the *scuola* is the **church of San Giovanni Evangelista** (at present open 10.00–12.00, 15.00–17.00. exc. Wed). It contains an organ built by Giovanni Battista Piaggia (1760) in an organ case designed by Giorgio Massari, and paintings by Jacopo Marieschi (*Last Supper*) and Domenico Tintoretto (*Crucifixion*). The good woodwork in the church is in need of restoration.

19 • The sestiere di Santa Croce

Numerous interesting churches are described in this chapter including the Baroque church of San Stae on the Grand Canal (with its own landing-stage) which contains 18C Venetian paintings, San Cassiano, which has three very fine paintings by Jacopo Tintoretto, the little Renaissance Santa Maria Mater Domini with some charming sculptures and paintings, San Giacomo dell'Orio, in an attractive large campo, which has a ship's keel roof and interesting paintings and sculptures, and San Giovanni Decollato with early frescoes in its lovely 12C interior. The Baroque Ca' Pesaro on the Grand Canal houses the Museum of Oriental Art (particularly important for its Japanese and Chinese works) and the Museo d'Arte Moderna, which has, however, been closed for many years. Also closed is the Natural History Museum in another building on the Grand Canal, the Fondaco dei Turchi. Instead, open regularly to visitors, is the Museo di Palazzo Mocenigo, a delightful example of a late 17C Venetian residence.

The little **Campo San Stae** opens on to the Grand Canal . Across the Canal (left) stands the 16C Palazzo Vendramin (see p 129), and, on this side just by the landing-stage, is Palazzo Priuli Bon with Veneto-Byzantine details.

San Stae

The church of San Stae (San Eustachio; Pl. 4; 7) presents a splendid Baroque façade to the waterfront. The work of Domenico Rossi, it was financed by Doge Alvise II Mocenigo in 1710. Concerts are held here (usually on Saturdays, sometimes on Tuesdays), and exhibitions in conjunction with the Biennale.

The bright white and grey **interior** (open 10.00–18.00; fest. 15.00–18.00) has an interesting collection of 18C paintings. **Right side**, first chapel, *Madonna in Glory and Saints*, by Niccolò Bambini. The **sanctuary** has an early work by Sebastiano Ricci on the ceiling and a series of good small early 18C paintings: right wall (lower row): Giambattista Tiepolo, *Martyrdom of St Bartholomew*; Gregorio Lazzarini, *St Paul*; Giovanni Antonio Pellegrini, *Martyrdom of St Andrew*; (middle) Giuseppe Angeli, *The Fall of Manna*; (upper row) Pietro Uberti, *Martyrdom of St Philip*; Niccolò Bambini, *Communion of St Jacob*; Angelo Trevisani, *Martyrdom of St Thomas*. On the left wall (lower row): Giovanni Battista Piazzetta, **Martyrdom of St Jacob*; Sebastiano Ricci, **St Peter freed from Prison*; Antonio Balestra, *Martyrdom of St John the Evangelist*; (middle) Giuseppe Angeli, *Sacrifice of Melchizedek*; (upper row) Silvestro Maniago, *St Mark the Evangelist*; Giovanni Battista Pittoni, *St Simeon*; Giovanni Battista Mariotti, *St Taddeo*.

Sacristy (admission on request). Over the altar, *Crucifix* by Maffeo da Verona and the *Dead Christ* by Pietro Muttoni. The two paintings with stories from the *Life of Trajan* are by Giustino Menescardi and Giovanni Battista Pittoni. **Left side** of the nave: sculpted *Crucifix* by Giuseppe Torretto, and funerary monuments of the Foscarini family by Torretto, Antonio Tarsia, Pietro Baratta, and Pietro Groppelli. Second chapel, Francesco Migliori, *Assumption*; first chapel, Jacopo Amigoni, *Saints Andrew and Catherine*. The organ above the west door is by Gaetano Callido (1772).

Beside the church is the charming little **Scuola dei Battiloro e Tiraoro** (goldsmiths), built in 1711. The salizzada leads away from the Grand Canal past the brick campanile with a 13C stone angel at its base. Calle Tron diverges right for Palazzo Tron (now owned by the University) which contains frescoes by Jacopo Guarana (admission sometimes granted).

Ca' Pesaro

From the campo a 19C iron bridge leads to Calle Pesaro which continues to the courtyard of Ca' Pesaro (Pl. 4; 7), which has an elaborate Renaissance well-head from the Zecca, with an Apollo by Danese Cattaneo. The great Baroque palace (see p 131) contains the Museo d'Arte Moderna and the Museo Orientale. The **Museo d'Arte Moderna** has been undergoing restoration since 1981 and it is still closed (for information, ☎ 041 721 127). The paintings and sculptures were mostly purchased at the Biennale art exhibitions. The collection includes: Marc Chagall, *Rabbi*; Gustav Klimt, *Salome* (*Judith II*); Pierre Bonnard, *La Toilette*; works by Georges Rouault, Kandinsky, Max Ernst, Joan Miró, Ben Nicholson, and Henry Moore. Portraits by Giacomo Balla and Umberto Boccioni; works by Filippo De Pisis, Lorenzo Viani, Antonio Donghi (*Donna al caffè*, 1931), Massimo

Campigli, Giorgio Morandi, Felice Casorati (*Ragazze a Nervi*, 1926), and Carlo Carrà. Santomaso, Emilio Vedova, Bruno Saetti are also represented. There is a fine collection of drawings and oil paintings by Guglielmo Ciardi (1842–1917).

There are also works by late 19C Venetian artists including Alessandro Milesi, Vincenzo Cadorin, Ippolito Caffi, Federico Zandomeneghi, Ettore Tito, Luigi Nono and Giacomo Favretto.

On the top floor is the *Museum of Oriental Art** (open 08.15–14.00 exc. Mon) devoted principally to Japanese and Chinese art, with specimens of Siamese and Javanese work. It includes paintings, sculpture, arms and armour, musical instruments, decorative arts and clothes. The Japanese paintings are especially interesting, and the lacquer-work and bronzes are of high quality. Notable also is the fine Khmer figure of Buddha (Cambodia; 12C).

Ca' Pesaro

The fondamenta leads down Rio Pesaro with a view of the fine **Palazzo Agnusdio**, by the bridge. It has a relief of three angels over the Gothic door, and a *patera* with the mystic lamb over the water-gate. Its window has good Gothic sculptures of the Annunciation and the four Symbols of the Evangelists. Calle del Ravano continues across Rio delle Due Torri (with a view left of the side façade of Palazzo Pesaro) to Calle Corner, at the end of which part of the huge **Ca' Corner della Regina** is visible (the main façade is described in Ch. 4) which houses the archives of the Biennale art exhibitions.

Calle della Regina and (left) Calle dei Morti continue to a bridge which leads into Campo San Cassiano. The church of **San Cassiano** (Pl. 4; 7) was founded early, but rebuilt (except for the 13C campanile) in the 17C. Open 08.00–12.00, 16.30–18.00; fest. 09.00–12.00, 17.00–18.00. Coin-operated lights.

The **interior** is covered with scaffolding for restoration work. In the **sanctuary** are three remarkable paintings by Jacopo Tintoretto; the *Crucifixion**, the *Resurrection*, and the *Descent into Limbo*. All three paintings are extremely unusual for their iconography: the *Crucifixion* is particularly memorable, and unlike any other painting of this subject. The tragic atmosphere of the picture is heightened by the menacing sky and line of soldiers with their spears on the low horizon, and the abandoned pink cloak at the foot of the Cross. The dramatic scene of the *Descent into Limbo* includes the nude figure of Eve and a splendid angel flying away. The *Resurrection* includes the figures of the patron saints of the church, St Cassiano and St Cecilia and charming putti, two of them holding wreaths of lilies. The altar front was carved by Enrico Meyring in 1696.

On the first altar in the **south aisle**, *St John the Baptist between Saints*, attributed to Rocco Marconi. In the chapel to the right of the high altar, *Visitation* (with a portrait in a tondo beneath of a member of the confraternity of the Scuola della Visitazione), *Annunciation to St Zacharias*, and *Birth of St John*, all by Leandro Bassano. **North aisle**. Next to the sacristy is a charming chapel (automatic light) which preserves its decorations of 1746, with an altar-piece (*Madonna and Child with St Charles Borromeo and St Philip Neri*) signed by Giovanni Battista Pittoni (1763), and *Christ in the Garden* by Leandro Bassano. The second altarpiece in this aisle is by Matteo Ponzone.

Palazzo Mocenigo

It is now best to return to San Stae (see above) and follow the Salizzada di San Stae away from the Grand Canal on the right of the façade of the church. It passes several fine (but dilapidated) palaces, including (no. 1988) a 13C building. Palazzo Mocenigo a San Stae (no. 1992; Pl. 3; 8) was left to the city of Venice in 1954 by the last descendant of this branch of the distinguished Mocenigo family (who provided the Republic with no fewer than seven doges). It now houses the **Museo di Palazzo Mocenigo** (open April–Oct 10.00–17.00, exc. Mon; Nov–March 10.00–16.00, exc. Mon).

From the **atrium**, with 18C benches and busts (being restored), the staircase leads up to the **portego** on the first floor which has a fine double doorway (early 18C) and portraits of the Mocenigo family. The first floor, or *primo piano nobile* is an interesting example of a late 17C Venetian residence once inhabited by the Mocenigo, with good furniture (17C–19C), including chandeliers from Murano, and Venetian mirrors. In most of the rooms there are now also charming displays of 18C costumes. A small **sitting-room** has delicate stucco decoration. The **red drawing-room** has a ceiling fresco attributed to Jacopo Guarana or Giambattista Canal. The *Portrait of a Contarini procurator* has a remarkable carved frame with elaborate allegories of the Contarini family, attributed to Antonio Corradini. The **green sitting room** has another ceiling fresco attributed to Jacopo Guarana, and interesting historical scenes of events in Mocenigo history, attributed to Antonio Stom. The **pink dining room** has a ceiling fresco by Giambattista Canal and three pastels by Francesco Pavona (also attributed to Rosalba Carriera). In the **bedroom** there is a *Madonna and Child with Saints John the Baptist and Peter* by the school of Bellini.

It is now necessary to return to the *portego*, across which is the **Room of the Four Seasons**, named after four monochrome allegories by Giambattista Canal. The **dining room**, has interesting panelling and furniture. The last room, the **library**, has a fine display of 16C–19C lace.

Theatre performances are sometimes held in the palace, which houses the **Centro Studi di Storia del Tessuto e del Costume**, with a remarkably complete documentation of costumes and materials from the 16C up to the 1950s.

Beyond the palace, Ramo della Rioda diverges left across two canals for the church of **Santa Maria Mater Domini** (Pl. 3; 8), a Renaissance building probably from a design by Giovanni Buora (1502–40), with an Istrian stone façade. The pretty interior has lovely sculptures and paintings (open daily exc. fest. 10.00–12.00). **South side**. The attractive first altar bears three marble figures of saints by Lorenzo Bregno (1524) and Antonio Minello; second altar, *Martyrdom of Santa Cristina* (1520), with a charming group of *angels, by Vincenzo Catena. On the south wall is a *Last Supper*, a copy by Bonifacio Veronese. On the right of the sanctuary is a delicately carved altar, attributed to Lorenzo Bregno. In the apse is a Tuscan high relief in terracotta of the Madonna and Child. On the altar on the left are two statuettes of Saints Mark and John by Lorenzo Bregno. On the north side, a 13C Byzantine marble bas-relief of the **Madonna in Prayer**, and above, *Invention of the Cross*, by Jacopo Tintoretto, and on the first altar, **Transfiguration**, by Francesco Bissolo.

The campo, with a fine well-head, has several good palaces. At the end (no. 2120) Palazzetto Viaro has a distinguished row of tall trefoil windows (14C) and a relief of a lion (almost obliterated). No. 2173 has ogee windows with, above, a frieze of Byzantine crosses and *paterae*. Opposite, no. 2177 has a quatrefoil decoration (almost completely ruined).

To follow the rest of this walk return to Salizzada San Stae (see above). Just to the left Calle del Tentor continues (right) roughly parallel to the Grand Canal, across two bridges. From the second, Ponte del Megio, Calle Larga leads into the large **Campo San Giacomo dell'Orio**, with its plane trees.

San Giacomo dell' Orio

San Giacomo dell' Orio (Pl. 3; 8), of ancient foundation, was rebuilt in 1225 (the tall campanile survives from this time), and altered in 1532.

The **interior** (open 10.00–18.00; fest. 15.00–18.00), recently restored, contains massive low Byzantine columns (12C–13C), one (in the south transept) of verde antico, and one (behind the pulpit) with a fine flowered capital. There is a beautiful 14C wooden ship's keel *roof. Around the west door (beneath the organ) are paintings attributed to Andrea Schiavone, including two prophets flanking the door. The huge stoup in Greek marble, was probably used as a font.

South aisle. Beyond a 16C painting of the **Last Supper**, the first altar has a Tuscan wooden statue of the **Madonna and Child**. In the south transept the old wall of the church has been exposed with interesting fragments embedded in it (the **Madonna in Prayer** dates from the 13C). The painting of the **Miracle of the Loaves and Fishes** is by Palma Giovane. Beside the door into the new sacristy is a statuette of St James by Bartolo Cabianca, and (above the door) an early 16C painting of the **Supper at Emmaus**. In the **new sacristy** is a ceiling painting of the **Allegory of Faith**, by the *bottega* of Veronese (restored) and four **Doctors of the Church**. The paintings include: **Madonna in Glory with Saints John and Nicholas**, and (opposite, above a fine carved fragment) **St John the Baptist preaching**, both by Francesco Bassano. The latter incorporates portraits of Bassano's family and Titian (on the extreme left wearing a red hat).

In the pretty domed chapel to the right of the high altar are vault frescoes by Jacopo Guarana, and paintings by Padovanino, Del Moro, and Palma Giovane. In the **sanctuary** the **Madonna and four Saints** is by Lorenzo Lotto (1546). Beneath it has been placed a relief from the old high altar, with the **Martyrdom of St James the Apostle**, dating from 1704. In the apse hangs a **Crucifix** attributed to Paolo Veneziano. On the walls are two large marble crosses, fine Lombardesque works. On the left pier, the statuette of the **Virgin Annunciate** was formerly over the door of Santa Maria Mater Domini. A charming Byzantine work, it shows the Virgin with a spindle in her hand.

The chapel to the left of the high altar has an altarpiece by Lorenzo Gramiccia (1770), and paintings from the old organ: two monochrome panels of **Daniel** and **David**, attributed to Gualtiero Padovano, and **St James** and **St John the Evangelist**, attributed to Schiavone. The **old sacristy**, with finely carved wood panelling, is entirely decorated with a cycle of *paintings, celebrating the **Mystery of the Eucharist**, by Palma Giovane (1575–81). Also here, a 14C bas-relief of the Madonna and Child with donor, and *Saints Sebastian, Roch, and Lorenzo*, by Giovanni Buonconsiglio.

North transept. *Saints Laurence, Jerome, and Prosper* (much restored), by Veronese, and two good early works by Palma Giovane with *Stories from the life of St Laurence*. **North aisle**. Above the door into the north porch is a painting of a *Miracle of St James*, attributed to Antonio Palma. The porch contains a 14C wood Crucifix, and an early 17C wooden Pietà. The first altar has a late 17C Crucifix.

To the south of the church (across a bridge), the name of Corte dell'Anatomia recalls the site of an anatomical theatre built here in 1671. The area north of the church, reached by Ramo dell'Isola, has boat-building yards and large warehouses which until recently, were surrounded on four sides by canals (now filled in except for Rio di San Zan Degolà).

From Calle Larga (see above) Calle del Capitello zigzags back to Calle Larga (right) which leads into the campo of the church of **San Giovanni Decollato** (Pl. 3; 8; San Zan Degolà), founded in the early 11C by the Venier family (admission 10.00–12.00, exc. fest.). The basilican interior has Greek marble columns and Byzantine capitals and a lovely ship's keel roof. In the left apse chapel are 13C fresco fragments of *St Elena* and *Four heads of Saints*, and an *Annunciation*, as well as a frescoed vault with *Symbols of the Evanglists* and a 17C carved Crucifix. In the right apse chapel, a charming late-14C fragment of *St Michael Archangel* was discovered behind the marble altarpiece.

From the campo, Calle dei Preti leads to the Salizzada dei Fondaco dei Turchi which leads up to the Grand Canal and the **Fondaco dei Turchi** (Pl. 3; 8), from 1621–1838 the warehouse of the Turkish merchants. Once the most characteristic Veneto-Byzantine palaces (12C–13C) in the city, it was virtually rebuilt after 1858 by Federico Berchet. In 1381 it was given to the Dukes of Ferrara, and here, as their guests, stayed John Palaeologus, the Byzantine Emperor in 1438, and Tasso in 1562. The building contains a **Natural History Museum** (closed some years ago for restoration) where the exhibits include a rare species of dinosaur, called an Ouranosaurus over 3.5m high and 7m long and a giant crocodile nearly 12m long, both found in the Sahara in 1973 and belonging to the Cretaceous period. The material from the Venetian lagoon includes an ancient boat.

On the other side of the Grand Canal rises the church of San Marcuola and (right) Palazzo Vendramin.

20 • San Marcuola to the Madonna dell'Orto

The church of San Marcuola, on the Grand Canal (with its own landing-stage), has some unusual paintings. From here a roundabout walk is followed leading north past a number of palaces and churches including San Marciliano, worth visiting for its ceiling paintings by Sebastiano Ricci. In a quiet area of the city, traversed by some particularly pretty canals, is the huge Scuola Grande della Misericordia by Jacopo Sansovino, which is to be restored, and the lovely church of the Madonna dell'Orto. This is extremely important for its works by Jacopo Tintoretto who lived close by (and it also has an altarpiece by Cima da Conegliano). Near by is the church of Sant'Alvise which contains paintings by Giovanni Battista Tiepolo.

The church of **San Marcuola** (Pl. 3; 6; or Santi Ermagora e Fortunato), by Giorgio Massari (1728–36), has an unfinished façade which faces the Grand Canal.

The **interior** (open 08.30–12.00, 17.00–19.00) contains statues by Giovanni Maria Morleiter and assistants. Around the two facing pulpits are some unusual paintings including the *Christ Child blessing between Saints Catherine and Andrew*, and the *Head of Christ* between two male portraits, thought to be by pupils of Titian (Francesco Vecellio?). On the left wall of the chancel is a *Last Supper*, a good early work (1547) by Jacopo Tintoretto; on the right wall is a copy of the *Washing of the Feet*, also by Tintoretto; the original is now in Newcastle-upon-Tyne, England, and is almost identical to another painting by Tintoretto in the Prado, Madrid. The original painting was substituted by this copy in the 17C. The church also contains paintings—on the ceiling, in the presbytery, on the high altar and in the 18C sacristy—by Francesco Migliori, a little-known 18C Venetian. The Callido organ dates from 1775.

The campo in front of the church has a landing-stage on the Grand Canal served by vaporetto no. **1**. The view takes in the dome of San Geremia (right) and, in the distance by the station, the façade of the Scalzi. Directly across the Grand Canal stands the Fondaco dei Turchi, and to the left are the granaries of the Republic and Palazzo Belloni-Bettagià with its two obelisks.

Behind the church the façade of the **Scuola del Cristo**, founded in 1644, can be seen. From here Ponte Storto (with a view over the Grand Canal of the end of the Fondaco dei Turchi) leads across Rio di San Marcuola. At the end of Calle Larga Vendramin is the land entrance to **Palazzo Vendramin**, the winter home of the Casinò (the façade is described in Ch. 4). In the courtyard is a fine 11C Byzantine well-head. A plaque records Wagner's death here in 1883 while a guest of the Duke of Chambord. The apartment where he lived can be seen by appointment on Saturdays (☎ 041 523 2544; entrance at no. 2079).

The Calle Larga Vendramin ends at **Rio terrà della Maddalena**, a crowded shopping street, dating from 1398. It passes (left) the 17C Palazzo Donà delle Rose (no. 2343) and the 15C Palazzo Contin (no. 2347). It ends at Ponte Sant'Antonio (good view left of Palazzo Diedo, see below) and the little Campo della Maddalena, with a fine well-head, surrounded by quaint old houses with tall chimney-pots. Palazzo Magno has a doorway with a Gothic lunette. The small round domed church of the **Maddalena** (Pl. 4; 5) is attractively sited on its canal. A neo-classical building by Tommaso Temanza (c 1760), it is closed to worship and is being restored.

The Strada Nuova continues across a bridge the Campo di Santa Fosca with a monument to **Fra' Paolo Sarpi** by Emilio Marsili (1892). Sarpi was born in Venice in 1552. He was a Servite friar, who became a great scientist (Galileo considered him his master) and historian (his history of the Council of Trent is of fundamental importance). But he is best remembered as the defender of the independence of the Venetian State against Papal interference, advocating that the temporal power of secular rulers should remain separate from that of the Roman Church. In a famous dispute between Doge Leonardo Donà and Pope Paul V over the rights of temporal rulers, the Pope, though he placed Venice under an interdict in 1606/7, was forced to give way, thanks largely to the able defence of the city's cause by Sarpi. His friend, the English ambassador Sir Henry Wotton (see p 129), who was quick to support him in his conflict with the Jesuits and the Pope, declared 'for learning, I think I may justly call him the most deep and general scholar of the world....His power of speech consisteth rather in the soundness of reason than in any other natural ability'. Sarpi died in 1623 and is buried in the church of San Michele in Isola.

The church of **Santa Fosca** (Pl. 4; 5; open 09.30–11.30) was founded in the 13C, and the domed brick campanile was reconstructed after damage in 1410. The church was rebuilt in 1679, and restored in 1741 when the façade was constructed. It contains (over the door on the north side) a damaged *Holy Family with a donor*, by Domenico Tintoretto, and (on the altar on the right of the sanctuary) a fine Byzantine painting of the *Pietà and two Saints* (recently restored). Also in the campo is the fine long 15C façade of Palazzo Correr.

A bridge leads across Rio di Santa Fosca on which can be seen (left), the 17C Palazzo Diedo, attributed to Andrea Tirali, and across another canal, the ex-convent and church of **Santa Maria dei Servi**, founded in 1318 and consecrated in 1491, and once one of the most important Gothic buildings in Venice. Most of it was destroyed in 1812 and only a Gothic doorway, and a 15C statue of the Madonna on the wall survives. To the right, on Fondamenta del Forner, is the noble Renaissance façade of Palazzo Vendramin.

Across the bridge Calle Zancani leads across another rio to the church of **San Marciliano** or San Marziale; (Pl. 4; 5; open 16.00–19.00; fest. 08.00–13.00). In the vault are *paintings in pretty gilded frames, by Sebastiano Ricci; they are among his best works. Titian's damaged painting of *Tobias and the Archangel* (c 1540) is to be placed on the first south altar after its restoration. On the second south altar is Jacopo Tintoretto's *St Martial and two Saints* (over restored), and on the second north altar a 15C wooden statue of the *Madonna and Child*. On either side of the chancel is Domenico Tintoretto's *Annunciation*.

The Strada Nova (see above) continues across another bridge from which there is a view (left) of the splendid 15C façade (with ingenious corner windows) of **Palazzo Giovanelli**. This was a gift from the Republic to the condottiere Francesco Maria della Rovere, Duke of Urbino (for his services to Venice) in 1538. It later became the property of Prince Giovanelli whose famous art collection included Giorgione's *Tempesta* (now in the Galleria dell'Accademia). From the bridge, in the other direction (right) there is a view of the façade of Palazzo Pesaro across the Grand Canal. The Strada Nova next passes the church of **San Felice** (Pl. 4; 7), which was founded in the 10C, restored 1276 and rebuilt after 1531. Above the west door on the canal is a carved 14C angel. On the third south altar is a painting of *St Demetrius and a donor* by Jacopo Tintoretto.

The pretty Fondamenta di San Felice (Pl. 4; 7) follows the rio which is fronted by a portico for part of its length. At the end is a private bridge without a parapet: most of the stone bridges in the city were originally built without parapets but this is the only one to have survived. In the distance there is a view of the lagoon and the island of Murano.

Ramo della Misericordia leads across the wide Rio di Noale to the Fondamenta della Misericordia on which is the large Palazzo Lezze, by Longhena (1654). The Fondamenta follows Rio di Noale past the massive walls of the **Scuola Grande**

della Misericordia (Pl. 4; 6), begun in 1532 by Jacopo Sansovino, but left incomplete at his death because of lack of funds—the huge façade which was to have been marble, remains unfinished in brick (a project designed by Palladio in the 1570s was never carried out). The building was finally opened in 1589 and contains a splendid lower hall. At the fall of the Republic it was used as a military store, and then as an archive, builders' yard, and sports centre. There are long-term plans to convert it into an auditorium for concerts.

A wooden bridge crosses the rio into the **Campo dell'Abbazia**, with its old pavement and well-head. The worn Gothic façade of the **Scuola Vecchia della Misericordia** (founded 1308; restored in the 15C) stands next to the façade (1659) of the deconsecrated church of Santa Maria della Misericordia. There is also a 14C relief of the Madonna which is Byzantine in style. The abbey buildings are now used as a restoration centre for works of art in stone and for paintings. An early 16C portico continues along Rio della Sensa and the Fondamenta dell'Abbazia passes Corte Nuova. Entered by a fine Gothic doorway with reliefs of the *Madonna of the Misericordia and Saints*, these were once the almshouses (1506) of the Scuola della Misericordia.

Corte Vecchia leads north to a bridge in a remote part of the town on the Sacca della Misericordia which opens on to the lagoon. There is a good view of the islands of San Michele, with its dark cypresses and church façade, and Murano, with its lighthouse and bell towers. Fondamenta Gasparo Contarini continues along the canal past the long 16C Palazzo Contarini dal Zaffo (no. 3539, with a garden) and Palazzo Minelli Spada with two obelisks. On the opposite side is the double façade of a simple low house with symmetrical chimneys and watergates, and the fine Palazzo Mastelli (or del Cammello) which bears a charming relief of a man leading a camel (a reminder that Venetian merchants brought merchandise, and in particular spices, from the East by caravan).

Madonna dell'Orto

The church of the Madonna dell'Orto (Pl. 4; 3), in a peaceful campo, contains important works by Jacopo Tintoretto who is buried here, in his parish church. Open 10.00–18.00; fest. 15.00–18.00.

The first church on this site, dedicated to St Christopher, was founded c 1350 by Fra Tiberio da Parma, general of the Umiliati order of Benedictines. After 1377 it became known as the Madonna dell'Orto from a miraculous statue of the Madonna and Child which had been abandoned in a nearby orchard.

The ***façade** is a fine example of Venetian Gothic, with good early 15C tracery in the windows. The statues of the Apostles in the niches are attributed to the Dalle Masegne brothers. Flanking the doorway are a Madonna and Annunciatory Angel, attributed as an early work to Antonio Rizzo. Above, the statue of St Christopher, traditionally attributed (as a late work) to Bartolomeo Bon, is now thought to be by the workshop of Niccolò di Giovanni Fiorentino. The campanile (1503), with its onion-shaped cupola is conspicuous from the lagoon towards Murano.

Interior. The nave and aisles are divided by columns of striped Turkish marble and the semi-circular apse is vaulted.

South aisle. On the first Renaissance altar is Cima da Conegliano's masterpiece of **St John the Baptist and four other Saints* (c 1493). It is still in its original frame, and was restored in 1999. The Cavazza family monument, richly decorated with polychrome marbles, is by Giuseppe Sardi (1657). Girolanno Cavazza (1588–1681) was a diplomat in the service of the Republic. Beyond the fourth altar, on the wall, is the *Presentation of the Virgin in the Temple*, by Jacopo Tintoretto. The use of a grand staircase (the risers of the steps in this painting are decorated in gold leaf) recalls Titian's painting of the same subject executed some 20 years earlier for the Scuola della Carità (see room 24 of the Galleria dell'Accademia). In the **Cappella di San Mauro** is the colossal stone statue (radically restored) of the *Madonna and Child* by Giovanni de'Santi, which gave the church its name (see above). A modest slab in the chapel on the right of the choir marks Tintoretto's resting-place. A plaque on the wall records Sir Ashley Clarke (1903–94), who, as a true friend of Venice, became an honorary citizen of the city. He was founder of the Venice in Peril Fund which has restored numerous monuments all over the city, including the fabric, sculptures and paintings of this church in 1968–70. It was the first Venetian building to be comprehensively restored after the flood of November 1966.

The **choir** is adorned by two huge paintings by Jacopo Tintoretto, the *Last Judgement* and the *Making of the Golden Calf*. 14.5m high and nearly 6m wide, they were probably painted in situ around 1562–64 (they fit the Gothic vault of the choir ceiling). Apart from the paintings for the Scuola Grande di San Rocco, these were considered Tintoretto's most important commissions and we know that he decided to donate them as a gift to his parish church. In the apse, flanking an *Annunciation* by Palma Giovane, is the *Vision of the Cross to St Peter*, and the *Beheading of St Paul*, by Tintoretto. In the vault, five *Virtues*, also by Tintoretto, except for the central one, *Faith*, which is by a 17C painter.

North aisle. The fourth chapel (Cappella Contarini) contains family busts, one by Danese Cattaneo, and the two in the centre by Alessandro Vittoria. Over the altar is another notable work by Tintoretto, *St Agnes raising Licinius*. The elegant Renaissance **Cappella Valier** (first chapel) was completed in 1526 by Andrea and Antonio Buora; it has a cupola and a semi-circular apse. The *Madonna* by Giovanni Bellini (c 1478) over the altar, in a charming sculpted tabernacle, was stolen in 1993, and has never been recovered. The organ by Pietro Bazzani (1878) has been restored.

In the campo, which retains its old paving in stone and brick, is the Scuola dei Mercanti (begun 1570) with a 16C relief.

A bridge leads over the rio into **Campo dei Mori** with three statues of mori, popularly supposed to be the Levantine merchants of the Mastelli family whose palace stands on the canal to the north (see above).

On the fondamenta overlooking the pretty Rio della Sensa, one of several parallel canals in this area, a plaque at no. 3399 marks Jacopo Tintoretto's charming house. He lived here from 1574 until his death in 1594. A quaint turbaned figure in a niche, standing on an ancient Roman altar, is incorporated in its façade (with several other ancient sculptural fragments), similar to those in Campo dei Mori. The cupola seen in the distance, at the east end of the rio, belongs to Santi Giovanni e Paolo.

In the other direction, the fondamenta leads along the canal over the Ponte Brazzo, from which you can see the façade of the Madonna dell'Orto. From the next bridge, Ponte Rosso, there is a view out to the lagoon. A palace (no. 3291) has a relief of St George and the Dragon. On the opposite side of the canal is a house with a double façade on either side of a calle connected by two arches. At the next bridge, Calle del Capitello leads north, and across the next rio is Campo Sant'Alvise, in a remote part of the city.

The church of **Sant'Alvise** (Pl. 3; 2) dates from the late 14C. The Gothic brick façade (being restored) bears an early 15C Tuscan statue of the titular saint. The **interior** (open 10.00–18. 00; fest. 15.00–18.00) has a nuns' choir (also being restored) at the west end. On the altar on the south side, is a seated polychrome wood statue of St Alvise (16C) and two statuettes of Saints John the Baptist and Anthony, perhaps early works by Girolamo Campagna. Beyond a *Last Supper* attributed to Girolamo Santacroce, are two fine works by Giambattista Tiepolo (*Crown of Thorns* and *Flagellation*). On the right wall of the sanctuary is Tiepolo's beautiful *Calvary* (1749). On the north wall of the church is the pulpit surrounded by paintings from the old organ doors by Bonifacio Veronese. The north altar has three 18C statues.

In the **sacristy** are eight charming little 16C tempera paintings with pretty landscapes, apparantly by different artists, showing the influence of Lazzaro Bastiani and Carpaccio. The subjects are: *Solomon and the Queen of Sheba, the Golden Calf, Rachel at the well, the Archangel Raphael with Tobias, the Finding of Joseph, the Colossus with feet of clay, Joshua taking Jericho*, and *the Poverty of Job.* The *Portrait of the donor* is attributed to Jacobello del Fiore.

Calle del Capitello and Calle della Malvasia return south away from the lagoon to Rio di San Girolamo near the Ghetto (see Ch. 21).

21 • Cannaregio and the Ghetto

This walk includes a number of churches near the station bridge: the Baroque church of the Scalzi, San Simeone Grande which contains good paintings and sculpture, the 18C church of San Simeone Piccolo with its conspicuous green dome, and San Niccolò da Tolentino, a 16C–17C church which is often closed.

The walk also covers part of the extensive sestiere of Cannaregio, with its attractive canal. At one end is Palazzo Labia which has important frescoes in the ballroom by Giovanni Battista Tiepolo (admission by appointment), and at the other end is the Franciscan church of San Giobbe, with a lovely Renaissance sanctuary and interesting works of art. On the other side of the canal is the area of the old Ghetto, where some of the synagogues and the Jewish museum are shown on tours.

Fom the station a bridge across the Grand Canal and a calle leads to a bridge across Rio Marin beyond which is the church of **San Simeone Grande** (San Simeone Profeta; Pl. 3; 7). The low interior (open 08.00–12.00, 17.00–19.00) has a wide nave with antique columns and statues above the arcade. On the north wall, near the main door, is a large painting of the *Last Supper* by Jacopo Tintoretto. Over the high altar is a *Presentation in the Temple*, by Palma Giovane. In the south aisle, in a niche, carved figure of St Valentine (Lombardesque), and, beyond, a 14C relief of St Simeon and an Abbot. On the end wall, above an arch, 14C carved angel.

In the chapel to the left of the main chapel is an *effigy of St Simeon, with an inscription of 1317 attributing it to Marco Romano. This powerful sculpture is a very unusual work, the only one signed and dated by Marco Romano, a Sienese sculptor who worked in Tuscany, Cremona, and Venice in the first two decades of the 14C. It had an important influence on contemporary Venetian sculptors. In the past some scholars have doubted the authenticity of the early date. In the sacristy is a painting of the *Trinity* attributed to Giovanni Mansueti. The flank of the church faces its campo on the Grand Canal. Beneath the portico is an interesting 14C relief of a saint.

Also close to the station bridge is the church of **San Simeone Piccolo** (Pl. 3; 7) on a stylobate with a pronaos, or vestibule with Corinthian columns and a high green dome. It is the best work of Giovanni Scalfurotto who built it in 1718–38 on a circular plan derived from the Pantheon in Rome (open only on fest. 10.30–12.00, and for concerts).

The fondamenta follows the Grand Canal to Rio dei Tolentini, across which is the **Giardino Papadopoli**, public gardens on the site of a church and monastery. To the east lies Piazzale Roma (Pl. 6; 1, 2) the busy terminal of the road from the mainland with its huge multi-storey car parks and bus stations. Behind the garage is the early Gothic church of **Sant'Andrea della Zirada** (Pl. 6; 1; closed to worship), which has a sumptuous altar by Juste Le Court (1679), and the church of the **Nome di Gesù**, a neo-Classical building (1815–21) by Gian Antonio Selva.

From the Giardino Papadopoli (see above) Fondamenta del Monastero follows the Rio dei Tolentini to a bridge which leads into the campo in front of the imposing church of **San Nicola da Tolentino** (Pl. 6; 4), often simply called **I Tolentini**. The fine Corinthian portico by Andrea Tirali (1706–14) is an unexpected sight. The Theatine Order, founded in Rome in 1524, escaped to Venice after the Sack of Rome three years later, knowing that Venice had supported the Pope rather than Charles V. The classical **interior** (often closed) by Vincenzo Scamozzi (1591–1602) recalls Palladian models, despite the heavy decorations added in the 17C.

South side, first chapel, paintings (right and left) by Padovanino; second chapel, three works by Camillo Procaccini, including *St Charles Borromeo in Glory*; third chapel, school of Bonifacio Veronese, *Banquet of Herod and Beheading of St John the Baptist*. Over the side door in the south transept, Gerolamo Forabosco, *Ecstasy of St Francis*. The tabernacle in the sanctuary by Baldassare Longhena, has sculptures by Juste Le Court; on the right wall, Luca Giordano, *Annunciation*. Outside the sanctuary (left), Johann Lys, **St Jerome visited by an Angel*. On the left wall, tomb of the patriarch Giovanni Francesco (d. 1678), by Filippo Parodi and *St Laurence distributing Alms* by Bernardo Strozzi. North side, third chapel, Palma Giovane, stories of *St Cecilia* and other *Saints*. Next to the church are buildings used by the University of Venice.

Church of the Scalzi

Beside the railway station (Stazione di S. Lucia) is the church of the Scalzi (Pl. 2; 8), belonging to the Carmelites, a fine Baroque building by Longhena (1670–80). The **façade** of Carrara marble is by Giuseppe Sardi (1672–80). The impressive dark Baroque **interior** (open 07.00–11.45, 15.30–18.45) is profusely decorated with marbles and sculptures, and a huge elaborate tabernacle fills the apse. The ceiling fresco by Giovanni Battista Tiepolo was destroyed by a bomb in 1915 and was replaced by a painting of the *Council of Ephesus* by Ettore Tito.

South side. The second chapel has a damaged vault fresco of *St Teresa in Glory* by Giambattista Tiepolo (1725), and on the two side walls, large scenes from the *Life of St Teresa* by Niccolò Bambini. The sculpted altarpiece of the *Ecstasy of St Teresa* is by Lazzaro Baldi or Enrico Meyring. In the pavement is the tomb slab of Doge Carlo Ruzzini (d. 1735). In the third chapel is a statue by Melchiore Barthel and a vault fresco by Pietro Liberi.

North side. The second chapel was the burial place Lodovico Manin, the last doge of Venice, who paid for the elaborate Baroque decoration of the chapel. The sculpture of the Holy Family is by Giuseppe Torretti, and the vault fresco by Ludovico Dorigny. Two remarkable huge turquoise blue glass candlesticks made in Murano in the early 18C have been placed here. In the first chapel there is a bas-relief by Giovanni Maria Morleiter, an 18C wax *Ecce Homo*, and more damaged frescoes in the vault (*Agony in the Garden*) by Giambattista Tiepolo.

The garish Lista di Spagna (with numerous hotels and souvenir shops) leads to Campo San Geremia. Here is the church of **San Geremia** (Pl. 3; 5; open 08.00–12.00, 15.00–19.00), a clumsy building by Carlo Corbellini (1753–60), although the fine campanile is among the oldest in Venice. The **interior** (the entrance is by the south door) is more successful than the exterior, but it is very cluttered with mementoes of St Lucy. When the body of St Lucy (martyred in Siracusa in Sicily in 304) was stolen from Constantinople in 1204 by Venetian crusaders, it was placed in the church of Santa Lucia. When Santa Lucia was demolished in 1863 to make way for the railway station her body was moved here (together with architectural fragments from the 16C church designed by Palladio). A painting of *St Lucy* by Palma Giovane is preserved with relics and church vestments in a room to the right of her chapel in the north transept; Palma also painted *St Magnus crowning Venice* (second south altar).

Palazzo Labia (Pl. 3; 5) has a façade in the campo by Alessandro (or Paolo) Tremignon (completed c 1750). The late 17C main façade on the Cannaregio canal is by Andrea Cominelli. The interior (now the regional headquarters of *RAI*, the Italian radio and television corporation) is shown by appointment when not in use (Wed, Thur, Fri 15.00–16.00). In the ballroom the trompe l'oeil frescoes by Gerolamo Mengozzi Colonna provide a setting for Giambattista Tiepolo's sumptuous **frescoes* of *Antony and Cleopatra*, subject of a recent controversial restoration. From the campo there is access to the public gardens behind Palazzo Savorgnan (see below), via Calle del Vergola.

The salizzada leads onto the **Cannaregio canal** (Pl. 3; 5), a busy waterway with two broad fondamenta, which runs through a distinctive part of the city. The stone Ponte delle Guglie (1580; restored 1777) has a pretty balustrade, and masks on the arch. In 1987 a ramp for the disabled was carefully incorporated into the design of the steps. Here is an entrance to the **Parco Savorgnan**, public gardens with a childrens' playground, with two more entrances from Campo San Geremia and Calle Riello.

Fondamenta Savorgnan leads along the Cannaregio canal past the huge Palazzo Manfrin (no. 342), built in 1735 by Andrea Tirali. Next, at no. 349, is Palazzo Savorgnan, built c 1663 to a design by Giuseppe Sardi. The fine garden façade behind can be seen from the public gardens here.

Beyond the red 15C Palazzo Testa (no. 468), is the entrance to a housing development, and an area formerly occupied by a factory, where Vittorio Gregotti began new buildings in 1992. Farther on the canal is crossed by Ponte dei Tre Archi, designed in 1688 by Andrea Tirali (the brick parapet was added in the 18C).

San Giobbe

In the secluded Campo di San Giobbe in the northwest-corner of the city is the church of San Giobbe (Pl. 2; 4; open 10.00–12.00, 16.00–18.00), built after 1450 by Antonio Gambello and enlarged by Pietro Lombardo who was responsible (with assistants) for the fine *doorway (the three statues are now exhibited in the ante-sacristy). In the lunette is a relief of St Francis and Job. The Gothic campanile can be seen from the courtyard once part of the convent which adjoined the church, which preserves an attractive portico next to a pleasant little garden. The **interior** is one of the earliest examples of a Franciscan Observant church plan; a single nave without aisles, with the monks' choir behind the presbytery.

A carved triumphal arch flanked by two smaller semi-circular chapels precedes the domed *sanctuary (c 1471), a masterpiece of Renaissance architecture and carving by Pietro Lombardo and assistants, built above the huge pavement tomb of the founder of the church, Doge Cristoforo Moro (d. 1471) and his wife Cristina Sanudo, which is beautifully carved with blackberries (*mori*). The tomb bears a simple inscription and has no religious references, and a portrait of the doge has been hung on the right wall. He was a friend of St Bernardine of Siena who stayed in the convent in 1443 and he dedicated the church to him. Behind the altar extends the long **choir** with 16C wood stalls.

South side. Second altar, Lattanzio Querena, *Vision of God to Job*, in a beautiful marble frame, which belonged to Giovanni Bellini's famous altarpiece, removed from here in the early 19C and now in the Galleria dell'Accademia. Beyond the monument to the French ambassador René d'Argenson by Claude Perrault (1651), composed of black and white marble supported by two bizarre crowned lions and with a fat putto above the sarcophagus, the fourth altarpiece is by Paris Bordone (*Three Saints*).

The two chapels at the beginning of the north side are beautifully decorated: in the first is a statue of St Luke by Lorenzo Bregno; the second (**Cappella Martini**) was built for a family of silk-workers from Lucca by 15C Tuscan artists. The vault is lined with majolica tiles and contains five pretty roundels, thought to be by Andrea della Robbia (early 1470s). The marble altar with statuettes of St John the Baptist and other saints is by a follower of Antonio Rossellino. The *Stations of the Cross* in the third chapel are attributed to Antonio Zucchi.

From the south side is the entrance to the **ante-sacristy**, part of a late 14C oratory, with a *Nativity* by Girolamo Savoldo. The sacristy has a 16C wooden ceiling and a charming little triptych of the *Annunciation between Saints Michael and Anthony* by Antonio Vivarini and Giovanni d'Alemagna (1440–50). Three statuettes from the main portal of the church are exhibited here. The 15C terracotta bust of San Bernardino da Siena attributed to Bartolomeo Bellano, was left to the church by Cristoforo Moro. At the other end of the room is a small painting in a very beautiful frame of the *Marriage of St Catherine* by Andrea Previtali.

Beyond Ponte dei Tre Archi the fondamenta continues to the edge of the lagoon past the huge **Macelli**, a slaughter-house built in 1832 by Giuseppe Salvadori. It was one of the largest in Italy after its extension in 1915, and only ceased to function as such in 1972. Since 1990 it has been undergoing restoration as premises for part of the University of Venice. The old brick buildings have been carefully preserved, and the alterations made in red steel in one of the most successful conservative restorations yet carried out in Venice. On the opposite side of the canal, on the Sacca di San Girolamo overlooking the lagoon, new municipal housing was built in 1987–90.

Across Ponte dei Tre Archi (with a view out to the lagoon) Fondamenta di Cannaregio leads back down the other side of the canal, passing (no. 967) Palazzo Surian, almost certainly by Giuseppe Sardi. This was once the French Embassy and Jean Jacques Rousseau was Secretary here in 1743–44. Just before Ponte delle Guglie, in a busy little shopping area, Sottoportico del Ghetto diverges left into the Ghetto (Pl. 3; 5, 3, 4). For admission to the museum and guided tour of the synagogues see p 46.

The Ghetto

The word ghetto is derived from the Venetian word *geto* indicating the place where metal was cast; there was an iron foundry here for making cannons until 1390 when it was transferred to the Arsenal. Although Jews from the East, northern Europe, Spain and Portugal had been coming to Venice for short periods (in which they were sometimes tolerated and sometimes expelled), it was not until 1516 that the *Maggior Consiglio* permitted Jews to live in Venice, but compelled them to inhabit only this part of the city. A curfew was enforced by guards who had to be paid for by the Jews themselves. The word Ghetto was subsequently used for isolated Jewish communities in other cities. The first settlement was on the island of Ghetto Nuovo (see below; named after a 'new' foundry); in 1541 it expanded to Ghetto Vecchio (the site of an 'old' foundry), and in 1633 to Ghetto Nuovissimo. It is estimated that as many as 5000 Jews lived here in the 16C–17C. Not until 1797 were Jews allowed (by Napoleon) to leave the Ghetto and live in other parts of the city. During the Austrian occupation the Jews were asked to return to the Ghetto, and it was only definitively opened in 1866. There are now some 500 Jewish residents in Venice, 30 of whom live in the Ghetto. The five main synagogues (or *scuole*) remain here, two of them still in use. Built for the first time in the 16C, they are named from the various different nationalities who erected them in their own distinctive style of architecture for their communities as meeting places and places of worship. The Jewish cemetery is on the Lido (see p 252).

At the beginning of the sottoportico are signs of the gate which closed the entrance at night. The dark calle leads past a stone (left) with a long list of the rules for 'converted' Jews who wished to return to the Ghetto inscribed in 1541. Beyond several carpenters' shops is **Campiello delle Scuole** with its two synagogues (on upper floors) still usually used for services, and a tall house with numerous windows, typical of this area (families were crowded into small flats with low ceilings). To the left, with an inconspicuous exterior, is the **Scuola Spagnola**, founded around 1585 as the Scuola Ponentina, with an interior rebuilt by Longhena c 1655. This is the largest of the Venetian synagogues. It has a fine elliptical womens' gallery (the women now sit below, but behind screens). The **Scuola Levantina**, opposite, probably founded around the same time as the Scuola Spagnola, and with a fine exterior, was erected by pupils of Longhena. The elaborate wood carving of the ceiling and pulpit are by Andrea Brustolon.

Ponte di Ghetto Vecchio leads over to the island of **Ghetto Nuovo**, the oldest area of the Ghetto, where large buildings were erected in the mid 15C by a Venetian merchant around a huge courtyard with three wells. The campo (on the site of that courtyard), with its three wells and clump of trees, is now partly surrounded by tall 17C houses, with numerous windows and some with as many as seven floors. Here, on the upper floors, are three more synagogues. Above a 19C portico of four columns is the **Scuola Italiana** (1575); it has five windows on the top floor and a cupola. The interior dates from 1739. In the corner of the campo is the **Scuola Canton** (1531), with its tiny wooden cupola just visible. It is now used by the Jewish community in Venice. Its name may be derived from its corner position, or from the name of a family (Cantono des Juif). It was connected by a passageway with the Scuola Italiana.

The **Scuola Grande Tedesca** the oldest synagogue in Venice (1528; to be restored), is now entered by a 19C staircase above the **Jewish Museum** (Pl. 3; 4; no. 2902/B), which has a well-labelled display of Jewish treasures (mostly 17C–18C).

On a wall in the campo, opposite the museum, bronze reliefs were set up in 1985 in memory of Jewish war victims, many of whom were deported to concentration camps in Germany, and another memorial dates from 1993. A hospice for the poor here was founded in 1890, which later became an old peoples' home. At no. 2912, under a portico, is the site of a pawn shop, known as the Banco Rosso. This was one of numerous such shops here run by the Jews, along with banking and exchange offices, and money-lenders, all of which were busy during the day with Venetian clients. A passageway (where the iron hinges of the doors which once closed the Ghetto at night can still be seen) leads into the **Ghetto Nuovissimo**, added in 1633, with more tall houses.

An iron bridge (guarded by two old sentry boxes where the Jewish guards were stationed) with decorative wrought-iron railings (1865–66) leads out of the Ghetto to Fondamenta degli Ormesini.

22 • The island of San Giorgio Maggiore

The church of San Giorgio Maggiore is in a superb position on an island opposite San Marco and the Palazzo Ducale. It is a masterpiece by Palladio, with a very fine façade, and on the walls of the chancel are two good paintings by Jacopo Tintoretto. From the top of the bell-tower, reached by a lift, there is a wonderful view. The rest of the island occupied by a Benedictine monastery (which has some buildings by Palladio), now owned the Giorgio Cini Foundation, is not open to the general public, except when exhibitions are in progress. There are frequent vaporetti services from San Zaccaria or the Giudecca (no. 82).

The lovely small island of San Giorgio Maggiore (Pl. 15; 4) was long occupied by a Benedictine convent; the most important in the lagoon. In 1951 the Giorgio Cini Foundation was established here and the buildings beautifully restored. It stands at the entrance to the city across the basin of St Mark's, separated from the island of the Giudecca by a narrow canal.

San Giorgio Maggiore

San Giorgio Maggiore (Pl. 15; 4) is one of the most conspicuous churches in Venice, in a magnificent position on a separate islet facing St Mark's. The white façade, tall campanile, and brick building reflect the changing light of the lagoon, and are especially beautiful at sunset. The original church dedicated to St George was probably founded in the 10C. The present building was begun in 1565 by Palladio and completed after his death by Simone Sorella. The **façade** was finished in 1610, almost certainly to a design by Palladio. It is modelled on a temple portico with four giant columns, and is particularly effective when seen from a distance across the water. The campanile was

The island of San Giorgio Maggiore

rebuilt in 1791 by Benedetto Buratti and is similar to that of St Mark's.

The white **interior** (open 10.00–12.30, 14.30–16.30) is remarkable for its clean architectural lines and the absence of decoration; it is enhanced by the proximity of water. The cruciform design has a central dome and a long choir separated from the chancel. On the west wall is a monument to Doge Leonardo Donà (d. 1612), the friend of Galileo, by Alessandro Vittoria. **South aisle**, first altar, Jacopo Bassano, *Adoration of the Shepherds*; second altar, wooden Crucifix, a Venetian work of c 1470; third altar, school of Jacopo Tintoretto, *Martyrdom of Saints Cosmas and Damian*, a well-composed painting.

South transept. On the altar, Jacopo Tintoretto (attributed), *Coronation of the Virgin*. Altar to the right of the high altar, Sebastiano Ricci, *Madonna and Saints*. The **chancel** is entered between two candelabra by Niccolò Roccatagliata (1598). The high altar, designed by Aliense, has a fine bronze group of the Saviour on a globe borne by the Evangelists by Girolamo Campagna, and two bronze angels by Pietro Boselli (1644). On the walls are two beautiful late works by Jacopo Tintoretto: *Last Supper (1594), and *Shower of Manna. In the choir behind, the Baroque *stalls and lectern are by van der Brulle and Gaspare Gatti (1594–98). The two small bronzes on the balustrade of St George and St Stephen are by Niccolò Roccatagliata (1593). On the altar to the left of the high altar, Jacopo Tintoretto (finished by his son Domenico), *Resurrection* (with portraits of the Morosini family).

North transept. School of Tintoretto, *Martyrdom of St Stephen*. As the inscription states, the body of St Stephen was brought to the church in 1110 from Constantinople.

A door on the right of the choir (at present closed) leads into a corridor with the tomb of Doge Domenico Michiel (d. 1130), to a design attributed to Baldassare Longhena, and, set in to the wall, the tomb slab of Bonincontro de' Boateri by the Dalle Masegne brothers. In the **Chapel of the Dead** (1592) is a moving *Deposition painted by Jacopo Tintoretto for this chapel in 1594. It is a very late work and he may have been helped by his son Domenico. A photograph of Carpaccio's *St George and the Dragon* which is housed in an upper chapel (only open for Mass at 08.00 on fest. in winter, or with special permission) where the Conclave met in 1799–1800 (see below) has been placed here. The tempera painting is another version (painted about eight years later) of the more famous work in the Scuola di San Giorgio degli Schiavoni (see Ch. 5).

On the other side of the choir is the sacristy which contains handsome dossals. The angel in the corridor, which formerly crowned the campanile, was struck by lightning in 1993, and replaced in situ by a bronze copy.

The **campanile** can be ascended by lift (open 09.30–12.30, 14.30–17.00) and provides one of the best views in Venice. To the **south** there is a view over the roof and dome of the church and the two cloisters of the monastery. The long island of the Giudecca can be seen on the right. Ahead is the lagoon with the islands of Le Grazie and San Clemente and, just to the right, Sacca Sessola. In the distance a tower marks the island of Spirito Santo. To the left is the spit of the Lido and Malamocco, with the island of San Lazzaro degli Armeni on the extreme left and Lazzaretto Vecchio nearer the Lido.

Looking **east** you can see the little port of the island, with the Lido straight ahead (and the island of San Lazzaro degli Armeni on the right). Beyond the Giardini is the brick tower of Sant'Elena and further left the white tower of San Pietro di Castello and part of the Arsenal. To the **north** there is a good view of the Basilica of San Marco and Palazzo Ducale. Straight across the water is the façade of the Pietà, with the tall campanile of San Francesco della Vigna, and the end of the island of Murano visible behind. Farther left the huge church of Santi Giovanni e Paolo can be seen, with the campanile of the Gesuiti conspicuous to the left. To the **west** there is another splendid view of the Bacino di San Marco, with Palazzo Ducale and the Punta della Dogana. The oil refinery of Marghera can be seen in the distance.

From outside the church there is a good view of St Mark's, the mouth of the Grand Canal, and the Punta della Dogana with its golden ball. The adjoining Benedictine *****monastery** is now part of the **Giorgio Cini Foundation**. It may be visited when exhibitions are being held.

In 982 Giovanni Morosini gave the island to the Benedictines. The monastery was rebuilt in 1223, and again in 1433 when Cosimo de'Medici was exiled here from Florence for a brief period. At this time his Florentine architect, Michelozzo, built the first library (later destroyed). In 1799–1800 the monastery was the scene of the Conclave that elected Pope Pius VII. After many years' use as barracks, it was restored in 1951–56 as the Giorgio Cini Foundation, set up as a memorial to Count Vittorio Cini's son who was killed in an air crash in 1949. It includes a Centre of Culture and Civilisation, an Arts and Crafts Centre, and a Naval Training School. Outstanding art exhibitions are held in a 19C wing.

The **first cloister** (entered to the right of the church) was designed by Palladio (1579). It is separated from the second cloister by the library wing designed by Longhena, which contains 17C woodwork by Francesco Pauc, and ceiling paintings by Filippo Gherardi and Giovanni Coli. The **second cloister** is by Andrea Buora (1516–40). Off it, and preceded by an anteroom with elaborate handbasins, is the handsome *****refectory**, another splendid work by Palladio (1560; now used as a conference hall). The *Marriage of the Virgin* by the school of

Tintoretto hangs here in the place of Paolo Veronese's *Marriage at Cana* (now in the Louvre; a copy of which is in the anteroom). From the first cloister a monumental double ***staircase** by Baldassare Longhena (1643–45) leads up to the Institute offices and exhibition rooms. The **dormitory** was begun when Michelozzo was staying in the convent (see above) and completed by Giovanni Buora (1494–1513). It closes the far wing of the second cloister and runs for 128 metres behind the church. It has a pretty gabled façade (with a relief of St George by Giovanni Battista Bregno, 1508) overlooking the little port. The two Istrian-stone lighthouses were designed by Giuseppe Mezzani and Romeo Venturelli in 1810–11. In 1829 the island became a free port (open to all boats from all countries and exempt from franchise duties). The Giorgio Cini training ship is usually moored here (it replaces a schooner built in 1894).

23 • The Giudecca

The Giudecca is an island beyond the wide Giudecca canal which has an atmosphere all of its own as many Venetians live here and it is seldom visited by tourist groups. It has some local shops on the waterfront and a few restaurants, but no hotels except for the Venice Youth Hostel and the 4-star *Cipriani* hotel. Its most important building is Palladio's church of the Redentore, with a superb façade and light interior (recently carefully restored). Here the little sacristy is also interesting. The rest of the island is worth exploring, although some of the gardens, churches, and industrial buildings have now been abandoned. Although the southern edge of the island is mostly inaccessible, there are wonderful views from the fondamenta along the Giudecca canal, always busy with boats.

The island of the Giudecca (Pl. 12, 13, 14, 15) is on the opposite side of the wide Giudecca canal from Dorsoduro. It was originally called *Spinalunga*, probably because of its elongated shape, but perhaps because thorn bushes used to grow here. Its present name could come from the fact that Jews (*Giudei*) established a colony here at the end of the 13C, but it is more likely that it comes from *giudicato (zudecà)* or judgement because here in the 9C allotments of land were conceded (by a judge) to families who were allowed to return to Venice from exile. Later on grand villas and pleasure-gardens were built here by the aristocracy, and it is known that Michelangelo stayed here in 1529.

Boat services The Giudecca has four landing-stages, *Palanca*, *Redentore* and *Zitelle* (*Sant'Eufemia* is closed in 2001 while repairs are being carried out on the fondamenta here). Vaporetto **82** stops at all of these (from *San Zaccaria* via the island of San Giorgio Maggiore), or from the railway station, *Piazzale Roma*, *Sacca Fisola* and *San Basilio* and the *Zattere* in the other direction. Vaporetto **42** also serves the Giudecca from *San Zaccaria*, and vaporetto **41** from the railway station, *Piazzale Roma*, *Santa Marta* and *Sacca Fisola* (for full details of these lines, see p 39). At night, there is an *ACTV* **ferry service** across the Giudecca canal to the Zattere (landing-stage near Santa Maria della Visitazione; see map p 42), and this is also usually guaranteed in fog, during *acqua alta* or vaporetto strikes.

Near the eastern point of the island, on the Giudecca canal, is the church of **Le Zitelle** (Pl. 15; 5; open April–Sept 09.30–12.30, and at 11.00 on Sun for a service). This was designed c 1570 by Palladio but built after his death in 1582–86. The attractive light interior is centrally planned with a dome. The high altarpiece of the *Presentation of Mary in the Temple* is by Francesco Bassano. On the left altar is a *Madonna* by Aliense, and on the right altar, *Prayer in the Garden* by Palma Giovane. Around the upper part of the walls are mid-17C paintings. The statue of the *Madonna and Child* is by Giuseppe Maria Morleiter.

Two wings of a hospice stand next to the church. It was founded in 1561 for young girls who were taught the art of lace-making. The **Antichi Granai** next to the convent have been restored and are used for exhibitions. To the left, the deserted fondamenta continues up to the entrance of the headquarters of the customs police (from here there is a fine view of San Marco). The Corte di Ca' Mosto has an overgrown garden. To the right of the Zitelle is the neo-Gothic **Casa di Maria** with an elaborate brick façade and three large windows, which takes its inspiration from Palazzo Ducale. It was built by the painter Mario de Maria as his studio in 1910–13, and is still in excellent condition.

Calle Michelangelo leads away from the waterfront through a stark modern district near a housing development, just opened, with tiny, claustrophobic dwellings, to the other side of the island (one of the few points where this bank is accessible from land—there is no fondamenta on this side of the island). The calle ends beside the **Villa Heriott**, a mock Gothic building dating from 1929 now owned by the Comune (and in very good conditon). From here there is a view of the island of Le Grazie. To the left, beyond the school and library, is the garden of the famous *Cipriani* hotel, perhaps the most exclusive and invisible of Venice's luxury hotels, which is usually approached by water.

Fondamenta della Croce continues along the Giudecca canal past ship-building warehouses and the Venice Youth Hostel. On the left can be seen the huge church of **Santa Croce** rebuilt in 1508–11, and now part of an institution for the elderly and under-privileged. Across the canal, Calle della Croce leads inland past a house with a handsome lion's masque above the bell and out onto the pretty Rio della Croce, lined with quaint old houses with boats moored alongside. A bizarre small bridge, made partly of wood and partly of iron, leads over the rio to a cypress which marks the entrance to the walled '**Garden of Eden**' (no admission), an English garden created after 1884 by Frederic and Caroline Eden, with the advice of the garden designer Gertrude Jekyll, who was Caroline's sister. On the site of an artichoke bed, it became one of the largest and finest private gardens in Venice, famous for its pergolas and lilies, and paved courts with tubs of oranges and lemons. Eden's diary *A Garden in Venice* published in 1903 describes the work they did on the garden. They also kept a small herd of cows here. At the end of the fondamenta there is a view out to the lagoon.

On the return to the Giudecca canal there is a view of the dome of Santa Maria della Salute in the distance, and (left) the dome of the Redentore. At the end of the Zattere, the golden ball of the Dogana and the campanile and domes of San Marco can be glimpsed.

The Redentore

Further along the Giudecca canal stands the Franciscan church of the Redentore (Pl. 14; 5), the most complete and perhaps the most successful of Palladio's churches (1577–92). The very fine *exterior, includes a handsome façade on the waterfront and a lovely dome crowned by a statue of the Redeemer, and two little turreted spires.

The Redentore was built in thanksgiving for the deliverance of Venice from the plague in 1575–77 which left some 46,000 dead (25–30 per cent of the population), and the doge vowed to visit the church annually across a bridge of boats which united the Zattere with the Giudecca. The feast of the Redentore (third Sunday in July) remains one of the most popular Venetian festivals, and a pontoon bridge is still usually constructed for the occasion. There are now some twenty Franciscan friars in the monastery attached to the church.

Palladio

The architect Andrea di Pietro dalla Gondola (1508–80)—by all accounts a pleasant, devout and modest man—was nicknamed Palladio, after Pallas, the Greek goddess of wisdom. He was born in Padua and settled in Vicenza in 1523. His distinctive Classical style of architecture, with its harmonious proportions, was later imitated in domestic architecture all over the world, especially in Britain and America, and he influenced both Vincenzo Scamozzi and Inigo Jones. After designing numerous country villas in the Veneto, and rebuilding Vicenza, he planned the two conspicuous churches of San Giorgio Maggiore and the Redentore in Venice towards the end of his life. He also built the delightful suburban Villa Malcontenta on the Brenta canal just before it enters the Venetian lagoon, although his design for the Rialto bridge was rejected.

The wonderful *interior (open 10.00–17.00; fest. 13.00–17.00), beautifully restored in 2000 and particularly well lit, has elements derived from Roman Classical buildings, with superb clean lines, and thermal windows in each side chapel, above the cornice of the nave, and in the apse. Beyond the lovely dome, the design of the chancel, with a curving row of columns, is particularly fine. The altarpieces on the **south side** are by Francesco Bassano (*Nativity*), the school of Veronese (*Baptism of Christ*) and the school of Tintoretto (*Flagellation of Christ*). Those on the **north side** are by Palma Giovane (*Deposition*), Francesco Bassano (*Resurrection*), and the workshop of Tintoretto (*Ascension*). On the Baroque high altar (by Giuseppe Mazza) are fine bronzes by Campagna of the *Crucifix, St Francis*, and *St Mark*.

The **sacristy** (entered through an inconspicuous door in the last south chapel, opened on request at the entrance to the church) is a charming little room with wooden cupboards, with precious paintings, sculptures, and reliquaries. The paintings include (on the entrance wall): a *Baptism of Christ* attributed to Paolo Veronese, a *Madonna and Child with Saints* by Palma Giovane, *St John the Baptist in the Desert* by Jacopo da Bassano, and two paintings of the *Madonna and Child and Saints* (displayed one above the other) by Francesco Bissolo and Rocco Marconi. The beautiful *Madonna in Adoration of the Child* is by Lazzaro Bastiani. Beneath are 18C reliquaries made in Murano. Another wall has cupboards with reliquaries, and a charming *Madonna in Adoration of the Child and two Angels*, by Alvise Vivarini, in an elaborate frame enclosing more relics. The *Crucifix* is by Andrea Brustolon. On the wall opposite the entrance the unusual bronze statuette of the *Madonna and Child* is attributed to Jacopo Sansovino. The realistic wax heads of Franciscans, preserved under glass domes, date from 1710: they were all made from one mould, but the features, including glass eyes made in Murano, were altered to represent supposed portraits of Franciscan saints who lived in the 16C and 17C. The paintings on this wall include an *Ecstasy of St Francis* by Carlo Saraceni, and four small paintings by a follower of Francesco Bassano.

The fondamenta continues to a wide rio, just before which is a plaque set up in 1995 in memory of martyrs of the Resistance movement in the Second World War. The rio is crossed by the Ponte Lungo, a long iron bridge constructed in 1895. The canal is filled with fishing boats. A brief detour inland may be made here (via Calle delle Erbe, Rio della Palada, and Corte Ferrando) through an area traditionally inhabited by fishermen. Beyond the Ponte Piccolo Calle del Forno leads to Corte dei Cordami where the row of houses have picturesque chimneys. The fondamenta ends at the church of **Sant' Eufemia** (Pl. 13; 5; open 09.00–11.00, 18.00–19.00; fest. 07.00–12.30), founded in the 9C, with a 16C Doric portico. The Rococo interior preserves the Veneto-Byzantine capitals. The first altar on the right has a charming painting of *St Roch and the Angel* (with a *Madonna and Child* in the lunette above) signed by Bartolomeo Vivarini (1480).

At the western extremity of the island rises the huge brick **Mulino Stucky**, a neo-Gothic flour-mill, built by Ernst Wullekopf in 1895, and completed in 1920. It is an unusual building for Italy, reminiscent of northern European industrial architecture. It dominates the view of the Giudecca from the Zattere and has been undergoing a radical restoration for many years for use as a cultural centre, and partly as residences. A long bridge connects the Giudecca to the island of Sacca Fisola (Pl. 12; 3), a modern residential area.

24 • The Arsenal

The Arsenal is beyond the end of Riva degli Schiavoni in the sestiere of Castello, and although this great shipyard constructed for the Venetian Republic's fleet and taken over by the Italian navy, is closed to the public, its great land entrance can still be seen guarded by ancient Greek lions. Close by is the well kept Naval Museum with a superb display of boats, models, and navigational instruments. The largest boats belonging to the museum are kept in an adjacent pavilion, temporarily closed for repairs. The little church of San Martino, also in the vicinity, is well worth a visit.

At the end of Riva degli Schiavoni Riva Ca' di Dio leads to the monumental Ponte de l'Arsenal, built in 1936, which crosses the Arsenal canal to Campo San Biagio (with the Museo Navale, described below) from which a fondamenta leads along the Canale dell'Arsenale past a neo-Classical guard-house built in 1829 by Giovanni Casoni during the Austrian occupation and the six big windows of the Officina Remi, where the oars were made for the Arsenal, now part of the Museo Navale (see below). At the end is the wooden bridge, which retains the form of previous bridges here (up until 1938 they were all drawbridges). The view embraces the oldest part of the Arsenal with the outlet onto the Fondamente

Nuove. On the other side of the bridge is the **land entrance to the Arsenal** (Pl. 10; 4) beside two massive towers (reconstructed in 1686) which protect the entrance from the lagoon. The great **gateway**, in the form of a triumphal arch, is one of the earliest works of the Renaissance in the city. It was begun in 1460 re-using Greek marble columns with Veneto-Byzantine capitals, by an unknown architect (it was for-

The entrance to the Arsenal

merly attributed to Antonio Gambello). Additions were made in the 16C–17C. The statue of St Justina above it is by Girolamo Campagna.

The gate is flanked by two colossal lions sent by Francesco Morosini from Piraeus as spoils of war and placed here in 1692. The one sitting upright on the left (which gave the name of Porta Leone to Piraeus) bears a (worn) Runic inscription carved in 1040 by Varangian guards from Byzantium, sent to Athens to put down an insurrection; its fellow possibly stood on the road from Athens to Eleusis. The two smaller lions, one also brought to Venice by Morosini and the other added in 1716 in celebration of the reconquest of Corfu, may have come originally from the Lion Terrace at Delos. Beyond the door, is a *Madonna and Child* signed by Jacopo Sansovino. In front of the doorway is a courtyard born on a little bridge designed in 1692–94, and surrounded by an elaborate railing with statues, by Giovanni Antonio Comino.

History of the Arsenal

The Arsenal was founded in 1104; it was enlarged from the 14C–16C, and now occupies 32 hectares (80 acres). It gave its name (from the Arabic *darsina'a*, meaning workshop) to subsequent dockyards all over the world. Here the Republic's ships were overhauled and repaired, and from the end of the 15C onwards shipbuilding was also concentrated here. Specialised workers made ropes and armaments and everything necessary to equip the warships and merchant galleys before they set sail. The workers, known as *arsenalotti* held a privileged position in Venetian society, as well as enjoying advantageous working conditions. At the height of Venetian prosperity they numbered some 16,000. They had the honour of carrying the doge in triumph in the procession immediately following his election. For centuries the Arsenal remained the symbol of the economic and military power of the Venetian Republic.

Dante visited the Arsenal in 1306, and again in 1321 when he was sent as emissary to Venice from Ravenna. He described it in the *Inferno* (Canto XXI).

The Arsenal (admission only on 4 November; at present used by the armed forces) is surrounded by crenellated walls with towers. Interminable discussions have been under way for many years about the long-term plans to convert part of the vast area of the Arsenal to civil use when the present military administration eventually relinquishes their claim to some of the huge monumental buildings (some of which are attributed to Jacopo Sansovino and are in urgent need of repair). *Thetis*, a consortium for marine technology, research and development, operates here, as well as an Institute for Strategic Studies, and some of the docks are to be used by *ACTV* for the maintenance of their fleet. The **Corderie**, where the ropes were made, and the **Artiglierie** building have been restored and opened as temporary exhibition centres in connection with the Biennale. Part of the northern area near the main canal of the Arsenale Vecchio and the archway opened in 1964 in its walls on the Fondamente Nuove, can be seen from the *Celestia* and *Bacini* vaporetto stops (nos. **41** and **42**), where the *Thetis* shipyard occupies the northern wharves.

San Martino

From the Arsenal gateway a short fondamenta leads along the side canal to the campo in front of the church of San Martino (Pl. 10; 5), founded in 932. The façade was remodelled in 1897. The interior (open 09.30–12.00, 15.30–19.00) was rebuilt in 1553 by Jacopo Sansovino on a Greek cross plan. The ceiling has 17C quadratura by Domenico Bruni, and *St Martin in Glory* by Jacopo Guarana. The Nacchini *organ was modified by Gaetano Callido in 1799 and has been carefully restored. On the organ case is a *Last Supper* by Girolamo da Santacroce (1549). Around the south door is a huge monument to Doge Francesco Erizzo by Matteo Carnero (1633), with an allegory of *Faith* in the vault above painted by Jacopo Guarana. The doge is buried in the centre of the church. In the chapel to the right of the chancel is a painting of the *Risen Christ*, by Girolamo da Santacroce, and a 16C bas relief on the altar frontal. In the chancel are frescoes by Fabio Canal and two paintings by Palma Giovane.

On the left of the north door is a late 15C altar by Lorenzo Bregno, supported by four charming kneeling *angels by Tullio Lombardo (completed by 1511), brought here from the demolished Oratory of the Santo Sepolcro. The Crucifix was probably made in the Arsenal for the mast of a ship which took part in the Battle of Lepanto in 1571. In the **sacristy** the frescoed vault which was white-washed in the 19C was rediscovered in 1960. It has frescoes by Antonio Zanchi and quadratura by Simon Guglielmini. Zanchi also painted the altarpiece, and the cupboards may have been designed by Baldassare Longhena. A Byzantine icon of the *Madonna and Child* (in an inappropriate bright red frame), a small 15C *Annunciation*, a 17C alabaster statuette of the Immacolata (with a ship beneath her feet), and three paintings of *Angels* and a *Deposition* by Palma Giovane are preserved here. The little **oratory** next door has a 15C relief of *St Martin and the Beggar*. The porch on the north side has two Corinthian columns.

A bridge leads across the rio dell'Arsenale which follows the high crenellated wall of the Arsenal and is used as a mooring for small boats. Beyond a secluded campo, Calle dell'Angelo leads to **Sottoportico dell'Angelo** where the low arch is surmounted by a fine statue of an angel between two hedgehogs in relief. At the end Calle Magno leads left to Campiello due Pozzi with a 14C house.

Museo Storico Navale

From the Arsenal gateway (see above) the fondamenta should be followed back to Campo San Biagio overlooking the Bacino di San Marco. Here in the former Granary of the Republic, is the *Museo Storico Navale or Maritime Museum (Pl. 10; 8). The exhibits are beautifully arranged on four floors, and the museum is superbly maintained. Since the labelling (in English) is extremely good, the following description has been kept to a minimum. Open 08.45–13.30 exc. Sun; the admission fee goes to an orphanage for sailors' children).

Ground floor. In **room 2** (left) is a torpedo, invented in 1935, which destroyed sixteen ships in the Second World War. **Room 3** (right), monument by Canova to Angelo Emo (1731–92), last admiral of the Venetian Republic. In **room 5** are cannon, one cast by Cosimo Cenni in 1643. **Room 6** contains models of the Fortezza di Sant'Andrea on the Lido. The fine display of arms includes late 16C arquebuses, 18C muskets and blunderbusses, two cannon donated by the British to Garibaldi, 19C rifles, and 18C–19C swords. **Room 7** is devoted to the Second World War, with an electro-mechanical gunfire computer and diving gear for underwater assault operations. **Room 8** has models of boats, including an ancient Egyptian boat, Phoenician boats (7C BC), material relating to the Roman boats (1C AD) found at the bottom of Lake Nemi, a 17C Dutch whale boat, 16C Venetian galleys, and the *Michelangelo*, the last large ocean-going liner built in Italy (1962).

First floor. At the top of the stairs **room 11** has a wooden sculpture of two Turks in chains, from the galley sailed by Morosini in 1684. **Room 12**. Nautical instruments and 17C charts. **Room 13**. Models of the Arsenal. **Room 14**. Models, including one of an ancient galley, or trireme. Elaborate 17C carvings from a Venetian galley. **Room 15**. Models of 16C Venetian galleys. **Room 16**. Models of 18C boats including a vessel built in the Arsenal by order of Napoleon which carried 80 cannon. **Room 17**. *Model of the last bucintoro (1728), the gala ship used for the ceremonial marriage of Venice with the sea, and a wooden statue of Venice as *Justice*.

Second floor. Rooms 21–27 illustrate naval history, including navigational instruments, warships and torpedoes. **Room 28** has naval uniforms.

Third floor. At the top of the stairs **room 31** has a model of the *Cristoforo Colombo* liner, and plans of the Arsenal. To the right, beyond **room 32** with models of ocean-going liners, **room 33** is almost filled by the *Lusoria*, an 18C boat. The walls are hung with ex votos. The Turkish caique was used until 1920 by the Italian ambassador in Istanbul to cross the Bosphorus. From here stairs lead up to a **mezzanine floor** with two rooms, both with splendid old roof beams, one illustrating the maritime relationship between Venice and Sweden, and the other displays a collection of some 2000 shells. There is a view from the window of the Arsenal gateway and the campanile of San Francesco della Vigna. Over the roof tops you can just see the lagoon and (on the extreme right) the top of the dome and campanile of San Pietro di Castello. **Room 34** has models of fishing vessels and part of an old 19C fishing boat from Chioggia. **Room 35** is devoted to gondolas (the wooden shelter, or *felze*, used to protect passengers in bad weather). **Room 36** displays more fishing vessels. **Room 37** contains *models of Far Eastern junks, and 18C Chinese embroidered panels.

The ex-naval church of **San Biagio**, next to the museum, is sometimes open to visitors, although it is closed to worship. On the site of a 10C church, it was reconstructed in the 18C, with ceiling frescoes attributed to Scagliaro. On the north altar there is an icon of *St Spiridon* by a Greek artist, Karousos (1818). The tomb of Angelo Emo, the last admiral of the fleet who died in Malta in 1792, has a good effigy by Giovanni Ferrari.

The 16C **Officina Remi**, part of the Arsenal where oars were made and wood stored, now called the **Padiglione delle Navi** (Pl. 10; 6) is also part of the Museo Storico Navale (entered from the Arsenal canal). The three huge halls still have their wooden roofs of 1546; meetings of the *Maggior Consiglio* were held here for a time after the fire in Palazzo Ducale in 1577. Displayed here are a miscellany of boats including an early 19C royal boat last used in 1959; a barge for divers built in the Arsenal; fishing boats with sails; a 19C vessel for heavy transport on the Po; Sicilian boats; a torpedo motor boat used in the last war and part of Marconi's wrecked *Elettra*, recovered from the sea near Trieste, which was used for his first radio experiments.

Riva Ca' di Dio (Pl. 10; 7) leads back towards San Marco past the **Forni Pubblici** (1473) with an ornamental marble frieze. These were the bakeries of the Republic which supplied the ships as they set sail from the Arsenal. On the next rio is the Ca' di Dio (restored), a pilgrim hospital founded in the 13C for Crusaders. In 1545 Jacopo Sansovino added a hospice wing along the rio (seen from the bridge, with its numerous chimney-stacks). Here begins the Riva degli Schiavoni (see Ch. 5) which returns to Piazza San Marco.

32 • Castello

This walk covers part of the sestiere of Castello at the extreme eastern end of the city. The walk follows the lively Via Garibaldi which leads away from the lagoon just beyond the Maritime Museum (described in Ch. 24) through a characteristic part of the city where many Venetians still live. The solitary church of San Pietro di Castello, once the cathedral of Venice, preserves some interesting works of art. From near the church of San Giuseppe di Castello, which also merits a visit, and the public gardens on the waterfront, it is worth taking a vaporetto (no. 1, 51 or 41; from the landing-stage of *Giardini*) to the next stop, *Sant' Elena* to visit the Gothic church of Sant' Elena (in urgent need of restoration), which is in an even more isolated position than San Pietro di Castello. It has a sculptural group by Antonio Rizzo over the portal. The Biennale exhibition grounds, overlooking the lagoon, are only open during the Biennale art show.

Across the bridge on Fondamenta San Biagio, rebuilt in 1927, the long broad **Via Garibaldi** (Pl. 10; 8) leads away from the waterfront. This was laid out by Napoleon in 1808 by filling in a canal (as the pavement, recently relaid, shows). It crosses a lively district of the city, with shops for the local inhabitants. The house at the beginning (right; plaque) was the residence of the navigators John Cabot (1420–98) and his son Sebastian (1477–1537), who were the first to touch the American mainland and explore the coast of America, from Hudson's Bay to Florida.

Farther on, Corte Nuova opens on the left with two well-heads and the Arsenal buildings in the distance. Just before the public gardens (right), a house (no. 1310) has a doorway with a good relief of Saints Dominic, John the Baptist, Peter Martyr and the Redeemer.

The church of **San Francesco di Paola** (Pl. 11; 7) stands opposite. In the interior the paintings on the ceiling are by Giovanni Contarini (1603); those around the top of the walls are by 18C artists including (second on the right) Gian Domenico Tiepolo (*Liberation of a Soul possessed*). Left side, first chapel, Marieschi, *Martyrdom of St Bartholomew*; fourth chapel, Palma Giovane, four *Virgin Saints*; right side (on either side of the last altar), four paintings attributed to Antonio Zanchi. The vault of the presbytery was frescoed by Michele Schiavone.

The calle beside the church leads down to Rio della Tana which follows the Arsenal wall (see Ch. 24); characteristic courtyards open off the fondamenta. Across the bridge, in Campo della Tana is the entrance to the **Corderie della Tana**, where the ropes were made for the Arsenal. The huge long warehouse was rebuilt in 1583 by Antonio da Ponte. It is now used for exhibitions in connection with the Biennale. Nearby, on the rio, is the incongruous white Palasport (1979), a sports arena.

In front of San Francesco di Paola, the **Giardini Garibaldi** (public gardens), laid out in 1808–12 by Gian Antonio Selva, extend to the waterfront and adjoin the Biennale gardens (see below). The statue of Garibaldi is by Augusto Benvenuti (1885). Near the entrance to the gardens, at no. 1310, the Gothic portal survives, dating from around 1375, of the Ospedale de le pute. It has sculptures of the Redeemer, and, below, Saints Domenic, Andrew and Peter Martyr, perhaps by a pupil of Filippo Calendario (restored in 1999). The hospice was founded by Doge Marino Zorzi in 1311, and after 1560 was used as a residence for officials of the Inquisition, but it was destroyed by Napoleon when the public gardens were laid out. Beyond a little street market is the end of Rio di Sant'Anna (no. 1132 is a Gothic house with Byzantine roundels).

The fondamenta on the left leads over a bridge (with a view, left, down Rio di San Daniele of the Arsenal wall and tower) to Calle San Gioachino, which bears left at the end of the next bridge. It passes a mid-15C relief of the Madonna and Child with Saints Peter and Paul and continues to the pretty Rio Riello lined with the small houses that are typical of this area, with washing lines stretched from one side of the canal to the other. Across the bridge a fondamenta leads beneath a portico down the right side of the canal and, at the end, diverges right through Campiello del Figaretto, where there is a little votive chapel with wrought-iron doors (1979). From here there is a good view of the campanile of San Pietro di Castello. From Campo Ruga, which has two fine palaces with balconies, Salizzada Stretta continues towards the Arsenal wall. Just before the canal, Calle Larga San Pietro leads right to a bridge, rebuilt in iron in 1883, over the wide Canale di San Pietro with its busy boatyards and the Arsenal conspicuous to the left.

San Pietro di Castello

On the solitary Isola di San Pietro (Pl. 11; 6), formerly known as Olivolo, near the eastern limit of the city, the grass-grown Campo di San Pietro with its grove of trees, opens out before the church and isolated campanile of San Pietro di Castello (Pl. 11; 6). Probably founded in the 7C, this was the cathedral of Venice from the 11C until 1807 when St Mark's was designated cathedral (see Ch. 1). The present church was built on a Palladian design of 1557.

In the light **interior** (open 10.00–18.00; fest. 15.00–18.00), on the west wall is the sarcophagus of procurator Filippo Correr (d. 1417). In the **south aisle** a venerable marble throne from Antioch has a Muslim funerary stele and is decorated with verses from the Koran. The sumptuous high altar was designed by Longhena. Behind it is the organ by Nacchini (1754). In the sanctuary is a large painting showing Doge Nicolò Contarini before Beato Lorenzo Giustiniani during the Plague of 1630. It was commissioned from Antonio Bellucci shortly after the canonisation of Giustiniani in 1690 (he was the first Patriarch of Venice in 1451). In the chapel to the left of the high altar is a dark wooden relief of the Crucifix with terminals in beaten copper (14C).

North aisle. The Baroque **Cappella Vendramin** was designed by Longhena in the 1660s; it contains coloured marbles and reliefs by Michael Fabris Ongaro. The altarpiece of the *Madonna of the Carmelites* is by Luca Giordano. Above the entrance to the Cappella Lando is a painting by Paolo Veronese, of *Saints John the Evangelist, Peter, and Paul*. The **Cappella Lando** contains an early pluteus (9C?) as an altar-front, and, in the pavement in front, an interesting polychrome mosaic fragment, thought to date from the 5C and showing the influence of Roman mosaic design. Also here, columns from the baptistery with Veneto-Byzantine capitals, and a 15C half-figure of San Lorenzo Giustiniani (see above). The isolated **campanile**, in Istrian stone, by Mauro Codussi, dates from 1482–88, with a cupola of 1670. On the house behind the campanile are 15C statues and reliefs.

The calle behind the campanile soon rejoins Canale di San Pietro beside a fine Renaissance relief of the Madonna and Child with St Peter. The calle continues to a bridge, first built in 1910 and one of the longest in the city (reconstructed in 1964), which re-crosses the canal near several busy boat repair yards. At the foot of the bridge is the abandoned church of **Sant'Anna** founded c 1240 and rebuilt in the 17C, next to an ex-naval hospital. Opposite, the canal is lined by a quaint row of old houses with typical chimney-pots. Campiello Correr diverges left from Rio Sant'Anna (see above) to cross an area laid out with rows of stark 19C houses.

Beyond the more colourful Secco Marina, Corte del Soldà continues across a bridge to the campo and church of **San Giuseppe di Castello** (Pl. 16, inset). The façade bears a relief of the Adoration of the Magi by Giulio del Moro. In the **interior** (usually open 10.00–12.00), the perspective ceiling is attributed to Giovanni Antonio Torriglia. **South side**. First altar, *St Michael and the Senator Michele Bon*, attributed to the workshop of Tintoretto. On the wall of the sanctuary is a monument to the procurator Giovanni Grimani (d. 1570), with a portrait bust by Alessandro Vittoria. Over the high altar is an *Adoration of the Shepherds* by Paolo Veronese. On the **north side**, the second altar bears a curious relief of the Battle of Lepanto. The huge monument to Doge Marino Grimani (d. 1605), son of Giovanni (see above), was designed by Vincenzo Scamozzi, with two bronze reliefs by Girolamo Campagna. It is one of the grandest doge's tombs in the city, and the doge himself commissioned it in 1601.

From Campo San Giuseppe it is a short way along the rio out to the waterfront and the *Giardini* landing-stage. It is one stop on vaporetto no. **1**, **41** or **51** from here to *Sant'Elena*. If you prefer to continue on foot (rather a long walk through a lonely and not very interesting part of the city) you leave Campo San Giuseppe (with a doorway leading into the public gardens on the waterfront), by following Rio terrà San Giuseppe to the left. Ramo Primo di Sant'Antonio leads round the outer wall of the Italian pavilion in the Biennale gardens (see below). A bridge leads over the canal, with a view of the gardens, and Viale XXIV Maggio continues through a residential quarter spaciously laid out in the early 20C. Viale Piave skirts a large harbour, beyond which the lagoon with some islands can be seen. The viale leads south along the Canale Sant'Elena.

At the end a bridge leads across to an avenue of plane trees which runs between the sports stadium and a military zone to reach the church of **Sant'Elena** (Pl. 16; 6), in a very remote part of the city. Dedicated to St Helena, mother of Constantine, it was founded in the early 13C by the Augustinians and rebuilt in 1435 when the Olivetan Benedictines moved here. They abandoned the church in 1807, but it was reopened in 1928 and now belongs to the municipality and is run by two friars of the community of the Servi di Maria. Over the doorway is a fine sculptured *group attributed to Antonio Rizzo, or to Niccolò di Giovanni Fiorentino (c 1467), representing Admiral Vittorio Cappello kneeling before St Helena. The fine vaulted **interior** (open 16.00–19.00; Mon 17.00–19.00), typical of an abbey church with a single nave and Gothic windows in the light chancel, is in urgent need of restoration (the roof is leaking). In the chapels on the south side are an *Annuciation* attributed to Francesco Vecellio (in urgent need of restoration) and a *Marriage of St Catherine* signed by Bernardo da Brescia (recently restored). The huge unattractive triptych which serves as the high altarpiece was painted in 1958 and hides the Gothic apse. The inappropriate lighting system was installed in the 1970s. The charming 15C cloister has an upper loggia on one side and the campanile dates from 1958.

The Canale di Sant'Elena ends on the waterfront near the landing-stage (*Sant'Elena*) of the vaporetti nos **1**, **42**, **52** which return to San Marco. The view encompasses many of the lagoon islands.

The Biennale Exhibition Grounds

It is a long but pleasant walk back towards San Marco, along the waterfront via the public gardens and past the entrance to the Biennale Exhibition Grounds (Pl. 16, inset). These are only open during the famous biennial (hence *Biennale*) international exhibition of modern art.

The first exhibition was opened in 1895, and during the 20C various nations have built permanent pavilions within the gardens. The park is dominated by the **Padiglione Italia** (the Italian pavilion), which has been altered over the years. The dome is frescoed by Galileo Chini (1909). In 1988 a competition for a new pavilion was won by Francesco Cellini, although the present structure by Duilio Torres (1932) will be preserved. The **Austrian pavilion**, in an enclosed addition to the park across the Rio dei Giardini, is by Vienna-Secessionist Josef Hoffmann (1934); the **Swiss pavilion** (1951) by Bruno Giacometti, brother of the sculptor. The **Venezuelan pavilion** is by Carlo Scarpa (1954), and the **Dutch pavilion** is by the De Stijl architect, Gerrit Rietveld (1954); the cabin-like **Icelandic pavilion** is by modernist Alvar Aalto (1956). The **British pavilion**, by E.A. Rickards (1909), is one of the earliest buildings in the gardens. The most recent additions have been the **Australian pavilion** by Philip Cox (1988) and the bookshop by James Stirling (1991).

Beyond the gardens, Riva dei Setti Martiri, and Riva Ca' di Dio continue to Riva degli Schiavoni (see Ch. 5) and San Marco.

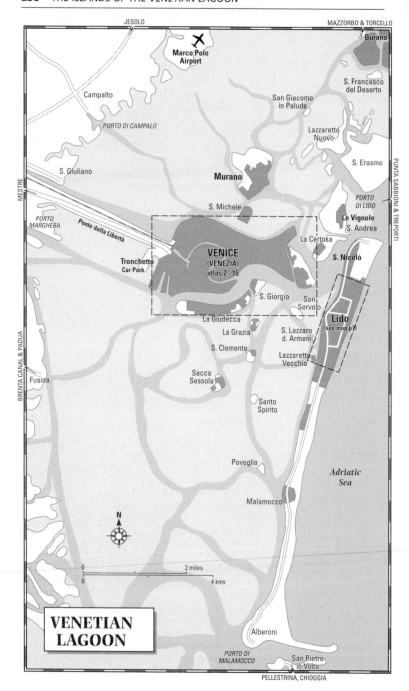

JESOLO

MAZZORBO & TORCELLO

Burano

Marco Polo
Airport

S. Francesco
del Deserto

Campalto

San Giacomo
in Palude

PORTO DI CAMPALO

Lazzaretto
Nuovo

S. Erasmo

MESTRE

S. Giuliano

Murano

PORTO
DI LIDO

PORTO
MARGHERA

S. Michele

Le Vignole
S. Andrea

Ponte della Libertà

La Certosa

PUNTA SABBIONI & TREPORTI

VENICE
(VENEZIA)
atlas 2 - 16

S. Nicolò

Tronchetto
Car Park

S. Giorgio

San
Servolo

Lido
(see map p7)

La Giudecca

S. Lazzaro
d. Armeni

BRENTA CANAL & PADUA

La Grazia

Lazzaretto
Vecchio

Fusina

S. Clemente

Sacca
Sessola

Santo
Spirito

Adriatic
Sea

Poveglia

Malamocco

N

0   2 miles

0   4 kms

VENETIAN
LAGOON

Alberoni

PORTO DI
MALAMOCCO

San Pietro
in Volta

PELLESTRINA, CHIOGGIA

The islands of the Venetian lagoon

For a general description of the lagoon, with notes on its ecology and conservation, see pp 74–76. In this chapter the islands in the lagoon, all served by *ACTV* public transport, are described. First the most important ones in the northern part of the lagoon, San Michele, Murano, Burano, and Torcello, then the sandbars of the Lido and Pellestrina which protect Venice to the east from the open sea, and the port of Chioggia. In the last part of this chapter the minor islands are described: San Servolo, San Lazzaro degli Armeni, Le Vignole, Sant'Erasmo, and the Lazzaretto Nuovo.

San Michele in Isola

Boat services to San Michele (*Cimitero*): vaporetti no. **42** and **41** (every 20 minutes; see map pp 42–43) which continue to the island of Murano. These are two circular routes: no. **42** calls at the station, and takes the Cannaregio canal to reach the Fondamente Nuove, while no. **41** runs from San Zaccaria via Giardini, Bacini, and Celestia to the Fondamente Nuove. For full details of these services, see p 39.

The walled island of San Michele (Pl. 5; 4) is Venice's cemetery. By the landing-stage is **San Michele in Isola** by Mauro Codussi (1469–78), the earliest Renaissance church in the city, in a site unfortunately extremely vulnerable to flooding by the excessive wash caused by the motorboats which pass close to the island.

The elegant and well-sited *façade* was the first church façade to be built in Istrian stone in Venice. It has an elegant doorway with a 15C statue of the Madonna and Child. The dome to the left belongs to the Cappella Emiliana (being restored; see below). A gateway surrounded by a Gothic carving of St Michael and the Dragon, leads into the 15C cloister, from which the church is entered if the main door is closed.

Interior (open 07.30–12.15, 15.00–16.00). The vestibule is separated from the rest of the church by the monks' choir decorated with marble carving on the pilasters. In front of the west door a marble lozenge in the floor marks the burial place of Fra Paolo Sarpi (see Ch. 20). The monument to Cardinal Giovanni Dolfin (d. 1622) around the west door is by Pietro Bernini, with a bust of the Cardinal by his son, Gian Lorenzo Bernini (1622). The 16C wooden sculptures of the Crucifix between the Madonna and St John were restored in 1999, and, beneath the monks' choir, is a stone statue of St Jerome by Juste Le Court.

The sacristy has an unusual ceiling of a painted vault in perspective. On the north wall of the church is an exquisitely carved Renaissance tablet (1501). At the beginning of the north side is the entrance, through a domed vestibule, to the charming little Renaissance **Cappella Emiliana**, by Guglielmo dei Grigi Bergamasco (1528–43). Hexagonal in form, it is beautifully designed with fine polychrome marble inlay and reliefs by Giovanni Antonio da Carona (16C). The chapel is being restored by the Venice in Peril Fund. The campanile was completed in 1460.

The **monastery** was occupied by Camaldolensian monks from 1212 to 1819, and it was famous as a centre of learning. Fra Mauro (1433–59), the cartographer, was a monk here, and in 1450–59 drew his map of the world (now in the

Library of St Mark's, see Ch. 2), forty years before the discovery of America. Silvio Pellico (1789–1854), the patriot writer and author of *Le Mie Prigioni* (1833), was imprisoned here by Austrians before being sent to the Spielberg, a notorious prison near Brünn. The monastery is now occupied by ten Franciscan friars, who sometimes show (on request) the monk's choir (with intarsia stalls), the Chapter House, with a fine 18C Venetian floor and *Madonna* by Sassoferrato, and the huge monastery in which a painting of **St Margaret of Cortona before the Crucifix** by Gian Domenico Tiepolo is hung for safekeeping.

The **cemetery**, planted with magnificent cypresses, is a neo-Gothic work by Annibale Forcellini (1871–72). It is open all day 07.30–dusk, and Roman numerals refer to the sections of the cemetery which are labelled and signposted. Near the west wall (VII; ask for directions from the custodian at the entrance) lies the writer Baron Corvo (Frederick Rolfe; d. 1913). The Protestant enclosure (XV) is on the far left. G.P.R. James (1801–60), who died as British consul in Venice, the composer Wolf-Ferrari, and Sir Ashley Clarke (1903–94), British Amabassador to Italy (1953–62), honorary citizen of Venice, and founder of the Venice in Peril Fund, are all buried here. Also, Ezra Pound (1885–1972) who published his first book of verse in Venice in 1908 at his own expense: *A Lume Spento* (at the Antonini printing press in Cannaregio). He was seized by partisans in Rapallo in a villa owned by Olga Rudge in southern Italy in May 1945 and handed over to the American command who accused him of treason for his Fascist sympathies and his broadcasts during the war to America in favour of Mussolini. They imprisoned him in solitary confinement in Pisa, and in the same year he was transferred to America and interred in a psychiatric hospital in Washington from which he was only released in 1958. He lived the last years of his life in Venice with Olga Rudge on the Zattere (252 Calle Querina) and died here.

In the adjacent Orthodox enclosure Serge Diaghilev (1872–1929) lies near his composer protégé, Igor Stravinsky (1882–1971) who died in New York.

Murano

Boat services The circular vaporetto services nos. **41** and **42** (every 20 minutes; see map pp 42–43) serve the island of Murano from the Fondamente Nuove. These are two circular routes: no. **42** calls at the station, and takes the Cannaregio canal to reach the Fondamente Nuove (taking 30 minutes), while no. **41** runs from *San Zaccaria* via *Sant'Elena*, *Bacini*, and *Celestia* to the Fondamente Nuove (taking 40 minutes). For full details of these services, see pp 39–40. On Murano the services call at the landing-stages of *Colonna*, *Faro*, *Navagero*, *Serenella*, *Museo* and *Venier* (see the plan p 241).

Boats leave roughly every hour from the *Faro* landing-stage, reached from Rio dei Vetrai (see below) via Viale Garibaldi for Burano and Torcello.

The pleasant island of Murano (plan on p 241) has 7500 inhabitants. Since 1292 it has been the centre of the Venetian glass industry, which under protective laws reached its zenith in the early 16C. It is now much visited by tourists for its numerous glass factories, in many of which the art of glass-blowing can be watched and items bought.

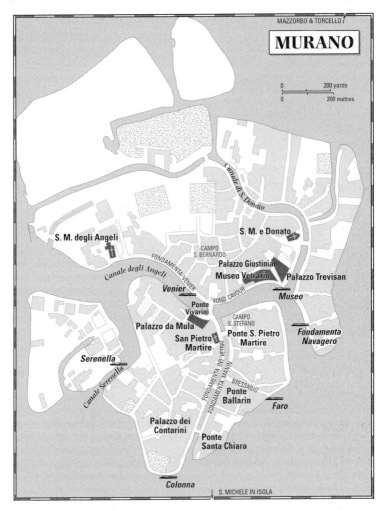

History of Murano

The island was first settled by refugees from Altino (on the mainland to the north) fleeing the Barbarian invasions. It had a considerable degree of independence from Venice as early as 1000, with its own governor, laws, and mint. The glass industry, established in Venice as early as the 10C, was moved here in the 13C from the city because of the danger of fire. The art of making crystal glass was rediscovered by the Venetians who retained the monopoly throughout the 16C. The special characteristics of Venetian glass are its elaborate design, lightness, and bright colour. After a period of decline at the beginning of the 19C the industry was revived at the end of the century under the impulse of Antonio Salviati and others, and the production of artistic glass is still thriving.

In 1441–50 Murano was the seat of a famous school of painters, headed by Antonio Vivarini and Giovanni d'Alemagna. At the beginning of the 16C it is estimated that there were as many as 50,000 inhabitants, and it was a favourite retreat of Venetian noblemen, many of whom built villas here.

From the landing-stage of *Colonna*, named after a column with a pretty base, the fondamenta along Rio dei Vetrai passes numerous glass factories (all of which welcome visitors). Palazzo dei Contarini (no. 27) is a Renaissance building which has suffered neglect and alterations. The name of Ponte Santa Chiara recalls the church and convent which once stood here. No. 37 is a simple Gothic house. Beyond, a few doors down, is a pretty small 14C house with an overhanging upper storey above a portico. Ponte Ballarin (with a lion on its arch) marks the centre of the island; proclamations were read here beside the column with the symbolic lion. On the other side of the canal the Bressagio leads past a charming chapel of 1753 to the waterfront and the vaporetto stop of *Faro* (where the Burano and Torcello boats also call). The houses diminish in size on the last stretch of the canal, as it bends left. To the right of Ponte San Pietro Martire opens Campo Santo Stefano with a bell tower on the site of a church demolished in the 19C. A trattoria here occupies an ancient house.

San Pietro Martire

San Pietro Martire is a Dominican Gothic church partly rebuilt in 1511 and restored in 1928, and again in 1981–83. The fine **interior** (open 08.00–12.00, 15.00–19.00) is hung with chandeliers made on the island at the beginning of the 20C. Much needed restoration is programmed. Above the nave arches are quaint 16C frescoes of Dominican saints. Around the walls are attractive early 20C dossals and confessionals. On the west wall are coin-operated lights. **South side**. The first Baroque altar has four twisted marble columns enclosing an altarpiece of *San Niccolò and Saints* by Palma Giovane. The altarpiece of the *Madonna in Glory with eight Saints* (1505–13) is usually attributed to Giovanni Bellini, and assistants. The *Madonna with Angels and Saints, and Doge Agostino Barbarigo* is signed and dated 1488 by Giovanni Bellini. It was commissioned by the doge who is represented kneeling before the Madonna to receive the blessing of Christ. St Mark is at his shoulder and his coat of arms is prominently displayed at the base of the Madonna's throne. The birds have a symbolic significance: the heron represents long life and the peacock, eternal life. Barbarigo left the painting to the convent of Santa Maria degli Angeli on Murano where two of his daughters were nuns with the express wish that they pray before it for the salvation of his soul. The *Baptism of Christ* is attributed as a late work to Jacopo Tintoretto. In the Cappella Ballarin is the funerary monument of Giovanni Battista Ballarin, Grand Chancellor of the Republic who died in 1666 in the war with Cyprus. The two interesting bas-reliefs show where he was imprisoned by the Turks, and his liberation from prison.

In the **sanctuary** are large paintings (1721–23) by Bartolomeo Letterini. In the **Gothic chapel** to the left, the good collection of paintings are to be returned here (after restoration). Right wall: school of Pordenone (Bernardo Licinio?), *Madonna and Child with Saints Lawrence and Ursula and Senator Pasqualigo*; (left wall) Agostino da Lodi, *Madonna and Child with Saints Jeremiah and Jerome and an angel*. The four *Angels* are by Niccolò Rondinelli. The Renaissance altar has a beautiful relief of the Pietà dated 1495, and to the left is a painting of a *Miracle of St Mark* attributed to Domenico Tintoretto.

On the north side, above the sacristy door, is a *St Jerome* by Veronese, and beyond, *St Agatha in Prison*, also by Veronese (both in very poor condition). Off the north side is the entrance to the **sacristy** and **Parish Museum** (open 09.30–12.30, 13.30–17.00; fest. 12.00–17.00). In the sacristy is finely carved *panelling (1652–56), extremely well preserved, by Pietro Morando. The charming museum, beautifully kept, contains 18C church silver, reliquaries, vestments and lanterns. On the north wall of the church is a huge painting of the *Deposition by Salviati and the first altar is decorated with luminous little tondoes of the Rosary, charming 18C works. In a niche on the west wall is a fine font in red marble surrounded by a balustrade.

On the left of the façade one side of the cloister survives and a well dated 1346.

Fondamenta dei Vetrai continues past a **pharmacy** with a ceiling painting by Francesco Fontebasso (1750–60; shown on request). Ponte Vivarini crosses the main Canale degli Angeli near **Palazzo da Mula**, one of the few grand palaces to have survived in Murano. It is partly Veneto-Byzantine but was largely restored in the 16C. Across the bridge, Fondamenta Venier leads left to **Santa Maria degli Angeli** in a remote part of the island (usually closed except for a service at 10.30 on Sunday). Over the gate into the churchyard, planted with trees, is a beautiful bas-relief of the *Annunciation* (both it and the garden are in need of restoration). The **interior** has a ceiling with panels painted by Pier Maria Pennacchi (c 1520; recently restored), and a high altarpiece of the *Annunciation* by Pordenone.

Museo Vetrario

From Ponte Vivarini, Fondamenta Cavour leads in the other direction to Palazzo Giustinian. This has been the seat of the *Museo Vetrario, the glass museum, since 1861, when the collection was founded by Vincenzo Zanetti. The glass, from the oldest Roman period to the 19C, is beautifully displayed. Open 10.00–16.00 or 17.00 exc. Wed.

The palace, built in the 15C, was transformed by the Giustinian family in the 17C, and in the 19C became the town hall. Beneath the **loggia** is a 14C well head with a rim worn from use, and a damaged 10C–11C Byzantine sarcophagus. In the little walled **garden** are three 15C well-heads. Excavations here in 1998 (since covered over) revealed traces of habitation from the 5C to the 17C.

On the **ground floor**, a room has archaeological finds including Roman glass from excavations carried out at the end of the 19C in Dalmatia (1C–3C AD). Four glass cinerary urns date from the 1C AD, and there is a fragment of a bowl engraved with the head of Isis (4–5C AD), and numerous bottles.

First floor. On the landing is a fine 14C relief of the Baptism of Christ from a demolished church in Murano. On the right is a room with an excellent display illustrating how glass is made. The **salone**, which survives from the Giustinian palace, is hung with three huge chandeliers, and has an allegorical ceiling fresco of the *Triumph of St Lorenzo Giustinian* by Francesco Zugno, and quadratura by Francesco Zanchi. In the centre is a remarkable 18C glass centrepiece, an intricate work reproducing an Italianate garden, acquired from Palazzo Morosini in 1894. Examples of 19C and 20C glass are exhibited here, including pieces by Pietro Bigaglia (1842–45) and Art Nouveau works (1884–90).

In the room to the left of the windows the earliest Murano glass to survive (15C) is displayed, including the famous dark blue Barovier marriage ***cup** (1470–80). The little hanging lamp is of a type which often appears in Venetian paintings of the late 15C (for instance in Giovanni Bellini's altarpiece in San Zaccaria, or Carpaccio's ***Presentation of Christ in the Temple*** in the Galleria dell' Accademia). There is also enamelled and decorated glass here from the Renaissance period. In two rooms off the other end of the Salone is a remarkable display of 16C and 17C glass including crystal ware and filigree glass. In the room off the Salone opposite the windows is 18C glass including examples from the Piratti workshops (showing the influence of Bohemian masters). The room at the end, with a 16C–17C wooden ceiling is arranged as an 18C interior.

Opposite the museum, on Canale di San Donato, stands **Palazzo Trevisan**, attributed to Palladio. It contains frescoed landscapes by Veronese, the only works by him left in Venice in a private building, and reliefs by Vittoria.

Santa Maria e Donato

Santa Maria e Donato

A little farther on is the splendid Venetian Byzantine basilica of Santa Maria e Donato. It stands on the former main square (the war memorial is on the site of the town hall) with its magnificent ***apse** facing the canal, once the entrance to Murano from the lagoon. The apse is beautifully decorated in an unusual and intricate design with two tiers of arches on twin marble columns, the upper arcade forming a balcony, and the lower arcade blind. It bears fine dog-tooth mouldings and carved and inlaid zigzag friezes, and carved Byzantine panels.

The church was founded in the 7C by several wealthy families from Altino. Restored in the 9C, the present church was rebuilt c 1141. In 1125, the body of St Donato, Bishop of Euraea in Epirus (Albania) in the 4C, was brought here from the Ionian island of Cephalonia, together with bones supposed to be those of the dragon he killed (four of its bones still hang behind the Baroque altar). In the early 18C the wealthy Marco Giustinian became bishop and damaged the church, destroying many of its most beautiful possessions. During a thorough restoration of the church in 1973–79, the foundations were strengthened.

The simple **façade** was formerly preceded by the baptistery (destroyed in 1719). It bears a late 14C marble relief of St Donato and a devotee, and two worn carved pilasters, good 2C Veneto-Roman works. In the beautifully proportioned **interior** (open 08.00–12.00, 16.00–19.00), with an early 15C ship's keel roof, the columns of the nave with Corinthian capitals (dating from the late Roman period to the 6C) support stilted arches. The splendid ***pavement** in mosaic opus sectile and opus tessellatum bears an inscription in the centre of the nave with the date of 1141. In 1977 the pavement was taken up, restored, and relaid on a concrete base, but it is now again in poor condition. The Byzantine style pulpit dates from the 6C, and the stoup is placed on a carved pillar (7C–8C). In the apse is a very beautiful 12C *mosaic of the Virgin with her hands raised in prayer on a gold ground. Beneath are 15C frescoes of the evangelists. A finely carved 9C sarcophagus in Greek marble, discovered in the 1979 restoration, now serves as the high altar. The unusual square Roman sarcophagus from Altino (2C), with an inscription saying that this was the gravestone of the Roman councillor, Lucus Acilius, in Altinum, is now used as the baptismal font.

North aisle. Large ancona of St Donato in low relief, dated 1310 and commissioned by the podestà of Murano, Donato Memo who is shown with his wife, kneeling. The lunette of the *Madonna and Child with Saints and donor* (the canon of the church, Giovanni degli Angeli) is by Lazzaro Bastiani (1484). The polyptych with the *Dormition of the Virgin* (mid 14C) formerly covered a large silver gilt altarpiece on the high altar. In the chapel off this aisle are Roman and medieval sarcophagi.

The nearest vaporetto stop to the church is *Museo* where no. **41** or **42** can be taken back to the Fondamente Nuove.

Burano

Boat services The quickest approach is also the most beautiful—the *ACTV* boat no. **12** (services every 30–60 minutes), from *Fondamente Nuove* via Murano (*Faro*) and *Mazzorbo* (Torcello in 35 minutes, Burano in 40 minutes). The boats usually call at Torcello first and then Burano. To reach the *Fondamente Nuove*, there are two circular vaporetto services nos **41** and **42** (every 20 minutes): no. **42** calls at the station, and takes the Cannaregio canal to reach the *Fondamente Nuove* (taking 30 minutes), while no. 41 runs from *San Zaccaria* via *Sant'Elena*, *Bacini*, and *Celestia* to the *Fondamente Nuove* (taking 40 minutes). Otherwise you can walk to *Fondamente Nuove* in about 20 minutes from San Marco.

A more leisurely approach is with the ACTV boat no. 14 (Burano in 80 mins, Torcello in 90 mins) which leaves from Ponte della Paglia (Riva degli Schiavoni). It runs about ten times a day via the Lido to the Bocca di Lido (with an interesting view of the long low stone wall which defends the sea entrance to the lagoon here). It then skirts the shore of Punta Sabbioni with its landing-stage and a few houses, calling at Treporti, in a remote part of the lagoon, near the wide Canale di San Felice. The boat now steers west along the Burano channel with low marshes on the right, through a particularly beautiful landscape with interesting bird life; tits, buntings, curlew, sandpipers and warblers can sometimes be seen. The boat passes the private Isola di Gravan, with a view on the left of San Francesco del Deserto, and the leaning bell-tower of Burano rising above the marshes. The channel then bends left, with a view right of the bell-tower of Torcello, to reach the brightly coloured houses of Burano.

For further details about *ACTV* transport, see pp 39–40, and map pp 42–43.

The private excursion launches which operate in summer from the Riva degli Schiavoni are much more expensive and make the round trip in 4 hours (including Murano, Burano, and Torcello), allowing only a very brief stay at Torcello.

Burano has a number of good trattorie and a simple hotel, see pp 36 and 27.

From the Fondamente Nuove the boat (no. **12**) passes the island of San Michele (see p 239) and calls at the *Faro* landing-stage on Murano (see p 242). It then skirts the east side of Murano before steering out into the lagoon, along a channel marked by wooden piles. The sandbanks to the right are part of Sant'Erasmo (described on p 263). Ahead, the green island of San Francesco del Deserto and the leaning campanile of Burano soon come into view, and, in the far distance, to the left of Burano, the cathedral and campanile of Torcello. The boat passes close to **San Giacomo in Palude**, an island abandoned in 1964. Marco Polo airport can be seen in the distance, to the left. The cypresses of San Francesco del Deserto are now more prominent to the right, rising out of the flat marshlands. The boat passes close to the island of the **Madonna del Monte** (right), and its dependent islet, where there was once an ammunition factory (abandoned after the Second World War), and where conservation work on the lagoon is in progress. Beyond, the canal forks left (the right branch goes on towards the conspicuous church of Santa Caterina; see below). The boat soon enters the pretty canal of **Mazzorbo**, lined with a few villas and a boatyard. Near the landing-stage is a campanile, behind the churchyard wall and next to a lone cypress, which belonged to the destroyed convent of Santa Maria Valverde. The *Trattoria alla Maddalena* is on the water-front here. The church of **Santa Caterina** dates from 1283–89. Above the door is a 14C bas-relief of the *Marriage of St Catherine*. It also has an interesting Gothic interior with a ship's keel roof, a 14C bas-relief and a high altarpiece by Giuseppe Salviati. The little settlement, where attractive low-cost houses were built in 1979–86 by Giancarlo de Carlo, is connected by a long bridge with Burano.

Burano is a cheerful little fishing village (5300 inhabitants) of immense charm, with brightly painted houses in a great variety of colours, and miniature canals (it has no cars). Most of the shops sell lace made on the island. From the landing-stage it is a short walk along a canal (left) to Via Baldassare Galuppi, the wide main street of the island with a number of restaurants.

Baldassare Galuppi (1706–85), known as il Buranello, the organist and composer of operatic and sacred music, was born here. He was music master at the Ospedale dei Mendicanti (1740–51) and later at the Incurabili (1768–76), and Maestro di Cappella at the Basilica of San Marco. He wrote music for works by Goldoni and collaborated with him at several theatres in Venice. Robert Browning celebrated him in verse (*A Toccato of Galuppi's*).

Galuppi is commemorated in a bronze half-figure (1989) in the piazza outside the parish church of **San Martino** (open 07.30–12.00, 15.00–18.00). The traditional foundation date of the church is 959, and it was reconstructed several times up until 1645. The entrance is through a corridor to the right. In the north aisle is a *Crucifixion* by Giambattista Tiepolo (removed for restoration), commissioned by a pharmacist in 1722 (who is shown in the oval portrait at the bottom of the painting). On the left wall of the sanctuary, *St Mark enthroned with four Saints* by Girolamo da Santacroce. At the end of the south aisle are three charming small paintings by Giovanni Mansueti (restored in 1999). They illustrate the *Marriage of the Virgin*, the *Nativity*, and the *Flight into Egypt*, and possibly once decorated a singing gallery. The seated figure on the left in the Nativity is probably the donor of all three paintings. The *Flight into Egypt* is full of charming naturalistic details with numerous animals, and all three works show the influence of Jacopo Bellini.

Opposite the church is the former Scuola del Merletto or lace-making school, now the **Museo del Merletto**, a lace museum (open 10.00–16.00 or 17.00 exc. Tues). Burano has for long been celebrated as the centre of the Venetian lace industry and the school was founded in 1872 to revive the industry which had decayed in the 18C. Lace was first made in Venice in the late 15C, and spread to France and in particular Flanders in later centuries. In 1871–72, when the lagoon was frozen over and the fishermen out

The island of Burano

of work, the home industry of lacemaking was reintroduced. Although the school has not taken students since 1991, it has a beautiful display of lace, and from Tuesday to Friday ladies from Burano still meet here to practise the art of lace-making. Their products are sold (for very reasonable prices) all over the island.

San Francesco del Deserto

The island of San Francesco lies to the south of Burano, in a deserted part of the lagoon, identified by its clump of cypresses. It can be visited (09.00–11.00, 15.00–17.15 only) by hiring a boat on Burano from the local fishermen (usually available on the waterfront near the church of San Martino). The journey takes about 20 minutes, and the boatman will wait for you while a friar conducts you round the island, which is said to have been a retreat of St Francis in 1220. In 1233, when it was known as the Isola delle Due Vigne, it was donated to the Franciscans by Jacopo Michiel. It took on its present name after it had been abandoned in the early 15C.

The church was built in 1460 on the site of an earlier foundation. There are also two cloisters. The buildings and gardens are kept immaculate by the ten friars who still live here. Recent excavations on the island have shown that the island was settled in the 5C AD, but was submerged by the waters of the lagoon at the end of the same century and only re-emerged at the beginning of the 6C.

Torcello

Boat services to Torcello also call at Burano and are described on p 245.

Torcello has three restaurants (two of them in the high price range; see p 36),

but it is also a beautiful place to picnic (it has no shops, so food must be brought from Venice). For accommodation, see p 26.

Torcello is the most beautiful and evocative place in the Venetian lagoon, inhabited before Venice itself. Though now only a remote small group of houses, it still preserves some lovely relics of its days of splendour. From the 7C to the 13C it was the island stronghold of the people of Altinum, who were driven from the mainland by the Lombard invaders. They had already taken temporary shelter here in the 5C and 6C. Bishop Paolo moved the bishopric of Altinum to Torcello in 639 bringing with him the relics of St Heliodorus, Altinum's first bishop (still preserved in the cathedral, see below). The foundation stone of the cathedral Bishop Paolo dedicated in the same year survives.

At one time Torcello is said to have had 20,000 inhabitants and was a thriving centre of wool manufacturing, but it had started to decline by the 15C. The rivalry of Venice and malaria—due to the marshes formed by the silting up of the river Sile—brought about its downfall. In the 17C the population had already dwindled to a few hundred, and it now has only a handful of inhabitants and no cars. However, during the day for most of the year it is disturbed by tourist groups.

Work has begun in an attempt to protect the island from flood tides and the force of the wash caused by speeding motorboats which bring tourists here. This includes renewing the inner canal walls and the quay along the main canal, but since reinforced concrete and steel have been used (instead of the traditional wood, brick and mud) conservationists took legal action to halt the work in 2000 because they feared that the measures taken were too drastic and might alter the delicate ecology of the lagoon, as well as the appearance of the island. A temporary path for visitors has been laid so that work can eventually begin on repaving the charming path which follows the peaceful canal from the landing-stage to the centre of the island. A walk of about 10 minutes, it passes two restaurants and a picturesque old stone bridge without a parapet and ends at the *Locanda Cipriani* with a famous restaurant. Just beyond is the group of monuments: to the left is Palazzo del Consiglio, ahead, the loggia of Palazzo dell'Archivio (both now museums) and to the right the cathedral and the church of Santa Fosca.

The cathedral

This superb Byzantine basilica is one of the most beautiful churches in Venice, famous for its mosaics (open every day Nov–March 10.00–16.30; April–Oct 10.30–17.30; combined ticket, for the basilica, bell-tower, and museum).

Dedicated to Santa Maria Assunta it was founded in 639 and is a Veneto-Byzantine building, derived from the Ravenna-type basilicas. Altered in 864, it was rebuilt in 1008 by bishop Otto (or Orso) Orseolo (later doge). In front of the façade are remains of the circular baptistery which was built as a separate building in the late 7C or early 8C, and joined to the basilica in the 11C (the foundations of the perimeter wall and bases of the columns are visible).

The dignified and cool aisled **interior** has 18 slender marble columns with well-carved capitals. The stilted arches of the colonnades were rebuilt in the 12C, and the vaulting is secured by wooden tie-beams. The superb **pavement** has a mosaic design in black, red and white marble. The splendid Byzantine **mosaics** were beautifully restored in 1977–84. An intricate Byzantine ***mosaic of the Last Judgement** covers the **west wall** (late 11C; the three upper registers were heavily restored in the 19C). The marble pulpit and ambo on the north side are made up from fragments from the earliest church. The iconostasis consists of four large marble ***plutei** (11C), elaborately carved with late Byzantine designs, and above the columns (with finely carved Corinthian capitals) are 15C local paintings of the *Virgin and Apostles*. Higher up is a wooden Gothic Crucifix. The choir has lovely marble panels (7C) in the apse, beneath which fragments of frescoed decoration and figures have been revealed. In the centre of the brick benches reserved for the clergy, steps rise to the bishop's throne. Below the high altar is a pagan sarcophagus (3C) which contains the relics of St Heliodorus. On the left, set in to the wall, is the foundation stone of the church (639).

In the semi-dome of the central apse, on a bright gold ground, is a **mosaic of the *Madonna**, one of the most striking figures ever produced in Byzantine art. We know that Greek craftsmen worked on the mosaics in the basilica and this remarkable icon of the Virgin has no equal in Constantinople itself. It is derived from a typical Byzantine image with Mary, as Mother of God, holding the Christ Child in her left arm and gesturing towards him, symbolising divine protection. Beneath are the apostles (mid-11C), and on the outer arch, the Annunciation, added in the second half of the 12C.

In the **south apse** are more ancient mosaics, *Christ in Benediction with Saints and Angels*, and a delightful vault decoration of *Four Angels with the Mystic Lamb* (11C, possibly replacing an 8C or even 7C mosaic), reminiscent of the mosaics in Ravenna. In this chapel is a tiny 8C tabernacle (right wall), recently restored. In front of the north apse is the pavement tomb of Nicola Morosini, bishop of Torcello (d. 1305).

The crypt, thought to date from the 9C, is water-logged at its lowest point. In the nave are two altars with gilded and painted wood tabernacles. Near the west door is a stoup carved with strange animals.

The tall square detached **campanile** (11C–12C) is a striking landmark in the lagoon, and has a wonderful peal of bells which ring out across the water. It is open at the same time as the basilica. A path leads along the south side of the basilica where the remarkable 11C shutters (hinged stone slabs) of the basilica's windows can be seen. A walkway provides a fine view of the east end of the basilica. The tower is ascended by a stone ramp, with a few steps: a very easy climb, and not at all claustrophobic. From the bell-chamber at the top there is a wonderful view of Torcello and of the entire lagoon with its islands and mudflats, and, on a clear day of the mainland and Alps in the distance.

The church of **Santa Fosca**, nearby, was built to house the body of St Fosca brought to the island before 1011. The remarkable Byzantine design, on a Greek-cross plan, probably survives from the 11C building, although it has been drastically restored. It is surrounded by an octagonal portico on three sides (probably added in the 12C). In the bare interior the beautiful marble columns have Byzantine capitals and support a circular

Santa Fosca

drum which once probably carried a dome. This may have been destroyed in an earthquake and it has been replaced by a low conical wooden roof.

Museo di Torcello

Palazzo del Consiglio houses the little museum of Torcello which contains an interesting collection of objects from the demolished churches on the island (which at one time numbered at least ten), and archaeological material. Open at the same time as the basilica except closed on Mon.

Ground floor. Mosaic fragments including two 7C heads of angels, and original 12C fragments from the *Last Judgement* in the cathedral; a 6C stoup with a Greek inscription: 'Take this water with joy since the voice of God is on the waters' (from Isaiah XII, 3 and Psalms XXIX.3); and a medieval lance with a runic inscription, thought to be an allusion to an ancient North German divinity, and astrological symbols. Among the architectural fragments are several plutei, and a 10C well-head. Part of the so-called *Pala d'Oro, formerly over the high altar of the cathedral, is soon to be returned here after its restoration. The thirteen fragments in gilded silver show the Madonna enthroned with archangels and saints, and two symbols of the evangelists. They are the work of goldsmiths from the Veneto working around the middle of the 14C. The altarpiece was formerly decorated with precious stones and enamels, and had 29 other plaquettes which were stolen in 1806.

Upper floor. The 15C Venetian wooden sculptures include the beautifully carved tomb of Santa Fosca. Also here: 11C Latin Cross in marble; St Christopher, an early 15C Venetian painting; ten small wooden panels (from a ceiling decoration) with Biblical scenes, attributed to Bonifacio Bembo da Cremona (15C); 16C paintings from the organ of Sant'Antonio; historical documents and illuminated antiphonals.

The **Palazzo dell'Archivio** is used as an archaeological museum. In the open loggia below are some fine Roman sculptural fragments. The top floor has material from the prehistoric era up to the 6C AD, including altars, funerary cippae, statues dating from the Late Empire (from Torcello and Altinum), small Roman bronzes, and Etruscan ceramics.

On the grass outside is a primitive stone seat known as Attila's chair.

It is not easy to explore the rest of the island, criss-crossed by narrow paths between fields of artichokes and vines, as most of them are on private land.

The Lido

Boat services Vaporetto no. **1** (every 10 minutes) and no. **51** (every 20 minutes) both from *San Zaccaria* in about 15 minues via *Giardini* and *Sant'Elena* (no. **1** calls also at *Arsenale*). For full details of these services, see pp 39–40. The return from the Lido is either by no. **1** or no. **52**. An express weekday service (no. **61**) runs from *Piazzale Roma, Santa Marta, San Basilio, Zattere, Giardini, Sant'Elena* to the Lido every 20 minutes in about 30 minutes (no. 62 makes the return trip).

Transport on the Lido The best way of seeing the south part of the Lido island and Pellestrina is by Bus no. **11** (from Piazzale Santa Maria Elisabetta (see p 251). For further details of navigation services, and bus services on the Lido see the Transport Information on pp 39 and 41 and map pp 42–43.

The **Lido** (18,800 inhabitants), is a long narrow island between the lagoon and the open Adriatic sea. The first bathing establishments were opened here in 1857 and by the beginning of the 20C it had become the most fashionable seaside resort in Italy. The name Lido was subsequently adopted by numerous seaside

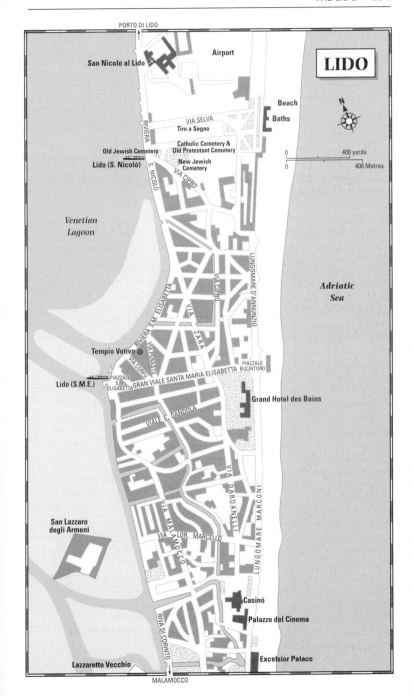

PORTO DI LIDO

Airport

San Nicolo al Lido

Beach

Baths

VIA SELVA

RIVIERA

Tiro a Segno

Old Jewish Cemetery

Catholic Cemetery &
Old Protestant Cemetery

Lido (S. Nicolò)

S. NICOLÒ

New Jewish
Cemetery

VIA CIPRO

N

0   400 yards
0   400 Metres

Venetian
Lagoon

VIA CIPRO

RIVIERA S.M. ELISABETTA

VIA ZARA

Adriatic
Sea

LUNGOMARE D'ANNUNZIO

Tempio Votivo

VIA PERASTO

VIA CORFU

PIAZZALE
BUCINTORO

Lido (S.M.E.)

PIAZZALE
S.M.
ELISABETTA

GRAN VIALE SANTA MARIA ELISABETTA

Grand Hotel des Bains

VIALE E. DANDOLA

VIA DARDANELLI

San Lazzaro
degli Armeni

VIA MALAMOCCO

VIA LOR. MARCELLO

LUNGOMARE MARCONI

Casinò

Palazzo del Cinema

RIVA DI CORINTO

Excelsior Palace

Lazzaretto Vecchio

MALAMOCCO

LIDO

resorts all over the world. The Adriatic sea-front consists of a group of luxurious hotels and villas bordering the fine sandy beach, which is divided up into sections, each belonging (except at the extreme ends) to a particular hotel or bathing area, with deckchairs, beach-huts and attendants. The rest of the northern part of the island has become a residential district of Venice, with fine trees and numerous gardens, crossed by several canals. The houses, mostly only a few storeys high, are spaciously laid out. The atmosphere on the Lido is very different from that in the city of Venice itself, as it does not have many canals, and cars and buses are the means of transport.

The landing-stage of *Santa Maria Elisabetta* (SME), where the vaporetti services from Venice terminate, is named after the church here of 1627. Buses to all destinations on the Lido (see p 41) pass through Piazzale Santa Maria Elisabetta.

The **Gran Viale Santa Maria Elisabetta**, the main street crossing the widest part of the island, leads from the piazzale (and the lagoon) past the tourist office, the post office, and numerous hotels and shops, to Piazzale Bucintoro on the sea-front. To the left, Lungomare d'Annunzio leads along the front to the public beaches of San Nicolò, while to the right Lungomare Marconi (with its numerous beach-huts and private beaches) passes the *Grand Hotel des Bains*, built by Francesco Marsich in 1905–09, which provided the setting for Thomas Mann's *Death in Venice*. Farther on is the **Casinò** and **Palazzo del Cinema** (to be rebuilt) where the international Venice Film Festival is usually held in summer. Both these conspicuous buildings were built in 1936–38 by Eugenio Miozzi and Quagliata. Just beyond is the famous *Excelsior Palace Hotel* (an elaborate building in Moorish style by Giovanni Sardi, 1898–1908), with its landing-stage on a canal (used by the hotel motor-launches, and the Casinò motor-boat).

The northern end of the island is reached by Bus A (from Lungomare Marconi, or Piazzale Santa Maria Elisabetta). The road skirts the lagoon past the conspicuous **Tempio Votivo** (or Santa Maria della Vittoria), a domed war memorial begun by Giuseppe Torres in 1925. Nearly 1km farther on Via Cipro leads to the **Catholic Cemetery**. In a corner of the newest part of the cemetery some 18C tombstones from the old **Protestant Cemetery** have recently been set up. This cemetery, in use from 1684–1810, was obliterated in the 1930s when the airport (see below) was extended. The tombstones include those of the collector and art dealer John Murray (1754–65) and the singer Catherine Tofts (d. 1756), who was the wife of consul Joseph Smith (1682–1770; his tomb slab was removed to the English church, see Ch. 12). Nearby is the **New Jewish Cemetery**, in use from 1774 onwards, where numerous older tombstones formerly in the Old Jewish Cemetery have recently been restored and set up in a corner by the gate.

On the main road, beside a row of seven cypresses, a small gate (signposted) precedes the **Old Jewish Cemetery** (open Sun 14.30, ☎ 041 715 359). The Jewish community was granted this land which belonged to the Benedictine convent of San Niccolò, overlooking the lagoon as a burial ground in 1386, the earliest recorded presence of the Jews in Venice. The cemetery, in use up until the 18C, had to be enlarged over the years and it grew to cover an area more than six times its present size. However, from the 17C onwards it was encroached upon by military installations set up in this strategic part of the lagoon, and in the process many of the tombstones were moved, damaged, or buried. Finally in 1774 a new cemetery was opened a few hundred meters to the east (see above). In the 19C what remained of the old cemetery was cleared and the site 'arranged' with the tombstones placed haphazardly in rows, and the enclosure wall was built and the memorial obelisk erected, according to Romantic concepts. It was fondly described by both Bryon and Shelley. In 1883–86, when the firing range was built close by, yet more tombstones came to light and were amassed in the new Jewish cemetery. In 1929 the area towards the lagoon (with the seven cypresses) was confiscated in order to widen the road.

In 1997–99 the old cemetery was cleared of undergrowth, and the marshy area furthest from the gate reclaimed and many tombstones salvaged from below ground and carefully re-erected or set up around the walls. It is now well kept and includes about 1200 tombstones, many of them decorated with beautifully carved Hebrew symbols. The fourteen 17C tombstones in the unusual form of columns decorated with Samson and the lion belong to a family from Cividale del Friuli.

The main road continues past the **Tiro a Segno**, a huge building (in need of restoration) erected in 1883–86 as a firing range and still in use, to a pretty bridge over an inlet, at the end of which can be seen the **Lido airport**, opened after the First World War and enlarged in 1934, now used only for private planes.

San Nicolò al Lido

Beyond is the church of San Nicolò al Lido (open 11.00–12.00, 16.00–19.00), now in a remote part of the island. The monastery and church were founded in 1044 and the present convent was built in the 16C. Its strategic position near the main entrance to the lagoon meant that the monastery was used by the doge as the official place to receive visitors. The emperor Barbarossa stayed here before his meeting with Pope Alexander III in San Marco in 1177, and elaborate celebrations were held in honour of Henry III, king of France in 1574. Domenico Selvo was elected doge here in 1071 while the basilica of San Marco was being completed. Above the door of the church is a monument to Doge Domenico Contarini, the founder. The **interior** has an interesting narrow choir with huge capitals. In the sanctuary is a 14C wooden Crucifix, and a high altar in pietre dure. The choirstalls, in excellent condition, were finely carved by Giovanni da Crema (1635).

Outside the church there is a view across the lagoon to the campanile of San Marco, and the dome and campanile of San Pietro di Castello. Near at hand is the green island of La Certosa. On the right of the church a paved lane leads down to the entrance (flanked by two 11C capitals) to the 16C Franciscan **convent**, which has a very grand staircase and a lovely cloister dating from 1530, with a wrought-iron well of 1710. Off the cloister the abandoned remains of the Romanesque church can be seen: its interesting polychrome mosaic floor (1043), with a geometric and floral design (removed for restoration), is the earliest to have been found in the lagoon, apart from that of San Marco.

On the other side of the church stands the **Palazzetto del Consiglio dei Dieci** (1520), probably on the site of a 14C building. The road continues past 16C military buildings to the northern tip of the island which overlooks the **Porto di Lido**, the main entrance to the lagoon and always strongly defended (at one time it was closed by huge chains to prevent the entrance of enemy ships). In November 1988 Mo.S.E. (*Modolo sperimentale elettromeccanico*), an experimental sluice gate was laid on the bed of the sea as part of the long term plans to install mobile flood barriers at all three entrances to the lagoon, in order to protect the city from flood tides (see p 75).

Facing the Lido, on the island of **Le Vignole**, is the **Fortezza di Sant'Andrea**, the masterpiece of Michele Sanmicheli (1543), the architect and engineer who had been appointed in 1534 to examine the defences of the lagoon. The Council of Ten finally gave their assent to the construction of a fortress here, despite the fact that Venice was renowned for the absence of heavily fortified buildings. It was one of the most important works of military architecture of its time, and a remarkable technical achievement since its foundations had to be laid on the lagoon bed. After years of neglect it has now been restored.

The ceremony of the Marriage with the Sea ~ Festa della Sensa

In the channel here the doge performed the annual ceremony of the marriage with the sea, when he threw his ring to his 'bride', the sea. By the 16C this was one of the most important and elaborate State occasions, but it has complicated and confused origins. According to tradition in 1177 Pope Alexander III gave Doge Sebastiano Ziani a golden ring and the right to 'wed' the sea with it, in gratitude to him for his support against the Emperor Frederick Barbarossa and his part in the reconciliation which took place between the Emperor and the Pope in San Marco on Ascension Day in that year. Another tradition dates the gesture to Doge Pietro II Orseolo, the victor in 1000 over the Slav pirates in Dalmatia, who is supposed to have blessed the sea here on Ascension Day every year. The legend of St Mark also incorporates an episode with a ring when, in the 14C, St Mark is supposed to have pursuaded an old fisherman to placate a storm at the mouth of the lagoon by overturning a boat load of demons and then present St Mark's ring to the doge (illustrated in Paris Bordone's painting in Room 23 of the Galleria dell' Accademia).

The ritual, symbolising the Republic's dominion over the sea, took place every year on Ascension Day when the doge was rowed out in the State barge (the bucintoro) in a procession of thousands of boats, welcoming on board also the Patriarch of Venice. They then attended Mass at San Nicolò and a State banquet was held. The ceremony also coincided with the evening in spring when the first Venetian ships were able to set sail again from Venice after the winter months in port. The *Festa della Sensa* is still celebrated on the first Sunday after Ascension Day when the mayor takes the place of the doge.

Across the channel is **Punta Sabbioni** on the mainland, connected by road with **Lido di Jesolo**, a popular seaside resort, between the old and new mouths of the Piave. It has over 450 hotels and numerous camping sites (bus connection with vaporetto no. **14**, see p 40). The old village of **Jesolo**, formerly Cavazuccherina, perpetuates the name of an early medieval centre, known also as *Equilium* (since horses were bred on the marshes here), the rival of Heraclea in the affairs of the lagoon.

Via Malamocco runs south from Piazzale Santa Maria Elisabetta (see above), a little inland from the lagoon, through a residential area with numerous gardens. The buildings become fewer as the island narrows.

Malamocco, is a quiet fishing village overlooking the lagoon. The ancient *Metamauco* was one of the first places to be inhabited in the lagoon by people from Heraclea in the northeast part of the lagoon,which had been an important episcopal and administrative centre in the 7C–8C. Metamauco became the seat of the lagoon government in the 8C. It was the scene of the famous defeat of King Pepin who had laid siege to the city in 810. Submerged by a tidal wave c 1107, the settlement was moved from the Adriatic sea front to this side of the island. It now consists of a small group of pretty houses, with a 15C Palazzo del Podestà in a little campo. In the church is a large painting by Gerolamo Forabosco, a carved polyptych of the *Dormition of the Virgin* (early 15C), and an early 17C painting of the *Madonna and Saints*. The campanile is modelled on that of San Marco. There is a view across the lagoon to Venice (on the extreme right), and in front, the port of Marghera is conspicuous. Just offshore lies the island of **Poveglia** (its hospital was abandoned in 1968).

Via Alberoni continues, now skirting the edge of the lagoon, to **Alberoni**, a little bathing resort, with the Lido golf course (18 holes), entered through the tunnel of an old fortress, and an extensive public beach. Fine walks can be taken along the edge of the sea between Alberoni and Malamocco. The road continues to the end of the promontory where there is a car ferry (used by bus No. **11**) for the island of Pellestrina.

Pellestrina

Bus and ferry services *ACTV* bus no. **11** from the Lido via a ferry c every 45 minutes going on to Chioggia (a remarkable scenic journey, described below, which can also be broken in order to visit San Pietro in Volta and Pellestrina on foot).

The bus departs from the beginning of Viale Santa Maria Elisabetta close to the vaporetti landing-stages on the Lido. It first runs towards the sea front which it skirts passing the *Hotel des Bains*, the Casinò, Palazzo del Cinema, and the *Hotel Excelsior*. It then turns towards the lagoon and leads through the southern part of the Lido past Malamocco and Alberoni (see above). The road ends at the southern tip of the Lido where a car ferry (in connection with the bus which drives straight on to it) crosses (in 5 minutes) the **Porto di Malamocco**, the narrow channel separating the islands of the Lido and Pellestrina, usually busy with large ships and oil tankers from Marghera. It is guarded by an amusing lighthouse, with its tower perched on top of a roof. The bus then continues (with request stops for San Pietro in Volta and Pellestrina) to the southern end of the island of Pellestrina where it terminates beside the passenger ferry landing-stage for Chioggia (services in connection with the buses).

A lovely **walk** can be taken from one end of the island of Pellestrina to the other, following the lagoon side at the villages of San Pietro in Volta and Pellestrina, and the dyke (or sandy beach) on the seaward side for the rest of the way.

The thin island of **Pellestrina** (10km long, and only a few hundred metres wide) is separated from the sea by a wall known as the **Murazzi**, a remarkable work of engineering, undertaken in 1744–82 by Bernardino Zendrini following a project drawn up in 1716 by the cosmographer Vincenzo Coronelli. This great sea wall which extends for the entire length of the island was formerly some 20 kilometres long running all the way from the Porto di Lido as far as Sottomarina. It was built of irregular blocks of Istrian stone and marble, and has been reinforced in places by huge blocks of concrete. The dyke is very well preserved and at intervals there are little flights of steps protected by ropes to the walkway along the top. There are numerous inscriptions recording the dates of the various stages in its construction and stones indicating distances. Since 1967 huge quantities of sand have been dredged from the sea and a fence erected to protect the seaward side of the wall.

The island is mostly well preserved and interesting for the colourful architecture of the two settlements of San Pietro in Volta and Pellestrina itself, which both face the lagoon. The houses, most of them in good repair (although the weather-proof doors, porches, and windows detract from their appearance), are often connected with low porticoes, between the narrow calli and small campi. Despite the remoteness of the area there is an air of well being and the island does not appear to be suffering from depopulation, although the market gardens on which the local economy was partly based have now been abandoned. Many of the inhabitants are fishermen who work both in the lagoon and the open sea, and their numerous fishing boats line the shore of the lagoon. The few shops are mostly in private houses without signs. Hardly any tourists come to this island, which is particularly peaceful (the only disturbing elements being the cars). The fondamente along the lagoon are being carefully restored.

The first settlement (with a request stop of bus no. **11**, about 2km from the Porto di Malamocco) is **San Pietro in Volta** (population 1600). From the main road and bus stop follow the lane which leads towards the lagoon along a moat which once surrounded a fortress, now in total ruin, to a bright red house in Art Nouveau style, near a water tower. The church of **San Pietro** was founded in the 10C but was rebuilt in 1777–1813. It has a fine organ decorated with sculptures. The house beside the church has a bas-relief of St Peter. Nearby, slightly inland, a monument records the 1966 flood which miraculously reached only the ground floors of the houses, so that the island escaped serious damage. There are just a few (inconspicuous) shops, and in the district of Portosecco, at the south end is the 17C church of Santo Stefano, with a neo-Classical façade, set back from the lagoon (usually closed). It contains an organ attributed to Gaetano Callido.

Pellestrina, with some 3600 inhabitants, is strung out for nearly 3km along the narrow sand-bar. The local industry of lace-making is disappearing, but most of the inhabitants are still fishermen. It is divided into four districts of Scarpa, Zennari, Vianello, and Busetto, named after local families sent here from Chioggia to settle the island after the sea battle with Genova in 1381, the descendents of many of whom still live here. A huge shipyard right on the lagoon adjoins the district of Scarpa where there is a tiny votive chapel with a pretty campanile (1862). The wider lane here is one of a series on the island called 'Carizzada' (each of them numbered): these were built from the lagoon to the seafront during the construction of the Murazzi: they were just wide enough for a cart (*carro*; hence 'carizzada') to pass with its load of heavy stones.

The church of **Sant'Antonio** was founded in 1612 but enlarged a century later. The third south altar by Baldassare Longhena has an altarpiece by Lorenzo di Tiziano. Beyond a playing field is the district of Zennari, with some bigger houses set back from the lagoon, with a well, school, and watertower. The town hall is in the district of Vianello together with the octagonal church of **San Vito**. This was rebuilt by Andrea Tirali in 1723 in honour of the lovely 17C *Madonna and Child* on the high altar, of Spanish origins. Formerly in a chapel on this site, it is greatly venerated (as the ex votoes in the sanctuary show) since it is associated with a miracle here in 1716 on the occasion of the defeat of the Turkish fleet at Corfu. Since 1923 the church has been named the 'Madonna dell'Apparizione'. The frescoes of four large prophets on the vault and over the sanctuary date from 1950–52. In a side calle there is an interesting little tabernacle, with miniature antique columns and a bas relief of the standing Madonna and Child, a rare survival. The last district, Busetto, has a few shops and a bar, and the very long church of **Ognissanti**, founded in the 12C and rebuilt and extended in the 16C and 17C. It contains a huge reliquary.

At the south end of the island is the cemetery and no. **11** bus terminus next to the landing-stage for the passenger ferry (in connection with the bus) to Chioggia. As the boat crosses the **Porto di Chioggia**, the third and last entrance to the lagoon, the Ca'Roman, a 16C fortification on the southern tip of the island, now inhabited by Cannossian nuns, can be seen (some services call here, on request). The boat takes a little under half an hour to reach Chioggia.

Chioggia

Bus and ferry services Bus **11** operates from the Lido (Santa Maria Elisabetta) via Malamocco, Alberoni, San Pietro in Volta and Pellestina (see pp 255 and 40). At Pellestrina (*Cimitero*) it connects with a boat which continues (25 minutes) to Chioggia. The whole journey, which is highly recommended, takes c 1.5 hrs.

Chioggia and Sottomarina can also be reached from the mainland by bus from Piazzale Roma (no. **25**) via Mestre in c 1 hr, but the approach from the Lido is much more interesting.

Chioggia (49,800 inhabitants), one of the main fishing ports on the Adriatic, is situated at the southern extremity of the Venetian lagoon, connected to the mainland by a bridge. The most important town after Venice in the lagoon, its unusual urban structure dating from the late 14C survives, with numerous narrow straight calli very close to each other on either side of the the Corso del Popolo and Canale Vena, with almost all the important churches and civic buildings in the centre. It is also visited for its beach at Sottomarina (see below).

Chioggia's history has been interwoven with that of Venice since it was first settled by inhabitants of Este, Monselice, and Padua, in the 5C–7C. Always loyal to Venice, Chioggia suffered destruction at the hands of the Genoese in 1379; but the Venetians under Vettor Pisani succeeded in shutting up the Genoese fleet in the harbour immediate afterwards, and its subsequent surrender marked the end of the struggle between the two rival maritime powers. The saltworks of Chioggia, first developed in the 12C, were the most important in the lagoon and survived until this century.

Famous natives include Cristoforo Sabbadino (1489–1560), the hydraulic engineer of the Republic, John Cabot (1425–c 1500), the navigator, Giuseppe Zerlino (1517–90), the musical theorist, Rosalba Carriera (1675–1757), the painter, and Eleonora Duse (1859–1924), the actress.

The boats from the Lido (and Venice) dock on the quay by Piazzetta Vigo, with its Greek marble column bearing the lion of St Mark. To the left Canale della Vena, used by the fishing fleet, is crossed by **Ponte Vigo** (1685), beyond which a calle leads to another bridge in front of the church of **San Domenico**. In the interior, on either side of the west door, are large historical canvases by Pietro Damini (1617–19). The first altarpiece on the **south side** of *Three Saints* is signed by Andrea Vicentino; beyond the second altar, *St Paul*, the last known work by Carpaccio (signed and dated 1520). On the right and left of the choir arch, *Deposition* and *Saints* by Leandro Bassano, and *Christ Crucified* and *Saints* attributed to Jacopo Tintoretto. On the high altar is a huge wooden Crucifix thought to date from the 15C or earlier. On the first north altar, *Martyrdom of St Peter*, by Andrea Vicentino.

*Corso del Popolo, the lively main street, with porticoes and cafés, starts from Piazzetta Vigo. It crosses the town parallel to the picturesque Canale della Vena (with some interesting palaces including Palazzo Grassi at no. 742 and Palazzo Lisatti at no. 609). On the left of the corso stands the church of **Sant'Andrea**, rebuilt in 1743, which preserves its detached Veneto-Byzantine campanile (13C). In the **interior**, the second south altar has a polychrome wood statuette of St Nicholas (16C). In the apse is a small oval painting of *St Andrew*, by the local painter Antonio Marinetti, known as Il Chioggiotto. The **sacristy** contains a *Crucifix and Saints* by an unknown 16C artist, and ivory reliefs in Baroque frames. In the **baptistery** is an unusual 16C marble tabernacle.

A short way further on in the corso is the low red building of the **Granaio** probably first built in 1322 (it preserves part of its old carved wood portico with stone columns), but restored in 1864. In the centre of the façade is a little tabernacle with a relief of the *Madonna and Child* by Jacopo Sansovino. The fish market on the canal behind (with specially designed slabs on which to display the fish) is awaiting restoration; for the time being the daily market takes place in a marquee on the Isola dell'Unione (see below). The large white **town hall** is a fine 19C building. At the far end is a flag staff supported by three giants (1713). Here is the church of the **Santissima Trinità**, rebuilt by Andrea Tirali (1703; being restored). The well-designed interior has an oratory behind the high altar. The two organs bear paintings by Giovanni Battista Mariotti. On the north altar is the *Presentation in the Temple*, by Matteo Ponzone. The oratory has a fine ceiling with paintings by the school of Tintoretto.

Across the canal can be seen the church of the **Filippini**. It contains (second south chapel) a *Visitation*, by Francesco Fontebasso, and (second north chapel), *Madonna and Child with Saints*, by Carlo Bevilacqua (1794).

On the corso is the **Loggia dei Bandi**, with an early 16C portico (now used as a police station). Beside a war memorial is the church of **San Giacomo**, with two campanili, one much taller then the other. The ceiling bears a fresco of *St James*, with remarkable perspective, by Il Chioggiotto. On the third south altar is a painting of *St Roch and St Sebastian* by the school of Bellini, incorporating a 15C fresco fragment. On the high altar, a *Pietà* by the 15C Venetian school is much venerated as the *Madonna della Navicella* (there are ex votos all over the church, including some in silver, recently restored). Farther on is the family mansion of Rosalba Carriera, later occupied by the playwright, Goldoni (plaque). On the other side of the corso is the little church of **San Francesco**. Beyond is the isolated early Gothic church of **San Martino** which has an interesting exterior (1392) in brick, with Romanesque and Gothic elements (it is used for exhibitions). Next to it is the **Duomo** with its detached campanile (1347–50). The **interior** (usually open 09.00–12.00) was reconstructed by Longhena in 1624. Beyond the third south altar is a small *Madonna and Child* by the school of Giovanni Bellini. The sacristy contains paintings (1593–98) of episodes in the history of Chioggia by Andrea Vicentino, Alvise dal Friso, Pietro Malombra and Benedetto Caliari. On the right of the sanctuary is a Baroque chapel decorated with marbles and stucco work by Giacomo Gaspari. The chapel also contains two oval paintings and a vault fresco by Michele Schiavone. The chapel to the left of the sanctuary contains six fine paintings by Giovanni Battista Cignaroli (attributed), Gaspare Diziani, Giambattista Tiepolo (*Torture of two Martyrs*), Giovanni Battista Piazzetta (attributed), Pietro Liberi, and Gian Mattei. On the north side is a statue of St Agnes signed by Antonio Bonazza, and a polychrome wood statue of St Roch dating from the late 17C signed by Filippo de Porris (recently restored). The marble baptistery contains three statues of Virtues by Alvise Tagliapietra.

The north side of the Duomo flanks a canal with a pretty marble balustrade decorated with 18C statues, including a venerated Madonna. Here, at the end of the corso, is the little **Torre di Santa Maria** (or Porta Garibaldi), the old entrance to the town. The bridge leads over to the ex-church of San Francesco fuori le mura, a large isolated building, where the **Museo Civico** was opened in 1997 (open Tues–Sun 09.00–13.00; Fri & Sat also 15.30–19.30; summer Fri & Sat 09.00–13.00; Thur–Sun 19.30–23.30; ☎ 041 550 0911). On the ground floor is archaeological material, including amphorae (1C–6C AD) found offshore between Malamocco and Sottomarina; displays relating to the sea defences in the southern part of the lagoon, and the changes in the coastline over the centuries; and the geology of the lagoon and its islands. Stairs lead up past a room with exhibits relating to Cristoforo Sabbadino, engineer of the Venetian Republic, and a display of ceramics dating from the 14C to the 18C found in the district of Chioggia. The rest of this floor is occupied by the town archives. On the top floor the splendid wooden roof of the former church can be seen and there are good views of Chioggia from the windows. Here are models of boats and fishing nets, and displays relating to boat building since the 18C.

From San Giacomo the Calle San Giacomo leads across Ponte San Giacomo and the Canale San Domenico (with a swing bridge) past the wholesale fish market, busy with lorries. Another bridge continues to the Isola dell'Unione, with a car park and public gardens, connected by another bridge to **Sottomarina**, once a village of fishermen and market-gardeners with narrow houses closely wedged together. It has now developed into a seaside resort with many small hotels lining the sandy beach on the Adriatic.

The minor islands

San Servolo and San Lazzaro degli Armeni

Boat services The small *ACTV* motor-boat no. 20 from Riva degli Schiavoni runs about every 40 minutes to San Lazzaro degli Armeni (in just over 10 minutes) calling at San Servolo on the way and the way back.

Admission Visitors are admitted to the island of San Lazzaro daily 15.20–17.00. With the present timetable, the 15.10 boat from Riva degli Schiavoni is the only one which coincides with the opening times of San Lazzaro. San Servolo is not officially open to visitors as it is occupied by various institutes and universities, and is used as a venue for international conferences.

From Riva degli Schiavoni the boat passes to the left of the island of San Giorgio Maggiore to reach the island of **San Servolo**, on the site of one of the oldest and most important Benedictine convents in the lagoon, founded in the 9C and dedicated to a Roman soldier martyred at the time of Diocletian. It became an important religious centre, and the buildings were transformed in the 18C by Temanza. Later used as a hospital, it is now owned by the Province, and some of the buildings are still being restored. A few palm trees grow on the island. Since 1980 it has been occupied by the workshops of the Venice European Centre for the Trades and Professions of the Conservation of Architectural Heritage (also called the Associazione Europea Pro Venezia Viva). The Venice International University was also opened here in 1997.

The Lido is now conspicuous ahead, and the little island of San Lazzaro degli Armeni with its tower amidst cypresses and pine trees.

San Lazzaro degli Armeni

The island of San Lazzaro degli Armeni, just off the Lido, is distinguished by its tall campanile crowned by an oriental cupola. Formerly the property of the Benedictines, it was used from 1182 as a leper colony. After a period of abandon, it was given to the Armenians in 1717 as the seat of an Armenian Catholic monastery, founded by Peter of Manug, called Mekhitar (the Consoler). The island has increased in size fourfold since the 18C, and is beautifully kept by the present community of about 20 Mekhitarian Fathers, some of whom are seminarists. The order is well known in academic and educational fields, and as a centre of Armenian culture. It was celebrated for its polyglot printing press, established here in 1789: the publishing house, which since 1994 has confined its activity to printing material for the Armenian Congregation, now operates on Punta Sabbioni, although the original presses have been kept on the island.

Visitors are shown the monastery by a father. Outside the entrance is a 14C Armenian memorial Cross, and a plaque commemorating Byron (see below). In the attractive cloister are some archaeological fragments. The **church** has 18C and 19C decorations, and stained glass made in Innsbruck in 1901. A fire in 1975 destroyed the sacristy and old library. In the **refectory**, where the fathers eat in silence while the Bible is read in classical Armenian, is a *Last Supper* by Pietro Novelli (1788). On the stairs are paintings by Palma Giovane, and ceiling frescoes by Francesco Zugno.

In the vestibule of the library, is a fine ceiling painting of *Peace and Justice* by Giambattista Tiepolo, and a delightful small collection of antiquities, with an incredible miscellany of objects. The **library,** which houses some of the 150,000 volumes owned by the monastery in 18C carved pearwood cupboards with their original Murano glass, has more frescoes by Zugno. The typical Venetian mosaic floor survives. The Egyptian objects displayed here include a mummy of the 7C BC, complete with its rare cover of glass and paste beads, donated to the monastery in 1825. Another room has been arranged as a small museum with Armenian books and porcelain and textiles. Steps lead down to **Byron's Room**, where his portrait hangs. He was a frequent visitor here, and studied Armenian as a means of conquering his boredom (he even helped publish an Armenian-English dictionary and grammar). In 1980 some of his books, formerly belonging to the Casa Magni at Lerici, were donated to the monastery. The plaster sculpture of the son of Napoleon (as the young St John the Baptist) is by Canova. The monastery also owns a rare 14C Indian throne.

A walkway leads across to the **Library Rotunda**, built in 1967 to house the ⁺collection of some 4000 Armenian manuscripts. Some of these are displayed, including the oldest known Armenian document (862), and an Evangelistery by Sarkis Pizak (1331), as well as rare bookbindings. A very fine Florentine polychrome terracotta relief (c 1400) is also kept here.

To the south, also close to the Lido, is the **island of Lazzaretto Vecchio**. A hospice for pilgrims was founded here in the 12C. The island was occupied by the Augustinian monastery of Santa Maria di Nazareth when in 1423 a hospital was set up here by order of the Republic for plague victims. It was the first-known permanent isolation hospital in Europe, and the name Lazzaretto (a corruption of Nazareth) was later adopted for all leper hospitals. After a period of use as a military deposit it was abandoned in 1965, and is now a home for stray dogs and cats. There are plans to open a sports centre here. The island of **La Grazia** was used until recently as an isolation hospital.

The hospital on the island of **San Clemente** was closed in 1992. The 17C church, with a fine series of Baroque monuments of the Morosini family, has been vandalised, but the sculptures have been recovered and are now kept in the Museo Diocesano in Venice. A large hotel is to be built on the island.

To the south is the island of **Santo Spirito**, the site of a famous monastery destroyed in 1656. It was later used as an ammunition factory and was abandoned in 1965. It is destined to become a sports centre. **Sacca Sessola**, a large island to the west, was occupied by a hospital until 1980. In 1993 it was given to the United Nations Industrial Development Organisation as a marine research centre, but more recently it has been decided to turn it into a hotel and conference centre. Poveglia, close to Malamocco, is mentioned in p 255.

Le Vignole, Lazzaretto Nuovo and Sant'Erasmo

Boat services Vaporetto no. **13** (about every hour) from *Fondamente Nuove* via Murano (*Faro*) to Le Vignole and Sant'Erasmo (which has three boat stops, *Capannone*, *Chiesa*, and *Punta Vela*). Before *Capannone*, the boat will sometimes stop at Lazzaretto Nuovo on request. The whole trip as far as *Punta Vela* takes about 1 hr. A few boats a day continue to Treporti.

After leaving the lighthouse of Murano, the boat runs straight across the lagoon, with views of the Arsenal and the tower of Sant'Elena on the right, to the secluded island of **Le Vignole**, with a handful of houses and two trattorie open in summer, and no cars. Most of the market gardens have now been abandoned (although the interesting system of irrigation channels with small locks to regulate the water survives in places) and most of the island is now a wilderness, but much of it is fenced off and not accessible, although some artichoke beds are still cultivated here. A grassy path leads from the landing-stage to a group of pine trees and a public water pump outside the little chapel with a miniature campanile of **Sant'Eurosia** whose pretty bust is above the door. A service is held here on holidays at 09.30 by the priest from Sant'Erasmo. The only bridge on the island leads over the canal where an old boat house built on stilts can be seen. At the end of the canal there is a view of the lagoon, and a path leads to the other side of the island where there is a view towards Venice: on the right is Murano and San Michele, the wall of the Arsenal and its cranes, and the apse, dome and white campanile of San Pietro di Castello, and further left the tower of Sant'Elena and some modern buildings. On the extreme southern tip of Le Vignole is the Fortezza di Sant'Andrea (described on p 253) guarding the Porto di Lido; at present it is not accessible by land.

The island of **La Certosa**, between Le Vignole and Sant'Elena used to be occupied by an explosives factory; it was abandoned in 1968, and may become a public park, but is at present closed to the public.

The Sant'Erasmo boat skirts the shore of Le Vignole and passes mud flats and marshes just above the level of the lagoon (*barene*). The landing-stage of *Capannone* on Sant'Erasmo (see below) is opposite the island of **Lazzaretto Nuovo** where a landing-stage has recently been built and where the *ACTV* boats sometimes call on request.

The island was called the Lazzaretto Nuovo when it was first used as a quarantine hospital to prevent the spread of the plague in Venice in 1468 to distinguish it from the Lazzaretto Vecchio, the island just off the Lido, which was already functioning as a hospital for plague victims. It continued to be used as such for a number of centuries and in the 19C it was occupied by the Austrian armed forces and used as a deposit for arms in connection with their defence system on Sant'Erasmo which at that time defended Venice from the open sea. The island was abandoned by the military in 1975 and restoration began here in the late 1980s with the cooperation of volunteers of a local branch of the Archeoclub d'Italia who still look after the island and show it to visitors by appointment, usually on Saturday and Sunday (☎ 041 244 4011; 📠 041 244 4010 or ☎ 041 710 515).

In the centre of the island is the **Tezon Grande**, one of the largest public buildings in Venice, more than 100 metres long, although internally it is divided in half. This was used to decontaminate the merchandise from the ships which were made to dock at the island (the goods were then fumigated outside, using rosemary and juniper). The arches were blocked up when it was later used as a military store, but the splendid wood roof has recently been restored. On the walls are some interesting inscriptions made by the sailors in the 16C. The original brick herring-bone pavement survives (the Austrians inserted a wood floor above it as can be seen from the raised stone blocks). Originally some 200–300 sailors could be housed on the island in small cells, each with their own kitchen and fireplace and court-yard, built against the perimeter wall. These were demolished by the Austrians, but the floors of some of them have recently been excavated. The gunpowder and ammunition from the ships anchored here was stored in two little edifices which formerly had pyramidal rooves but were altered in the 19C (one of them has been restored as a delightful little museum dedicated to the history of the island, which contains finds from excavations including prehistoric flints, Greek and Roman coins, and ceramics from later centuries).

Two well-heads survive on the island, one decorated with the lion of St Mark. Excavations, still in progress, have also revealed remains of a church here (it is known that the Benedictines were on the island in the 12C). A second line of walls built by the Austrians survives, and in one of the turrets a little observation platform has recently been built which provides a good view of the lagoon. A path on the outside of the walls leads right round the island in about half an hour from which there is a very good view of the lagoon and its islands as well as its wildlife (including herons, cormorants, swamp hawks, kingfishers and egrets) and vegetation. There are long-term plans to use the Teson Grande as a museum dedicated to the plague or to the natural history of the lagoon. A sea dyke has recently been constructed on the west side of the island in an attempt to protect it from *acqua alta*, and a pilot project is being carried out here to demonstrate that water can be purified by plant biology.

Sant'Erasmo is a much bigger island than Le Vignole. It is a tongue of land formed by sediment from the sea, which became important to the defence of the lagoon. Artichokes and asparagus are now cultivated here. The inhabitants (about 800) use vespas or little vespa vans (*ape*) to get about. It is an exceptionally peaceful place, with narrow surfaced roads, and very few fences. The vegetation includes aster, laurel, blackthorn and temerisk, and white herons, some of them almost tame, abound. Hand-painted notices welcome visitors and indicate the various itineraries. A paved lane (built by the Austrians to connect the defences with the island of Lazzaretto Nuovo) leads straight from the *Capannone* landing-stage past market gardens to the other side of the island and the **Torre di Massimiliano**, a low circular fort built in 1813, and occupied by Daniele Manin in 1848, now in urgent need of restoration, surrounded by beds of artichokes. Here a shack serves as the only bar on the island (and restaurant in summer). There is a view from here straight out to sea through the Bocca di Lido, the northernmost channel which connects the lagoon to the sea: on the left can be seen Punta Sabbioni and on the right the end of the Lido.

The island which can be seen here is Le Vignole with the fortress of Sant'Andrea on the water. Private boats can dock near the bar, and near a bridge there is another good view taking in the tower of San Francesco della Vigna on the right. Just to the right of a large building, in the far distance, the camanile of San Marco can be seen, and the dome and tower of San Pietro di Castello.

After the landing-stage of *Capannone* the boat follows a channel between the low wall which protects the island and the marshes: the main settlement on the island is at the landing-stage of **Chiesa** (with a church and a shop) which can also be reached on foot (a pleasant walk) from Capannone. From the last stop, **Punta Vela**, there is a good view of the island of San Francesco del Deserto with its cypresses, and Burano and Torcello in the distance. A few boats a day continue to Treporti.

Glossary

albergo, small room used for committee meetings on the upper floor of a Scuola

altana, terrace made of wood, on the roof of a Venetian house

ambo (pl. *ambone*), pulpit in a Christian basilica; two pulpits on opposite sides of a church from which the gospel and epistle were read

ancona, retable or large altarpiece (painted or sculpted) in an architectural frame

androne, principal ground floor hall behind the water entrance of a Venetian palace

architrave, the lowest part of an entablature, the horizontal frame around a door

archivolt, moulded architrave carried round an arch

atlantes (or telamones). male figures used as supporting columns

atrium, forecourt, usually part of a Byzantine church or a classical Roman house

attic, topmost storey of a classical building, hiding the spring of the roof

baldacchino, canopy supported by columns, usually over an altar

bardiglio, marble streaked with blue and white

basilica, originally a Roman building used for public administration; in Christian architecture, an aisled church with a clerestory and apse, and no transepts

bas-relief, sculpture in low relief

bottega, the studio of an artist; or the pupils who worked under his direction

bozzetto, sketch, often used to describe a small model for a piece of sculpture

campanile, bell-tower, often detached from the building to which it belongs

Ca' (casa), Venetian term for palace (or important residence)

calle, narrow Venetian street

campiello, small Venetian piazza

campo (*pl. campi*), Venetian term for piazza (or square)

capital, architectural element at the top of a column

chalice, wine cup used in the celebration of Mass

chiaroscuro, distribution of light and shade, apart from colour in a painting

ciborium, casket or tabernacle containing the Host

cipollino, greyish marble with streaks of white or green

cippus (pl. *cippae*), sepulchral monument in the form of an altar

cloisonné, type of enamel decoration, divided by narrow strips of metal

condottiere, captain-general of a city militia, soldier of fortune at the head of an army

corbel, a projecting block, usually of stone

cornu (or *berretta*), peaked ducal beret in red velvet, worn over a white linen skull cap

corte, courtyard

crenellations, battlements

cupola, dome

diptych, painting or ivory tablet in two sections

dossal, altarpiece

duomo, cathedral

exedra, semi-circular recess

ex voto, tablet or small painting expressing gratitude to a saint

fondaco (fontego), trading post

fondamenta, street alongside a canal

forno, bakery

Greek cross, cross with arms of equal length

herm, quadrangular pillar decreasing in girth towards the ground, surmounted by a bust

iconostasis, high balustrade with figures of saints, guarding the sanctuary of a Byzantine church

intarsia, inlay of wood, marble, or metal

Latin cross, cross with a long vertical arm

liagò, upper floor loggia which protrudes from a Venetian palace façade

lista, a lane which led up to an ambassador's palace

loggia, covered gallery

lunette, semi-circular space in a vault or ceiling often decorated with a painting or relief

magazen (magazzino), warehouse

merceria, market

matroneum, gallery reserved for women in early Christian churches

monstrance, a vessel for displaying the Host

narthex, vestibule of a Christian basilica

niello, a black inlay using silver, lead, copper, sulphur and borax

ogee (arch), shaped in a double curve, convex above and concave below

opus alexandrinum, mosaic design of black and red geometric figures on a white ground

opus sectile, mosaic or paving of thin slabs of coloured marble cut in geometrical shapes

palazzo, palace; any dignified and important building

pali, wood piles used as foundations for buildings in Venice; and the mooring posts in front of palaces showing the livery colours of their proprietors

Pantocrater, the almighty, the ruler of the Universe

paten, flat dish on which the Host is placed

patera (pl. *paterae*), small circular carved ornament (often Byzantine), sometimes used as a decorative feature on façades in Venice

pavonazzetto, yellow marble blotched with blue

pax, sacred object used by a priest for the blessing of peace, and offered for the kiss of the faithful, usually circular, engraved, enamelled or painted in a rich gold or silver frame

pendentive, concave spandrel beneath a dome

piano nobile, the main floor of a house, and usually the principal architectural feature of the façade

pier, a square or compound pillar used as a support in architecture

Pietà, group of the Virgin mourning the dead Christ

pietre dure, hard or semi-precious stones, often used in the form of mosaics to decorate cabinets, tabletops, etc.

piscina, place where a basin of water connected to a canal formerly existed

pluteus (pl. *plutei*), marble panel, usually decorated; a series of them are often used to form a parapet to precede the altar of a church

polyptych, painting or panel in more than three sections

porphyry, an extremely hard red rock quarried in Egypt, often used for sculpture by the Romans

portego, the central hall of a Venetian house, usually running the whole depth of the building

predella, small painting attached below a large altarpiece

pronaos, porch in front of the cella of a temple

proto, 'protomagister', chief architect

putto (pl. *putti*), sculpted or painted figure, usually nude, of a boy

quadratura, painted architectural perspectives

quatrefoil, four-lobed cusp (on an arch)

ramo, offshoot (of a canal)

reredos, decorated screen rising behind an altar

rio, canal

rio terrà, street in the course of a filled-in rio

riva, wharf

rood-screen, a screen below the Rood or Crucifix dividing the nave from the chancel or a church

ruga, street

rustication, huge blocks of masonry usually with rough surfaces, often used on palace façades

sacca, stretch of water where canals meet

alizzada, paved street

scuola (pl. *scuole*), lay confraternity, dedicated to charitable works

sestiere, district of Venice

soffit, underside or intrados of an arch

sottoportico, Venetian term for a street which passes beneath a building, or a street entered under arches

spandrel, surface between two arches in an arcade or the triangular space on either side of an arch

stilted arch, round arch that rises vertically before it springs

stoup, vessel for Holy Water usually near the west door of a church

stylobate, basement of a columned temple or other building

telamones, see **atlantes**

tenebroso, dark-toned, shadowy

tessera, small cube of marble, glass, etc. used in mosaic work

thermal window, semicircular window derived from those used in ancient Roman public baths. A characteristic feature of Palladian architecture

tondo (pl. *tondi*), roundel

transenna, open grille or screen, usually of marble, in an early Christian church

trefoil, three-lobed cusp (on an arch)

triptych, painting or tablet in three sections

vera da pozzo, well head

verde antico, dark green marble from Tessaglia

villa, country house with garden

volute, spiral scroll, the distinguishing feature of an Ionic capital

zoia Doge's horned cap decorated with jewels for state ceremonies

Index to artists

A

Agostino (Giovanni) da Lodi (pseudo Boccaccino: c 1500)   168, 242

Alberegno, Jacobello (died c 1379)   162

Alberghetti, Alfonso (16C)   114

Alberti, Camillo (fl. 1520)   90

Albertinelli, Mariotto (1474–1515)   175

Aliense (Antonio Vassilacchi: c 1556–1629)   86, 87, 88, 99, 120, 122, 145, 175, 225, 228

Alvise dal Friso (1569–1609)   186, 208, 259

Amigoni, Jacopo (1675–1752)   180, 210

Ammannati, Bartolomeo (1511–92)   107

Andrea di Bartolo (died 1428)   194

Andrea del Castagno (1423–57)   86, 90, 135

Andrea da Murano (fl. 1462–1502)   167

Angeli, Giuseppe (c 1710–98)   136, 154, 157, 180, 206, 209, 210

Antico (Pier Jacopo Alari Bonacolsi: 1460–1528)   194

Antonello da Messina (c 1430–79)   102

Antonello da Saliba (c 1466–1535)   124, 168

Antonio da Negroponte (15C)   150

Antonio da Ponte (c 1512–97)   109, 117, 118, 123, 128, 176, 235

Antonio dal Zotto (1841–1918)   146, 188

Aspetti, Tiziano (c 1559–1606)   104, 117, 131, 150, 151

B

Bacci, Baccio Maria (1888–1974)   172

Baccio da Montelupo (1469–1535)   202

Bachiacca (Antonio Ubertino: 1494–1557)   175

Baldassare d'Este (Estense: c 1440–1504)   100, 170

Baldi, Lazzaro (17C)   221

Balestra, Antonio (1666–1740)   135, 183, 210

Balla, Giacomo (1874–1958)   171

Ballini, Camillo (fl. 1540–92)   129

Bambini, Niccolò (1651–1736)   157, 175, 179, 183, 210, 221

Bandini, Giovanni (dell'Opera: 1540–99)   114, 121

Baratta, Pietro (c 1659–1729)   145, 210

Barthel, Melchiore (1625–72)   221

Bartolomeo di Paolo (fl. 1389–1404)   102

Barzaghi, Francesco (1839–92)   157

Basaiti, Marco (fl. 1496–1530)   103, 162, 168, 169, 174, 203

Bassano, Francesco (da Ponte: son of Jacopo: 1549–92)   120, 122, 213, 228, 229, 230

Bassano, Gerolamo (1566–1621)   117

Bassano, Jacopo (da Ponte: c 1510–92)   117, 167, 225, 229

Bassano, Leandro (da Ponte: 1558–1623)   87, 122, 120, 123, 141, 146, 148, 152, 167, 211, 212, 258

Bassi, Alvise (18C)   183

Bastiani, Lazzaro (c 1425–1512)   99, 137, 103, 141, 168, 169, 194, 219, 229, 245

Index

INDEX
to colour atlas

KEY
to maps

🏨ᵃ   Hotel

🛈   Tourist information

▮   Building of interest

✚   Church

▮   Other building

Arsenale   Vaporetti waterbus stop

....   Vaporetti waterbus route

━━━━   Railway line

scale of maps

0   100 yards

0   100 Metres

N

1

ISOLA DI
SAN MICHELE

2   Railway Station

Canale di Cannaregio

3   GHETTO

Grand Canal

4   Madonna dell'Orto

5   Gesuiti

6   Piazzale Roma Car Park

7   S. Maria Gloriosa dei Frari

8   Ponte di Rialto   Grand Canal

9   Santi Giovanni e Paolo   San Marco   Piazza San Marco   Palazzo Ducale

10   Arsenale

11   S. Pietro di Castello   inset, page 16

inset

16   S. Pietro di Castello   S. Elena

12   S. Sebastiano

13   Ponte dell'Accademia

14   S. Maria d. Salute

15   S. Giorgio Maggiore

G I U D E C C A

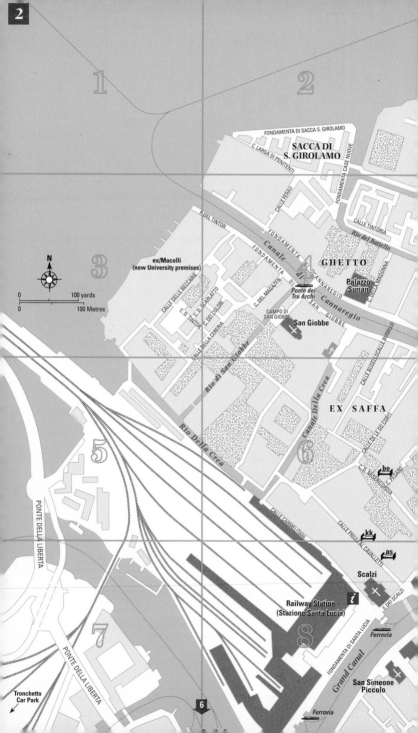

SACCA DI
S. GIROLAMO

FONDAMENTA DI SACCA S. GIROLAMO

C. LARGA DI PENITENTI

CALLETERAU

FONDAMENTA CASE NUOVE

CALLE TINTORIA

Rio del Battello

GHETTO

F. DEL TINTOR

FONDAMENTA DI CANNAREGIO

Canale di Cannaregio

FONDAMENTA DI SAN GIOBBE

ex/Macelli
(now University premises)

CALLE DELLE BECCARIE

C. D. TINTOR

C. D. SCARLATTO

C. DEI COLORI

CALLE DELLA CERERIA

C. DEL MAGAZEN

Ponte dei
Tre Archi

Palazzo
Surian

C. DELLA MADONNA

CAMPO DI
SAN GIOBBE

San Giobbe

Canale di Cannaregio

CALLE BUSELLO CALLE BUSELLO

Rio di San Giobbe

Canale Della Crea

EX SAFFA

CALLE LE DO CORTI

Rio Della Crea

be

CALLE D. MISERICORDIA C. D. ESADO

kk

CALLE CARMELITANI

CALLE PRIULI AI CAVALLETTI

as

PONTE DELLA LIBERTA

Scalzi

i

Railway Station
(Stazione Santa Lucia)

F. DEI SCALZI

Ferrovia

PONTE DELLA LIBERTA

FONDAMENTA DI SANTA LUCIA

Grand Canal

San Simeone
Piccolo

Tronchetto
Car Park

Ferrovia

N

0   100 yards
0   100 Metres

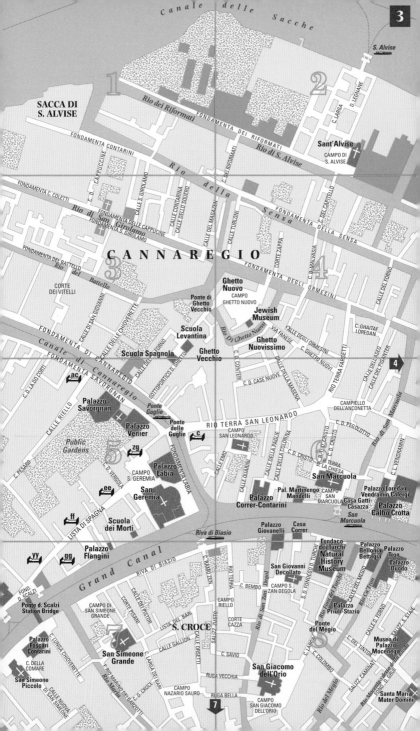

Canale delle Sacche

S. Alvise

SACCA DI
S. ALVISE

1

2

FONDAMENTA CONTARINI

Rio dei Riformati

FONDAMENTA DEI RIFORMATI

C. LARGA

D. LEGNAME

Sant'Alvise

CAMPO DI
S. ALVISE

Rio di S. Alvise

FONDAMENTA C. COLETTI

C. D. CAPPUCCINE

CALLE S. GIROLAMO

CALLE CONTARINA

CALLE DELLO SQUERO

CALLE DEL MAGAZEN

CALLE TURLONI

RIO della

FONDAMENTA DELLA SENSA

Sensa

C. DEL CAPITELLO

Rio di San Girolamo

FONDAMENTA DELLE CAPPUCINE

FONDAMENTA S. GIROLAMO

CORTE ZAPPA

C. D. MALVASIA

FONDAMENTA DEL BATTELLO

Rio del Battello

C A N N A R E G I O

FONDAMENTA DEGLI ORMESINI

CALLE DEL FORNO

CORTE
DEI VITELLI

3

4

Ghetto
Nuovo

CAMPO
GHETTO NUOVO

FONDAMENTA DI CANNAREGIO

CALLE DE SAN GIOVANNI

CALLE DELLE CHIOVERETTE

Ponte di
Ghetto
Vecchio

Jewish
Museum

CALLE DEGLI ORMESINI

C. GHAITAF
LOREDAN

Canale di Cannaregio

FONDAMENTA SAVORGNAN

CALLE SPORINO

Scuola
Levantina

Rio Di Ghetto Nuovo

VIA FANESE

Ghetto
Nuovissimo

C. GHETTO NUOVI

RIO TERRA FARSETTI

CALLE BELLISSEO

CALLE DE PIGNTER

ac

Scuola Spagnola

SOTTOPORTICO D. GHETTO

Ghetto
Vecchio

C. D. CONTER

C. D. CASE NUOVE

CAMPIELLO
DELL'ANCONETTA

RIO DI PALAZZO

C. D. LA DO CORTI

CALLE RIELLO

C. D. VERGOLA

Palazzo
Savorgnan

Ponte
Guglie

Palazzo
Venier

Ponte
delle
Guglie

RIO TERRA SAN LEONARDO

CAMPO
SAN LEONARDO

C. D. CASE NUOVE

CALLE DELLA MASENA

C. D. PEGOLOTTO

CALLE VENDRAMIN

RIO DI PALAZZO S. MARCUOLA

4

Public
Gardens

5

zg

C. PESARO

Palazzo
Labia

CAMPO
S. GEREMIA

FONDAMENTA LABIA

CALLE EMO

CALLE DELLA PAGLIE

CALLE DELLA COLONNA

C. D. CRISTO

R. TERRA
D. CRISTO

C. D. CRISTO

RIO TERRA
D. LA CHIESA

San Marcuola

C. VENDRAMIN

Palazzo Loredan
Vendramin Calergi

ee

San
Geremia

CAMPO
S. MARCUOLA

Palazzo
Calbo Crotta

ff

LISTA DI SPAGNA

Scuola
dei Morti

CALLE QUARINI

Pal. Martinengo
Mandelli

Palazzo
Correr-Contarini

Casa Gatti
Casazza

San
Marcuola

yy

gg

Palazzo
Flangini

Riva di Biasio

Palazzo
Giovanelli

Casa
Correr

Fondaco
dei turchi

Palazzo
Bellona
Bettaqua

Palazzo
Tron

FOND.
D. SCALZI

Grand

Canal

RIVA DI BIASIO

C. RAMO ZEN

RIO TERRA

Natural
History
Museum

Palazzo
Duodo

Ponte d. Scalzi
Station Bridge

CAMPO DI
SAN SIMEONE
GRANDE

CALLE PISANI

CALLE DEI PISTOR

San Giovanni
Decollato

C. BEMBO

CAMPO S.
ZAN DEGOLA

S. D. FONDEGO D. TURCHI

Palazzo
Priuli-Stazio

Ponte
del Megio

C. DEL TINTOR

Palazzo
Foscari
Contarini

C. LUNGA CHIOVERETTE

RIO MARIN O D. CROCE DI GARZOTTI

CAMPO
RIELLO

CORTE
CAZZA

CALLE DEL BARI

RIO DEL MEGIO

Museo di
Palazzo
Mocenigo

C. DELLA
COMARE

San Simeone
Piccolo

CALLE LARGA DEL BARI

San Simeone
Grande

7

C. SAVIO

RUGA VECCHIA

C. LARGA

C. COLOMBO

San Giacomo
dell'Orio

SALIZZ. S. STAE

C. DEI TINTORI

RIO MARIN

CALLE INDRIA
DI SAN SIMEONE

S. CROCE

SALIZZ. JUSTO

CALLE ORSETTI

C. D'OLO

CAMPO
NAZARIO SAURO

RUGA BELLA

CAMPO
SAN GIACOMO
DELL'ORIO

Santa Maria
Mater Domini

7

1

2

3

4

Madonna dell'Orto

CAMPIELLO PIAVE

Madonna dell'Orto

CAMPO DELLA MADONNA DELL'ORTO

C. GRADISCA

C. LOREDAN

FONDAMENTA MADONNA DELL'ORTO

C. BRAZZO

ca

Palazzo Mastelli

3

C. DEI MORI

Rio della Madonna dell'Orto

FONDAMENTA GASPARO CONTARINI

FONDAMENTA DEI MORI

C. TINTORETTO

CANNAREGIO

Rio della Sensa

C. LARGA

Ponte dei Muti

FONDAMENTA DELLA MISERICORDIA

CORTE VECCHIA

C. DEL TREVISAN

FONDAMENTA DELL'ABBAZIA

Sacca della Misericordia

FONDAMENTE NUOVE

Scuola Vecchia della Misericordia

Abbazia della Misericordia

FOND. DELL'ABBAZIA

3

Santa Maria dei Servi

Rio della Misericordia

Rio di S. Girolamo

FOND. CANAL

FOND. O. MORO

Palazzo Lezze

CALLE LARGA LEZZE

CALLE LUNGA SANTA CATERINA

CALLE MARCO FOSCARINI

R. T. D. MADDALENA

Ponte Sant'Antonio

FOND. DEI TRAPOLIN

San Marciliano

Palazzo Vendramin

Scuola Grande della Misericordia

CAMPO DELLA MISERICORDIA

Rio di Noale

Santa Caterina

Rio di S. Caterina

CAMPO S. CATERINA

Oratorio dei Crociferi

Palazzo Zen

FONDAMENTA S. CATERINA

CAMPO D. MADDALENA

CAMPO D'ORO

Maddalena

S. FOSCA

Rio della Maddalena

Santa Fosca

Palazzo Giovanelli

bf

VIA V. EMANUELE

CALLE DELLA RACCHETTA

CORTE SQUERO VECCHIO

F. S. ANDREA

CALLE ZANARDI

C. DEL SARTORI

F. D. SARTORI

Palazzo Soranzo

Palazzo Erizzo

Palazzo Marcello

Palazzo Emo

Palazzo Molin

C. NOAL

Palazzo Barbarigo

C. BARBARO

FOND. DI CHIESA

Rio di San Felice

FOND. SAN FELICE

CALLE CORRENTE

C. PRIULI

R. T. BARBA FRUTTAROL

Palazzo Gussoni-Grimani della Vida

San Felice

CAMPO S. FELICE

C. D. FORNO

Rio di S. Sofia

RUGA DUE POZZI

Rio di Ca' Dolce

S. Stae

Pal. Da Lezze

Pal. Boldù

Pal. Contarini-Pisani

C. PISTOR

C. DELLE VELE

C. PRIULI

R. T. D. FRANCESCHI

CAMPO S. STAE

Pal. Foscarini-Giovanelli

Ca' Pesaro Gallery of Modern Art

Pal. Fontana

Santa Sofia

CAMPO S. SOFIA

STRADA NUOVA

C. D. FORNO

CALLE VERDE

SALIZADA DEL PISTOR

C. L. D. PROVERBI

cc

San Stae

Museum of Oriental Art

Pal. Corner della Regina

ao

Ca d'Oro

Pal. Pesaro-Rava

Pal. Sagredo

S. FELICE

Santi Apostoli

bs

CAMPIELLO D. CASON

Rio delle Pergola

C. DEL RAVANO

CALLE DELLA REGINA

CALLE CORNER

Casa Bragadin Favretto

Palazzo Morosini-Brandolin

Ca' d'Oro

Pal. Foscari

Pal. Michiel d. Colonne

Pal. Michiel Dal Brusa

CAMPO DELLA PESCHERIA

Ponte Santi Apostoli

Pal. Falier

R. D. SANTI APOSTOLI

R. T. BAGATIN

Santa Maria Mater Domini

S. CROCE

San Cassiano

CALLE DEL CAMPANILE

C. D. BOTTERI

R. D. RIVA D'OLIO

Pescheria

Pal. Mangilli-Valmarana

Ca' da Mosto

Pal. Morosini Sagredo

Pal. Michiel Dal Brusa

CAMPO S.S. APOSTOLI

C. D. MAGAZEN

CAMPO S. MARIA MATER DOMINI

8

5

MURANO

St Michele
in Isola

C e m e t e r y

**ISOLA DI
SAN MICHELE**

1

2

3

4

Canale delle Fondamente Nuove

FONDAMENTE NUOVE

Gesuiti

Oratorio
dei Crociferi

Pal.
Zen

CAMPO DEI
GESUITI

Rio dei Gesuiti

Fondamente
Nuove

CALLA LARGA DEI BOTTERI

5

6

C. VENIER

**Palazzo
Contarini-Serriman**

CAMPIELLO
D. PIETA

CALLE DEI CORDON

CALLE DEL FUMO

RIO TERRA
BARBA FRUTTAROL

CALLE STELLA

Rio della Panada

RIO TERRA BIRI

CALLE DEL SQUERO

Rio dei Mendicanti

FONDAMENTA DEI MENDICANTI

FONDAMENTE NUOVE

S. Lazzaro
d. Mendicanti

7

8

Rio Terà Santi Apostoli

Rio di S. Caterina

CALLE BANDO

CAMPIELLO
WIDMAN

CALLE
WIDMAN

**San
Canciano**

CAMPO
SANTA MARIA
NOVA

F. PIOVAN

C. LARGA G. GALLINA

**Pafazzo
Bembo Boldu**

**Scuola Grande
di San Marco**

9

Ospedale
Civile

**S. Maria
d. Pianto**

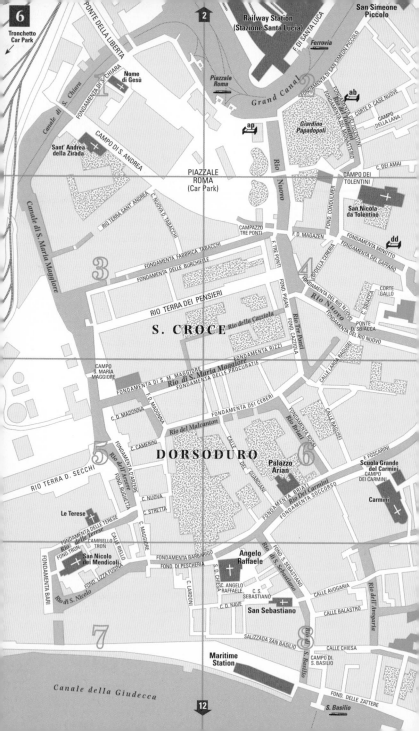

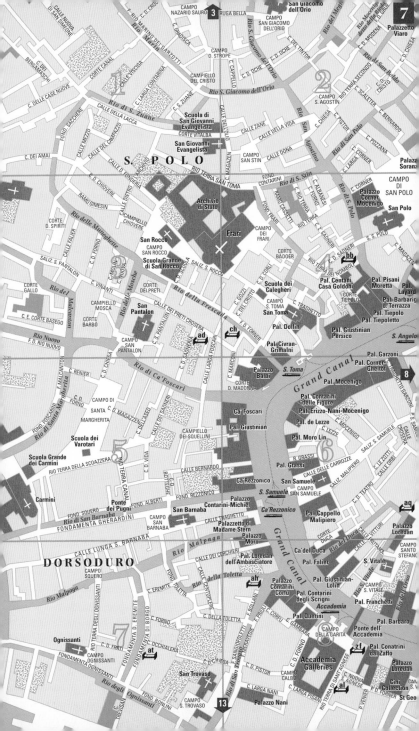

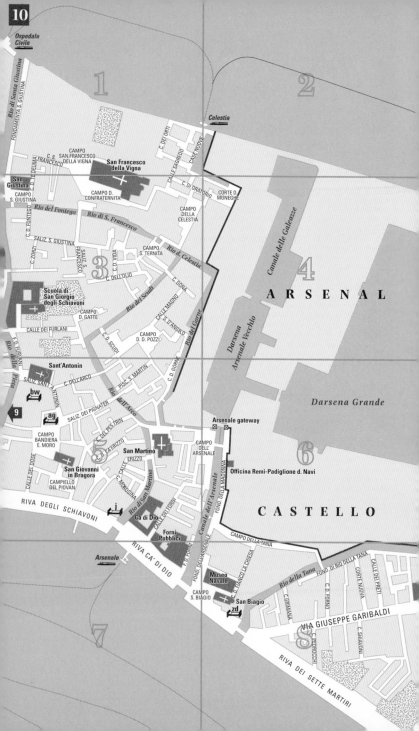

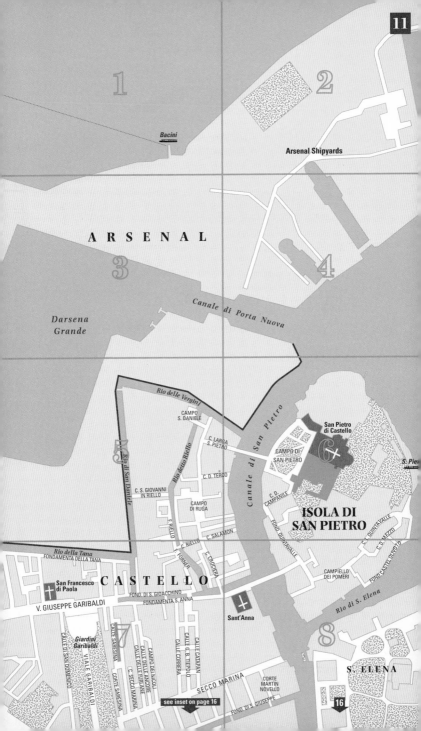

Bacini

Arsenal Shipyards

A R S E N A L

1

2

3

4

*Darsena
Grande*

Canale di Porta Nuova

Rio delle Vergini

CAMPO
S. DANIELE

C. LARGA
S. PIETRO

C. D. TERGO

C. S. GIOVANNI
IN RIELLO

CAMPO
DI RUGA

5

F. RIELLO

F. RIELLO

F. FORNER

C. SALAMON

C. CRICHERA

San Pietro
di Castello

CAMPO DI
SAN PIETRO

6

S. Pie

C. D.
CAMPANILE

**ISOLA DI
SAN PIETRO**

FOND. QUINTAVALLE

C. D. QUINTAVALLE

C. D. MEZZO

CAMPIELLO
DEI POMERI

FOND. CASTEL DUVOTO

Rio di S. Elena

Rio della Tana
FONDAMENTA DELLA TANA

San Francesco
di Paola

C A S T E L L O

V. GIUSEPPE GARIBALDI

FOND. DI S. GIOACCHINO

FONDAMENTA S. ANNA

Sant'Anna

*Giardini
Garibaldi*

7

CALLE DI SAN DOMENICO

VIALE GARIBALDI

CALLE SARESINA

CORTE SARESINA

C. SECCO MARINA

CAMPO DEI INCOLI

CALLE DELLE ANCORE

CALLE DELLE FURLANE

CALLE CORREERA

CALLE CATAPAN

CALLE G. B. TIEPOLO

SECCO MARINA

CORTE
MARTIN
NOVELLO

FOND. DI S. GIUSEPPE

8

S. ELENA

see inset on page 16

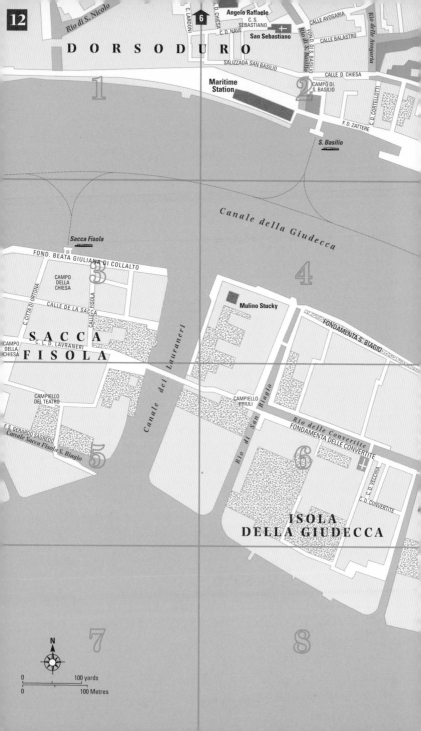

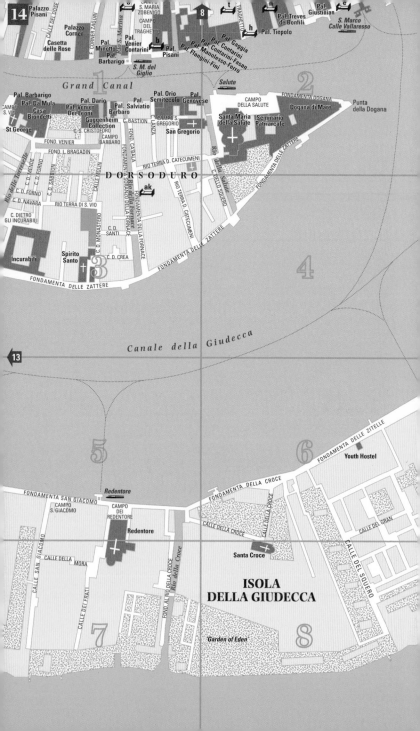

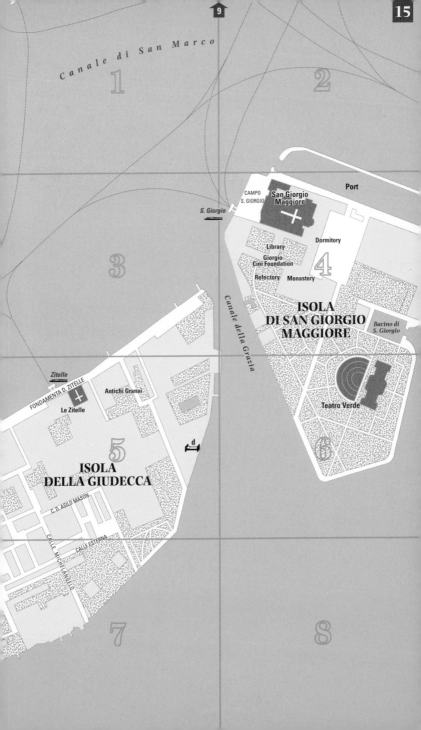

Canale di San Marco

1

2

3

Port

CAMPO
S. GIORGIO

San Giorgio
Maggiore

S. Giorgio

Dormitory

Library

Giorgio
Cini Foundation

Refectory   Monastery

4

ISOLA
DI SAN GIORGIO
MAGGIORE

Bacino di
S. Giorgio

Canale della Grazia

Zitelle

FONDAMENTA D. ZITELLE

Antichi Granai

Le Zitelle

Teatro Verde

6

d

5

ISOLA
DELLA GIUDECCA

C. D. ASILO MASON

CALLE ESTERNA

CALLE MICHELANGELO

7

8

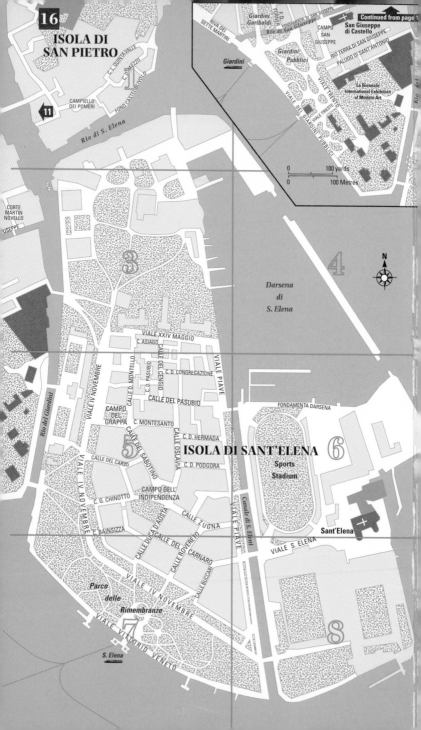

16

ISOLA DI SAN PIETRO

ISOLA DI SANT'ELENA

Continued from page 1

CAMPIELLO
DEI POMERI

11

Rio di S. Elena

CORTE
MARTIN
NOVELLO

USEPPE

Giardini
Garibaldi

F. D.
TORNER

RIVA DEI
SETTE MARTIRI

Rio di San Giuseppe

FONDAMENTA DI SAN GIUSEPPE

CAMPO
SAN
GIUSEPPE

San Giuseppe
di Castello

Giardini
Pubblici

RIO TERRA DI SAN GIUSEPPE

PALUDO DI SANT'ANTONIO

Giardini

VIALE DEI GIARDINI PUBBLICI

VIALE TRENTO

VIALE TRIESTE

La Biennale
International Exhibition
of Modern Art

Rio dei

0   100 yards
0   100 Metres

C. L. QUINTAVALLE

C. DI MEZZO

FOND. CASTELFORTE OLIVOLO

N

3

Darsena
di
S. Elena

4

VIALE XXIV MAGGIO

C. ASIAGO

CALLE D. MONTELLO

C. D. PASUBIO

CALLE DEL CENGIO

C. D. CONGREGAZIONE

VIALE IV NOVEMBRE

VIALE PIAVE

CALLE DEL PASUBIO

CAMPO
DEL
GRAPPA

C. MONTESANTO

CALLE DEL SABOTINO

CALLE OSLAVIA

C. D. HERMADA

FONDAMENTA DARSENA

ISOLA DI SANT'ELENA

Sports
Stadium

6

5

CALLE DEL CARSO

C. D. PODGORA

Rio del Giardini

C. G. CHINOTTO

CAMPO DELL'
INDIPENDENZA

Canale di S. Elena

Sant'Elena

VIALE IV NOVEMBRE

C. BAINSIZZA

CALLE DUCA D'AOSTA

CALLE ZUGNA

CALLE DEL ROVERETO

CALLE CARNARO

VIALE PIAVE

VIALE S. ELENA

CALLE BUCCARI

Parco
delle
Rimembranze

VIALE IV NOVEMBRE

7

S. Elena

8

VIALE VITTORIO VENETO